FROM THE FLAG TO THE CROSS

FROM

THE FLAG

TO

THE CROSS

OR,

SCENES AND INCIDENTS

OF

CHRISTIANITY

IN THE WAR.

THE CONVERSIONS, PRAYERS, DYING REQUESTS, LAST WORDS, SUFFERINGS AND DEATHS OF OUR SOLDIERS, ON THE BATTLE-FIELD, IN HOSPITAL, CAMP AND PRISON;

AND A DESCRIPTION OF

DISTINGUISHED CHRISTIAN MEN AND THEIR LABORS.

BY A. S. BILLINGSLEY,
LATE CHAPLAIN U.S. ARMY.

"*Stand by the Flag, and cling to the Cross.*"—E. M. SCHNEIDER, 57th Mass. Vol.

SOLID GROUND CHRISTIAN BOOKS
Birmingham, Alabama USA

Solid Ground Christian Books
2090 Columbiana Rd, Suite 2000
Birmingham, AL 35216
205-443-0311
sgcb@charter.net
http://solid-ground-books.com

FROM THE FLAG TO THE CROSS
Scenes and Incidents of Christianity in the Civil War

Amos S. Billingsley (1818-1897)

Taken from 1872 edition by New World Publishing Co., Philadelphia, PA

Solid Ground Classic Reprints

First edition April 2006

Cover work by Borgo Design, Tuscaloosa, AL
Contact them at nelbrown@comcast.net

Special thanks to John Wega of The U.S. Christian Commission for his encouragement to pursue this project and for writing a helpful Introduction to this precious book.

1-59925-070-5

To the Memory

OF THE

DEPARTED SOLDIERS, SAILORS AND OFFICERS OF THE
UNION, WHO FOUGHT, BLED, AND DIED FOR THEIR
COUNTRY; AND IN HONOR OF THE SURVIVING
SOLDIERS, SAILORS, AND OFFICERS WHO
FOUGHT AND SUFFERED IN QUELL-
ING THE LATE REBELLION,

This Book

IS GRATEFULLY INSCRIBED AND HEARTILY DEDICATED

BY THE AUTHOR.

Heroes of the Faith

During the Civil War in America, over 600,000 men died serving in a conflict that is hard for us to imagine. A nation birthed in liberty just some 80 years before fought a war on its own soil, between its own people, that nearly destroyed the nation. Only the hand of providence could have re-birthed this young nation out of the ash heap of the Civil War, to become one of the greatest nations on the timeline of freedom.

Many theologians, historians and philosophers have debated the providential hand of God and where it acted through this terrible chapter of our history. Few have put down the telescope, in order to pick up the magnifying glass and look into the lives of the men who fought and to see not whose side God was on, but where He was.

> "Yea, though I walk through
> the valley of the shadow of death,
> I will fear no evil;
> *for you are with me;*
> Your rod and your staff,
> They comfort me."
> - Psalm 23:4

Even the most cursory reading of Civil War history makes apparent the "valley of death" that the soldiers walked through in the Civil War. Scenes from Dante's *Inferno* pale in comparison to the reality of Civil War battlefields and hospitals. Brave men on both sides of this struggle walked through the valley of death and stared into the belly of hell. But there is a story woven throughout the Civil War that has remained relatively unknown. That is the story of a living God walking among the men; a Savior granting men true and eternal life in the midst of this "shadow of death." And a story of heroic men and women that went to the battlefields, not to fight for the blue or the grey but to fight for the souls of men and for the sake of the gospel. Their instruments of battle were not rifles or bayonets; their instruments of battle were Bibles, bandages and the love of Christ. These were the military chaplains and the men and women of the United States Christian Commission.

New Introduction

One such man was Amos Stevens Billingsley, Chaplain of the 101st Pennsylvania, who in addition to being a lifelong servant of His Master was a prolific writer. His story from the hospitals and battlefields represents thousands of others, who like Billingsley, went to war under the banner of the Cross.

From the Flag to the Cross is the Northern counterpart to the widely read *Christ in the Camp*, that chronicles the movement of God in the Southern armies. You will discover that these stories of faith from the battlefields reveal the presence of almighty God and neither blue nor grey color the tone of these stories. It is beautiful to see how these accounts can be overlaid like your right and left hand and you see the power of the gospel at work in both the northern and southern armies. For God's desire is that no man should perish without coming to the knowledge of His Son and inherit eternal life.

We have recently re-founded the U.S. Christian Commission to tell these stories of faith and courage during the Civil War. These stories will inspire true believers to take up their spiritual weapons of war and go to the battlefields of this world we call life. Just as Chaplain Billingsley went to the battlefields with the gospel, we are called to do no less in our own world.

If you have not yet met Jesus Christ in a real way and found Him as one that sticks closer than a brother, making Him alone your Lord and Savior, I encourage you to read this book with your eyes and heart open and listen to the words of dying men, confident of their eternal home that lies only in Christ.

We stand in the shadows of men like Chaplain A.S. Billingsley, who exhibited heroic faith in "the valley of the shadow of death." To him and those that served alongside him under the banner of the cross, we gladly and humbly salute and earnestly pray that we not just stand in their shadow, but upon their shoulders.

John A. Wega
Executive Director
United States Christian Commission
P.O. Box 4037
Gettysburg, PA 17325

To learn more about the modern day ministry of the United States Christian Commission, please visit our website at www.usccgettysburg.org

PREFACE.

THE late war was one of the greatest conflicts that ever stained the historic page. Involving the life of the nation and the great question of man's self-government, its results will very materially affect the progress of Christianity and the destiny of the world for generations to come. When we look at the extent, the duration, and the severity of the mighty struggle, the number of men engaged, the number of lives lost, and the glorious victory achieved, for awfulness, grandeur, and glory, it excels all modern warfare.

And as such a war occurs only once in an age, it is well to have its history recorded as fully as possible. And although it has already given rise to a great many books, — yet, as those already issued relate more particularly to the cause, rise, and progress of the Rebellion, and the great sacrifice and mighty uprising of the North in putting it down, together with the military genius and heroic achievements of great generals and officers, — there seems to be a demand for another, giving a more detailed account of the sufferings, piety, and heroism of the *private soldier and patient in the hospital.* Thus far there seems to be a tendency in the historian to ascribe *too much* honor and glory to the officer, and *too little* to the private soldier. There were, doubtless, among the rank and file of the late Union army and navy *many unknown heroes,* whose piety, worth, and heroism deserve to be written on leaves more durable than brass; men whose sagacity, courage, and military genius, if fully developed, would to-day shine as bright in the galaxy of military glory as many of those whose names will go down to posterity crowned with glory and honor. Now, to record some of the sufferings, hardships, prayers, conversions, sayings, and dying messages of the

Patient in the Hospital and of the Captive in the Prison, and to aid a little in giving the Private Soldier the honor due him in the great conflict for our national preservation, and to comfort the soldier's bereaved mother, widowed wife, and orphaned child, is the object of this little book. Laboring for a long while in the United States General Hospital, Fortress Monroe, Va., one of the largest in the country during the war, and visiting daily from seven hundred to nine hundred patients, canvassing the hearts of the worst cases and noting down their religious experience as they gave it in their own words, the writer had a fine opportunity of becoming acquainted with the general character and moral condition of our soldiery.

We have written out but a very small proportion of the number of patients visited whose spiritual diagnosis we recorded in our diary; but in making our selections we have taken some from all classes, so that the reader can see at a glance the general moral character of the American soldier. Thus furnished with the *materials*, at the request of friends the author now sends forth to the world this little volume, with the hope that it may be a source of comfort to the soldier's bereaved friend, praying that it may lead some wandering soul, who has so long borne his country's flag, to take up and bear the Cross of Christ.

NEW BRIGHTON, PA.

CONTENTS.

INTRODUCTORY.

PAGE

Tour to the Rocky Mountains — The Devil Outflanked — "The Biggest Gun ever Fired in America" — Plucking Flowers and Making Snowballs at the Same Time — Gathering up the Lost Sheep — Preaching to Colorado Volunteers — Late Papers "go off like Hot Cakes" — The Mighty Struggle waxes Hotter — Going to the Army — Visiting and Bidding Good-bye to Friends — Touching at Pittsburg and Baltimore, We enjoyed a very Pleasant Foretaste of Army and Hospital Life at Washington, Fortress Monroe, and Newbern — Another Sail brought us to Plymouth 17

CHAPTER I.

ENTERING THE SERVICE.

Arrival at Plymouth — Found our Regiment, the 101st Pa. Vol., comfortably Housed — The Garrison Hungry for the Gospel — Christmas Sermon — Big Turn-out — The Rebels Captured and Drove us off . . 21

CHAPTER II.

SKETCHES OF SOLDIERS AND OFFICERS.

A Fort-Fisher Hero — A Heroic Soldier: "I Don't Backslide" — "Jesus is All I Want" — "Stand by the Flag, and Cling to the Cross" — "All is Well!" — A Soldier's Farewell — Capt. Tresouthick — Lieut. Ransom: His Dying Prayer and "Glory to God" — Capt. Fee: His Request, "Please Pray for Me" — A Rolling Chaplain — "You Saved My Life" — A Dying Soldier's Letter — Lieut. Merrill: Baptized at Midnight — The Dying Captain: "Hurrah for Jesus." By Chaplain Marshall. . 22

CHAPTER III.

SKETCHES OF SOLDIERS.

"When I go into Battle, I put Jesus in Front" — A Hero of Plymouth: "I will Fall right into His Arms" — "Jesus is Precious to Me Now" — "Why did You Call Me back?" — "I don't Fear Nothin' at all" —

"The World is Hollow and Empty "— "I came out to Conquer or Die "— "They left Me for Dead "— "Good-bye, Old Arm!"— "Put the Bright Side out to Mother," he said, as he died — "Oh, if I only could!" — "I am Happy, Day and Night" — Value of the Union: "Pray, Labor, Fight for it." 46

CHAPTER IV.

THE FALL OF PLYMOUTH.

The Rebels Attack Us, April 17, 1864 — The Garrison numbered about Nineteen Hundred Men fit for Duty — Excitement Great — Alarmed Women fled to Me, crying, "Come and Pray for Me!" "Come in and Pray for Us!" — The Army and Navy both Engage at once — The Scene was Grand, Awful, Sublime — Rebel Iron-clad attacks our Gunboats — Fight Severe — Lieut. Flusser Killed — The Garrison Overawed by the Rebel Ram — "The Combat Deepens" — "In the Last Ditch" — Hard Fighting — The Capture — Gen. Wessels Surrenders — Massacre at Plymouth — Visiting the Wounded — Preached in a Rebel Hospital — Prayed for a Rebel Soldier. 63

CHAPTER V.

GOING TO LIBBY.

Order: "Be Ready to Start for Richmond To-morrow Morning at Four" — Sail up the Roanoke to Halifax — Take Cars — Enter Libby with Loud Shouts of "Fresh Fish! Fresh Fish!" — They took our Money — Life in Libby — All Sorts of Things going on — Very Hard Place — Preach to the Prisoners — Big Congregation — Visited the Hospital — Not Allowed to Preach to the Sick — Released — Farewell to Libby — The Exchange — We Cheered the Dear Old Flag — Rebels Handle our Men very Roughly — Belle Isle — U. S. General Hospital, Annapolis, Md. — Labors in, etc. 71

CHAPTER VI.

U. S. GENERAL HOSPITAL, FORTRESS MONROE, VA.

Location Fine — Buildings Splendid — Chesapeake Hospital — Bethesdian Chapel — Interesting Meetings — Reading-Room and Library for Patients — Hampton Hospital, Organized 1862 — Head-Quarters — "New Camp" — Contraband Hospital — All Consolidated into One General Hospital in 1864 — Called by the Above Name — **Disbanded in March, 1866** — Managed by Dr. Eli McClellan, Assistant Surgeon U. S. A. — Hospital Garden — Very Extensive — Twenty-five Thousand Head of Cabbage — Hospital Hennery — Camp Distribution — Soldiers came and went by Thousands — Chaplain Marshall Preached to Them by Night — Military Prison — Preaching to the Spirits in Prison — Gan-

CONTENTS.   ix

PAGE

grene Camp — Interesting Scenes — "None but Christ" — Arrival of Patients: from Two Hundred to Eight Hundred a Day — Transferring Patients — Voyage to New York with a Load of Patients — Big Job for the Chaplain — A Patient Kissed my Hand — A Weeping Mother and Hard-hearted Surgeon — "All Fast on the Potomac." . . 79

CHAPTER VII.
THE RELIGIOUS WORK AT HAMPTON HOSPITAL.

The Harvest, Great and White — The Prayer-Hall — No Church — Soldiers' Earnest Prayers and Eloquent Exhortations — It was the Eloquence of the Heart Melting All into Tears — Ward Prayer-Meetings — Interest Increasing — The Power of Prayer — Soldiers' Prayer-Meeting — Bush Prayer-Meetings — Preaching to Men on their Death-Beds — "The Last Morning." 93

CHAPTER VIII.
WRITING LETTERS FOR THE PATIENTS.

A Dying Soldier's Letter to his Brother — Solemn — His Will — "Yours in Death" — "Letters of Death" — "I am Ready" — Letters from the Bereaved: No. 1. The Bereaved Wife — No. 2. The Bereaved Brother — No. 3. The Weeping Widow — No. 4. The Dying Husband's Letter to His Wife — No. 5. A Weeping Southern Family — Canvassing Patients' Hearts — Diagnosis of the Whole Hospital — "Oh, Chaplain, Stay, and Talk to Me more about Jesus!" — "Before I would cry, 'Fort Pillow, and Let 'em have it!'" — "Save Me, Lord! Save Me, Lord!" . . 107

CHAPTER IX.
THE WOMEN OF THE HOSPITAL.

Their Valuable Services highly Appreciated by the Patients — Chesapeake Hospital well Supplied — Here Mrs. Mary B. Dully was Directress and Head of Sanitary Department — "She did what she Could" — Miss Amos, of Baltimore, Kind, Faithful, and True — Mrs. Chaplain E. P. Roe — "She went about Doing Good" — Mrs. Meecham and Many Others did Likewise — Mrs. Carver, with her Tent, Cooking-Stove, and Provisions, did much for the Patients — Mrs. Mary Alexander — Plain, Earnest, Heroic, Loved the Soldiers Ardently — "Bury Me with Them when I Die." 118

CHAPTER X.
SKETCHES OF SOLDIERS.

"Past Feeling" — Patchwork won't do for Eternity — "Jesus Saved Me Twice" — "I Never Forget My Saviour" — The Blind Exhorter — "I have very Sweet Communion with God" — His Death — Letter from

His Wife — Corporal John Creed, 23d Ill., Co. B — Honored for His Bravery — Soldiers Die Clinched — Courage of Pompey — Joy an Element of Strength — Ananias Montgomery — "He had a Ball in His Side, and God in His Heart" — "I Feel Happy" — The Backslider — "I Lost My Religion" — "Now I am Miserable" — George H. Vanloan — "I do Love Him" — "It would be Hard to Live in the Army without Religion" — The Fixed Heart — "I Pray Often" — "I do Feel Happy" — "I am Too Wicked for That" — "I Swear a Great Deal" — "I Can't Pray" — "It's Too Late" — "I am a Great Sinner" — "I Have Given Up" — "It is Better to Die" — "I am Willing to Go" — "All is Well" — Midnight Calls — "O Chaplain, I Feel Most Awful!" . . 124

CHAPTER XI.

SCENES IN ANDERSONVILLE.

The Prison — Its Condition — Cruel Treatment — "Can this be Hell?" — Prisoners' Awful Condition — Mortality One Hundred and Fifty a Day — Apathy of U. S. Government toward Them — Hundreds Died of Broken Hearts — Many went Deranged, and turned Maniacs — A School and Church there Now — "The Dead-Line" — Execution of Union Prisoners — Band of Robbers and Murderers — Six Tried, and Condemned to be Hung — Awful Tragic Scene — They Expected to the Last to Escape — The Crisis of Andersonville — Murder will Out — Patriotism in Andersonville — "I would rather have Died a Dozen Deaths" — "I am not Sorry that I Enlisted" — Your Patriotism never Dies: "It is Stronger than Death" — Died Praying for Victory — Andersonville Hospital: an Awful Place — No Beds but Bare Ground — Rations — Diet — Enlarged — The Food would Produce Disease among Swine — The Moonlight Prayer-Meeting — Religion Sweetens the Bitterest Cup. 151

CHAPTER XII.

THE EXCHANGE.

Long Looked for — Many Exchanging Time for Eternity — They Cheer the Old Flag — "It never Seemed so Dear" — They Wept Profusely — Rejoicing — Sung the "Battle-Cry of Freedom" — What a Happy, Grateful Crowd — Furloughed Home Thirty Days — The Departure — "Be Ready to Depart" — Filled with Rejoicing — They Cried "Thank God! Thank God!" — "The Year of Jubilee is Come" — Loud Shouts of Joy burst from Thousands — Farewell, Andersonville — Sad Disappointment — It was no Exchange: Only a Removal — "Hope Deferred maketh the Heart Sick." 164

CHAPTER XIII.

ANDERSONVILLE CEMETERY.

Contains Fifty Acres — Thirteen Thousand and Seven Hundred and Five Graves — Who are the Dead? — What did They Suffer? — How did

They Die? — As They Lived and Fought — The First Prisoners Buried There — The Last One — The Stars and Stripes Wave over Them — Captain Wirz — His Birth — Entering the Rebel Army — Promoted for His Cruelties to the Prisoners — Proven Guilty of Conspiracy against the United States — "I will give you Bullets for Bread" — He Shot a Prisoner — "Oh, do Let Me Down!" — His Last Days — Found Guilty — Received Sentence to be Hung very Coolly — Attended by the Priest — No Signs of Sorrow — His Execution — Hurries to the Gallows — The Closing Scene 169

CHAPTER XIV.

SKETCHES OF SOLDIERS.

"My Heart is so Hard, I Can't Pray" — Converted on the Field of Battle — "I Went to Church Cursing, and Came away Praying" — "I Can't Get Religion" — "I Can't Help but Pray" — A Hero of Andersonville Saved by His Wife — A Boat-Load of Andersonville Prisoners — "Converted on Picket by Two Men Talking to Me" — "I am Resolved to Quit Swearing" — Died Calling to the Chaplain to Pray for Him — "I am Ready to Die" — "Tell Them I am Happy" — "Converted through a Sister's Letters" — "If I go to Hell, I will go Praying" — "Prayer is a Great Privilege" — "Oh, that I had Ventured Before!" — "I am Guilty of Everything but Theft and Murder" — "I Expect to get Religion when I get Home" — Bleeding to Death, yet "Resting on Christ" — "Praying for Sport" — "I Gave My Heart to Jesus" — "Christ is Everything to Me" — "My Sins are Great and Heavy" — "Satan is Often at My Heels" — James Ward, 81st N. Y., Co. I — A Soldier's Creed — "I See so much Bad Christianity, I am Discouraged" — "Jesus is Still Precious" — "I Still Hold on to God" — "I Pray much in Battle" — A Soldier with Seven Wounds — "I can Afford to Suffer" — A Happy, Shouting Soldier — "I would Like to be a Christian, if I Could Keep It" — "I Can't Live without Prayer" — "The Lord is Mine" — "I Can't Pray" — "I Found Jesus" — "I Leave it all with the Lord" — A Swearer Brought to Tears. . . . 178

CHAPTER XV.

SKETCHES OF SOLDIERS — CONTINUED.

The Bomb-Proof Prayer-Meeting — "Are You Ready to Go?" — Little Lizzie's Letter — "I Prayed in the Street" — "I Love Everybody" — "I Have no Fear" — Sergeant James Tustison: "I am Dying, But I am very Happy" — "I have Got It!" — Satan Repulsed by Prayer — "Hell Seems to be Gaping for Me" — "I am Happy in the Lord" — "Converted in the Army through Sin" — "Do You Trust in the Lord?" — "Urge Him to Come to Jesus" — "Thank God for My Wound" — Sergeant Dwight Kneeland: "My Work is Done" — Died Calling for the Chaplain — "Just as God Wishes" — "Tell My Mother I Died Happy" — "It is Easier to Serve Satan" — "I am Better in the Army than at Home" — William J. Johnson, 142d N. Y., Co. D — "All is Well" —

"Old Jacob," the Grave-Digger — "The Bible Better than Greenbacks" — "Somehow It Worked upon Me" — "God Still Sticks to Me" — "O Chaplain, What Will I Do?" — "I am on the Devil's Side" — "Pray for Me, Chaplain, till I Die:" His Bereaved Wife's Letter — "I would as soon Go to My Heavenly Home" — "I am Too Wicked to Come to Jesus" — "God Grabbed Me into His Heart at Once" — "I Prayed on, and God Changed My Heart" — "The Devil Coaxed Me Off." . . 210

CHAPTER XVI.
EXTRACTS FROM THE AUTHOR'S DIARY.

Preaching in the Wards — A Melting Prayer-Meeting — Hospital Church Organized — Church Creed — A Weeping Scene at the Grave — The Naked Heart — Mortality Increasing — "Try Again" — A Soldier's Prayer-Meeting — Catholics Turning Protestants — Christmas Dinner — Holidays in U. S. Hospital — Week of Prayer — The Lord's Supper — Revival in Hospital. 256

CHAPTER XVII.
MISCELLANEOUS FACTS.

Celebration of Washington's Birthday — Religious Interest in New Camp — Soldiers' Entertainment — The Fall of Richmond — Unbounded Rejoicing — Lee's Surrender — Death of President Lincoln — Largest Interment — Dedication of New Hospital Chapel — Arrival of Fort Fisher Wounded. 279

CHAPTER XVIII.
BOMBARDMENT OF FORT FISHER.

The Wounded Arrive at the Hospital — They are very Jubilant — Admiral Porter Commands the Fleet — "The World never Saw such Fighting" — The Scene Awfully Grand and Sublime — Great Slaughter of Sailors — Awful Hand-to-Hand Fight for Hours — The Surrender — Buoyant Wounded from Richmond — Dying that the Nation might Live — Hospital Variety Monotonous — Desire to go Home. . . . 288

CHAPTER XIX.
LINCOLN'S FUNERAL.

Lincoln's Funeral — Deep Feeling: Solemn, Impressive — The Author's Address at the Funeral — Sudden Change from Rejoicing to Weeping — His Death a Loss to the Entire World — National Grief Unspeakable — His Character — The Great Emancipator and Friend of the Slave — Self-Made — The Saviour of His Country — Religious Character: Brought up to Pray, and Read the Bible — His Last Request: "Pray for Me" — "I Leave Myself, my Country, and All in the Hands of God." 294

CHAPTER XX.
THE STREAM OF DEATH.

The First Soldiers Killed in the War — Rebel Cruelty to the Dead —

Death of Col. Baker — Gen. Lyon's Bravery and Death — Death in the Mississippi Valley and on the Peninsula — Removal of Gen. McClellan — Gen. Rosecrans' Bravery at Stone River — "The Bloodiest Battle of the War" — The Battle of Gettysburg the Death-blow of the Rebellion — Gen. Grant Assumes Command in Chief — "On to Richmond" — Death of Gen. Sedgwick — Battle of Coal Harbor — Simultaneous Movement of Armies — Gen. Sherman at Atlanta — Gen. Sheridan's Victories in the Shenandoah Valley — Battle at Franklin, Tenn. — Gen. Sheridan's Stratagem at Cedar Creek — Lincoln Calls for More Volunteers — Gen. Sherman Completes His "March to the Sea" — Slavery Abolished by Congress, Jan. 31, 1865 — Grant's Last "Great Strike" — Fall of Richmond, Flight of Jeff. Davis, and Surrender of Gen. Lee — Mortality During the War — The Deserter. 300

CHAPTER XXI.
THE NATIONAL CEMETERY AT FORTRESS MONROE, VA.

Number of Graves — The Place of Many Prayers, Sighs, and Tears — The Old Man Weeping at his Son's Grave — Who are the Dead? — How did They Die? — Soldiers' Dying Words — The Monument — The Inscription — Burying the Dead — National Cemeteries — General Summary. 315

CHAPTER XXII.
SKETCHES BY CHAPLAIN MARSHALL — THE U. S. CHRISTIAN COMMISSION.

A Theatre turned into a Religious Meeting — Masses of Soldiers in Camp Distribution — Their Profanity — Burlesque Military Drill — The Chaplain's Resolution — A Shout upon his Entrance — Theatrical Preparations — They Black Themselves up — They Sing — Devotion Rises — God Helps — The Chaplain Reads, Speaks, Prays — They Sing with Great Power — They Visit the Reading-Room — Great Good done in a Short Time — "No more Swearing" — Sunday Night with the Dying — The Dying Sergeant sends for the Chaplain — The Weeping Father prays for his Dying Son — The Dying Lieutenant desires to be Prayed for — The Dying Captain's Warm Grasp — The Friendship of Christ — The U. S. Christian Commission — Its Origin — Officers — First Meeting — Its Spirit and Zeal — Head-Quarters — Its Object — Fidelity of its Delegates — Its Efficiency and Contributions — Its Popularity. . 326

CHAPTER XXIII.
DISTINGUISHED CHRISTIAN MEN IN THE WAR.
REV. P. D. GURLEY, D.D.

His Birth — Pious Mother — Babyhood — Desire for the Ministry — His Education — Works his own Way through Union College — His Piety when a Boy — Studied Theology at Princeton — His Standing in his Class — Graduates at Princeton, and Receives a Call to Preach in Indianapolis — His Marriage — His Ordination — Successful Labors —

Accepts a Call to Dayton, Ohio — Leaves Dayton, and goes to Washington, D. C. — Summoned to Lincoln's Death-Bed — Impressive Scene — Prays at his Death — Presides at a Meeting of the Clergy of the District of Columbia — Preaches at Lincoln's Funeral — Dr. Hall reads the Episcopal Burial-Service — Bishop Simpson's Opening Prayer — "Cling to Liberty and Right" — Composed a Hymn for the Funeral — Bishop Simpson's Sermon at the Grave — Dr. Gurley's Christian Character — His Ability in Prayer — Successful as a Minister — His Gifts — He Comforts the Afflicted — His Popularity — His Death — His Rapturous Foretastes of Heaven — His Dying Requests to his Family and Friends — Last Words — Dr. Sunderland's Remarks at the Funeral — His People's Affection for him. 334

OLIVER O. HOWARD.

His Birth — Boyhood — Early Religious Training — A Christian Gentleman — He Graduates at Bowdoin College; also at West Point Academy in 1854 — His Patriotism — Appointed Colonel of Third Regiment Maine Volunteers — Is Promoted for Bravery — Joins Army of the Potomac — Wounded at Battle of Fair Oaks — Had his Arm Amputated — Returns Home the Next Day — Lectures the People, and Urges Them to Come to the Rescue of the Country — He Returned in Time for the Battles of Bull Run, Antietam, Fredericksburg, and Chancellorsville — His Position at the Battle of Gettysburg — His Calmness in Battle — Is Temperate — Gen. Sherman's High Opinion of him — His Warm Attachment for Capt. Griffin — He Prays with him, and Bids him a Final Farewell — "It is the Last Time" — Appointed Commissioner of the Freedman's Bureau — Howard University a Monument of His Benevolent Efforts. 343

BISHOP SIMPSON.

His Nativity — His Education — Enters the Ministry — His Popularity — Elected President of Asbury University — Elected Editor of "Western Christian Advocate" — His Success — Elected Bishop — His Success and Administration — His Patriotism and Zeal in Quelling the Rebellion — Lincoln's Trusted Friend — His Prayer at Lincoln's Funeral — His Preaching Abilities — His Oration at Lincoln's Grave — Powers of Discrimination — Delineates Lincoln's Characteristics, and Points out the Secret of his Power — His Style of Preaching — He Preaches Christ — What he Covets — His Tour to the Rocky Mountains — Intimate with the Presidents of the United States — Appointed by President Grant to Visit San Domingo — His Present Standing, Influence, and Power — His Touching Peroration at Lincoln's Tomb . . . 346

ADMIRAL FARRAGUT.

A New Era in Naval Affairs — Fight between the Monitor and Merrimac — Progress in Destroying and Saving Man — Satan's Whetting his Sword should Arouse the Church — Farragut's Birth — Enters the U. S. Navy — His First and Second Engagements — Heroic Courage — Wounded — Highly Esteemed by his Commander — His Heroism Sleeps — Sails all over the World — Promoted — His Loyalty — Went North — Commands a Naval Expedition *vs.* New Orleans — His Large Fleet — Captures New Orleans — Daring Feats in Capturing Vicksburg — His Stratagem and Heroism in Capturing Mobile — Lashed Himself to the Rigging of his Ship in Battle — Calls upon God for Help and Direction — Severe Fight with a Rebel Ironclad — He Whipped Her — She Surrenders — Promoted Again — His Habits — Decorating his Grave — His Prayer in the Battle of Mobile Bay — "Go Forward" — His Religious Life — Testimony of Lieut. Montgomery. 353

GEORGE H. STUART.

Sketch of, by Dr. Wylie — His Birth — Parents — Education — Arrival in this Country — Religious Profession — Elected Ruling Elder — His Christian Zeal and Liberality — Missionary Spirit — A Sabbath-school Worker — Suggested the National Presbyterian Convention, and Presided over it — His Suspension from the Church — Refused a Position in President Grant's Cabinet — A Successful Merchant — His Natural Talents — Christian Character — An Expert Presiding Officer — His Natural Eloquence — Attractive Speaker and Successful Beggar — He Always Succeeds — Goes about Doing Good — His Marriage — Family — Personal Appearance — His Labors in the Christian Commission — Its Leading Spirit and President — His Qualification and Devotion to the Work — Secret of His Success — Distributes Books — Overcomes an Infidel — The People's Faith in Him — Money Flows in at his Asking — His Importunity Prevails — His Zeal to Supply the Needy Soldiers — His Kindness to the Rebels — Rebels Weep at Northern Kindness — His Fondness for Army Relics — "His Generalship in Prayer" — He can always have Prayer — "An Eminent Christian at Work" — His Christian Sagacity — His Popularity — An Eloquent Speaker — His Speech in England. 364

HENRY WARD BEECHER.

His Distinguishing Traits — A Great Worker — His Style — Oratory — His Birth — Lost his Mother — Early Religious Impressions — Inured to Hardship — A Bashful, Stammering, Unpromising Boy — His Education — Went to School Barefooted, and Hemmed Towels at Recess — Fond of Flowers and Full of Jokes — Drilled in Elocution — Tired of School — Wishes to "Go to Sea" — Subject of a Revival — Unites with the Church — Naval Project Given up — Attention Turned to the Ministry — Enters College — Choice of Studies — Preferring Rhetoric, Studies to Know "What to Say," and "How to Say it" — Strictly Temperate — Conducts Prayer-Meetings — His Creed — Religious Impressions — Troubled — Believed — Buoyant — Teaches School — Lectures and Preaches — The Slave's Friend — Graduates — Studies Theology — Perplexed about Entering the Ministry — Marries — First Pastoral Charge — Did Everything Himself — Moves to Indianapolis — Style of Preaching — His Popularity — Revival in his Church — Moves to Brooklyn — Visits England and Europe — Lectures in England, and,

Braving all Opposition, Pleads America's Cause Successfully — His
London Letter glowing with Joy and Gratitude to God, and Love to his
Enemies — Impression Favorable — Affectionate Enthusiasm for him —
His War Sermons — Oration at Fort Sumter. 383

DWIGHT L. MOODY.

Power of Individual Effort — Earnestness the Secret of Success — A
Great Want — The Church and the World Asleep — His Birth — Lay-
preaching Encouraged — Paul's Great Success — Labor, Labor! —
Moody's Early Religious Views — His Conversion — Joins the Congre-
gationalists — Education Limited — His Labors Successful — A Great
Worker in Sabbath Schools — Organized Mission Sunday School in
Chicago — Its Growth — Started Prayer-Meetings — Labors Blessed —
Young Men's Christian Association Begun — Daily Prayer-Meeting —
His Trust in God for a Living — No Salary — His Active Labors in the
Army — His Zeal at the Battle of Fort Donelson — Goes to God for
Direction — Efficient in Building — Calls to go Abroad — Crosses the
Atlantic — Organized Daily Prayer-Meeting in London — Labors in
Sunday-School Convention — Successful — Deeds, not Words, a True
Sign of Principle — His Success as an Organizer; as a Speaker; as a
Revivalist — How to "Get up a Revival" — His Large Audiences in
Chicago — His Popularity at Home — His Personal Influence over Others. 395

GARRETSON I. YOUNG.

Solemn Warning — "Be Ye also Ready!" — His Birth — Parents — Boy-
hood — Education — A Diligent Scholar — His Academical Course at
Calcutta, Ohio — Enters Jefferson College — Graduates — His Habits —
Taught High School — Studies and Practises Law — Elected Probate
Judge — A Neat Book-keeper — Marries — Early Religious Training —
Read the Bible Daily — Joins the Episcopal Church — His Military
Position — Labors in War Department — Resigns, and Returns Home —
Purchased the "Buckeye State" — Edits it — His Success — Elected to
the Ohio Legislature — His Character — Patriotic — Winning Ways —
Noble Traits — "He Made Friends Fast" — His Sudden Death — Im-
pressive Scenes at the Capitol; and at his Home — His Funeral —
Marked Honors Paid him by the Governor and State Legislature —
Eulogies by the Members. 403

CHAPTER XXIV.

FAREWELL TO THE HOSPITAL.

A Brief and Solemn Review — Number of Patients in Hospital — Average
Daily and Total Mortality of the War — Interviews with Soldiers —
Chaplains much Exposed to Disease — Solemn to Part — Farewell to the
Chesapeake; to the Chapel; to the Matrons; to Hampton; to the Chap-
lains — Farewell to the Christian Soldiers — Appeal and Farewell to the
Impenitent — Farewell to the Dead — The Great Christian Victory —
The Rebellion Dissected — Source of the Victory — Munificent Gifts —
Americans and Europeans Whetting One Another — Go Forward. . 411

LIST OF ILLUSTRATIONS.

	PAGE.
Abraham Lincoln	15
Fort Sumter in 1861	16
Street in Cincinnati in the early part of the War	20
Harper's Ferry	32
Rev. Jas. Marshall, U. S. Army	42
Pratt Street, Baltimore	46
Rev. E. P. Roe, U. S. Army	59
Hampton Hospital	92
Hospital Scene	119
Pittsburg Landing	124
Cooper Volunteer Refreshment-Saloon, Philadelphia	210
Uncle Jacob	235
The President's Reception Room during the War	283
View of the Antietam Battle Ground	300
National Cemetery, Fortress Monroe, Va.	315
Rev. P. D. Gurley, D.D.	334
Rev. Matthew Simpson	346
Geo. H. Stuart, Esq.	364
Henry Ward Beecher	383
Independence Square, Philadelphia	418

ABRAHAM LINCOLN

A. Lincoln

CHRISTIANITY IN THE WAR.

INTRODUCTORY.

Tour to the Rocky Mountains — The Devil Out-flanked — "The Biggest Gun ever Fired in America" — Plucking Flowers and Making Snowballs at the Same Time — Gathering up the Lost Sheep — Preaching to Colorado Volunteers — Late Papers "go off like Hot Cakes" — The Mighty Struggle waxes Hotter — Going to the Army — Visiting and Bidding Good-by to Friends — Touching at Pittsburg and Baltimore, We Enjoyed a very Pleasant Foretaste of Army and Hospital Life at Washington, Fortress Monroe, and Newbern — Another Sail brought us to Plymouth.

THE present is an eventful age — an age for intellectual research, discovery, scientific investigation; and for great and mighty changes and revolutions in the social, moral, civil, and religious world, is unparalleled in the history of man.

It is peculiarly a *fast* age. Kingdoms and empires now rise, flourish, fade, and fall, almost in a day. And the human mind ever on the alert in search of new truths, under the present march of mind, we often see old creeds and platforms give way, and give rise to new and better ones. Although our country has just emerged from a baptism of blood, and although Satan is whetting his sword and rallying his forces, yet with oceans traversed with telegraphs, and continents spanned with railroads, knowledge is running to and fro, and Christianity is spreading rapidly.

When the nation's indignation was stirred at the rebel bombardment of Fort Sumter, April 12, 1861, the writer was winding his way across the boundless plains of Nebraska, to Denver, and the Rocky Mountains of Colorado. Leaving Omaha, Neb., April 21, after riding over six successive days and nights in the coach, and travelling over six hundred miles up the broad waters of the Platte, we reached Denver, and put up at the Cherokee House, at twelve dollars a week for boarding and lodging. It was here, in this bustling city, that we first felt the gloom that overspread the country, occasioned by the signal defeat at the first battle of Bull Run. Here we spent several months in preaching, and gathering up the scattered sheep of Israel, and preaching occasionally to small squads of Colorado volunteers. It was at Laurette — far beyond Pike's Peak, at the foot of the snowy range, between two lofty spurs of the backbone of North America, in the regions of perpetual snow, where in July you can pluck flowers with one hand and make snowballs with the other — that the glorious news of Lincoln's Emancipation Proclamation first fell upon our ears. A mountain merchant then said, " *It is the biggest gun ever fired in America;* " while Lord John Russell, of England, pronounced it " *an act of vengeance on the slave-holder.*"

Meeting here, beneath the shade of the lofty peaks and rocky cliffs, for preaching, prayer, and praise, we often enjoyed precious times of refreshing. On one occasion, we out-flanked the devil, and broke up a Sabbath-evening auction, and had the pleasure of seeing the Sabbath-breaking auctioneer haul in his unsold goods, and come to church himself. And although we were separated from the seat of war by a distance of some two thousand miles, yet we watched the movements of the two mighty armies with intense interest. Every mail was looked for with the greatest anxiety, and the late papers, by thousands, " went off like hot cakes." But seeing the mighty struggle for our national existence waxing hotter and hotter, and feeling deeply anxious to aid in quelling the rebellion, we pulled up stakes and struck for home, and hastened to lend our assistance as chaplain of the 101st Regiment of Pennsylvania Volunteers. Having visited my friends, and bidden farewell to a kind and affectionate sister

FORT SUMTER IN 1861.

and her family, we took the cars at New Brighton, Pa., and soon landed in the thronged streets of Pittsburg and Alleghany. Leaving these smoky twin cities, in the Pennsylvania Central Express, with lightning speed we hurried across the lofty Alleghanies, with their beautiful curves and deep ravines, and soon found ourselves promenading the broad pavements of Pennsylvania Avenue, overlooked by the splendid dome of the national capitol at one end, and the " White House " at the other. Here we visited a few U. S. General Hospitals, and, for the first time, enjoyed the privilege of preaching to the sick and wounded soldiers, lying upon their narrow couches, in their airy wards. It was in Douglas Hospital, chaplained by Rev. W. Y. Brown, U.S.A. Having enjoyed this little foretaste of hospital life, we hastened back to Baltimore, where we fell in with G. S. Griffith, Esq., president of the Maryland Branch of the U. S. Christian Commission, who, though a stranger, received me very kindly, and gave me a rich supply of Testaments, books, papers, and tracts for my regiment. Embracing the first opportunity, we sailed down the broad bosom of Chesapeake Bay to Fortress Monroe, Va., and soon made our way up to the Chesapeake Hospital, where we met with a very kind reception from Chaplain James Marshall, U.S.A., stationed at that point, faithfully laboring for the welfare of the large number of patients collected at that noted place. Waiting for transportation, we spent a few days here very agreeably; preaching for the chaplain Sabbath morning to his patients, and to a regiment of colored troops, in Camp Distribution, in the afternoon. Having enjoyed this, another little taste of hospital life, early Tuesday morning we bade farewell to the thronged wharf of Fortress Monroe, and sailed in the splendid steamer *Spaulding* for Beaufort, N. C., rounding the dangerous coast of Cape Hatteras in the night, while wrapped in the sweet embraces of sleep, entirely unconscious of the danger encountered. But rocked by the raging billows of the troubled ocean, upon leaving my berth in the morning, I found my head so light, and my stomach so disturbed, that I could not walk for sea-sickness. But having fully recovered before reaching Beaufort, we hurried, " by rail," to captured

Newbern, surrounded with fortifications and soldiers without, and teeming with colored people within. Here we visited soldiers' camps, chaplains' quarters, hospitals, and delegates of the Christian Commission, preaching as often as we could; and thus enjoyed another very profitable initiatory step into the panorama of hospital and army life. After waiting a few days, a Government transport arrived, and sailing down the broad Pamlico and up the placid Albemarle Sounds, we arrived at Plymouth, N. C., Dec. 19, 1863, where we found the brave boys of the 101st comfortably housed in their warm winter-quarters, and met with a very warm reception from Col. A. W. Taylor, then commanding the regiment.

CHAPTER I.

ENTERING THE SERVICE.

ARRIVAL AT PLYMOUTH — FOUND OUR REGIMENT, THE 101ST PA. VOL., COMFORTABLY HOUSED — THE GARRISON HUNGRY FOR THE GOSPEL — CHRISTMAS SERMON — BIG TURN-OUT — THE REBELS CAPTURED AND DROVE US OFF.

ON arriving at Plymouth, we found the garrison, containing some two thousand men, made up of the following regiments and companies: the 103d Pa. Vol., Col. Leghman; the 85th N. Y. Vol., Col. Fidello; the 101st Pa. Vol., Lt.-Col. A. W. Taylor; the 16th Conn. Vol., Col. Beech; a New York Independent Battery, and parts of the 12th N. Y. Cavalry and the 2d Mass. Heavy Artillery, all commanded by Brig.-Gen. H. W. Wessels. They had been there a long time, and were almost entirely destitute of preaching. Col. Taylor preached occasionally, and the Rev. Mr. Morris, a faithful delegate of the U. S. Christian Commission, had just arrived, and held service one or two Sabbaths. At his request, I preached the first Sabbath evening after my arrival, and announced a Christmas sermon for the following Sabbath evening. At the hour appointed, the large Methodist church, seating some eight hundred, was crowded to overflowing: hundreds, they said, had to go away for want of room. Several ladies, Gen. Wessels, and his staff, graced the wide-awake audience with their presence. I gave them a sermon on the advent of the Saviour, (Gal. iv. 4, 5,) and they listened with rapt attention. From that time on, we had a crowded house every Sabbath. The soldiers and officers seemed to be *hungry for the gospel*. The field was great, white, ready to harvest. It was a delightful work to preach to them. We had a large, interesting Bible-class, and a semi-weekly, well-attended prayer-meeting. Our meetings were usually very interesting, solemn, and impressive; and at one time we seemed to be on the eve of a great revival, but the rebels came, and drove us off before we enjoyed it. The colored people had preaching or prayer-meeting in the same house every Sabbath afternoon, and a flourishing Sabbath-school, conducted by a sergeant of the New York Battery. Chaplain Dixon, of the 16th Conn. Vol., and Chaplain Rawlings, of the 103d Pa. Vol., soon arrived, and took part in the regular services of the Sabbath. Many of the soldiers and officers took an active part, and seemed to be deeply interested. The whole garrison, without any distinction of sects, together with a few of the citizens of the place, met together. We had no church organization, but whenever we met a man apparently bearing the image of Christ, we treated him as a brother in the Lord. Graced with a well-played melodeon, we had a fine choir, which gave life and animation to the services. Each chaplain labored with his own regiment during the week, and being well supplied with religious papers, tracts, and books, from the Christian Commission, our religious work went on finely until the attack by the rebels, April 17, 1864, which resulted in our capture, after a hot siege of three days.

CHAPTER II.

SKETCHES OF SOLDIERS AND OFFICERS.

A FORT-FISHER HERO — A HEROIC SOLDIER: "I DON'T BACKSLIDE" — "JESUS IS ALL I WANT" — "STAND BY THE FLAG, AND CLING TO THE CROSS" — "ALL IS WELL!" A SOLDIER'S FAREWELL — CAPT. TRESOUTHICK — LIEUT. RANSOM: HIS DYING PRAYER AND "GLORY TO GOD" — CAPT. FEE: HIS REQUEST, "PLEASE PRAY FOR ME" — A ROLLING CHAPLAIN — "YOU SAVED MY LIFE" — A DYING SOLDIER'S LETTER — LIEUT. MERRILL: BAPTIZED AT MIDNIGHT — THE DYING CAPTAIN: "HURRAH FOR JESUS." BY CHAPLAIN MARSHALL.

THE following sketches of patients, on to page 62, were taken from the U. S. General Hospital, Fortress Monroe, Va.

STREET IN CINCINNATI IN THE EARLY PART OF THE WAR.

A FORT FISHER HERO.

John B. Duncan, Co. B, 3d N. H. Vol., was wounded at the capture of Fort Fisher, N. C., Jan. 15, 1865. Eager for victory, after having fought several hours, he mounts the fort, and while there battling for his country, about fifteen minutes before the surrender, a minie-ball passed through his shoulder, entering just above the right lung. He was brought here Jan. 19, and I preached to him and his ward the next evening, from the Saviour's last farewell promise, "Lo, I am with you alway." Blessed with patience and courage, though he suffered severely, he bore it all very patiently like a young hero. Not a murmur fell from his lips. Approaching his bed one day, he said, "I want you to talk to me, chaplain." We found him very tender, anxious, prayerful, and penitent. He said he had been awakened at Hilton Head, S. C., last May, and had been praying ever since. He said "he trusted in Christ, and that he was dear and precious; *that he felt prepared, and was not afraid to die.*" Having with undaunted courage fought the rebels at Fort Fisher, and shared in the honor of the glorious victory there achieved, and trusting in Him "who hath abolished death," he now prepares to meet "the last enemy," death, and says, "If I die, send my Testament (much worn by use), my portfolio, and my jack-knife to my mother, and tell her not to mourn for me, for I feel that I can die happy, and am willing to go, and hope and pray we will all meet in heaven."

I talked, read, and prayed with him. He was *very anxious* to be talked to, and hear about Jesus. On the last morning of his life he said, "*I feel happy in the Lord.*" On going into the ward to preach on Saturday evening, we found him worse, and breathing very hard. We asked him if he would like to hear. He said, "Yes;" and while we were singing, "I am going home to die no more," he *went*, and, doubtless, through grace, achieved a victory far more glorious than that won at Fort Fisher. His serene countenance, *resignation*, and easy departure seemed to say: "O death, where is thy sting?"

"To die is gain." How sudden the change! How striking the contrast of his condition on the field of battle with his condition in heaven! Here all is war, blood, and death; there all is life, joy, and peace! Here he was clothed in garments stained with blood; there in robes white and clean! Here he was surrounded with the dead and dying; there with the redeemed and living! Here his wounds were bathed in blood; there in the waters of the river of life! Here he shouted on to victory; there on to glory! Here he bore a sword; there he wears a crown! And "though dead, he yet speaketh." His tongue, though now mute in death, seems to say to every surviving soldier, "*Be ye also ready* — PREPARE TO MEET THY GOD."

A HEROIC SOLDIER.

Elias Babcock, 10th N. Y., Co. B., was wounded at the last battle before Petersburg, and brought here April 4, with his left leg amputated above the knee. He had been sick before the battle; and although his stump seemed to do pretty well for a while, he always looked like a man that was going to die. His ward was full of stumps or amputated limbs, fresh from the bloody field and fierce conflict that gained the glorious victory that put Jeff. Davis to flight, brought down Richmond, and led to Lee's surrender and the overthrow of the great rebellion.

On my first approaching him, I found him a prayerful, decided Christian. He said, though in the army, "*I don't backslide.*" I visited him very frequently, and often preached to him and several others on their death-beds in his ward. He seemed to enjoy it very much. Though pale and weak, he would always put out his arm to shake hands on my approach. A few days before his departure, he said, "I thought I was dying last night, and my thoughts reverted to the place of my conversion four years ago." "All was bright — I felt very happy." "This wound is God's rod to comfort me; it is for my good." "Oh, the precious promises in God's word!" "I am not afraid to die." "I believe I could die happy." "Men may live along with religion, but when they get wounded and begin to look into eternity, and feel the near approach of heaven, it is far better." He spoke of, and seemed to realize deeply, the great sacrifice God requires us to make for Christ. At another interview, when I spoke to him about Christ knocking at the door for admittance into the sinner's heart, he said, "I have let him in long ago." Here the solemn scene beggars description. With his weeping wife standing at his side, and with eyes streaming with tears, and clasped hands lifted up toward heaven, and gazing into eternity, he said, "It is far better." But passing this lofty attainment, and rising higher and higher, and drawing nearer and nearer to God, apparently "filled with the Holy Ghost," he seemed to realize "a joy unspeakable."

Though he suffered long and severely, he bore it all very patiently; not a murmur fell from his lips. Blessed with God's sanctifying grace, his wounded limb was a healing balm to his soul. And his dying words, "This wound is God's rod to comfort me; it is for my good," should strengthen the heart and cheer the soul of every wounded soldier. "Behold, happy is the man whom God correcteth." His last words were, "I am happy." Thus passed away the heroic soldier, doubly crowned — crowned with victory on the field, and with glory in heaven. "To die is gain."

"JESUS IS ALL I WANT."

Man is a creature of vast desires — so vast that the world with all its grandeur and glory will not satisfy him. Though he really *wants* but little, "nor wants that little long," yet "the more he gets the more he wants." Let a man own all the gold of earth, possess all the wealth of the universe, command all thrones, wield all sceptres, control all commerce, scale all heights, fathom all depths, enjoy all the pleasures that this world can afford, and yet there remains an empty void within. The insatiable heart still cries, "Give! give!" and longs for more.

But is there no adequate portion? Is there no remedy for this insatiable thirst? Must man live and die famishing upon the empty vanities of this fleeting world? No; he need not.

There is the infinite God, and the all-comprehensive Saviour, filled with all the fulness of God, before whom "all nations are as nothing, and counted less than nothing and vanity."

Yes, man of the world, here is Jesus, infinitely rich in wisdom, honor, power, and glory, waiting to make you infinitely rich in all the joys of earth, and in all the glories of heaven. Jesus is here willing to be "made unto you wisdom, righteousness, sanctification, and redemption."

The following incident shows, in a very striking manner, the all-sufficiency of Christ as a satisfying portion. Walking over the field of battle, shortly after a severe fight, a chaplain stepped up to a wounded soldier lying on the cold ground, apparently in severe pain, and said: "Can I do anything for you?" "Oh, no," replied the soldier; "I want nothing. I have Jesus here with me, and he is all I want." "But," said the chaplain, "you can't live but a few minutes longer!" "I know it; but I am in perfect peace. I have no fear of death. Please put my blanket over me and cover my face, and let me shut out all but Jesus; so let me die."

Oh, what wonderful words! "I want nothing!" How rich the dying soldier! Go and gaze upon the wonderful scene. See! There he lies with his mangled body bathed in his own blood, and wrapped in a thin blanket, and yet he says, "I want nothing." No earthly friend is near; not a prayer was offered for him; not a tear was shed over him; not an emotion of sympathy to console him; and yet the warm response rises from his gushing heart, "*I want nothing*" — nothing of the world; and why? His soul, his heart, was full of Jesus. "I have Jesus here, and he is all I want." Oh, what a rich possession! What an all-sufficient portion! Where is the worldling that can say as much? Search creation through, explore all heights, examine all kingdoms, ascend all thrones, muster all millionnaires, and where can you find one out of Christ that can say, "I have all I want." No, it is not in the riches, honors, or pleasures of the world to satisfy the cravings of the immortal mind. Then let us pray to be crucified to the world and consecrated to God; so that when we come to die we may be able to say, "I have Jesus, and he is all I want."

"STAND BY THE FLAG, AND CLING TO THE CROSS."

Every age produces some vivid, remarkable, and sublime sayings, words glowing with intense thought, lofty fervor, and heroic devotion. Bacon's " *Knowledge is power;*" Patrick Henry's " *Give me liberty or give me death;*" Gen. Grant's "*I am determined to fight it out on this line;* " and Abraham Lincoln's " *Charity for all and malice toward none*" will live until the close of time. So will the immortal words, " *Stand by the flag, and cling to the cross.*" They are the dying words of Edward M. Schneider, of the 57th Mass. Regiment, to his brother in the navy. When the regiment was being formed, young Schneider was at school in Philip's Academy, Andover, Mass.; but fired with a lofty patriotism, he dropped his books, laid down his pen, girded on the sword, and boldly marched to the defence of his country, though strongly opposed by his friends.

During the weary march from Annapolis to the Rapidan, though but seventeen years of age, he steadily kept his place in the ranks, and receiving a slight wound on the North Anna, was sent to Port Royal for transportation to Washington; but preferring the field to the hospital, and longing to go, he returned to his regiment, and joined them at Coal Harbor; and being so full of fight, he said to his chaplain, while preparing to charge upon the enemy near the " Dunn House," "*I intend to be the first one to enter their works.*" The charge was made. On they rush, with a full determination to conquer or die; and with an eager heart young Schneider led the advance, keeping several paces ahead, as they approached the awful crisis. He was almost there, near enough to feel the hot flash of the rebel musketry in his face, when a fatal ball pierced his body and brought him to the ground. He was carried back to the hospital, with six hundred and fifty of his comrades, where he lay all night with his wound undressed, waiting his turn. He suffered severely, yet, possessing a heroic patience, not a murmur fell from his lips.

The chaplain, Rev. Mr. Dashiell, visited him, looked at his wound; and the suffering soldier, anxiously looking him in the face, asks, "What do you think of it, chaplain?" Seeing that it was mortal, the chaplain was so deeply affected that he could neither reply nor restrain his tears. Edward interpreted the meaning of his silent tears that his wound was mortal. "Don't weep, chaplain," he said; "it is God's will. Please write to my father, and tell him that I have tried to do my duty to my country and to God." He disposed of his effects, giving ten dollars to the U. S. Christian Commission, twenty dollars to the American Board, and trifles to his friends. Then, in the simplicity of his heart, he said, "I have many good friends, schoolmates, and companions. They will want to know where I am, and how I am getting on. Tell them I am gone, and that I die content. And the boys in the regiment, chaplain, I want you to tell them *to stand by the dear old flag*. And there is my brother in the navy, write to him, and tell him *to stand by the flag, and cling to the cross of Christ*." The surgeon came, examined his wound, and said, "It is my duty to tell you that you will soon go home." "Yes, doctor, I am going home. I am not afraid to die. I don't know how the valley will be when I get to it, but it is all right now." Then, gathering up his waning strength, he calmly and solemnly repeated the verse often sung by the soldiers, who, amid all the whirl and shock of battle, never forget their loved ones at home,—

> "Soon with angels I'll be marching,
> With bright laurels on my brow:
> I have for my country fallen;
> Who will care for sister now?"

"The night passed away, death came on apace;" he still suffered intensely, yet without a complaining word. Sabbath morning came, and, with the dawning of the light, his blood-washed soul passed away on the 17th of June, 1864, just eighty-nine years after the battle of Bunker's Hill. It was sad news to send to his father, then a well-known missionary of the American Board at Aintab, Turkey. It was a great loss to lose such a noble son; yet it was glorious to die such a triumphant death.

His work is done. His destiny is fixed. He died that his country might live. His death was a triumphant victory. And although he was not permitted to stand *first* upon the ramparts of the enemy's works at Petersburg, yet, having died such a glorious death, no doubt to-day he stands among the first within the ramparts of heaven.

His grave is by the roadside, marked by the rude palings erected by Chaplain Dashiell. "The summer-breeze sweeps through the sighing pines overspreading the heaved-up mound. Mournful, yet sweet, the music of the wind-harp — mournful, because one so young, so full of life, and capable of such a future, should go so soon; sweet, in that he did his work so well." "Had he lived a century, he could not have made it more complete." "And," says Carlton, to whom we are indebted for the facts, and part of the language of this sketch, "I have stood by the mouldering dust of those whose names are great in history; whose deeds and virtues are cut in brass and marble; who were reverenced while living, and mourned for when dead,— but never have I felt a profounder reverence for departed worth than for him who sleeps beneath the pines, uncoffined, unshrouded, wearing, as when he fell, the uniform of his country."

His last words —

"STAND BY THE FLAG, AND CLING TO THE CROSS!"

will live as long as the flag of our country waves, or the cross of Christ endures. "They are the emblems of all our hopes, both for time and for eternity." How heroic the patriotism! and how strong and sublime the faith that prompted them! What lofty conceptions of duty! What *earnest, whole-hearted* consecration do they indicate! They are the very cream and essence of the young hero's life, and the sum and concentration of man's *whole* duty. What power, grandeur, and glory do they inspire and carry along with them! Dudley Tyng's immortal words: "STAND UP FOR JESUS," have fired the hearts of millions; but they only impress us with our duty to God; but the heroic soldier, with a heart glowing with Christian zeal and patriotic ardor, with his dying breath pleads most earnestly both for his country and his Saviour.

God grant that his inspiring words may be deeply impressed upon every Christian's heart.

"ALL IS WELL!" A SOLDIER'S FAREWELL.

ELNOR WINSLOW, 203d Pa., Co. C, was mortally wounded at the capture of Fort Fisher, N. C., Jan. 15, 1864, and brought to the hospital shortly after. Brave and courageous, he rose above all fear in battle; and, eager for victory, he ventured within a few feet of the rebel guns, and there, amidst whizzing balls and bursting shells, battling for his country, he received a wound, which, after a few months of severe and patient suffering, closed his career on earth. Though blessed with a religious education, he enlisted in the service of his country before he enlisted under the banner of the Cross, and was converted in the army. At my first interview with him, he said he had been seeking religion for some six months; and that he began to pray while posted at Camp Cadwalader, near Philadelphia, Pa. It was there, it seems, he first began to realize his lost and undone condition, and to feel his need of a Saviour. It was then he began to cry, "God be merciful to me a sinner!" I pointed him to the Lamb of God that taketh away the sins of the world, and urged him to look unto him. Orthodox in his views, and with a clear conception of the plan of salvation by faith in Christ, at our next interview we found him indulging a hope, and he said, "I think, now, I am a Christian." And now having tasted something "of the heavenly gift," he thirsts for more, and realizing his dependence upon God for it, he very frequently goes unto him in prayer, earnestly pleading for an increase of light, grace, and strength. Possessing a heart glowing with an ardent, lofty patriotism, he prayed much for his country. Though pale and weak in body, he appeared to be strong in the Lord, and would very often make most beautiful, earnest, touching prayers. I visited him often; and when I preached in his ward, he seemed to enjoy the services very much. He was remarkably mild, patient, and resigned. Notwithstanding the duration and severity of his sufferings, yet in patience possessing his soul, he seemed to lie passive in the arms of Jesus, patiently waiting God's time. Not a murmur fell from his lips. Rising above all fear of death, he said, " I feel happy in the Lord, and am not afraid to die." Deeply concerned for the salvation of his comrades, he frequently urged them to be faithful to God and their country. At another call, some ten days before his death, full of bright hopes of eternal glory, with Christ precious to his soul, he said, "ALL IS WELL." " Yes, dying for your country, and dying in the Lord, all *must* be well. When Rev. S. B. Bangs was approaching the eternal world, full of assurance, he exclaimed, 'Not a doubt! not a cloud!' '*All is well!* more than well,' and looking out at the window, he said, 'The sun is setting; mine is rising.' 'I go from this bed to a crown,' and, bidding all farewell, he went home to glory. And here you lie, with a body pierced with rebel bullets, expecting soon to bid farewell to this weeping world, and, rising above all doubts and fears, be enabled to say, glory be to God, '*all is well!*'" Oh, how glorious the approximation! How lofty the achievement! Victory over the enemy on the field of battle is glorious. Having shed his own blood for his country, and with his soul washed in the blood of Jesus, there he lies patiently waiting the summons, "Come up higher!" And God keeps him here among his comrades. And *why?* Doubtless to give them further warning by his example, exhortations, and prayers. Yet, like Paul, having a desire to depart, he prays, "Lord, can't you as well let me go now as any other time?" In the language of the sainted Toplady, he seemed to cry, "Oh, how this soul of mine longs to be yours! Like a bird imprisoned in a cage, it longs to take its flight! Oh, that I had wings like a dove, then would I fly away to the realms of bliss, and be at rest forever! Oh, that some guardian angel might be commissioned; for I long to be absent from this body, and to be with my Lord forever." "Come, Lord Jesus, come quickly!" And yet this brave hero lingers; the grave yawns. Death knocks at his door, yet withholds the fatal stroke; and his noble soul still cleaves to its clay tenement. Gather round, and gaze upon the solemn scene, and learn how a heroic soldier can die! His dear comrades weep around him; angels hover over him, till at last, March 14, 1864, God, in mercy, snaps the silver cord, and his emancipated soul took its flight home to glory.

CAPTAIN TRESOUTHICK.

This brave officer was brought to the Chesapeake Hospital early in July, 1864, with one leg amputated above the knee. In what engagement he was wounded, we do not recollect. But having proven his love for his country on the bloody field, he comes to the hospital to complete the sacrifice. With a robust frame, a dark, heavy brow, and a countenance beaming with honor and integrity, his appearance was quite prepossessing.

Delighting in the law of the Lord, he kept his Bible at his side all the time, drawing from its exceeding great and precious promises strong consolation. Blessed with the skilful surgical attendance of Dr. Rush, Surgeon of the U.S. volunteers, and nursed by a tender, faithful matron and an affectionate brother, he was well cared for, and received the best attention the hospital could afford. And although his loss was great and suffering severe, yet, "counting all things but loss" for the salvation of his country, he was not only composed and resigned, but he seemed to enjoy an inward peace the world knows nothing of.

I preached occasionally to him and his large ward of sick and wounded officers, in all some one hundred and fifty patients, once on the nature and necessity of regeneration, and again on the nature of God's presence and the rest it affords, urging upon them all the great importance of "fleeing the wrath to come, and immediately to lay hold of the hope set before them in the gospel." Fond of the word of God and prayer, the captain felt himself neglected, if Chaplain Marshall or I did not go every evening and read and pray with him. Consequently we did this very often. At the close of the day, just as the sun was setting beneath the bloody sky, we would go, in a quiet, easy way, and read to him about the Sun of Righteousness, and, after a few words of explanation, kneel down by his bedside and pray with him, commending him, soul and body, to the watchful care of "Him who neither slumbereth nor sleepeth." He had commenced to study for the ministry, but with a heart swelling with patriotism, at his country's call he laid down theology, grasped the sword, fought, and fell a martyr in the noble cause of liberty and truth.

Giving satisfactory evidence of the gracious state by his words and deeds, we never felt like questioning him particularly on his religious experience. But his meek, forgiving spirit and heroic devotion evinced that there was laid up for him a crown of glory. The weather became extremely warm. He lingered along the shore of the eternal world until late in July, when, robed in white, and crowned with a martyr's crown, and singing a victor's song, he passed the precincts of mortality, and went, we trust, to swell the ranks of the blood-washed throng in heaven.

LIEUTENANT C. M. RANSOM.

The following brief sketch of Lieut. Ransom was written by the author, and published in the "American Messenger," New York.

CHESAPEAKE HOSPITAL,
FORTRESS MONROE, VA., July 25, 1865.

Rev. A. S. Billingsley, a devoted chaplain of this hospital, writes, Lieut. C. M. Ransom, 98th N. Y. Vol., was wounded at Petersburg, Va., on the 6th, and brought here on the 8th of July. He soon became very restless, slept but little, and seemed to suffer intensely. I visited him very often, and frequently spoke to him of Jesus, and told him that he is a precious, merciful, all-compassionate Saviour, able and willing to save even to the very uttermost, and urged him to come unto him.

On one occasion I read and explained to him the interesting story of "blind Bartimeus," Mark x., and kneeling by his bedside besought God for his salvation, and prayed that that poor beggar's prayer, "*Jesus, thou son of David, have mercy on me!*" might go forth from his heart. As I prayed, he cried, "Amen! amen!" and exclaimed, "Glory to God; glory to God." Prayer being over, and convinced of his approaching death, he said to me, with deep emotion and tears, "*Tell my mother, brothers, and sisters that I died for my country, and with a Christian heart, and hope they will do the same.*" Soon after he offered an audible prayer. Let us thank God for such a victory. How glorious such a death. "To die for our country, and to die with a Christian heart," is the chief end and highest attainment of man.

Shortly after his death his brother came to see him, and learning he was dead and buried, was *deeply anxious* to know if he died with hope in the Lord. When I told him of his dying words and bright prospects, with a smitten heart he exclaimed, "Thank God! thank God!" and burst into tears, weeping like a child.

Such is the anxiety of one brother for another, and such the strong consolation "to die with a Christian heart" affords. Let Christian laborers, soldiers, and officers "thank God, and take courage."

CAPTAIN FEE.

Capt. JOHN A. FEE, Co. I, 48th N. Y. Vol., was severely wounded in the right shoulder and arm, June 30, 1864, while defending his country's honor, and brought to Chesapeake Hospital shortly after. Brave, frank, and free in conversation, with a generous heart, although he possessed many noble traits, yet he made no pretensions to piety. His wound never seemed to do well. In spite of all the surgeons could do, it would occasionally bleed profusely, thus rapidly reducing his strength. But being lively and jovial, he bore up under it very well. Easy of access, we had no trouble in approaching him on the subject of religion, and frequently we had lengthy conversations about the "one thing needful." I recollect one occasion particularly, on the 12th of July, when I read to him the fifty-third chapter of Isaiah, pointing him to the Saviour "who was wounded for our transgressions, and with whose stripes we are healed." "Jesus received five wounds for the salvation of our souls; you, captain, have received only one for our country. He was pierced through his hands and feet, you only through the shoulder." And having explained to him the plan of salvation, upholding Christ to him in all his offices of prophet, priest, and king, urging upon him the necessity of regeneration, and the importance of immediate repentance, I besought him by every motive under heaven *at once* to fly to the Saviour. On July 9, his wound bled again profusely, and made another heavy draw upon his vitality. The surgeons tied the artery, but erelong it broke loose again; and, after consultation, the doctors decided to take his arm off. Laying him on a stretcher, he was carried to the "operators' tent;" and feeling deeply interested in his welfare, I went along to witness

HARPER'S FERRY

the operation. All ready, they lay him upon the hard table; and conscious of the danger of losing his life (in the operation), I spoke to him about his future prospects, and asked him, "If you should die in the operation, captain, do you feel prepared to go?" "No," he said; "*I don't know as I do.*" Firm and composed, the captain exhibited no signs of fear. They gave him chloroform; and as it began to take effect, he began to say bad words. The surgeons hesitate; waiting, it was said, for the advice of the surgeon in charge. The stupefaction passes off, and I began to persuade him to repent and come to Jesus. Endeavoring to impress his mind with the importance of making his peace with God immediately, and to encourage him, I referred him to the striking, encouraging case of the thief on the *cross*. I told him "man's extremity is God's opportunity." "There hangs the dying thief. It is his last opportunity. This may be your last. There he hangs upon the cross — here you lie upon the fatal amputation-table. There he went a hardened sinner — here you have come an open swearer. He died a malefactor for his crime. You may soon die a martyr for your country. With him it was the last extremity; with you this is probably the last opportunity. Oh, then, trifle no longer with your soul's salvation. There he hangs, a thief and a robber — here you lie, a patriot soldier. A regular Jew, he had been brought up to hate and despise the Saviour. You have been brought up to love and serve him. How thrilling the scene! There he hangs right beside the bleeding Saviour. Hark! do you hear that voice? It is the voice of prayer,— the dying thief praying to the dying Saviour. 'Jesus, Lord, remember me when thou comest into thy kingdom.' Oh, what a prayer was that! It is not only short, direct, earnest, comprehensive, but it was a prayer of wonderful *faith* and *power*. Look at the circumstances, how dark and unfavorable to elicit faith and secure confidence! There hangs the Saviour, nailed to the cross, dying as a malefactor; yet with divine light flashed upon the thief's soul, his faith penetrates the dark cloud, and recognizes the expiring Redeemer as '*Jesus, Lord,*' and flies to him for salvation. How critical the moment! It is the crisis of his soul. It is salvation *now*, or never.

It was his last prayer. And was it heard? Did it prevail? Did Jesus remember him? He did, and replied, 'To-day shalt thou be with me in paradise.' Yes, that very day, with his soul washed in Christ's blood, he went home to glory, translated from the cross to the throne. Oh, then, my dear captain, be encouraged. Look to Jesus. Look and live, believe and be saved. Pray like the publican, 'God be merciful to me a sinner.' Pray like sinking Peter, 'Lord, save me.' Pray like the dying thief, 'Jesus, Lord, remember me,' and I can *assure you*, your prayer will be heard, your sins pardoned, and your soul saved.

"Doubtless it will soon be with you, as it was with that dying thief, your *very last* chance. Now is the crisis of *your* soul. It is salvation *now*, or never; it is believe and be saved *now*, or refuse and be lost forever; it will soon be salvation or damnation! *Now* is the accepted time; oh, then, let this be the day of your salvation! Just think, captain, of the Saviour's love in suffering and dying to save us, and of his ability and willingness to save you; think, too, how lamentable it will be to die for your country and lose your own soul! Think of the torments of hell; of the lashings of a guilty conscience; of the gnawings of the undying worm; of 'the everlasting fire;' of the weeping, wailing, and gnashing of teeth, you will soon bring upon yourself, unless you soon repent! Then let these things alarm you; let the love of Christ constrain you, and his spirit woo you. Gaze upon the compassionate Saviour lying in a manger. View him agonizing in Gethsemane; suffering, groaning, bleeding, dying upon Calvary, crying unto you, 'Give me thy heart!' and let the cry go forth from your heart, 'Here, Lord, I give myself away!'" And perceiving his heart beginning to yield, I asked him, "If he had not been a great sinner?" He replied, "Yes;" and feeling a sense of his sins, and realizing his need of a Saviour, he said, "Chaplain, will you please pray for me?" and then, while he lay on the hard board, surrounded with doctors and surgeons, I knelt down on the ground: I prayed, and besought God, for Jesus' sake, to have mercy on him. Then urging him still further to surrender himself to the great Captain of our salvation, and beseeching him to let go of everything else, and to step right out upon the promises of God, and throw himself into the arms of Jesus, we left him. They cut off his arm, and carried him back to his ward. At my next call, I said to him, "Do you feel sorry for your sins, captain?" "Yes," he replied. "Seek ye the Lord while he may be found. O captain, just surrender yourself *at once*, and come to Jesus. *Now* is your best time. *Now* is God's time. Delay is dangerous. It is glorious to die for your country; but it is lamentable to die, and be lost. Go to Calvary; see how Jesus suffered, bled, and died that you might live! And *can* you, *will* you refuse him? May God bless you, captain." He said, "He loved the Saviour, and that he was precious to him." He grew pale and weak, and his attendant brother sent for me just as he was dying, July 15, 1864; but it was then too late, even to pray for him again. We trust he went happy.

A ROLLING CHAPLAIN.

The son of Dr. Eastman, Secretary of the American Tract Society, was a chaplain. His horse, plunging during a battle, struck him on the knee-pan. His leg swelled and stiffened until the pain became almost unendurable. When he could no longer stand, he gave his horse up to a servant, and had himself to lie on the ground. The pain was intense. Darkness settled over him. He had to take a wounded soldier's place alone that night. As he lay on his back, suffering and thinking, he heard a voice: "*O my God!*" He thought, can any body be swearing in such a place as this! He listened again, and a prayer began. It was a wounded soldier praying. *How can I get at him?* was his first impulse. He tried to draw up his stiffened limb, but he could not rise. Then he grasped a sapling, drew up his well foot, and tried to lift the other up and extend it without bending, that he might walk; but he fell back, in the effort, with a heavy fall, that jarred through him like a stab! He then thought, "I CAN ROLL." And over and over, in pain, he rolled in blood and over dead bodies, until he fell against the dying man, and *there he preached Christ, and prayed*. At length one of the line-officers came up, and said, "Where is the chaplain? Where is the chaplain? One of the staff-officers is dying." "Here he is! here he is!" cried out the suffering hero. "Well, such an officer is dying; can't you come out and see him?" "I cannot move; I have just rolled up alongside of this dying man to talk to him." "If I detail two men to carry you, may they do it?" "Yes." They took him gently up, and carried him. And that live-long night those two men rode him over the battle-field, and laid him down, in blood, beside bleeding, dying men; and he preached Christ to them, and prayed. He had to look up then, brethren; he could look no other way from that position, not even into the face of the dying; and with God's stars shining down on him, and heaven bending over him, he had to preach Christ, and pray!

> "I can do all things, and can bear
> All sufferings, if my Lord be there;
> And pleasure mingles with my pains,
> While his right hand my head sustains."
>
> *Extract.*

"YOU SAVED MY LIFE!"

It was on a hot, sultry night, about twelve o'clock, in the summer of 1864, when all was calm and quiet, that I heard a quick rap at the door of my quarters. "Who's there?" I inquired, hastily. "The nurse from room number eleven, first ward!" replied the nocturnal visitor. "What do you want?" "Lieut. D. is very bad, and wants you to come up and see him — *right quick.*" Immediately I got up, put on my clothes, and hurrying up the long, winding stairs, by the lamps dimly burning, made my way to his lofty apartment, and found him lying on his bed in the sixth story of the hospital. On approaching his bed, he reached out his hand, and giving each other a warm, tender shake, I said, "What's the matter, lieutenant?" "O chaplain, I feel most awful. I have long been a professor of religion, and have enjoyed much comfort in it; but now I feel that I have lost it all. I am afraid I am going to die, and be lost. Oh, what shall I do?" "Look to Jesus, *look to Jesus*, He is the

CHRISTIANITY IN THE WAR. 37

great Physician, able, willing, and mighty to save and comfort! And he is right here — *here in this room,* in all his loveliness, tenderness, and compassion, waiting to dispel your doubts and fears, and restore unto you the joys of his salvation. Are you in darkness? He is light. Are you weak? He is strength. Are you guilty? His blood cleanseth from all sin. Are you afraid you'll be lost? He is '*mighty to save.*' Are you in trouble? He says, 'Be of good cheer.' Then, '*fear not;*' don't be discouraged; there is no danger of your going to die now, and be lost. God's promises run parallel with a man's life. 'Cast thy burden upon the Lord, and he will sustain thee.' '*Only believe,*' and your doubts and fears will leave you. Jesus says, 'My grace is sufficient for thee.'. . . The temptations of army life have, perhaps, led you away from the Saviour, and God has, in mercy, thrown you into the furnace of affliction, to whip and bring you back. God is, no doubt, only *trying* your faith, and he says, 'Think it not strange concerning the fiery trial that is to try you.' Troubles and trials don't come by chance; no, they are sent in infinite wisdom, love, and mercy for your good; and if through their sanctified use you are brought nearer to God, you ought to be thankful for them. Basil's prayer was, 'Saviour, give me *any cross* that may bring me into subjection to *thy* cross.' Then be patient: 'All things work together for good.' Job says, 'Though he slay me, yet will I trust in him.' Oh, then, *fly* to Jesus — throw yourself right into his arms, and cry, like sinking Peter, '*Lord, save me,*' and God will lift you out of this 'doubting castle.' If the dying thief, when hanging upon the cross, trusted a dying Saviour amidst all the darkness, horror, and gloom of the crucifixion, *surely you* can trust him here in the hospital. Besides these encouraging facts, it is very common for Christians at times to become cast down, and get into a state of soul dejection. Job, with all his patience, piety, and assurance, on one occasion so lost his sense of God's presence, that he exclaimed, 'Oh, that I knew where I mind find him!' David, though we find him, at times, soaring aloft and basking in the blessed enjoyment of full assurance, yet, again, we find him cast down, watering his couch with tears, earnestly exclaiming, 'Why art thou cast down, O my soul? Why art thou disquieted within me?' So you need not be discouraged, if, amidst all the whirlpools of temptation incident to a soldier's life, you do sometimes get into the fog, and wander away into the Slough of Despond. Besides, your trouble and distress of mind may arise from the disease of your body."

Thus, sorely troubled, and being very anxious to have his doubts and fears removed, he began to inquire about the nature and evidences of love to the Saviour. Answering his inquiries as well as I could, and recounting to him some of the principal marks of the gracious state, and endeavoring to console him, after reading to him the fourteenth chapter of John, and praying that God would dispel his dark clouds, and pour into his soul the consolations of his Spirit, his doubts and fears began to leave him. After pointing him again to the Saviour, and upholding him in all his offices and attractiveness, drawn from the melting scenes of Gethsemane and Calvary, I bid him a tender farewell for the night. Hastening up early next morning, I found him all bright and clear. The lowering cloud had passed away, and, enjoying the bright rays of the Sun of Righteousness, he was very gratefully rejoicing in his happy deliverance. I visited him frequently afterward, and always found his heart overflowing with gratitude and thanksgiving. He soon got well, and went back to his regiment; served his time out, and went home. I labored on in the hospital long after Lee's surrender: the rebellion was quelled, the slave was freed, and the country saved; but of the lieutenant I heard nothing more until the fall of 1868, when he saw and recognized me in the church while attending the Presbyterian Synod in Ohio. Finding out my lodging-place, he came round next morning to see me; and on entering my room, as we shook hands, he said, with a good deal of warmth, *"Do you know me?"* Looking at him a moment— "No; I guess not," I replied. And says he, "YOU SAVED MY LIFE!" "I saved your life?" greatly surprised. "Yes, I believe you did." "When and where?" "In Chesapeake Hospital." "Who are you?" "Lieut. D——, 143d Ohio Vol. Co. E. Don't you remember coming up late, one night, to see a sick man in room number eleven, first ward?" "Yes; I remember it very well." "I am the man," and then, with joy, I recognized him at once. It was a very happy re-union. How glad we were to see one another again! He was unspeakably thankful for what I had done for him, and I was very glad to learn that I had been the means of relieving him and saving his life. I had not known it until now.

At his kind request, with great pleasure I went out and spent a night with him and his family, near C——; and, as I reached the house, found his noble wife waiting for me at the door. As I approached her, she gave me a very warm shake of the hand, saying, "You are very dear to me, because I believe you saved the life of my husband." Thanking her heartily for her compliments and kind reception, we went in, and found them living very comfortably with his parents. Instead of dying, and being lost in the hospital, as he feared he would be that awful night, Mr. D—— still lives, a highly-respected, consistent Christian gentleman.

Reader, let this striking case encourage you to labor on, and be faithful, even though you do not *see* the fruits. It is not given us always to *know* what good we are doing. *The blessing is of God.* It is man's duty to *labor;* it is God's prerogative to *bless.*

A DYING SOLDIER'S LETTER.

We copy the following from a late number of the "Detroit Free Press:"

Many of the friends and acquaintances of the late Col. Brodhead have expressed a great desire to see his last letter,—the one which, it is generally known, he wrote to his wife from the fatal battle-field. To gratify this desire, we have requested, and have been able to obtain, a copy of the letter, and to publish it, with the restriction, however, that the names referred to in it should not be mentioned:

"My Dearest Wife:—I write to you mortally wounded from the battle-field. We are again defeated, and ere this reaches you your children will be fatherless.

"Before I die, let me implore that, in some way, it may be stated that Gen. —— has been outwitted, and that —— is a traitor. Had they done their duty as I did mine, and had led as I led, the dear old flag had waved in triumph.

"I wrote to you yesterday morning. To-day is Sunday, and to-day I sink to the green couch of our final rest.

"I have fought well, my darling; and I was shot in the endeavor to rally our broken battalions. I could have escaped; but I would not till all hope was gone, and was shot — about the only one of our forces left on the field. Our cause is just, and our generals, not the enemy's, have defeated us. In God's good time he will give us victory.

"And now good-by, wife and children. Bring them up, I know you will, in the fear of God and love for the Saviour. But for you and the dear ones dependent, I should die happy. I know the blow will fall with crushing weight on you. Trust in Him who gave manna in the wilderness.

"Dr. Nash is with me. It is now after midnight, and I have spent most of the night in sending messages to you.

"Two bullets have gone through my chest, and directly through the lungs. I suffer but little now, but at first the pain was acute. I have won the soldier's name, and am ready to meet now, as I must, the soldier's fate. I hope that from heaven I may see the glorious old flag wave again over the undivided Union I have loved so well.

"Farewell, wife and babes, and friends! We shall meet again.
  "Your loving
                                    "THORNTON."

LIEUTENANT FRANK L. MERRILL.

This noble officer of the 3d Regiment N. H. Vol., Co. H, was brought into Chesapeake Hospital, July 2, 1864, with his left leg amputated below the knee. Mild and affable in his manners, he was always an agreeable patient to wait on. Frank and free in conversation, we found no difficulty in approaching him on any subject. Touching his religious character, he said he had been brought up by Baptist parents; and although not a professor of religion himself, he was moral, and had often been deeply impressed with religious things, yet, he said, "I am satisfied I am not a Christian." Still he was deeply concerned about his salvation, and, at his request, I read and prayed with him very frequently; sometimes three or four times a day. He seemed to hunger and thirst for salvation. And in the plainest manner I pointed him to Christ, explaining to him the simplicity of faith, urging him to prayer, and by the mercies of God besought him to repent, and come to Jesus. By the thrilling and encouraging example of the thief on the cross, I endeavored to impress upon his mind the *willingness* and *ability* of the Saviour to save even to the uttermost; beseeching him, Peter-like, to launch forth and step right out upon the promises of God, and throw himself into the arms of the compassionate Saviour, and be saved.

Time fled, the heat became more intense, his wound grew worse, mild lockjaw set in, his appetite began to fail, and frail nature began to give way. At our next call, with his noble countenance lit up with smiles, we found him indulging a hope; and with a spirit of meek submission, he said, "I feel perfectly resigned and happy lying here. I can say from the heart, not my will, but thine, O God, be done, in my case." "I suppose that rebel shot through your leg has, by grace, knocked the spirit of rebellion out of your heart, and brought you in submission to God's will. Oh, how rich the blessing to be resigned!" Recently I heard a wounded soldier say, "I thank God for my wound; it has brought me to the point." At times the lieutenant suffered very severely, yet he never murmured.

Two days before his departure, we warned him of his danger and probably approaching dissolution; yet without an emotion of fear, and resigned to God's will, he seemed to say, in the language of old Eli, "It is the Lord; let him do as seemeth him good." Entertaining a hope that he had passed from death unto life, and giving bright evidence of a change of heart, a few days before his death, at his own request, after due examination, we baptized him in the name of the triune Jehovah. How solemn the scene! There lies the brave hero, away up in the fifth story of the massive building, cheered and soothed by the warm-hearted kindness of Mrs. Dully, principal matron of the hospital. It was about midnight when we applied the outward emblem of the washing of regeneration. And having again invoked the blessing of God to accompany the administration of the ordinance, we gave him the right hand of fellowship, and his heart seemed to throb with thanksgiving to God and gratitude to man.

Resigned to his fate, he had no fear of death. And fond of the word of God and prayer, I still read and prayed, two or three times a day, with him until the last. It is now July 13, near two o'clock in the morning, and he is still failing. His last sands are running, and yet how sensible and composed. Having given me some ringlets and precious mementos to send home to his friends, as his last dying request, he said, "Give my dying love to my father, mother, wife, brothers, and sisters." He stood the conflict of life till near twelve the next evening, when the silver cord was broken, and his noble spirit took its flight, we trust, to the realms of endless bliss. His mortal remains were sent home in a few days.

The following letter from Chaplain James Marshall, U.S.A., will be read with much interest. This captain died in Chesapeake Hospital.

THE DYING CAPTAIN.

When Capt. P—— was brought to the hospital, he said *that slight wound through his wrist could not kill him*. The bones were fractured, and his whole hand was badly inflamed. The surgeon was anxious to amputate, as soon it would be impossible to cut off the disease, when the whole system would become diseased by absorbing the poison. The captain refused to have his hand amputated, as he could not well support a wife and a family of small children with only one hand. His heart was blessed with good natural affections, but piety did not ennoble them. They were the beautiful flowers springing up amid the most noxious weeds around a den of vipers. His heart grew hard as his hand grew worse. His frame grew weak; amputation now would only hasten death, if not cause it at once. The surgeon might cut off the wrist, but he could not the disease. One Sabbath morning, while in his room, he told me *he might not live,* and evinced great anxiety about sending home at once his effects. He wanted to get his pay, to settle up with the Government, and then send money and effects to his wife. When earthly affairs were properly arranged, I very plainly referred to

the necessity of preparing to settle his account with his God, and asked him how he felt in regard to death, and his own personal preparation for such an event. Lying with his right side to the room, he cast his eyes upon the wall, shook his head, his face looking despair, and said, "I don't know. Pretty hard case." This very remark was a rebuke to a life of sin and neglect to prepare for death while in health. I spoke freely to him of Christ as the satisfier of divine justice, as the atoner for sin, as the mediator between God and man, and as the present intercessor at the court of Heaven for all sinners who would cheerfully and willingly trust in the great work he had done, and was then doing by his Holy Spirit, to save the most guilty among men. He was most solemnly attentive. I did not pray with him; but the story of the Cross was fixed in his mind. He was silent and thoughtful, and his manner spoke more than words. As I left him for other sick beds, whose occupants I wanted a word with before the religious services of the day, I heard his voice saying, "Come again soon: I can't talk; but I love to hear you talk."

About ten o'clock at night he sent for me. I was weary and worn; had visited and prayed with a number of wounded men that day, four of whom died within a month; had preached at 10 A. M.; held a Bible-class for soldiers at 2 P. M., and a Sunday-school for colored servants of these officers at 3½ P. M.; had preached at 4½ P. M. in the military prison to about five hundred rebel refugees, blockade-runners, Union deserters, etc., and had conducted a most interesting meeting of soldiers for prayer and conference in the evening. But I went at once to his room. Just as soon as I entered, he told the story of preparing his effects that day to send to his family. I satisfied him that his pay could be drawn on the morrow, and all sent home with little trouble and expense. When satisfied on these things, I inquired how he had spent the day, and how he felt after our conversation in the morning. He replied, "I feel very serious — very serious indeed."

"You want to be a Christian, a friend of Christ, do you, captain?"

"I do. I believe there is a reality in religion, and I want it."

I then prayed with him, after trying to prepare his mind to come to Christ. During prayer, he would exclaim, "God grant it!" "Come, Jesus; come just now!" He was failing — growing weaker. I repeated the promises, and pointed out the significance of God's providences, and Christ's mercy; his willingness to pardon and give peace, if he were only willing to give up family, house, friends, the world, *all* for Christ's sake; let him cast himself a helpless sinner upon the merits of Christ's work: believe in *what* he had done for sinners.

"But I have been," he said, "such a vile, guilty man!" After showing him that the fact that he felt so convicted of his sin was cause for gratitude, — for it was evidence God's Spirit was working in his heart, — I removed quietly to one side, as he was tired and exhausted, and I wanted him to sleep. But soon he seemed in silent prayer, and whispering, in most plaintive, beseeching breath, "O Jesus, just now! O Jesus, just now! Come, O Jesus, bless my soul just now!" Then he spoke out, apparently to himself, "I can't understand; I can't understand." Arousing up, I asked him what it was he could not understand. "Oh, I can't understand how to get religion." Here man's weakness is so plain, I felt like leaving the bedside in despair. But Christ says, My grace is sufficient. Repeating those blessed promises, and urging him to trust his Saviour as a little child trusts his parents, he said, "Oh, yes; I am willing to trust the Saviour. I have the *disposition*, but I haven't the *ability* to come to Christ. If I could only get a *foothold* — something to stand on."

How true that experience. How childlike had become that rough, courageous, brave, profane, proud man! Only divine grace can make such changes. After talking in quieting, cheering, comforting words, I sat one side to let him go to sleep. Soon he was in prayer again. His hand he waved over his face in form of cheering, whispering, "Hurrah for Jesus! hurrah for Jesus! Oh, come, just now!" Then he broke out in a strong voice, "Oh, glory, glory, hallelujah!" and sang, in a most beautiful strain,

"Jesus, my all, to heaven is gone," etc.

He was a changed man. He sang "The Star of Bethlehem," and other most beautiful hymns, showing he had had a religious training. The nurse had been giving him water at times, and observing most intently his experiences. After singing "The Star of Bethlehem," he said, " Oh, I feel that I had a most joyful night." He kept talking, and praying, and singing for some time. At one time he would grieve for his sins. "Oh, that I had served the Lord in the days of my youth." Again: "I wish I was able to grasp the very *essence* of religion." The wife of another wounded officer in an adjoining room had come in to see him, and, while getting him some ice-water, he asked for some. I told him Mrs. J—— was getting some. "Is she? God bless her! I came here a perfect stranger, and how many have been my friends. Everybody has been so kind to me. How thankful I am. It shows there is a blessed reality in religion. How I have been prayed for! The church, the congregation, my father and mother, and friends, God bless them! how they have all prayed for me. But what an ungrateful, wicked sinner I have been — a poor, despised sinner." Then he broke out into prayer, "O Jesus, save me! O Jesus, save me just now!" He spoke of his family with such deep interest, — of his little children; related some anecdotes of them; wished he could see them once more. When telling him that a Christian character was the richest legacy he could leave them, " I know it," said he. " I believe it; oh, yes. I wish I could have them here to-night, arranged along before me; how I would like to talk to them — give them good advice; but God wills it otherwise." I told him freely that life's hardest lesson, which he was learning by trial, was to submit to God's holy will. He knows best. We should be thankful for this world, where, through the Holy Spirit, we can prepare and fit ourselves to meet our Saviour and our earthly relatives and friends in another and better world. Then, his face glowing, he sang out —

> "Cheer me onward,
> Cheer me onward,
> Cheer me onward,
> Just now!"

Becoming reconciled and quieted, he passed into a rest which seemed the peace of heaven. Thus passed the night until three o'clock A.M., when I left him asleep.

He lived eight days from that time in which God converted his soul. Nothing but grace on the heart, teaching the joys of heaven and the hope of glory through Jesus Christ our Lord, makes such changes in these dying men. He was all this time mild, cheerful, gentle, submissive, resigned to God's will; and when he died, it seemed as though he was gazing upon the very splendors of the eternal throne, so clear and implicit his trust in the mercy and power of the Lord and Saviour.

CHAPTER III.

SKETCHES OF SOLDIERS.

"When I go into Battle, I put Jesus in Front"—A Hero of Plymouth: "I will Fall Right into His Arms"—"Jesus is Precious to Me Now"—"Why did You Call Me back?"—"I don't Fear Nothin' at all"—"The World is Hollow and Empty"—"I came out to Conquer or Die" "They left Me for Dead"—"Good-by, Old Arm!"—"Put the Bright Side out to Mother," he said, as he died—"Oh, if I only could!"—"I am Happy, Day and Night"—Value of the Union: "Pray, Labor, Fight for It."

"WHEN I GO INTO BATTLE, I PUT JESUS IN FRONT."

AT my first interview with LEWIS LOVETT, 2d Regiment U. S. Colored Vol., Co. C., we found him prayerful, penitent, patient, brave, and fluent in religious conversation. He said he had been serving God thirty-two years, and seemed to be a decided, earnest Christian. I said to him, "How does the Saviour appear to you?" He replied, "He is dear and sweet; and I am determined to hold on to him, let what else may come." "*When I go into battle, I put Jesus in front; and if I fall, I will hold him*

PRATT STREET, BALTIMORE.

fast." "I have no fear in battle." "No fear?" "No." "Why not?" "Because I put Jesus in front; and if I fall, I know he will save me." "Perfect love casteth out fear. Oh, what an exalted privilege! What a glorious attainment! ready and willing to die for your country, and prepared 'to die in the Lord.'" Thanks be to God for such faith and heroic patriotism. It is worth more than earth's loftiest throne, or brightest laurel ever won upon the field of battle. "Don't the shock of battle, the roaring cannon, the whizzing bullet, and the bursting shell, affright you? Don't the streaming blood, the groans of the wounded and dying intimidate you?" "No; with Jesus in front, none of these things move me; neither count I my life dear to myself, so that I may win victories, aid in quelling the rebellion, and, if need be, die for God and my country. I go in for crushing out the rebellion at all hazards, though blood flow to the horse's bridle, and death come up to the window." "You seem to have courage like a martyr, and faith almost equal to Abraham." "I don't know, but I suppose not. I am a poor sinner; but with Jesus in front, and the everlasting arms beneath, I fear no evil. God says, 'No evil shall touch thee.' With God for my help, and with Jesus in front, and holding him fast, striving, watching, and praying, I expect to go on fighting the 'good fight of faith' until God says, 'Depart, and come up higher.'"

"You seem to have no doubts of salvation?" "No; I passed the Slough of Despond and doubts long ago, and now, by offering up prayers and supplications, with strong crying and tears, I strive to 'go on to perfection,' and I feel very happy. With Jesus in front to direct, guard, protect, and sustain me, I fear nothing but sin, and nobody but God. I expect soon to die; but I have no fear of death. Death is only a *change*—nothing but a *departure*. 'To die is gain, and to depart is far better.' I won victories on the field of battle, but when I die, I expect to win a far more glorious victory."

"How did you attain to this high degree of assurance and comfort?" "Besides striving to 'walk worthy,' I just take God at his word, and try to *act* as though I believed what he says. I stagger not, but *step right out* upon the promises of God, like intrepid Peter, when he walked upon the water to go to Jesus. Jesus said, 'Come,' and Peter stepped forth, treading the mighty deep, 'nothing doubting.' When God commanded Abraham to sacrifice his son, he went forth and offered him without waiting, doubting nothing. When God bade Noah build an ark, he obeyed, went forward and built it." "So, I suppose, it is with you, when God says do this or that; you go forward with implicit faith and do it." "Yes, that's it — WHOLE-HEARTED FAITH IN GOD, DOUBTING NOTHING. When I ask God in faith, I expect, believe, and know he will hear me." "You colored people have long prayed for liberty?" "Yes; we have long prayed and wrestled with God for it." "You expected it?" "Yes; we were *sure* of it. We knew that God said, 'Let the oppressed go free,' and we knew he would bring it to pass." "The great secret of attaining this assurance is UNSHAKEN FAITH IN GOD. It is all summed up in *two words* — BELIEVING and DOING." "Yes, that's it, — *believing* and *doing* with *all* your heart. Just take God at his word, and *do* what he says. I strive to be faithful to God and my country; and I expect to cling to the cross and stand by the flag till I die."

A HERO OF PLYMOUTH: "I WILL FALL RIGHT INTO HIS ARMS."

I became acquainted with JOHN H. BARNETT, Co. H, 101st Pa. Vol., some two years ago, at Plymouth, N. C. At our first interview, he said, "The army has been a good place for me;" and he went on and gave me an account of his conversion, which occurred since he enlisted in 1861, at New Brighton, Pa. He endured the hardness of the Peninsula campaign, and for many months the miasmatic atmosphere of swampy North Carolina, and the shock of all the battles in which the 101st was engaged. He was regularly at prayer-meeting, at church, Bible-class, and a frequent, welcome visitor at my quarters, to get religious books, and talk about religion. He would often meet with a few colored people, read the Bible, talk and pray with them, and had concluded to study for the ministry. He often assisted me in distributing papers and tracts to the regiment. His captain called him "Our Chaplain."

He was severely wounded April 19, 1864, while supporting the pickets during the heavy siege at Plymouth. When the battle was over, after he had lain on the cold ground for several hours, the rebels took him into the hospital, and laid him down near the fire with their wounded, and seemed to treat him kindly. Here I visited, read, preached to and prayed with him, surrounded by some forty wounded rebels. Though apparently mortally wounded, he was calm, patient, composed, and resigned. Not an expression of fear or complaint fell from his lips. Intimating to him, one evening, that he would probably die before morning, and pointing him to Jesus, I said, "Do you think he will save you?" "Yes," he said; "*I will fall right into his arms!*" How glorious to fall on the field, battling for his country, and yet fall into the arms of Jesus! Putting his hand into his pocket, he drew out his Testament, stained with his own blood, and gave it to me, together with his diary, pocket-book — containing some sixty-seven dollars — and his coat-buttons, to send home to his widowed mother. Though unable to get up, or turn himself as he lay on the floor suffering from his wounds, he took it all very patiently, as though he was reposing "in the arms of Jesus." He was a good fellow, a faithful soldier, and evidently a devoted Christian.

At my last visit, at his request, I read, kneeled down by him and prayed for his salvation. Oh, how very much I regretted to leave him and the rest of our wounded. With weeping eyes I bade him a long farewell, to meet no more on earth. He died, I heard, shortly after, and doubtless "fell into the arms of Jesus," and his soul went from a rebel hospital home to heaven, where there will be no more war, pain, nor death.

Very early next morning, we, Gen. Wessels, his staff, and a few other officers, started for Libby on an old tug-boat, up the Roanoke River.

A. S. B——,
Late Chaplain 101*st Pa. Vol.*

"JESUS IS PRECIOUS TO ME NOW."

The wharf to which the patients of the U. S. General Hospital, Fortress Monroe, Va., were brought, was near three-fourths of a mile from the hospital, at the mouth of Hampton Creek. Here they were brought in on Government steamers at the rate of from one hundred and fifty to eight hundred a day. From this point the patients either walked, were hauled in ambulances, or were carried on stretchers, to the wards, and laid on their narrow beds to suffer, get well, or bleed and die, and fill a soldier's grave, as God had appointed them. It was a sad sight to see a large steamer crowded with brave men, bearing scars of honor, with bleeding wounds and amputated limbs, patiently waiting the attention and comforts of the hospital. Here, on these crowded transports, we walked among the living and the dead, and often found the suffering heroes, some in the last stages of life, and others in the agonies of death. Here they lie, strewn all over the boat, calm, quiet, and composed, and sometimes, when they had just come off the gory field flushed with victory, as at the capture of Fort Fisher, or the fall of Richmond, with hearts glowing, and eyes sparkling with patriotism, they were in the best of spirits, and full of jubilation. And while some were thus exulting over victories won by valor and courage upon the field, others we found glorying in the Cross, and rejoicing in Him who conquered on Calvary, and through whom we can conquer, even to the last enemy — Death!

On one of the dog-days of August, 1864, three boat-loads of patients (some four hundred in all) were brought down from Deep Bottom, among whom were two dead officers, and a great many very severely wounded, with amputated legs and arms. It was while passing around among these brave heroes, endeavoring to learn their spiritual condition and catch the dying words of the dying, that we came to one suffering severely, whose first words, after he recognized me, were "JESUS IS PRECIOUS TO ME NOW." "Jesus precious to you now? Oh, how rich and striking this spontaneous manifestation of faith, joy, and comfort. Yes, although just from the gory field of battle, with the loss of an arm and much blood, and lying among the dead and dying, yet with Jesus precious to your soul, you must be very happy?" "Yes, chaplain, I am happy. With Jesus precious, whether in sickness or in health, whether in prosperity or adversity, in life or in death, we can say, '*all is well.*' It is not in the *place* we occupy on earth; it is not in the friends about us; it is not in worldly engagements or earthly emoluments. No; it is in enjoying Christ's gracious presence that makes us happy. Enjoying his smiles, though the world may allure and devils prowl, we have nothing to fear, and can rejoice with a joy unspeakable and full of glory."

Jesus is a friend that sticketh closer than a brother; and although he may, for a while, sometimes withdraw his smiles from his children, to *try* them, yet when they have sufficiently felt the rod, he withdraws the frown and restores the joys of his salvation. All earthly friends may forsake us, but Jesus never. It is a law of his kingdom never to forsake the least of his subjects. Hence his farewell promise, "Lo, I am with you always," should always give comfort and consolation to his followers, whether at home, abroad, or amidst the clash of arms and the shock of battle. It will matter but little who else may be absent, or whatever may be your circumstances, with a sense of God's presence and with Jesus precious to your soul, your peace will flow like a river.

"WHY DID YOU CALL ME BACK?"

It was early in May, 1864, while making my regular rounds among the sick, wounded, and dying, that I came in contact with Moses Bowman, 15th Va., Co. F, whom I found, at our first interview, indulging a hope that he had passed from death unto life. In God's good providence, it seems, enlisting under his country's flag had been the means of his enlisting under the banner of the Cross. There is something connected with army life and with battle scenes well calculated to impress and awaken the sinner. The solemn pause, the awful suspense just before a battle, together with the dread of death and the awful forebodings of the eternal world, are well calculated to arouse the most *careless*. Hence, conversions among the most wayward are not unfrequent in the army. It was some such impressions, it seems, received during the thrilling scenes of battle, that led the subject of this sketch to repentance. "God, who out of the mouths of babes has ordained strength, has his own way of doing his work." He who shoots his arrows when, where, and how he pleases, can make the whizzing of a bullet, the groans of the dying, or the lightning's vivid flash, the means of the soul's salvation. And aroused from his slumber and convinced of his sin, Moses Bowman began to pray on the field of battle; and there, pleading for mercy, it seemed darkness fled, light dawned upon his soul, God smiled, the Spirit wooed, Satan was dethroned, and Christ enthroned upon his heart; and with a soul leaping for joy and a heart swelling with gratitude, he was enabled to exclaim, "All is bright," and "I am happy in God." Yes, though clothed in garments stained with blood, and surrounded with the dead and dying, with the stern reality of eternity rising in full view before him, yet calmly reposing in the arms of Jesus, and longing to depart, he said, upon recovering from a sinking spell, which brought him nigh unto death, "*Why did you call me back?*" "I saw *Jesus* and the angels waiting to receive me." And now with his enraptured soul so filled with joy that he was enfeebled thereby, or from his wound, he said, "My mind is so weak, I can't enjoy it well." The Rev. John Welsh, an earnest Scotch divine, who spent eight hours out of twenty-four in prayer, when about to depart, enjoyed such an ecstasy of joy that he exclaimed, with his dying breath, "It is enough, O Lord; it is enough: hold thy hand; thy servant is a clay vessel, and can hold no more!" Somewhat similar seemed to have been the feelings of Moses Bowman as he stood upon the threshold of glory. His last words to me, according to my record, were, "*God blessed me.*" Whether he got well, or soon went home to heaven, I know not.

"I DON'T FEAR NOTHIN' AT ALL."

A sense of shame and the fear of man are two great hindrances in the discharge of religious duties. Perseverance and courage are equally alike necessary to win and conquer at the foot of the Cross as they are upon the field of battle. Yea, more; for it requires more strength and moral courage to face the world, the flesh, and the devil, than it does to face the blazing charge and the belching cannon's mouth. To stand firm for your country's flag requires much undaunted courage; but it requires more to stand firm for the cross of Christ.

And it was while we were passing through "New Camp," canvassing the hearts of the colored patients, that the brave words heading this article fell from the lips of the brave Edward Draper, 45th U. S., Co. H., while he lay upon his bed, suffering with rheumatic pains, as I was talking to him about the matchless love of Jesus, and he telling me about what great things the Lord had done for him. "And have you no fear?" "No." "No fear of death?" "No; I trust in de Lord all de time for everything." "And so you are satisfied?" "Yes; God gives me what I need, and '*I don't want.*'" "Will you please give me a brief sketch of your history? When were you converted?" "About two years ago." "Where?" "In New Jersey." "What led to your conversion?" "*Light.* I prayed to de Lord, and I received light; then I knew I was in darkness." "How did you feel, when you received the light?" "Me felt I was a very great sinner." "How did your sins appear to you?" "My sins seemed very great and heavy, and my heart felt hard, and me felt very bad and unhappy. Then me prayed on to de Lord; me broke off from my evil ways, and all of a sudden, when I was prayin' and meditatin' about de blessed Saviour, I felt as though a great burden rolled off my back, and dare, while wrestling with de good Lord, I believe Christ was formed in my poor soul, and I felt a great change come over me. And now I pray day and night, and feel ready to go whenever de Lord calls me." "No fear? no want? and ready to die any time?—what a glorious attainment! How did you make such progress in holiness?" "Oh, *I just trust in de Lord*, and pray day and night. Christ is *very dear and precious.* I goes to church, when I can, to hear of Jesus. I serve him. And it is a glorious thing!" "What is a glorious thing!" "Religion, and to enjoy this assurance of salvation? I would not be without it for all the world. What is a man profited, if he shall gain the whole world, and lose his own soul? Yes, it is a glorious thing! By it, Christ, the glorious Saviour, is made unto the believer 'wisdom, righteousness, sanctification, and redemption.' Through it we achieve a glorious victory, and receive a glorious crown. It is glorious on earth; it will be far more glorious in heaven. That by which we rise above all 'fear' and 'want,' and by which we are made *heirs of God*, and receive Christ in all his fulness, and are made to reign and rule with him on his throne (Rev. iii. 21) in heaven, must be perfectly glorious. All earthly glory and honor is nothing compared with the honor and glory the glorious gospel reveals."

"THE WORLD IS HOLLOW AND EMPTY."

Notwithstanding the general similarity in the soldier's experience, we find, on some points, a shade of difference in every individual case. Accustomed to hardness, suffering, and death, even with a well-grounded hope, they generally expressed no fear of death. At our first interview with John B. Moore, 1st Texas, Co. D, though conscious of his being mortally wounded, yet with an abiding hope, he said, "I feel perfectly resigned." Blessed with courage and self-reliance, I said to him, "You seem very calm, cheerful, and lively." "Yes, I do feel so; and it is because I love God." Love to God is enough to calm the most turbulent and rebellious, and cast a lasting smile upon the most forlorn of earth. Linked to God's throne by the ties of this heavenly grace, it soothes the sorrows of the distressed, binds up the broken in heart, and comforts in circumstances the most adverse and trying. Constrained by the fire and strength of divine love, the heroic martyr dies at the stake with joy and triumph. And fired with this most noble of all principles,—of love to country and love to God,—the faithful dying soldier, though weltering in his own blood, in defending the honor of his country's flag and the glory of his Saviour's cross, will shout victory in the last agonies of death upon the gory field of battle. Constrained by this most powerful of all motives, our country has been deluged with blood and ridged with graves. And to buoy up, encourage, and console the suffering soldier in the hospital, there is nothing like it. Conscious of his own sins and unworthiness, John B. Moore seemed very penitent, and manifested a strong desire to live a righteous life, and die a triumphant death. His tender emotions, his anxious desires, his resigned and prayerful spirit, all gave evidence that the love of God was shed abroad in his heart. With a high appreciation of things spiritual, and a deep sense of the instability and vanity of things temporal, he said, "The world is hollow and empty." "Yes," I replied,—

> "'This world is all a fleeting show,
> For man's illusion given:
> Deceitful shine, deceitful flow,
> There's nothing true but heaven.'

Solomon, with a very rich and a most varied experience, rolling in wealth and grandeur, and crowned with a brilliant success as a ruler on the throne, yet with all his wisdom and understanding, at the close of a most eventful life, in speaking of the emptiness of earthly things, exclaimed, "Vanity of vanities! vanity of vanities! all is vanity." What, we ask, signifies all the gold of Ophir, if a man is without the pearl of great price? What signifies the most extensive intellectual attainments, if a man is without an experimental knowledge of the way of salvation? Of what value are all the laurels and victories won upon the field of battle, if the conqueror is at last conquered by Satan? What, we ask, does it signify to sit on the loftiest throne of earth, if at last you make your bed in hell? Then let us with meek humility sit low at the foot of the Cross, and learn how to be wise, useful, and good. In talking about the ministers of Texas, I asked him if he had ever seen the distinguished Dr. Baker. "Yes," he said; "I have often fed his horse when he was stopping at my father's house. He was the first man that ever showed me the Cross." With ups and downs, John Moore survived the struggle of life till Nov. 1, 1864, and gave up the ghost.

"I CAME OUT TO CONQUER OR DIE." "THEY LEFT ME FOR DEAD."

To hear the brave soldier recount the thrilling incidents of battle — the deadly charge, the hand-to-hand fight, and the bloody conflict — is enough to warm the heart and stir the soul of the most indifferent and unpatriotic. Returning from visiting the sick and wounded, one day, as I approached my quarters, I fell in conversation with Robert Curtis, 1st U.S., Co. C, who gave me an astonishing account of his inhuman treatment, severe punishment, and wonderful escape from the enemy. He was from Salem, N. J., and seemed to be a confiding, steadfast Christian; said "he started to serve God twenty-two years ago," and, trusting in the Lord, appeared to have no fear of death. He was in the fight at "the springing of the mine," near Petersburg, Va., July 30, 1864. Said he, "As we went into it, I said, '*It's God's* work, and I am going into it. I came out to conquer or die;'"

and urging his colonel to go forward, in they plunged with twelve hundred men in his regiment, and so destructive was the battle, they came out with only nineteen. The idea that "*it is God's work,*" urges on the religious devotee more than all things else besides. Impress the Turk or Mohammedan with this principle, and they will fight to the very death. Coming in close contact in that battle, Robert Curtis said, "One rebel ran his bayonet through my body, another shot off one of my fingers and bit my left arm." "Why, you must have had a real hot time of it!" "Yes, chaplain, it was hot." "And what did you do to the bloodthirsty rebels in this severe conflict?" "I shot five of them dead; got one by the throat with my teeth, and tried to bite his big vein, but I failed to do it; and while he had me by the arm, I got loose from him, picked up a gun and shot him dead; and falling down by him, the rebels jumped up and down on me, till the blood gushed out of my side so profusely they left me for dead. I laid there for three days, got better, and in three days the 'rebs' came around and took me into the hospital, and I got well." Such is his wonderful story; and did he not bear about with him in the body the marks of those ruthless rebels, we would look upon it as being almost incredible; but when we saw the print of their voracious teeth in his arm, and saw the rent in his side, we could no longer doubt. "Your sufferings have been very severe indeed; but they are nothing compared with the sufferings of Christ. You received five wounds on the gory field; he received five on the bloody cross. You suffered pain of body; Christ suffered agony of soul. You suffered the frowns of enemies on earth; Christ suffered the frown of his Father in heaven. You suffered for the salvation of your country; Christ for the salvation of the world. You suffered without seeing death; Christ suffered the ignominious death of the cross."

The following extract is from the distinguished Chaplain McCabe. It denotes strong courage and a lofty patriotism in the wounded hero. Such acts of heroism deserve to be published all over the earth. I never learned the hero's name.

"GOOD-BY, OLD ARM!"

In an hospital at Nashville, a short time ago, a wounded hero was lying on the amputation-table, under the influence of chloroform. They cut off his strong right arm, and cast it, all bleeding, upon the pile of human limbs. They then laid him gently upon his couch. He woke from his stupor, and missed his arm. With his left arm he lifted the cloth, and there was nothing but the gory stump! "Where's my arm?" he cried; "get my arm; I want to see it once more — my strong right arm." They brought it to him. He took hold of the cold, clammy fingers, and, looking steadfastly at the poor dead member, thus addressed it with tearful earnestness: "Good-by, old arm! We have been a long time together. We must part now. Good-by, old arm! You'll never fire another carbine nor swing another sabre for the Government;" and the tears rolled down his cheeks. He then said to those standing by, "Understand, I don't regret its loss. It has been torn from my body that not one State should be torn from this glorious Union." He might have added:

> "Some things are worthless, some others so good
> That nations that buy them pay only in blood:
> For freedom and Union each man owes his part,
> And here I pay my share, all warm from my heart."

This is what that man gave. What is your share and mine?

"PUT THE BRIGHT SIDE OUT TO MOTHER."

Filial affection is one of the strongest propensities of the soul; implanted in the human breast by God himself, it is a ruling passion of the heart. To love one's mother ardently is natural. A striking example of which is seen in the case of a little drummer-boy, as he lay dying in the awful abodes of Andersonville prison. The little hero had long endured the hardships and deprivations of prison-life with great patience and heroism; but the severe suffering and exposure at last proved too much for him. Reduced by hunger and disease, and crushed with rebel cruelty and revenge, frail nature gives way, and, with his cup of suffering almost full, the day of his relief draws nigh. How sad and mournful the scene! Draw nigh, and gaze upon the noble patriot. There he lies. Once cheering the home, and gladdening the heart, of his widowed mother, — now he lies low in the agonies of death. The heart that once throbbed with patriotic devotion is now sinking in death. The king of terrors closes in upon him, and, though dying amidst all the heart rending scenes of Andersonville, yet, with a heart gushing with filial affection and love, his thoughts fly home to the parental roof; and having cheered and comforted his dear mother during life, he is most tender and faithful to her in death. And being well aware of the severe stroke his death would prove to her, he endeavors to lighten it; and, with his dying words, pours into her smitten heart the living words of strong consolation. It is the last act of his life; and, commending his soul to God, he bids his comrade come to him, and, as he bent down to catch his last words, he whispered into his ear: "PUT THE BRIGHT SIDE OUT TO MOTHER!" And with a few more struggles, his noble soul passed away, crowned with the honors and glories of martyrdom.

"Thank God! the battle is fought; the victory won; and his soul is saved. But, alas!" said his faithful friend, as he bowed his head, and wept bitterly, "*what side is bright in this terrible prison - life?* It is all darkness, horror, and gloom." His remains were interred in the gloomy graveyard close by; but his comrade's life was spared to tell the sad story to his bereaved mother.

Mark the sublime courage, strong, filial affection, and patient resignation of this noble boy. Though his soul was harassed, and his heart pierced with rebel cruelty, yet not a murmuring word fell from his lips. Oh, what deep depths of filial affection, moral grandeur, and glory breathe through those immortal words, "*Put the bright side out to mother!*" What a noble and magnanimous *principle* they exhibit! They deserve to be written in letters of gold, and embedded in the heart of every youth. Let them be written upon the broad canopy of heaven, that every son and daughter of the land may read them. How sublime and Christ-like this example of filial affection! It is second only to that exhibited by the Saviour himself on the cross. Having loved and served his Saviour in his *life*, here we see how he *acts* like him in his *death*. Jesus, with his soul wrapped in the deepest agonies of the cross, laying down his life for his

E. P. ROE.

people, with a heart gushing with care and affection for his mother, charges his disciple, John, to take care of her, and, with his dying words, says to him, "*Behold thy mother.*" * The drummer-boy, though dying amidst all the horrors of Andersonville, laying down his life for his country, with a heart glowing with filial affection, says to his comrade, "*Put the bright side out to mother!*" The Saviour and the drummer-boy both seemed to be more concerned about their mothers' sorrows than about their own sufferings.

"OH, IF I ONLY COULD!"

At my first interview with SAMUEL WILLIAMS, 104th Pa., Co. E, I found him careless and prayerless. Though low with rheumatism, he still remained impenitent, yet not destitute of religious emotions and desires. I endeavored to explain to him the simplicity of the plan of salvation; and when I urged and besought him by the mercies of God to repent and come to Jesus, he earnestly exclaimed, "*If I only could! Oh, if I only could!*" "You *can*, if you *will*," I replied. "What hinders you from coming?" "Oh, I don't know; but I feel as though I cannot." "Perhaps you have never tried it? Did you ever try to pray?" "No, not much." "There is nothing to hinder you but *yourself*. God is willing; the Spirit is wooing; and Jesus is able and waiting. Yes, the Lord *waits* to be gracious.

'Jesus ready stands to save you,
Full of pity, love, and power.'

Jesus having made 'all things ready,' now most earnestly warns and most tenderly invites you to look and live, believe, and be saved. If you refuse to come, and go down to eternal death, it is your own fault. It is the sinner's *voluntary* '*cannot*' that keeps him away from the Saviour. Jesus nowhere says '*Ye cannot;*' but he expressly says, '*Ye* WILL *not* come to me, that ye might have life.' (John v. 40.) Look with what a gushing heart the compassionate Saviour cried to wicked Jerusalem: 'O Jerusalem! Jerusalem! how often would I have gathered thy chil-

---

* That is Mary, the mother of Jesus.

dren together, even as a hen gathereth her chickens under her wings, and *ye would not.*' Yes, it is the sinner's 'ye *would not*' and '*will not,*' not his '*cannot,*' that keeps him away from the Saviour. Whose fault then is it that the sinner is lost? Is it the fault of the church? No. Is it the preacher's fault? No. Is it Satan's fault? No. Is it Christ's fault? No; for he has made an atonement sufficient to save the whole world, if they will only accept of it. Jesus has fulfilled the law, satisfied divine justice, given himself a *ransom,* paid the price, 'redeemed us by his blood,' wrought out salvation, and given his Spirit to *apply* it, and now says, 'What could have been done *more* to my vineyard that I have not done.' Then let the important question come home to every sinner's heart, Whose fault is it, if he is lost? It is his *own* fault. He loses *his own* soul. He works out his *own* destruction. 'And,' says an old orthodox divine, 'he dies, because he *will* die.' Going on in sin, he is treasuring up 'wrath against the day of wrath.' And yet you say you can't come to Christ. You *can,* if you *will.* Only make up your mind, and resolve, like the penitent prodigal, '*I* WILL *arise,*' and go, and you will soon find the way. Perhaps you have never sought God earnestly, and say you *can't* without making the proper effort. God says, 'Ye shall seek me, and find me, when ye shall search for me with *all your heart.*' (Jer. xxix. 13.) Are you *willing* to come to Christ?" "Oh, yes; I am willing, if I only could." "Christ's *ability* and *willingness* to save you is beyond a doubt. He says, '*Whosoever will,* let him come.' Jesus is '*mighty* to save.' You seem to *thirst* for salvation. And the risen Saviour says, Ho, every one that *thirsteth,* 'come.' To the man with a withered hand, God said, 'Stretch *forth* thy hand;' and immediately he stretched it forth, made whole as the other. God said to the valley of dry bones, '*hear,*' and they heard. He said to them '*live,*' and they lived, rose, and stood upon their feet, an exceeding great army. And although you may think yourself unable to come to Jesus, yet if, like Peter, you will only make the *effort,* strive with all your might, and throw yourself right into the arms of Jesus, he will grasp and save you. Oh, then, rise; come with all your hindrances; come with all your weakness; *come just as you are;* look and live; believe, and be saved. May God help and bless you."

"I AM HAPPY, DAY AND NIGHT."

JAMES A. CUNNINGHAM, Co. C, 96th Ohio Vol., constrained by a sense of duty to his country, volunteered in her service in August, 1862. After a few months' hard service, he shared in the honors of the first battle of Vicksburg, in the following December, and shortly after he took sick; and after suffering severely for months, from exposure, was taken to the U. S. Floating Hospital, at Milliken's Bend, La., by Rev. B. W. Chidlaw, whom he afterward called to him, as he was passing through the hospital. After a short interview, by way of introduction, the minister inquired into his religious prospects and feelings; whereupon he replied, "*I am happy, day and night!*" "Happy, day and night, here, so far from friends and home, floating on this sickly, frail craft?" "Oh, yes; Jesus is my all in all, and I am happy." It is not the place nor surroundings that make us happy. No; if "without God," we may have all that heart could wish, and still be miserable. But if we can only say from the heart, "*Jesus is my all,*" we will always be happy anywhere. With Jesus for our prophet, priest, and king, we may say with the Psalmist, "In thy presence is fulness of joy;" and then

> "Let cares like a wild deluge come,
> And storms of sorrow fall —"

And let the world allure; the flesh entice; and Satan shoot his fiery darts dipped in sin's poisonous bowl; yet, with God for our portion and Jesus for our all, we can "bid farewell to every fear," and say "*all is well.*" In a letter to his father, a short time before his death, he said, "Father, I feel satisfied. I hope I have no fear of death. I have my Bible and, more than all, my God, near me day and night; and I pray secretly to him to watch over me, and prepare me for every trial that awaits me on earth, and fit me for entering that rest where the wicked cease to trouble, and the weary are at rest." Patient, and resigned to his Father's will, and enjoying his smiles, he rejoiced in tribulation.

Although for a long time severely afflicted with rheumatism and chronic diarrhœa, yet, sustained by God's grace, he lingered till May 3, 1863, when "the silver cord was loosed, and the golden bowl was broken." God gave him his discharge, and, doubtless, took him home to heaven, a few days after he had received his honorable discharge from the service of his country. His mortal remains were taken home to his native place in Delaware County, Ohio, and decently interred, amidst the tears of a bereaved mother, father, brothers, sisters, and friends.

The following extract is taken from one of the author's letters, written before he entered the army, while laboring in the Rocky Mountains of Colorado.

ATLANTIC SLOPE, ROCKY MOUNTAINS,
BUCKSKIN JOE, C. T., Oct. 15, 1862.

The religious operations of this isolated territory are moving on as usual; interrupted, of course, more or less, by the all-absorbing interests of the war. Detached, as we are, from the seat of the great, fierce, and mighty conflict, we feel it perhaps less than most other sections. Yet we feel it sensibly here in the Rocky Mountains. Colorado has furnished her full quota of troops to defend the glorious old flag. My eyes fill with tears while penning these lines, when I think of the gross, indignant contempt with which that flag has been used. God grant that it may again soon wave untarnished over our *whole* country. For this let us *unitedly* pray, act, and fight. How awful, terrible, and oh, how *humiliating*, this war! And yet we fear the people are not yet humbled because of it. Some have asked the question, Is the principle at stake worth all that it is costing us in treasure, blood, agony, and tears? Yes, and infinitely more! What is treasure, what is *life*, and what is *death*, when a great eternal *principle* is at stake? What is half a million of lives, and all the gold in America, to the life of a great and prosperous nation? Yes, what is *all* this to the life of civil and religious liberty? Oh, then, let every loyal heart gird on the sword; and let Zion awake, and put on her strength, plead and pray for deliverance from this unhallowed rebellion.

CHAPTER IV.

THE FALL OF PLYMOUTH.

THE REBELS ATTACK US, APRIL 17, 1864 — THE GARRISON NUMBERED ABOUT NINETEEN HUNDRED MEN FIT FOR DUTY — EXCITEMENT GREAT — ALARMED WOMEN FLED TO ME, CRYING, "COME AND PRAY FOR ME!" "COME IN AND PRAY FOR US!" — THE ARMY AND NAVY BOTH ENGAGE AT ONCE — THE SCENE WAS GRAND, AWFUL, SUBLIME — REBEL IRON-CLAD ATTACKS OUR GUNBOATS — FIGHT SEVERE — LIEUT. FLUSSER KILLED — THE GARRISON OVERAWED BY THE REBEL RAM — "THE COMBAT DEEPENS" — "IN THE LAST DITCH" — HARD FIGHTING — THE CAPTURE — GEN. WESSELS SURRENDERS — MASSACRE AT PLYMOUTH — VISITING THE WOUNDED — PREACHED IN A REBEL HOSPITAL — PRAYED FOR A REBEL SOLDIER.

IT was on a mild, beautiful Sabbath-day, April 17, 1864, about five o'clock, P. M., when all was quiet, that the rebels, under command of Gen. Hoke, began the siege of Plymouth. They commenced the assault with a heavy fire of artillery upon Fort Gray, some two miles above the town, on the Roanoke River, commanded by Capt. John Brown, of the 85th N. Y. Vol., who, with his brave few, gallantly defended it to the last. About the same time an attack was made upon our pickets in front; whereupon a small detachment of the 12th N. Y. Cavalry was sent out to see, who, after a short skirmish with a loss of one man killed, and Lieut. Russell wounded, soon returned to announce a strong force in that quarter. The alarm now suddenly spread all over town, and many of the women, frantic with fear, came to me, trembling and weeping, crying, "*Come and pray for me!*" "*Come in and pray for us!*" all with most intense anxiety inquiring what to do to be saved?

I had preached in the morning, and Chaplain Dixon, of the 16th Conn., was to preach at night; but the distraction and excitement were so great that the sexton failed to ring the bell; and we had no evening service. A few of the praying men of my regiment had a prayer-meeting in their quarters. It was a good time to pray.

A little after dark, the spirited firing at Fort Gray ceased; and, aside from the activity occasioned by sending our sick and the ladies to Roanoke Island, on a small steamer, a solemn silence pervaded doomed Plymouth, with the men all at their posts, ready for any emergency. An attack had been expected for several days; and Gen. Wessels, with characteristic sagacity and foresight, made due preparations for it. Early Monday morning, the stillness of the night was broken by sharp firing above the town, indicating the rebels' determination to take Fort Gray; and in the struggle, the *Bombshell*, a small gunboat, was so disabled that she dropped down the river, and sunk opposite Plymouth.

Nothing of special notice occurred on Monday, but occasional firing by the enemy, and a warm skirmish along our picket-line, wounding Capt. Burke.

The *Massasoit* returned from Roanoke Island with some two hundred men, commanded by Capt. Mays, of the 101st Pa. Vol., just in time to engage in the severe conflict. Now comes the tug of war in earnest. The fierce struggle for swampy Plymouth begins to wax hotter and hotter. The bloodthirsty rebels thus far had fired only upon our outposts; but now, Monday evening, just at sunset, a heavy line of infantry, emerging from the woods, drove in our pickets in front; and obtaining a favorable position for their artillery, they soon opened upon the town, with shells flying from five or six batteries at a most terrible rate, paying particular attention to Fort Williams, where Gen. Wessels had established his head-quarters. It was just after supper; and having gone over to the head of my regiment, the band of the 16th Conn. Vol. struck up and played a few patriotic airs, to animate and encourage the soldiers' hearts for the approaching struggle.

Presently the music ceases; and although it was dangerous, yet fearing no evil, I was not afraid as, though unconscious of danger, I stood undismayed amidst whistling bullets, balls, and shells, while all around me dodged and juked behind the breastworks. By this time (little after dark), all the artillery on both sides, and our gunboats on the river, were brought into action, and the fierce conflict now presented a scene brilliant and grand. Graced with the silver light of the full moon shining brightly, dimmed only by the smoke of battle, and eager for victory, there they fought for some three hours with perfect desperation. The long sheet of flame issuing from the rebel lines in front, and the heavy storm of balls and shells bursting forth from our artillery and the gunboats, filling the air with balls, shells, and burning fuses, together with the groans of the wounded and dying, presented a scene awfully terrible, grand, and sublime. Men who had been through the Peninsula campaign said, for awfulness, grandeur, and glory, it excelled anything they had seen. Finding, with a heavy loss, after a long, persistent attempt, their efforts to storm our works and take the town proved unsuccessful, and feeling that our fire was too hot for them, they abandoned the fight for the night, to renew it again with increased vigor.

Meanwhile, an assault had been made upon Fort Wessels, a small detached work lying about a mile to the right front, commanded by Capt. Chapin, 85th N. Y. Vol., who, with a handful of heroic men, bravely repulsed heavy charges of the desperate odds of a brigade, frequently driving them back with the bayonet and hand-grenades, until their ammunition gave out, and the brave, noble-hearted captain, receiving a mortal wound, was overpowered, and finally compelled to surrender, having, it was said, killed nearly as many rebels as he commanded men. He died soon after. Peace be to his ashes. Encouraged by the capture of this fort, the enemy now sent in a staff-officer, under a flag of truce, and demanded a surrender of the garrison. This, of course, was peremptorily refused, notwithstanding a rebel force of some fifteen thousand was said to confront us.

SEVERE NAVAL FIGHT.

Very early Tuesday morning, just after the setting of the moon, embracing the darkness of the hour, the iron-clad rebel ram *Albemarle* came floating quietly down the Roanoke River, and passed Fort Gray (receiving a few shots) and our 200-pounder at Plymouth almost unobserved; and approaching our little fleet of wooden gunboats, she ran into the *Southfield*, commanded by Lieut. French, as she lay tied to the *Miami*, and soon she began gradually to sink. Lieut. Flusser, the brave commander of the fleet, soon began to move upon the iron-clad with the *Miami*, endeavoring to sink her; and while the ill-fated *Southfield* was gradually sinking, she was taking the *Albemarle* down with her. During this time, a most severe hand-to-hand fight was going on between the rebel crew and our seamen. Thirsting for victory, Flusser commanded a gun himself; but, most unfortunately for the fleet and the garrison on shore, he was struck by a ball rebounding from the *Albemarle*, discharged from his own gun, and fell mortally wounded on the deck of his own ship, with the lanyard in his hand, and soon after expired. "The command now devolved upon Lieut. French, who left his sinking ship," says Lieut. Longnecker, "and sprang aboard the *Miami*, and sailed down the river, whereupon the *Albemarle* was enabled to withdraw from the sinking *Southfield*, and she came to the surface with three feet of water in her hold, coming very nigh sinking. But the unfortunate *Southfield* went down, and," continues Lieut. Longnecker, "more than one hundred brave but deserted sailors were left to go down with her, and find a watery grave on the decks where they so bravely fought for their country." Some were fired upon by the hard-hearted rebels while attempting to swim ashore, calling for quarter. Says the same lieutenant, "Their drowning cries could be distinctly heard from where I stood. Only a few escaped." When day dawned, the *Albemarle*, now to us "the terror of the seas," was seen sailing about in the river below, and nothing but the smoke-stack and pilot-house of the *Southfield* could be seen. Thus deprived of our invaluable gunboats, and cut off from all possibility of reinforcements, the unwelcome prospect of a rebel prison began to stare us in the face. Yet "none of these things moved me."

Nothing special occurred during Tuesday but frequent firing and shelling from Fort Wessels and the *Albemarle*, from which, to screen themselves, the men constructed bomb-proofs. I found it no trouble to dodge a cannon-ball discharged a mile distant. Passing along the lines, I found the men, though fatigued, of good courage, and ready for more fight. It was astonishing to see what desolation the rebel ram had wrought at Compher redoubt. But there were five companies of the 101st Pa. Vol., commanded by Capt. Compher, all still unterrified. This was the evening before the capture next morning.

THE LAST STRUGGLE.

Toward Tuesday evening, the rebels were seen moving and massing their forces on our left to assault the town at our weakest point; and about midnight they opened a brisk cannonade on our picket-line, near Canoby bridge, to which our men spiritedly replied; but, after a most desperate contest, were by overwhelming numbers overpowered, and compelled to give way. They fell back fighting, gallantly contending for the ground inch by inch.

Here David Fisher, Co. H, 101st Pa. Vol., was killed; two more mortally and several others severely wounded. We were now in "the last ditch;" for a few hours before, all was comparatively quiet; but it was a quiet that precedes the storm, for about daylight, artillery opened along the rebel lines — it would seem as a signal for a general assault — and in a few minutes more, a whole brigade, led by Gen. Ransom, furiously charged on us on the left, defended mainly by the 101st Pa. Vol., commanded by Lieut.-Col. A. W. Taylor, concentrating their main force on Compher redoubt, commanded by Capt. Compher of the 101st Pa. Vol., who, with five companies of his own regiment and part of a company of the 2d Mass. Heavy Artillery, most bravely defended it to the uttermost against overwhelming odds, until the rebels, rushing in, compelled them to give away. The rebels now rushed into town, and our men forming again gave them battle in street after street, repulsing them at different points; and thus bravely contended for their old quarters to the very last. In this severe conflict six of our horses were shot down on a caisson in quick succession. It was now about sunrise, Wednesday, April 20, 1864; and the enemy, having got possession of the town, pillaged the houses, robbed the stores, and took several hundred prisoners, I among the rest, who were marched over the rebel dead lying around Compher redoubt, and on the left, some two miles down the Columbia road. The loyal North Carolinians and colored troops, after fighting nobly, and seeing that all hope of successful defence was gone, and well knowing their awful fate if captured, fled to the adjoining swamps. But our forces still held part of our works. Gen. Wessels, with the 103d Pa. Vol., commanded by Col. Leghman, and a company of 2d Mass. Heavy Artillery, and part of the 16th Conn., still held Fort Williams, and over it our dear old flag still waved in all its glory. Gazing upon it *then* and *there*, surrounded with hosts of rampant rebels, as we marched out of town, prisoners of war, it seemed peculiarly dear and precious. An irregular engagement took place between the rebel sharpshooters and our forces in and about Fort Williams, amidst which Gen. Wessels stood calm and serene. A short truce followed, when terms of surrender were proposed, which our general refused, and firing was again resumed. No further advantage was gained by either side until about eleven o'clock, A. M., when our flag was very reluctantly lowered, and the place surrendered.

Thus ended the siege. Gen. Wessels, with a force of eighteen hundred men, defended the place for nearly three days against a rebel force of some fifteen thousand. The rebel loss in killed and wounded was estimated at about fifteen hundred; ours at two hundred and twenty-five. The 101st Pa. Vol. had twenty-one privates and two officers wounded, and five privates killed. The 103d Pa. Vol. had sixteen privates and two officers wounded, and one lieutenant killed. The 85th N. Y. Vol. had twenty-one privates and one officer wounded, and ten privates and one captain killed. The 16th Conn. had some twelve or fourteen privates wounded; killed, unknown. The N. Y. Cavalry had one officer and one sergeant wounded.

MASSACRE AT PLYMOUTH.

"During the whole afternoon after the surrender," says Lieut. J. H. Longnecker, adjutant of the 101st Pa. Vol., a very reliable man, "we could hear the sharp crack of rebel rifles along the swamps, where they were hunting down the colored troops and loyal North Carolinians. I cannot say that the latter were shot, but the former were shot down wherever found. They were massacred after the surrender." I heard a rebel colonel say, with an oath, "That they intended to shoot every '*buffalo*,' i.e. (North Carolinian) and negro they found in our uniform; and, as far as I know, they managed to redeem the promise." For two days after the surrender, I heard very frequent firing in an adjoining swamp, and I always believed they were shooting our men. The Richmond Dispatch, quoting from the Philadelphia Inquirer, speaking of this awful tragedy, says, "Two full companies of the 2d N. C. Union (colored) Vol. were among the captured; the most of whom were led out and shot by the enemy after surrendering."

RAVAGES OF THE FIGHT.

After returning from below, we were marched about a mile out the Washington road, where our captured host quartered the first night after the fall, before starting to our destined prisons. Through the kindness of a rebel major, I got permission to return to town for my satchel, and on entering my room found everything topsy-turvy. My diary was torn up; several of my most valuable devotional books gone. Library scattered, desk broken, trunk broken open and rifled, the house-floor torn up, papers, tracts, and letters scattered, coats, shirts, pants, blankets, satchel, Bible, sermons all gone, and everything in a state of perfect desolation. I filled my trunk with the scattered books and left them with Mr. Latham, an old resident, who let a rebel officer carry them off. I never saw nor heard of them afterward. Here, in this room, I pointed the anxious soldier to Christ; and here in this room, while rebel shot and shell were pouring into the town for our destruction, my prayers ascended to

God for our defence and protection. Going up into Col. Taylor's room, I picked up an old Bible, which I carried through Libby, used during the war, and brought it home for daily use. With stores and houses plundered, buildings demolished, riddled with balls and shell; with the gunboats sunk and swept away; with the hospitals crowded with wounded, the streets strewn with the dead and dying, and the dear old flag lowered, North Carolinians and negroes massacred, and bereaved widows mourning for their husbands, and weeping because they were not, fallen Plymouth now presented a scene of horrible desolation and distress.

VISITING THE WOUNDED.

During our stay at Plymouth, after the capture, surgeons and chaplains had the privilege of visiting the wounded. Several of our wounded were put in the same hospital with theirs. On one occasion I went in to see three of our men lying crowded in a room with theirs, and while conversing with and pointing them to Christ, a small, wounded North Carolinian boy, who seemed to be in deep anguish, beckoned me to come to him; and as I approached him, he put out his feeble hand, grasped mine, and earnestly said, "Will you please pray for me?" I knelt by his side, asked God to lead him to repentance, forgive his sins, and save his soul. He thanked me most heartily. The approach of death seemed to knock the spirit of rebellion out of him. He seemed very tender, penitent, and anxious to be saved. The scene was solemn and impressive. Bidding him farewell, I said to him, "Trust in the Lord, and prepare to meet thy God." He died soon after. This was in the officer's messroom of the 101st Pa. Vol., where we formerly passed many a lively joke, and enjoyed many a social confab. How changed is all now! Here, where we cracked jokes and ate crackers, now lie dying rebels, bleeding soldiers, and heroic wounded patriots dying for their country. At the request of one of our mortally-wounded heroes, lying in another hospital amidst some forty rebels, I preached, sung, and prayed, and, with close attention, the meeting was deeply solemn and interesting. I counted hundreds of rebel wounded quartered in the largest houses in Plymouth.

In visiting a large hospital down on Water Street, I found P. B. Mortimer, Co. F., 103d Pa. Vol., mortally wounded in the abdomen. Upon canvassing his heart, I found him, though conscious of approaching death, composed and tender, trusting in the Lord, and resigned to his fate. Although suffering severely, and with death staring him in the face, he gave no signs of fear or complaint. Having fought a "good fight," and now about finishing his course, he seemed to be waiting to receive a crown of righteousness laid up for him. Bidding him a long farewell, we parted to meet no more until the trumpet of God shall sound, summoning us to judgment.

CHAPTER V.

GOING TO LIBBY.

ORDER: "BE READY TO START FOR RICHMOND TO - MORROW MORNING AT FOUR" — SAIL UP THE ROANOKE TO HALIFAX — TAKE CARS — ENTER LIBBY WITH LOUD SHOUTS OF "FRESH FISH! FRESH FISH!" — THEY TOOK OUR MONEY — LIFE IN LIBBY — ALL SORTS OF THINGS GOING ON — VERY HARD PLACE — PREACH TO THE PRISONERS — BIG CONGREGATION — VISITED THE HOSPITAL — NOT ALLOWED TO PREACH TO THE SICK — RELEASED — FAREWELL TO LIBBY — THE EXCHANGE — WE CHEERED THE DEAR OLD FLAG — REBELS HANDLE OUR MEN VERY ROUGHLY — BELLE ISLE — U. S. GENERAL HOSPITAL, ANNAPOLIS, MD. — LABORS IN, ETC.

HAVING spent some three days in captivity at Plymouth, about 11 o'clock, Friday night, orders came to our quarters, "Be ready to start for Richmond by four o'clock to-morrow morning." Now came the trial of leaving our wounded, whom, though apparently quite well provided with provisions, surgeons, and nurses, it was hard to leave. Bidding them farewell, and gathering up a few scattered books, blankets, etc., with

Gen. Wessels, his staff, and a few other officers, nineteen in all, we were marched down to the river before day, and got aboard an old tug-boat, and in a short time we bid good-by to Plymouth, and set sail up the beautiful Roanoke, under command of a wounded rebel major. Our fare was tolerably respectable. They furnished us two colored servants to wait on us, and prepare our meals. Being without any, we made wooden knives and forks to eat with. Sailing up the river, we were the object of all gazers. Having reached Halifax, we left our old tug, and took the cars for Richmond, and reached there early Monday morning. Having registered our names at the provost-marshal's office, we were marched down to Libby, and were jocosely received by the inmates with loud shouts of "Fresh fish! fresh fish!" As we went in, Major Turner, the prison-keeper, searched us for arms, registered our names and rank, and took our money. One of our men gave him six hundred dollars. But, to our great surprise, they refunded the money again. For this, we give them due credit.

LIFE IN LIBBY.

Libby prison is a large three-story brick building, one hundred and twenty by eighty feet, formerly occupied by "Libby & Son, ship-chandlers and grocers." It contained, when we were there, nine hundred and thirty captured officers, ranking from the brigadier-general down to first lieutenant. Sometimes the number rose to twelve or thirteen hundred. Some had been there, enduring all the hardships and deprivations, for twelve or fifteen months. With very scant, poor, rough, and unwholesome diet, with some one hundred and fifty men crowded into a room, with no glass in the windows, and no beds but a blanket each man had the good fortune to provide himself, it was a very hard, miserable place. And yet with all these deprivations, with buoyant spirits and patriotic hearts, the men seemed to get along and look better than we would naturally suppose. Every morning there was a general skirmish and severe fight with the invading hosts of "graybacks."

The employment in Libby was various. What did they do

there? How did the captured patriots spend the long, wearisome months in captivity? From splendid portrait painting down to card playing, they had a great variety of exercises. The men were usually divided off into small squads or messes. Every man had his own quarter and sleeping-place on the floor, though densely crowded all around him. Walk around, and see: There you see a man with his slate and pencil studying arithmetic; there is another at geography; there is another writing home to his friends. A little farther on, you see two men busily engaged in making a wooden clock; and then, off to one side, you see a small squad playing cards or chess to kill time. Approach that table, and there you see an Italian portrait painter minutely drawing the features and expression of a dark-eyed major. Twice a day we were all made to pass through a narrow door, and counted one by one, by the guard, in order to be sure no one had escaped. While thus dragging out a life so intolerable in these wretched abodes, our unterrified men were fighting the battles of our country on the field. Some of the prisoners often received boxes from home, and thus procured something respectable to eat. I took tea with a kind friend one evening, and our fare was respectable, considering. There was a stove and fuel for cooking, and soap for washing. The fare was a small ration of *very rough, coarse* corn-bread and a few worm-eaten black peas. The Richmond daily papers were brought in for sale every morning. With this daily routine, it was a hard way of serving our country. They had lectures, debates, etc., to break the dull monotony.

PREACHING IN LIBBY.

I had not been long within the massive walls of that terrible place until they found out I was a chaplain, and invited me to preach. A room was selected, an hour appointed, and the people invited; Bible and hymn-books procured, and, at the appointed time, we met in the name of Him who said, "Lo, I am with you always!" and we had a very large, attentive congregation and a solemn, interesting meeting. I chose for the text God's precious, encouraging promise to Moses and the children of Israel, when they were in troubles and trials, journeying through the wilderness to Canaan, "*My presence shall go with thee, and I will give thee rest.*" (Ex. xxxiii. 14.) God's presence, *essential* and *gracious*, and the *rest* it affords. GOD IS PRESENT, that, though prisoners of war, shut up in this stronghold in the rebel capital, yet the "Lord of hosts is with us," "God is our refuge and strength, a very present help in trouble," that Jesus Christ is here, waiting to be gracious, waiting to sustain, guide, guard, comfort, and save us. Though encompassed with the strong rebel guard, yet God was with us, and it was good to be there. The next day but one, I preached again on *the attractions of the cross*; and many were drawn together, and seemed by Christ's constraining love to draw very near to God; and the congregation was much larger and the services more solemn and impressive. Some of the Richmond clergy came in and preached occasionally, until one spoke contemptibly of our flag, and he could never get a hearing afterward. The people seemed to be hungering for the gospel, and anxious to hear preaching. Libby was a good, *promising* field for preaching, and therefore, with all its hardness and deprivations, I regretted, in some respects, to leave it.

LIBBY HOSPITAL.

The hospital, containing some forty patients, was down in the lower story of the same building. Through the permission of Major Turner, accompanied by a guard, I went down to see the patients, and having encouraged the hearts of the sickest ones and pointed them to Christ, besought them, by the mercies of God, to come to Jesus, and "be of good cheer." At their request I consented to stay, take supper, and preach for them that evening; but the hard-hearted major would not allow it, and I had to go back to my own place, with the guard, before dark. The sick fared better than the well. They had bunks, mattresses, pillows, etc., but all were so awful dirty, that it was enough to make a man sick to sleep on them. There were but few very bad cases.

FAREWELL TO LIBBY.

During my short stay I made the acquaintance of many noble, generous, patriotic fellows, whom I regretted very much to leave incarcerated in that horrible place of torment. But now having witnessed something of the panorama of prison-life in Libby, right beneath the frown of "old Jeff," and having shared in their sorrows and trials, early Saturday morning orders came "for all chaplains, surgeons, and some twenty-five others, to get ready to start for the flag-of-truce boat." As the list of exchanged officers was read out, all stood with profound silence, every one with intense anxiety waiting to hear his own name called. By hurrying, we soon got ready, and, hastening downstairs, stood in double file in front of the prison, waiting "marching orders," with the prison windows densely crowded with anxious hearts witnessing our departure; and as we started, many exclaimed, "Good-by, chaplain — good-by, chaplain," and with a hearty response, and with a falling tear, commending them to the God of all grace, we bade them farewell, sorrowing most of all to leave them in their forlorn, suffering condition. On reaching the boat, we found it heavily loaded and densely crowded with some three hundred and fifty half-starved Union prisoners from Bell Isle and Richmond. Many of them were mere skeletons, and pale as death from disease and starvation. On arriving upon the boat, they gave us small rations of good wheat bread and a kind of briny soup, which, not suiting my taste, I threw into the river; but the wheat bread tasted very well, after living so long on coarse corn and the hard, scanty fare in Libby.

THE EXCHANGE.

On arriving at City Point, the place of exchange, we again beheld our dear old flag, and cheered it heartily. What a change from the rebel to the Union flag! from Libby prison to the sweet air of liberty, sailing down the flowing tide of the beautiful James. It was like emerging from darkness to light. As we stepped off their boat into ours, we felt as though a heavy burden had rolled from our backs.

And now began the exchange of the poor suffering soldiers. While their men, fresh from our prisons, looked stout and rugged and well-fed, nearly all ours looked pale, weak, and half starved to death. And how shocking to see how awfully rough they handled our men. I could but weep to see them toss them about almost like dead hogs. It was most cruel. Laboring hard, I did what I could to comfort the poor fellows while going to Annapolis: I begged bread from the cook, and fed the most hungry. I preached and prayed with them, pointed them to the Saviour, and tried to comfort them with the consolations of the gospel. Sailing down the river, and it being the Sabbath-day, at the request of Col. Beech, I gave them a short sermon in the cabin.

Touching at Fortress Monroe, we sailed up the broad Chesapeake Bay to Annapolis, Md., where our half-starved, sick, and dying patriots were taken to the hospital and well cared for; and all the officers were granted twenty days' leave of absence to go home. But I chose to remain and labor "for the welfare of the poor suffering soldiers." Having registered my name, and supplied myself with a little necessary clothing, and being refreshed with a good night's sleep, after writing out a brief sketch of the fall of Plymouth for a New York paper, we started out in search of the hospital, to see how those suffering soldiers were faring. And upon entering one of the wards of the naval hospital, my attention was drawn to a half-starved, fine-looking soldier, for whom we had begged bread on the boat two days before, now struggling in the agonies of death, soothed by the tender affection of two kind lady-nurses. How solemn the scene! Gaze upon the brave soldier, now fighting his last battle, dying for his country! See how he struggles! the conflict rages; the soul clings to its clay tenement; death presses his claims; frail nature gives way; reason is dethroned; and it is now too late to inquire into his spiritual condition,— but the calm smile resting upon his noble brow, the manifest submissive spirit, together with his serene countenance, seemed to tell that he was getting the victory over the last enemy! There he lies. time flies; life ebbs away; he gasps, struggles, and, though he seemed to die easy, yet the twitching of his face evinced that he felt the pain of dying! He breathes on, till, presently, the wheel at the cistern stands still, and his immortal spirit, washed in Christ's blood, we trust, went home to God!

UNITED STATES GENERAL HOSPITAL, ANNAPOLIS, MD.

And now, looking around us, we found ourselves in one of the finest hospitals in the country. Occupying the neat, comfortable buildings and beautiful grounds of the U. S. Naval School, and washed by the swelling tide of the pure water of Chesapeake Bay, it is most delightfully situated, and enjoying the sweet, refreshing breeze rolling up from the "old ocean," and surrounded with a salubrious atmosphere, rendered it very conducive to the health and comfort of the patients. Superintended by the discriminating and exacting Dr. Vanderkeiff, Assistant Surgeon U.S.A., everything was carried on with good order. Well supplied with surgeons and a good corps of faithful lady-matrons, and good rations, the patients fared very well.

With a good chapel, organ, and choir, we had a good attentive congregation and very interesting prayer-meetings. With a very large, well-selected library and a good supply of papers, the patients were very well supplied with reading matter.

Yet, with all these comforts and appliances, they could not keep death out of the camp. In spite of all their skill and attention, "the king of terrors" would invade their thick brick walls and tent wards and pluck off his victims daily. To see the brave heroes drop off, and four or five consigned to the tomb in a day, was, to one not accustomed to such rapid mortality, deeply impressive. Here we met with a kind and generous friend in the laborious Chaplain H. C. Henries, U.S.A., at whose request we took charge of the religious work of the hospital during his absence East. And now there opened before us a fine field for Christian effort. Preaching, visiting the patients, and burying the dead, kept us very busy all the time. And, without time to particularize minutely, we had many very interesting cases and interviews with the patients, and here we formed many pleasant acquaintances.

BELLE ISLE.

Hard by Libby was the cruel Belle Isle, a prison for cruelty more severe than Libby, situated on an island in the James River, opposite Richmond, on a low, sandy, barren waste, where the prisoners were exposed to severe heat in summer and extreme cold in winter. Here the rebels practised cruelties upon our unfortunate soldiers in a manner almost impossible to describe. With but a few ragged tents, about one-half of the men had no shelter at all. It was my privilege to labor for and preach to a boat-load of some three hundred and fifty men from this place of torment; and such a half-starved, distressed appearance as they presented, was enough to make an angel weep. With eyes sunken, hair dishevelled, countenances pale and wan, and reduced to skin and bones, they looked more like walking skeletons than living men.

To hear them relate their hardships, deprivations, and sufferings was truly heart-rending. There, they told me, "many starved to death, and many froze to death." One day a dog ran into camp, they said, and he was quickly snatched up, killed, skinned, and devoured by the prisoners with the appetite of a vulture. I have now in my possession a ration of corn-bread given me over five years ago by one of those half-starved fellows as we sailed from Richmond to Annapolis; it is less than two inches square, and less than an inch thick. This, with a gill of rye coffee in the morning and a gill of soup in the evening, twice a day, was all they had to sustain life. "Sometimes some of them got a mouthful of meat." Having there dragged out a life more intolerable than death itself, in this horrible place, many of them were sent down to Annapolis to die. But a day of retribution awaits those unmerciful oppressors and tyrants. Yes, it has already come upon them. Less than a year after, Richmond, the stronghold of rebeldom and of this unparalleled cruelty, was wrapped in flames, and the arch-traitor, Jeff. Davis, driven from his throne, caught, manacled, and imprisoned. "The way of the transgressor is hard. Be sure your sins will find you out."

CHAPTER VI.

U. S. GENERAL HOSPITAL, FORTRESS MONROE, VA.

LOCATION FINE — BUILDINGS SPLENDID — CHESAPEAKE HOSPITAL — BETHESDIAN CHAPEL — INTERESTING MEETINGS — READING-ROOM AND LIBRARY FOR PATIENTS — HAMPTON HOSPITAL, ORGANIZED 1862 — HEAD-QUARTERS — " NEW CAMP " — CONTRABAND HOSPITAL — ALL CONSOLIDATED INTO ONE GENERAL HOSPITAL IN 1864 — CALLED BY THE ABOVE NAME — DISBANDED IN MARCH, 1866 — MANAGED BY DR. ELI MCCLELLAN, ASSISTANT SURGEON, U. S. A. — HOSPITAL GARDEN — VERY EXTENSIVE — TWENTY-FIVE THOUSAND HEAD OF CABBAGE — HOSPITAL HENNERY — CAMP DISTRIBUTION — SOLDIERS CAME AND WENT BY THOUSANDS — CHAPLAIN MARSHALL PREACHED TO THEM BY NIGHT — MILITARY PRISON — PREACHING TO THE SPIRITS IN PRISON — GANGRENE CAMP — INTERESTING SCENES — "NONE BUT CHRIST" — ARRIVAL OF PATIENTS: FROM TWO HUNDRED TO EIGHT HUNDRED A DAY — TRANSFERRING PATIENTS — VOYAGE TO NEW YORK WITH A LOAD OF PATIENTS — BIG JOB FOR THE CHAPLAIN — A PATIENT KISSED MY HAND — A WEEPING MOTHER AND HARD-HEARTED SURGEON — "ALL FAST ON THE POTOMAC."

STANDING off Hampton Roads, some two miles north of the fort, is the old *Chesapeake Seminary* building. Built of brick, it is massive and substantial, one hundred and sixty by sixty feet, six stories high, and well devised. With grand and lofty columns, and a towering dome surmounted with the glorious "stars and stripes," and overlooking the busy fort, Hampton Hospital, the mouth of James River, and the long lines of ships and steamers playing therein, it is most beautiful for situation. Washed by the swelling tide, and fanned by the bland, invigorating breeze of the ocean, it is one of the most pleasant and desirable places in the United States. Captured in 1861, it was used a while for regimental hospital purposes, and was organized into a United States general hospital in March, 1862, by Dr. John M. Cuyler, then medical director at the fort. This is generally known as Chesapeake Hospital.

Having spent about a month, immediately after my release from Libby prison, in the U. S. General Hospital at Annapolis, Md., I reported in person to the Secretary of War, who gave me, unasked, under his own signature, a leave of absence for twenty days. But not wishing to go home, and Fortress Monroe being the head-quarters of the department to which I belonged, I was afterward ordered to report there for duty. Here I arrived June 1, 1864, and reported to Gen. Butler, and was ordered to the above hospital for duty the next day. Here I met the laborious Chaplain James Marshall, U. S. A., who had been laboring here for the spiritual welfare of our brave heroes for some two years. Through his persevering efforts, he had succeeded in raising funds at the North, and had erected a very neat, comfortable little chapel, hard by Camp Distribution and close by the Chesapeake. Here the chaplains, delegates of the U. S. Christian Commission, visitors, patients, officers and soldiers, matrons and all, met from time to time; and we often enjoyed most precious seasons of refreshing. Here the suffering patients, after lying for months upon their wearisome beds, when at all able to get out, would drag their crippled limbs and mangled bodies, on crutches, to church and the semiweekly prayer-meeting, where many would relate their religious feelings and experience with deep interest and powerful effect. Sometimes the whole congregation would rise to be prayed for. Here Chaplain Marshall and myself labored together, and for some three months preached in turns, and I always found it good to be there. The pulpit was very often supplied by delegates and visitors. Having no organized church, the converts were never counted. In this main building I quartered and boarded till mustered out. Close by it were two large wooden star-barracks and a few tents, accommodating in all some eight hundred patients.

Mr. Marshall collected a valuable and well-assorted library of some fifteen hundred volumes, which, together with a great variety of pamphlets, periodicals, and a rich supply of secular and religious papers and tracts, made a very interesting reading-room. Here the reader could always find on file "The Army and Navy Journal," and the daily papers from all parts of the country. Here the soldiers went, read the news, wrote letters, and obtained books as they chose. The reading-room was a great light among the patients. It was in connection with the chapel. They had a Sabbath-school and Bible-class also. This hospital was the scene of much severe suffering, of many prayers, many tears, many deaths, and of some very striking conversions. Here many a sick and wounded officer and soldier, after suffering for months most severely, was at last relieved by death, and laid in a soldier's grave. Here, too, many a weeping wife and bereaved mother faithfully watched and tenderly nursed their sick and wounded, dying, sons and husbands. You could tell the patient's condition, whether better or worse each day, by the nurse's countenance and expression. If the patient's prospects were encouraging, and bidding fair to get well, you could see the cheerful expression beaming from the nurse's countenance as we sat by them at the table. On the other hand, if all looked discouraging, and death seemed to be approaching, you could see a solemn sadness in the eye of the anxious wife or mother.

To this noted hospital and camp the coming and going of patients, soldiers, officers, prisoners, surgeons, visitors, and matrons were like the ebbing and flowing of the tide of the ocean. Superintended by Dr. Eli McClellan, assistant surgeon of the U.S.A., surgeon in charge, noted for his good executive ability, and managed more directly by the skilful surgeon, Dr. Rush, surgeon of U.S. Vol., and executive officer of this division, with all the modern improvements, and carefully managed internally, by Mrs. Mary B. Dully, directress, who, like Mary of old, "did what she could" to provide for and comfort the sick and wounded, the patients generally fared very well. It was called Chesapeake Hospital, and sometimes known as the Officer's Division. It was closed August 1865.

Having labored here some three months, owing to the diminution of patients in this division, I went over to the

UNITED STATES GENERAL HOSPITAL, HAMPTON, VA.,

which was organized August 18, 1862, by Dr. J. M. Cuyler, Assistant Surgeon, U.S.A. Dr. E. McClellan was the first surgeon in charge, and was continued nearly three years. It was only about half a mile from the Chesapeake. It contained twenty-five good frame wards, well furnished with single iron bedsteads and good bedding, with everything convenient and comfortable. Each ward would accommodate about sixty patients. It was beautifully laid out, and built in the form of a sharp triangle, or wedge, with comfortable board-walks all through it, and with two large dining-halls and two "*side-kitchens*" in the centre, with linen-room, dispensary, baggage-room, library, post-office, and head-quarters, at the base—all were very conveniently arranged.

Besides those twenty-five "wooden wards," there were several large tent-wards, containing each about one hundred patients, which, together with the guards and attendants, made in all usually about twenty-five hundred patients in this division.

Built upon a level plain, hard by the old aristocratic town of Hampton, always kept clean and neat, and overlooked by the lofty dome of the Chesapeake, and the Tyler House, and overshadowed by the dear old flag, and surrounded with hospital tents, it looked like a little city, and presented a very neat appearance. Here I met with the efficient Chaplain E. P. Roe, U.S.A.; and we labored together very agreeably until several months after the war closed. This division was the scene of much severe suffering and many deaths. It was devoted, during my stay, exclusively to private soldiers; and, being the head-quarters of all the other divisions, in the fall of 1864 it was very much enlarged. Here the surgeon in charge had his office, to which all the other divisions made their regular reports. In July or August, 1865, all the other divisions were consolidated into this. Soon after the fall of Richmond, the hospitals at the front began to disband, and the patients were brought here. About the 20th of July, 1865, Dr. McClellan, the old surgeon in charge, was relieved, and Dr. J. H. Frantz, Assistant Surgeon, U.S.A., succeeded him.

NEW CAMP,

or Division No. 2, established in the summer of 1864, and chaplained by Rev. Dr. Charles Raymond, U.S.A., was composed entirely of tents. Situated upon a little eminence close by Hampton, and washed by the swelling tide, and favored with a fine refreshing breeze, the location was fine. It contained from ten to twelve hundred patients, comfortably situated in good tents. Everything about it was kept clean and neat, so that it was an interesting place to visit. Here, a great many brave soldiers fought their last battle, and many, too, gave every evidence of triumphing over death. It was afterward used exclusively for colored patients. Chaplain Raymond, having charge of the public schools of the department, was absent very often, and consequently had pious soldiers appointed to go round, read, talk, and pray with the sickest or worst wounded patients, and note down their religious experience and the dying messages of those that died, and send them home to the bereaved friends. I very often visited this camp and did what I could in pointing the patients to Christ, warning and beseeching them to trust in the Lord. Here I met with many very interesting cases in religious experience.

THE CONTRABAND HOSPITAL,

or Division No. 4, accommodating about one hundred and sixty patients, was situated over beyond Hampton, in a very pleasant place. Although it was devoted more especially to the accommodation of the contrabands, colored soldiers were often sent there for treatment. They had no chaplain; and when I could find it convenient, I went over, visited, conversed with the worst cases, and preached to them all. They seemed to appreciate it highly.

During the summer and fall of 1864, this vast institution was rather a *receiving hospital*, where the patients were coming and going nearly all the time. They came at the rate of seven hundred, or more, a day; sometimes, and often, from two hundred and fifty to four hundred per day in Government steamers. They were sent North by ship-loads; often in a state of health so low that several would die on their way North. All the different divisions were consolidated into one general hospital in the summer of 1864, under the name of the *United States General Hospital*, Fortress Monroe, Va., and so remained until March, 1866, when it was all disbanded. Blessed with an almost constant refreshing sea-breeze, and being almost surrounded with water, the location was fine, and very conducive to health. For nearly three entire years of the bloody war, the whole was commanded by Dr. E. McClellan, Assistant Surgeon, U.S.A., who displayed fine executive ability in managing it so successfully.

THE HOSPITAL GARDEN.

Close by Hampton Hospital was the hospital garden. With a rich, fertile soil in a fine state of cultivation, and superintended by Chaplain Roe, it was well managed, and worked by the patients and convalescents; it was well tilled, and yielded abundant crops. It was the biggest garden I ever saw. There must have been some sixty acres under cultivation, yielding the finest kind of vegetables, and many of them of a very early growth. The yield in the year 1865, according to the report of Chaplain Roe, was 25,000 head of cabbage, 800 bushels of beans, 100 bushels of carrots, 20 bushels of cucumbers, 75 bushels of beets, 5 bushels of peppers, 20 bushels of salsify, 25 bushels of parsnips, 100 bushels of squashes, 250 bushels of tomatoes, 2693 ears of sweet corn, 1100 cheese pumpkins, 1500 watermelons, 325 egg-plants, 1000 bushel of Irish potatoes, 1100 bushels of lettuce, 104 bushels of spinach, 364 bushels of pease, 11,760 bunches of onions, 11,465 bunches of radishes, 800 heads of cauliflowers, and large, fine patches of strawberries, etc. Many of the patients having been so long without vegetables, they gave them a double relish for them. A nice dish of fine strawberries was very refreshing to the sick and wounded soldier. The officers shared largely in the products of the garden. Dr. McClellan frequently sent a box of vegetables to Gen. Barnes, Surgeon-General, U.S.A., at Washington City. When the strawberries and watermelons began to get ripe, the garden was put under guard. The garden was a fine thing for the hospital. The vegetables were conducive to the recovery of the patients.

THE HOSPITAL HENNERY.

Owing to the great demand for eggs and chickens in the hospital, and well aware of the value of this kind of diet among the patients, the surgeon in charge got up a hospital hennery hard by the hospital garden and graveyard. It contained some five or six acres of ground, traversed by a small ravine, with a little bayou of a small arm of the adjoining bay. Inclosed with a very high paling, it was very difficult for the fowls to escape. It was well furnished with neat, comfortable hen-houses and roomy coops. Here the doctor gathered in some fifteen hundred chickens, turkeys, and ducks. Overseen by a detached soldier expert in the business, the institution was well managed. And although the hens laid thousands of eggs and hatched over a thousand chickens, yet, owing to their being too much crowded, or from some other cause, they never seemed to do well. Yet the craving appetite of many a needy soldier was satisfied and his languishing system strengthened by the eggs, soup, and chickens furnished from this poultry yard; and no doubt many a patient's life was saved by these refreshments.

CAMP DISTRIBUTION.

Hard by Chesapeake Hospital was Camp Distribution. Washed by the swelling tide of the limpid waters of Hampton Roads, overlooking the fort and the mighty ships and flying steamers ploughing the wide surrounding waters, the location was fine. With extensive barracks, and inclosed with a strong fence, with a secure guard, it formed a safe retreat for the sojourning soldier. Here the new recruit, the drafted soldier, the volunteer, and the returning veteran poured in from the North by thousands and thousands, and during the last eighteen months of the war some hundred thousand passed through this often crowded camp. Like the ebbing and flowing of the tide, they came and went daily by hundreds and thousands to all parts of the army and navy. Commanded by Capt. Blake, and guarded by Battery F, of the 3d Pa. Heavy Artillery, everything was kept clean and neat. With large crowds collected in these barracks, it afforded a very good opportunity for preaching. And here Chaplain Marshall would go, night after night, and administer to their spiritual wants. Entering the vast crowd at dark, he would commence by singing an interesting hymn, and having thus attracted their attention, he would preach to them the simple truths of the gospel, earnestly urging them, as they had enlisted in the service of their bleeding country, to enlist in the cause of a bleeding Saviour. Commencing in his attractive, winning way, he always succeeded in getting their attention, and then, in a warm, earnest manner, he gave many of the heroic patriots their last warning and urgent invitation, as they were going forth to fight for the salvation of their country, first to secure the salvation of their immortal souls. The meetings were solemn and interesting. And the chaplain, feeling that it was doubtless the last opportunity with many of them, with his heart warmed and soul stirred with the solemnity and importance of the occasion, was enabled the more earnestly to beseech them, by the mercies of God, "to flee the wrath to come," repent, and come to Jesus. Eternity alone will reveal the good accomplished in these meetings.

Immediately adjoining this camp was the *military prison*, into which were gathered all sorts of criminals from the Union army, and hosts of rebel prisoners of all grades and characters. To see a gang of "Johnnies" stripped of their arms, clothed in tattered gray, with countenances fallen, hearts discouraged, each one dragging a flimsy blanket surmounted with a rusty canteen, presented quite a shabby appearance. In this stronghold, or " bull pen," as it was generally called, Union soldiers and officers were often, for very small offences, kept in confinement for months. They repeatedly sought redress, but it was difficult to get, and always slow in coming. They had comfortable barracks, partitioned off into small rooms, to dwell in; but no beds but blankets in their bunks to sleep in. When any got very sick, they were taken to the rebel ward in the hospital.

Their spiritual wants were supplied with Testaments, religious books, tracts, and papers. Besides, they usually had preaching on the Sabbath — sometimes by a stranger, or a delegate of the Christian Commission, but generally by Mr. Marshall. Here this laborious chaplain would go with an armful of papers and tracts, and having distributed them to the hungry inmates, many of whom read them with avidity, he would assemble them together in the open air, and preach to them "Jesus, and the resurrection," telling them of their sins, warning them of their danger, and beseeching them by the mercies of God to repent, and embrace the Saviour. Here, too, I went occasionally, distributed papers and tracts, and "preached to the spirits in prison," urging them by the love of Christ, by the pains of hell, and by the joys of heaven, to cling to the cross.

GANGRENE CAMP.

A little to the left of the apex of Hampton Hospital, situated alongside of a little swamp, headed by a fine spring of good water, was the lonely Gangrene Camp; made of tents, some good and some inferior, some with plank floors and some without, yet being well kept, with the streets swept clean, it presented rather a neat appearance.

The cooling spring, so convenient, added very much to the comfort of the wounded heroes. This camp was the scene of much very severe suffering. It was not until a patient's wound became badly gangrened, and they began to despair of recovery, that he was brought here, as the place of the last resort. Here the brave heroes would undergo the most severe pain for months and months, and finally die at last. Here they put in nearly the whole winter of 1864-'65, without any fire in their tents, which added much to their suffering from wounds and disease. Stoves were put up late in the winter, and added much to the comfort of the patients. Although this camp was furnished with a surgeon, ward-master, nurses, wound-dresser, and all the appliances of the hospital, yet, being off to one side, it was generally a somewhat forsaken and neglected place. Sometimes persons visiting it were not allowed to go immediately into other wards, lest they should convey the gangrene to other wounded patients.

Besides, many did not wish to see so many severe "wounds, bruises, and putrefying sores." I visited it, preached to, read and prayed with, the patients very often; urging the impenitent to repentance, and comforting the believer with the consolations of the gospel.

It was on a cold, chilly night in November, near the hour of twelve, when I was called by the nurse to go and visit a patient lying nigh unto death in this lonely, cheerless camp. The pale moon was dimly shining, and the dim light feebly burning in the tent, when I lifted the curtain where the brave hero was lying, earnestly praying for his soul's salvation. On approaching him, he warmly grasped my hand, and, upon inquiring how he was, he replied, "I am very weak; I don't think I am going to live long; and I have sent for you, hoping you could administer a word of comfort, and write a letter of sympathy and consolation to my wife and children." "I trust you are not without hope?" "Oh, no! I have a glorious hope. Christ is my only hope, and he is growing more and more precious every hour."

"The pious, heroic John Lambert, with his legs burned to the stumps, with his body pierced with ruthless halberds, with his fingers flaming with fire, with dying breath exclaimed, 'None but Christ! NONE BUT CHRIST!' Think you would be afraid to die?" "No, I think not. I die for my country, and, dying for Him who died for me, I have nothing to fear; I don't fear death, thank God! I trust He will give me the victory over it." "You seem to have it *already*." "I have *got* the victory!" said the dying Rutherford, and he left the world shouting glory. I asked him, "What word shall I send to your wife and dear children?" "*Tell them I died happy in Christ.*" He lingered a few hours, and God took him home. How striking the transition! how glorious the change! from a lonely, dreary gangrene camp to the throne of God in heaven! Here, he wore a soldier's garb; there, robed in white, he wears a crown of glory, and bears palms of victory. I visited two other patients at the same call; one of which was so far gone, it was then too late to get his dying message to send home to comfort his bereaved friends. He was a good man. Such were my visits to this suffering camp.

Here we have witnessed some most glorious, triumphant deaths. Big sinners saved — "brands plucked out of the fire"— rejoicing in the Lord, shouting glory to God, and giving thanks for saving grace. Here we saw a wounded soldier with whom we had often conversed, read, and prayed, after several days' earnest seeking and praying, while we were trying to explain to him the way of salvation, and urging him to fly to Christ, all of a sudden exclaim, "I have got it! *I have got it! I have got religion!*" and he went on shouting "glory to God and hallelujah to the Lamb" to such an extent that it roused the whole camp. Here, too, we have seen the affectionate wife, burdened with anxiety, come several hundred miles to see her wounded husband; and on arriving, to her most sad disappointment, find him struggling in the agonies of death, with reason dethroned, unable to recognize her. It was a severe trial. But such is life, and such is death in the hospital. Here, too, we have seen the intelligent New England colored soldier, with his face and eyes so badly swollen with erysipelas that he could not see; yet, enlightened by God's Spirit, and seeing Jesus with the eye of faith, give important instruction and advice to dying comrades lying around him, urging them, as the *last* act of his life, and in a most tender manner beseech them, be reconciled to God. With an eye and a countenance beaming with intelligence and probity deeply stamped with the image of Christ, and possessing clear and distinct views of the plan of salvation, he was able in a few words, in an appropriate manner, to point the sick and wounded soldier, lying close by him, to Him whose blood cleanseth from all sin.

ARRIVAL OF PATIENTS.

During the time of the most destructive fighting, we often received from two hundred to five hundred patients in a day, and some days the number reached nearly eight hundred. And our hospital having better accommodations than those at the front, they usually sent us the worst and most dangerous cases. We often sent them North by ship-loads of five or six hundred each, to make room for more. During the summer of 1864, like the mighty waves of the sea, they came and went all the time. We frequently received large boat-loads of patients all wounded, many of them seriously and mortally wounded; yet it was surprising to find them so calm, patient, and resigned. Inured to hardness on the march and in battle, and filled with a heroic spirit, they had learned not to complain. To see a large steamer crowded with them, lying upon their narrow couches, with bleeding wounds, shattered bones, amputated limbs, and parched tongues, was enough to move the compassion and rouse the sympathies of the hardest heart. And to gaze upon so many brave hearts, with limbs riven from their bodies, that not a State be riven from the Union, would stir the loyalty of the coldest patient.

TRANSFERRING PATIENTS.

During the summer of 1864, Hampton Hospital was more of a *receiving* hospital than a *home* for the sick and wounded soldier. Like the ebbing and flowing of the tide, the patients kept pouring in and flowing out all the time. They were brought in from "the front" by boat-loads, and transferred North by ship-loads. After a man had tried the realities and trials of hospital life a few months, he usually began to think about getting a furlough home. And often patients severely wounded, and *low* with disease even, sometimes, when they were unfit to go, were gathered up and transferred. Sometimes ten or twelve would die on board during one trip to New York or Philadelphia They were often a good deal crowded, and frequently suffered for the want of air. Although a change of climate, besides the voyage, together with the idea of going home or homeward, were well calculated to inspire new life and vigor into the poor sufferers, yet many found a watery grave by the way instead of the smiles of kind friends and the comforts of home. While some were transferred when unable and unfit to go, yet doubtless many an emaciated patient, run down with chronic diarrhœa, and breathing an unwholesome air, and often fed on an unsuitable diet, died in the hospital, who would have got well had they been discharged or furloughed and sent home. But, somehow or other, they were retained in the hospital until reduced to mere skeletons, and at last death came as a relief and closed the solemn scene. And although the patients were often handled quite roughly in being taken to and from the transport, yet, tired of hospital life, and very anxious to go home, they were nearly always ready to start.

VOYAGE TO NEW YORK.

Late in July, 1864, I sailed with a load of five hundred and fifteen patients on the beautiful ocean-steamer *Atlantic*, Capt. Eldridge, in charge of Dr. Smith, Surgeon, U. S. Vol., for New York. The *Atlantic* was a very fine, large, fast-running ship, well fitted up for transferring patients, and, being so large, she could not get near the hospital; hence the patients had to be taken out to her in tugs and small crafts, which occasioned another handling of them to their disadvantage. With the last patient on board, taken in at a small hole in the side of the sable *Atlantic*, it was about noon, and the old gray-headed captain gave the bell a ring, and we set sail amidst the surging waves of the old Chesapeake lashing the bustling wharf of Fortress Monroe. On reviewing the patients, and learning their condition, we soon found that we had got into "a big job," for there were many bad, needy cases. One brave veteran, with an arm and leg both off, fatigued with his removal, fell from his bed, and hurt his wounds till they bled afresh. Yet, full of pluck, he bore it all very patiently. Others we found apparently nigh unto death, needing much attention; but they all survived the voyage. Some of the nurses seemed rather negligent, and, by administering to his wants, I believe I saved the life of one poor frail old man. The labors of a chaplain are very much needed on board, when so many patients are being transferred. In making my rounds, we found one very low, weak patient, with whom we conversed and prayed in the hospital before we started, lying on his back, unable to sit up; and, as I approached him, he was so glad that he grasped and kissed my hand most affectionately, as he lay upon the floor attended by his kind brother. And though weak, yet within that frail body there throbbed a warm heart, beating high with gratitude to God and his friends. Trusting in the Lord, he bore all very patiently, and seemed to have no fear of death. Lying in the same ward in the ship was the unfortunate soldier who was shot in the head, who lay beside him in the same tent in the hospital, accompanied by his kind, affectionate mother. Crowded into a place poorly ventilated, they both, with all in that ward, suffered for the want of fresh air; and he who carried the minie-ball in his head grew worse by the fatigue of the trip. And it was very hard, when he was carried off the *Atlantic*, to see the surgeon in charge of the patients received at New York, refuse the weeping mother the privilege of taking her dear son to the city hospital. "No," the surgeon sternly replied; "he must go to David's Island, with the rest of the patients;" and the grieved mother wept like a child, saying, "The Government will get no more of my sons for the army." Although the opportunity for preaching on the transport was not favorable, we gave them one or two short sermons during the trip. We had many very interesting seasons of prayer for and with the patients during the pleasant voyage. Frequently they would request to be prayed for. The weather was cool for the season, and the patients, with good beds and good rations, generally fared well. We reached quarantine, ten miles below New York, in less than thirty-six hours, where we lay all night, and landed at the foot of Canal Street by seven o'clock next morning, July 29th, and by one P.M. we had all the brave boys transferred to another boat for David's Island, some twenty-five miles above the city. Though the work was laborious, I enjoyed the trip very much. It was an encouraging field for usefulness. Though duty called, we parted with the maimed and suffering heroes with reluctance. Having been detained two days in New York, we sailed Friday morning for Alexandria, Va., for another load of patients. And having rounded Fortress Monroe, with all its beautiful attractions, and sailing up the broad, beautiful Chesapeake Bay, we entered the wide-mouthed Potomac, with a fine view of Point Lookout on the right, Saturday evening at six, and soon anchored for the night, July 30, a little above Blackstone's Island. A beautiful Sabbath morning dawned, and by

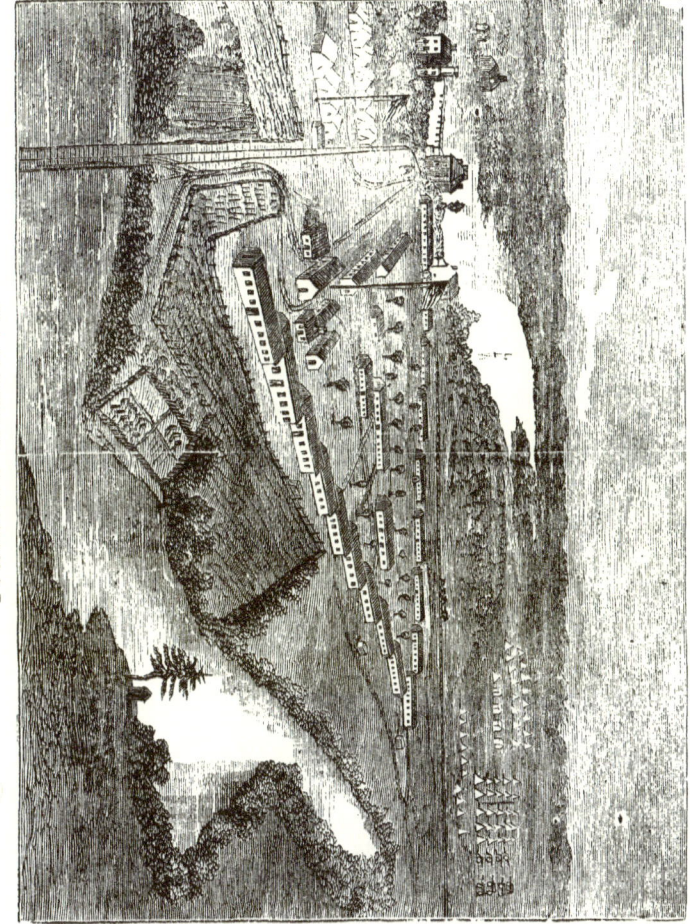
HAMPTON HOSPITAL.

five we weighed anchor, and the gigantic *Atlantic* went on sublimely, ploughing the murky Potomac, regardless of the Lord's day, until half-past six, when she ran aground on Kettle Bottom Shoals, opposite Homini cliffs, hard by the birthplace of General Washington. Now came a hard day for the old gray-headed captain. At the stupidity of the pilot, he was sorely vexed. He, the crew, and the nurses, all worked very hard all Sabbath-day to get loose, but failed. They hitched on tug after tug to pull her off, but, being so deeply moored in the sand, she stuck fast. Sabbath evening I gathered up all I could in the cabin and preached to them. We had a very good meeting. Yet it was a hard way spending the Lord's day, which is so awfully disregarded in time of war, and by boatmen generally. Having spent the Sabbath "all fast on the Potomac," we got loose on Monday, and sailed for Fortress Monroe; and I was glad to get back to the hospital.

CHAPTER VII.

THE RELIGIOUS WORK AT HAMPTON HOSPITAL.

THE HARVEST, GREAT AND WHITE — THE PRAYER-HALL — NO CHURCH — SOLDIERS' EARNEST PRAYERS AND ELOQUENT EXHORTATIONS — IT WAS THE ELOQUENCE OF THE HEART, MELTING ALL INTO TEARS — WARD PRAYER-MEETINGS — INTEREST INCREASING — THE POWER OF PRAYER — SOLDIERS' PRAYER-MEETING — BUSH PRAYER-MEETINGS — PREACHING TO MEN ON THEIR DEATH-BEDS — "THE LAST MORNING."

OWING to the diminution of patients at the Chesapeake, and having heard the Macedonian cry on the other side, we went over, and commenced laboring regularly in Hampton Hospital about the first of August, 1864. Here, with a large hospital, containing some two thousand patients, the field was great, white, ready to harvest; and God, in his providence, as well as the sick and dying soldier, loudly called, *"Thrust in the sickle, and reap."*

Before we quit laboring at the Chesapeake, we occasionally visited Hampton. At the first prayer-meeting we attended there, June 17, 1864, the people seemed cold and backward in taking part. The meeting was small, and, conducted on the *voluntary* principle, it seemed to drag. The time wasted between prayer and praise denoted a want of interest. Yet praying right in the midst of so many sick, wounded, and dying soldiers, we deemed it a great privilege to be there; and, at the request of the chaplain, we took part in prayer and exhortation. The touching song, "Just before the battle, mother," sweetly sung by a few ladies at the close, was deeply impressive. Such was the first prayer-meeting at Hampton, where we met so often afterward and enjoyed such precious times of refreshing. A few days after, we again visited Hampton, and, after calling with a few of the old patients from the Chesapeake, we went back to the house of prayer, and we had a very good meeting. The spirit of the Lord was with us, and there was much more life and devotion in the exercises. Several soldiers spoke and prayed. It was good to be there.

Here we met with a generous, agreeable, fast friend in Chaplain E. P. Roe, U.S.A., in charge of the spiritual interests of this division of the hospital, with whom we labored, hand-in-hand, till long after the rebellion was quelled and the country saved. Mild, modest, and unpretending in his nature, and progressive in his views, Chaplain Roe had a good tact to get Christians to labor in the vineyard of the Lord.

THE PRAYER-HALL.

Being without a chapel, we met in one of the dining-halls situated in the centre of the triangular hospital. The building was a mere shell — an upright frame, some two hundred feet long and about thirty wide, with a dingy table in the middle, around one end of which we met twice a week for many long, bloody months, and poured out our souls and hearts unto God for the salvation of the patients, the bereaved and loved ones at home, and for the salvation of our bleeding country. Being without any fire, and the hall being open, it was very cold in winter, and very uncomfortably warm in summer. But it was the best we could get, and, knowing that the blessing to be obtained through the prayer-meeting did not depend upon the house or place we met in, but upon the state of the hearts that meet, here we met regularly, and enjoyed many seasons of refreshing. Paul and Silas had a very happy meeting in the Philippian jail, with their feet fast in the stocks. And within the murky walls of this sombre hall the faithful soldier of the cross would drag his emaciated, mutilated frame upon crutches, to sing and pray. Accustomed to feats of daring and courage, men are less bashful in the army than at home. Trained to fight upon the bloody field, they are not so slow and backward to take up the cross in the house of prayer. Partaking less of "*the form*," our prayer-meetings in the hospital seemed to enjoy, or possess, more of "the *power of God*" than those usually at home. To see men hobbling along to the prayer-meeting when scarcely able to walk, and so earnestly engaged in the great work of salvation, was truly encouraging and refreshing to the soul. The warm, earnest exhortation, and the fervent, heart-gushing prayer, told that many of the soldiers lived near the throne of grace.

Sometimes the recital of religious experience, incidents, and purposes was most touching, eloquent, and powerful. Their little speeches were not composed, far-fetched or fine-spun phrases: no; it was the eloquence of the *heart*—big, earnest thoughts, bubbling up from the depths of the soul, struggling for utterance, and when they fell from lips set on fire by the Holy Ghost, it was like rain upon the mown grass. Gushing right out from the heart, their words were sharp, quick, and powerful, and, steeped in prayer, they sunk down deep into the heart and made a deep, lasting impression. Men, illiterate, with souls burning with zeal, would sometimes so electrify the whole congregation that all would melt into tears. To hear the young converts relate their own experience often arrested the careless, and stirred the soul of the lukewarm professor. The interest was often so great, and the disposition to pray so strong, that it was very difficult to get through in reasonable time. Sometimes we had fifteen or twenty prayers at one meeting. The hall being used for eating purposes in the daytime, we always met at night, and with but a few candles "dimly burning," stuck up along the rough sides of the hall, it always presented a gloomy appearance; yet with our souls lit up by God's Spirit, and stimulated by the crisis of the dying soldier's soul, we often got very near the throne of grace, and the men often prayed as though they felt "I will not let thee go, except thou bless me." Praying-men from all quarters of the country putting up their prayers from this noted place, the prayer-meetings became quite a *power* in the hospital. The happy seasons there enjoyed by thousands will, doubtless, be remembered throughout eternity. Such a spirit of *union* pervaded the meeting that we seldom inquired to what church a man belonged. Denominationalism was swallowed up in the great interests of the soul.

These meetings were usually led by Chaplain Roe, but often by the author. We generally commenced by singing a hymn, and after reading a few verses of Scripture, accompanied with prayer and a few words of exhortation by the chaplain, the meeting was thrown open, and all *cordially* invited to lay aside all restraint and take part freely, and the liberty in praying and speaking fully evinced that the Spirit of the Lord was with us.

In this same gloomy hall we had preaching every Sabbath night. In this the chaplains took turns, except when visitors, or the delegates of the Christian Commission, by request, filled the pulpit. The attendance was usually good, and sometimes very large, reaching five hundred or six hundred attentive hearers. With a good choir, graced with a well-played harmonium, they made the dusty walls of the old hall ring again with their enchanting music. We usually used "the Army and Navy Hymn-book," published by the American Tract Society.

WARD PRAYER-MEETINGS.

Seeing the field was so great, and the work so arduous, the chaplains labored to secure *Christian effort* among the patients. In this Mr. Roe succeeded well. And in this way we induced the patients to hold prayer-meetings in their own wards by themselves. In several wards those little praying-circles were kept up regularly for months, and some of the more active Christians would go round and look up the scattered sheep, and gather the wayward into the fold. And in this way, we believe, much was accomplished. One soldier told me he was led to Christ by two men talking to him, one night, on picket. Another, while lying on his sick-bed, he said, was converted by hearing a man of the world read a chapter out of the Bible. I have frequently seen the Christian soldier earnestly talking Christ into his comrade, and beseech him to be reconciled to God. This was obeying the divine command, " *Go*, WORK *in my vineyard*." And if *all* Christians would only obey it, the cause of Christ would advance tenfold faster. " *Why stand ye here all the day idle ?* "

Tired of the lonely monotony of hospital life, the sick or wounded soldier, who has lain for months on his bed sore-back, is always willing and glad to hear a word of prayer and praise, and, coming from a soldier, it is often more effectual than from a chaplain. There was one good boy, George, of the 188th Pa. Vol., recently converted in the hospital, who took a deep interest in this work. He would often go round, talk to, read and pray with the patients, earnestly beseeching them to repent, and come to the Saviour.

The ward masters and matrons also did a good work in this way in their own wards. With these, besides the labors of the delegates of the Christian and Sanitary Commissions, together with the regular visitations of the chaplains and the rich supply of books, periodicals, tracts, and all sorts of papers, the spiritual as well as the intellectual wants of the patients were well provided for. In visiting the patients we usually noted down their religious experience, and when they died, we sent home their dying messages to comfort and console their bereaved friends To go round thus, daily bending over the sick, wounded, and low-fevered cases, endeavoring to catch their last dying words, and learn their hopes and feelings, exposing ourselves to disease, though the work was hard and laborious, yet we delighted in it.

INTEREST INCREASING.

After laboring a short time in Hampton Hospital, preaching daily in the wards, and by prayer, exhortation, and conversing with the patients, urging them to repent, and come to the Saviour, together with the regular Sabbath evening preaching and semi-weekly prayer-meetings in the dining-hall, in connection with the distribution of tracts, religious papers, pamphlets, and books, through the blessing of God, the interest soon began to increase. Clouds of mercy gathered and burst upon us, and God's gracious presence and the strivings of his Spirit were evinced not only by the attentive ear, but by the enlarged attendance upon the preaching of the gospel, and increased interest in the regular prayer-meetings.

The weather was now very warm, and the battles raging at the front, boat-loads of patients were brought in almost daily, with many very severely wounded, with arms and legs off, and shot in all parts of the body. Hence the stream of death rose very high, and flowed all through the hospital, carrying away from ten to twenty suffering heroes a day. The average mortality during the month of August, 1864, was a little over ten a day. And while death was raging so furiously, as though the people were warned and impressed with the solemn fact, the desire for spiritual life increased. While some, being so "used to death," rather "made light of it," others, seeing so many dear comrades snatched away, wrapped in their winding-sheets, and borne to the dead-house on stretchers, were deeply impressed, and acting as though they felt, "I don't know but it may be my turn to go next," they began to consider their ways, and to prepare to meet their God. Still, death reigned: God's Spirit was poured out, and there was quite a shaking among the dry bones, and the people were enabled to speak and pray with great power. And while our armies at "the front" were winning glorious victories on the field, through grace the sick and wounded were achieving greater victories on their beds in the hospital. Although they could no longer wield the sword nor fire a cannon, yet, with their hearts fired with the Holy Spirit, they could wield an instrumentality in defence of their country still more powerful than either of these. What was it? PRAYER! *faithful, earnest prayer.* "Prayer moves the arm that moves the world." "Prayer is literally, actually, and positively a *means of power.*" "When Ethelred, the Saxon king of Northumberland, invaded Wales, and was about to give battle to the Britons, he observed near the enemy a host of unarmed men. He inquired who they were, and what they were doing. He was told that they were monks of Bangor, praying for the success of their countrymen. 'Then,' said the heathen prince, 'they have *begun* the fight against us; attack them first.'" How clear and strong the king's faith in prayer as a means of power. "Prayer is no fiction." No: it is a reality. "It is," says Dr. Phelps — and God has purposed that it should be — "a link of connection between the human mind and the divine mind by which, through his infinite condescension, we may actually move his will."

The orifice of the throttle connecting the boiler with the cylinder of a steam-engine is very small; but it is an engine of mighty power. Gaze upon the *Great Eastern* as she lies upon the placid ocean. Not a wave is to be seen; not a wheel or a paddle in motion. All is calm and quiet. Lift the valve, the steam escapes, enters the cylinder, starts the piston, moves the huge crank, turns the ponderous wheel, and in a moment all is in motion, and the mammoth steamer ploughs the mighty ocean and heaves the very earth. And all done simply by lifting a little valve. "Behold how great a matter a little fire kindleth." So it is with earnest, importunate prayer; though apparently a small, weak instrumentality, yet it is "mighty through God." Gaze upon the earnest supplicant in his closet; there, upon his bended knees, he lifts the valve of his gushing heart; his desires escape, reach God's throne, and thus moves the powers of heaven and earth. The Saviour says, "If ye shall ask anything in my name, I will do it." "And *all* things whatsoever ye shall ask in prayer, *believing,* ye shall receive." "The effectual, fervent prayer of a righteous man availeth much." Jacob prayed, and had power with God, and prevailed. Gaze upon the thrilling scene of Peniel, and mark the power of prayer. Jacob had supplanted his brother Esau, and caused his furious wrath and murderous indignation to burn against him, and, being afraid, Jacob fled to Padan-aram for refuge. After a sojourn of twenty years he returned, and finds Esau's vengeance still burning against him; but Jacob resolves to meet him, and to try the power of prayer to effect a reconciliation. And having sent his family and flocks over the brook Jabbok, he retires alone, prays, and wrestles with God, and prevails. The heart of Esau is touched, the rebellion knocked out of him, and his fratricidal revenge is turned to brotherly love and affection; and when he met him, he embraced him with a kiss and the warmest affection.

And although our success in quelling the rebellion is generally attributed to the sagacity and ability of great generals and the hard fighting of brave soldiers, yet, doubtless, we owe it very much to the prayers of God's people. If the revenge and rebellion of Esau were quelled in answer to Jacob's prayer, could we not expect God's loyal people to pray down the rebellion of the South? If God delivered the captive hosts of Israel in answer to the prayers of Daniel, could we not expect deliverance from the great rebellion in answer to the prayers of the North? What! without fighting? No. But the prayers of faith are always mixed with works. Hence, while the faithful Christian soldier prays as though God had to do everything, he fights and labors as though he had to do everything himself. Washington and Cromwell fought bravely, doubtless, because they prayed fervently. The colored people had been praying for liberty for years before their emancipation. God says: "Call upon me in the day of trouble, and I will deliver thee." And endowed with the spirit of prayer, there commenced about this time among the nurses and patients of the hospital

A SOLDIERS' PRAYER-MEETING.

U. S. Hampton General Hospital,
Fortress Monroe, Va., Sept. 17, 1864.

It was on Friday evening, August 12, 1864: a few of us had just returned from burying the mortal remains of five soldiers, and left seven more in the dead-house for want of graves. The meeting was opened with reading the tenth chapter of Isaiah, by Chaplain Roe, followed with some appropriate remarks, and the singing of a few verses from the Army and Navy Hymn-book. The meeting was then thrown open to all, and the chaplain said, "We wish to have *a free, social soldiers' meeting.*"

Soon one rose, and said, "The past week has been the happiest of my life. On this night a week ago, I went round, after prayer-meeting, and gathered up four comrades, and we went out in the woods to pray. We all prayed, and had a very happy time." He also spoke of the last words of a poor, dying soldier, who said, "*The Lord is mine.*"

Another rose, and said, "I never felt so happy;" and, requesting the prayers of the congregation, sat down in tears.

Another rose, and, with a trembling heart and stirred spirit, confessed his sins, acknowledged his unfaithfulness, and earnestly besought the prayers of all that he "*might do right.*"

Another, like the trembling jailer, "desired to be a Christian." He said he had Christian parents, and asked to be prayed for, "that God might bless his soul;" to which many responded, "Amen! Amen!"

Another boy, George, aged sixteen, said, "I have tried to be a Christian a week. I received a letter from my good old mother, and she encourages me much;" and with a smitten heart he sat down, "all filled up." This same boy speaks and prays with wonderful power and effect. He goes about in the wards, talks and prays with the patients, and gathers up a little company, and goes out into the woods every day to have prayer-meeting. He says they always come back much refreshed. "Let us thank God, and take courage." Toil on, George, God will reward you.

Another, more aged, soldier said, "I am filled full. I thank God for what I have felt to-night. Some say we can't be Christians in the army; but we can be better here than anywhere else." He closed with shouting "glory," and seemed very much stirred up — said he felt happy.

Another said, "It is twenty-five years, next Monday, since I found Jesus in a sugar-grove in Ohio. God found me a sinner. I feel very happy to-night."

Another said, "It is *good* to serve God. I have tried it, and would recommend it."

It was a happy, powerful meeting — a real "time of refreshing." Some of the speeches were really eloquent; it was the eloquence of the heart — the Spirit of God speaking through the quickened soldier. We could but weep. It was truly good to be there.

The gracious work still goes on, deepening and widening. The frail soldiers turn out very well. Some walk with crutches; others, scarcely able to walk at all, drag their frail bodies to the dining-hall to sing and pray. We now have a hospital Union church of over fifty members, and still they come. Last night we had a most precious time. I scarcely ever saw such a disposition to pray. After the chaplain ended his remarks, he picked up the hymn-book to give out a hymn to sing; but before he had time to open his mouth, some soldier was on his knees praying. We "go it on the voluntary system;" and very often, when one ceased praying, two more began at once. Eighteen led in prayer last night. We did n't take time to sing much.

Brethren, pray for us! "O Lord, revive thy work!"

A PRAYER-MEETING IN THE BUSHES.

When God's Spirit is powerfully poured out, it always draws men to their knees; and when man, just converted, gets a glimpse of the great things God has done for him in "pulling him out of the fire," with a heart overflowing with gratitude and burning with desire for the salvation of souls, he cannot help but pray. Such was the feeling of the small squad of soldiers in Hampton Hospital. And wooed by the Spirit, and desiring a more retired place than the crowded, suffering ward afforded, they retired to the leafy copse daily for prayer and supplication. Armed with the sword of the Spirit, and the little Army and Navy Hymn-book, thither this little band of suppliants would daily resort to pour out their hearts unto God for the preservation of the country, and for the salvation of the sick and wounded. There, secluded from the world, and shut in with God, with no covering but the canopy of heaven, and no altar but the cross of Christ, they read, sung, and prayed; and while the earth was drinking the blood of our brave veterans at the front, dying for the salvation of their country, their prayers ascended to God for the salvation of their souls.

And so eager were they in this blessed work, that sometimes a few of them would collect and go out to pray, after the regular weekly prayer-meeting, late at night. And there, overshadowed by the darkness of the night, yet with their souls lit up by the light of God's Spirit, they found the way to the throne of grace, and got so nigh unto God that one says, "We all felt very happy." Another active spirit in these bush prayer-meetings says, "We always come back much refreshed." "What a blessing! how encouraging! Always come back much refreshed!" "Yes!" "Why, George?" "Well, I don't know, chaplain; but so it

CHRISTIANITY IN THE WAR.

is. We go out into the bushes. God meets with us; and, by singing and praying, we endeavor to get very near to God, and always come back much refreshed." What the cooling brook is to the thirsty hart, or the thirsty soldier on a long march on a warm day, prayer is to a thirsty soul — *always refreshing.* "And doubtless, George, it is your drinking so deeply of the wells of salvation that proves so refreshing to your longing hearts." "Yes; I suppose, chaplain, that is so. We always find the nearer we get to God, and the more earnestly we pray, the more refreshed we feel." "Yes, God is an inexhaustible 'fountain of life;' and the oftener you draw, and the deeper you drink, the more refreshed you will be.

"Then, George, let me entreat you, go on with your prayer-meetings. As you have got the fire burning in the bushes, fan it, and keep it burning until it spreads all over the camp, and burns upon the altar of every sinner's heart, so that when the patients go back to the front, they may go armed with weapons not carnal, that they may be mighty through God to the pulling down of the strongholds of the rebellion. Oh, then, George, *pray on.* Gather up the forces, and lead them on in the battles of the Lord! You have every encouragement. It was in answer to the prayers of eleven apostles that the Holy Spirit was poured out on the day of Pentecost, when three thousand souls were converted in a day. In answer to the prayers of the church, the chains fell off of Peter, and he was released from prison. It was after Rev. John Livingstone had spent the previous night in prayer, that he preached that *most powerful sermon* on 'the new heart' (Ezek. xxxvi. 25, 26), at Shotts, in Scotland, June 21, 1630, under which about five hundred sinners were converted.

"Thus you see what great things God has wrought in answer to the prayers of his people. How very encouraging to pray on, George! Then go on with unfaltering determination."

PREACHING TO MEN ON THEIR DEATH-BEDS.

Overburdened with labor, and surrounded with so many critical cases of sick and wounded men requiring prompt attention, our ingenuity was sometimes taxed to know how to meet them to the best advantage. Hence, on entering a ward, and seeing so many brave heroes lying upon the verge of eternity, and others, perhaps, just passing the crisis of the soul, and all anxiously inquiring what to do to be saved, and not being able to reach them all in due time in *personal* conversation, we were led to adopt the plan of preaching in the wards, where we could at the same time instruct, beseech, and implore all in the whole ward to come to the Saviour at once. This plan seemed to work very well. A word of prayer and praise, accompanied with a plain, pointed, brief sermon, was a relief to the patients, tired of the dull monotony of the hospital. After entering a ward, and securing the approbation of the ward-master, we usually commenced the solemn service by singing some appropriate hymn *full of Christ*, the soldiers joining in, followed by reading a short passage of Scripture, such as the parable of the prodigal son, the case of the Philippian jailer, or the story of blind Bartimeus, etc. Then followed the sermon, which we always endeavored to make searching, powerful, and practical; always endeavoring to convince the sinner of his sins, the imminent *danger* of his course, and the great importance of *immediate* repentance; urging them by the love of Christ, by the pain of hell, and by the eternal glories of heaven, "to flee the wrath to come," and fly to the cross at once. With the sick, the dead, and the dying around us, and with the stern realities of eternity rising before us, and God's Spirit stirring within us, the services were usually very solemn and interesting. Preaching to men lying upon their death-beds, who had laid down their lives for their country, and feeling that it was "*the last time*," and the *last* warning to some of them, and that their salvation, under God, hung suspended upon the decision of the hour, seemed to add much to the solemnity of the occasion, to heighten our responsibility, and to help and strengthen us for the arduous, important work. This work, though very laborious to the chaplain, was to me very pleasant and delightful. To point out the way of eternal life to him who had sacrificed his life for his country, though a sad, was no melancholy, duty. The patients enjoyed it much. And very often would they express their gratification, as I passed their couches, in such words as these. "You don't know, chaplain, how much good that sermon did me. Please come in and give us another as soon as you can."

A colored soldier said to me, "*I liked to jumpt out of bed while you was preaching, last night, I felt so happy; my very heart seemed to leap with joy.*"

I preached on this way, averaging more than a sermon a day, for several months. Very often I preached two or three times a day, besides writing letters for the patients, burying the dead, and canvassing the hearts of the most dangerous cases, noting down their religious experience and prospects for the future.

There, standing between the living and the dead, we endeavored to hold forth the cross of Christ as the only way of salvation; endeavoring to comfort and console the suffering patient by the meek submission of Him who died upon Calvary that guilty sinners might enjoy eternal life.

The following extract will give the reader an idea of our manner of addressing the patients in the wards.

THE LAST WARNING.

AN APPEAL TO WOUNDED SOLDIERS IN HOSPITAL.

Having spoken to the Christian soldier and to the backslider, we come now, my impenitent friends, to give you a word of warning and encouragement. You have had many warnings. The thrilling, heart-rending scenes of battle — dear comrades falling, bleeding, dying at your side, beseeching you with their last breath, "*Be ye also ready*" — the departed spirits of half a million slain in this war, whose tongues are now mute in death, bid you "*Prepare to meet thy God.*" The daily funeral notes of the death march of the escort bearing a cart-load of dead soldiers to the grave is but the voice of God warning you "to flee the wrath to come." The gushing tears and earnest prayers of a tender mother, an affectionate wife, and anxious sister, warn you; trust in God and fly to Jesus. And yet, withal, here you are to-night, still impenitent, lying prostrate upon your couches, and, doubtless, many of you upon your death-beds, dying for your country, and yet rejecting Him who died for you. You kill men for rebelling against the government, and yet you still live in rebellion against God. Your sufferings for your country have been terribly severe, but they are *nothing* compared with the sufferings that await you if you die impenitent. You have felt the raking fire of long lines of rebel heavy artillery, but that is nothing to the "unquenchable fire," artillery, and torments of hell. And here you are still careless and insensible to your danger. Careless! insensible! with the grave yawning, the devil seeking, and hell moving to destroy you! Insensible! with God smiling, the Spirit striving, and heaven stooping to save you! Oh, then, we beseech you, by the mercies of God, by the love of Christ, and by the joys of heaven, bestir yourselves; repent, and come to Jesus. This is, without doubt, the *last* warning to some of you. It is now or never; to-morrow, doubtless, will be too late. "Now is the accepted time." I heard a dying soldier say, last night, with his life-blood flowing from him, "IT IS TOO LATE! TOO LATE!" And so it will be with you, unless you soon repent. Oh, then, let this be the day of your salvation! May God bless you! And yet the Lord *waits* to be gracious. Jesus is here waiting to forgive your sins, and wash your souls in his own blood. Jesus is here earnestly crying, "Turn ye! *turn ye!* for why will you die!" And *will* you die, patriot soldier? WILL you die with Jesus, "the Prince of Life," at your hand, waiting to give you eternal life? You may die, die here in the hospital, covered with glory and honor defending your country — that is glorious — but, oh, if you die to save your country and lose your own soul, is not that lamentable? Die for your country! Die beside the Prince of Life, and to enter "the second death," which never dies! Die for Him who died for you, and yet die and be lost! Oh, how lamentable! Oh, my dear friend, stop, think, consider, turn, look, and come to Jesus, and come *now!* May God have mercy on you, and bless you! May the love of Christ constrain you! Jesus is *here* — *here* in this ward — *here* in all the plenitude of his power, readiness, and willingness, to give you life, pardon, peace, and salvation —

> "Jesus ready stands to save you,
> Full of pity, love, and power."

As the compassionate Saviour cried to the anxious throng around the lovely heights of Jerusalem, "Come unto me, and I will give you rest," so he still cries to you, my impenitent friends, in tones of love and mercy, with the same gushing heart and encouraging promise, "*How often would I have gathered you!*" Yes, *you*, my dear soldier; and *must* it, *shall* it, be said of *you*, as of them, "*ye would not?*" Oh, remember, I pray you, only think of the Saviour's "I WOULD," and your own, "*ye would not!*" And are you not *willing* to be saved? Are you willing to *die* for the salvation of your country, and not willing to be saved "without money and without price?" And *will* you, *can* you, reject such a Saviour, who has suffered, bled, and died to redeem you? "Who of God is ready to be made unto you wisdom, righteousness, sanctification, and redemption." Oh, then, come unto him! "Come, for all things are now ready." Come, for yet there is room. Yes, room for every patriot soldier; room in the church below; room in the church above; and room in the Saviour's bleeding heart. See how he pleads! hear how he entreats! by the thrilling scenes of Bethlehem, Gethsemane, and Calvary he cries, Come! by his bleeding hands and dying groans, he cries, Come unto me, and I will give you REST — rest from sin — rest from error and doubt — rest from sorrow and suffering — rest in heaven, where there will be no more sorrow, pain, nor death; for God himself shall wipe away all tears. Oh, then, come! Come *where?* Come *here!* Come *when?* Come *now!* Come *how?* Come JUST AS YOU ARE! But, oh, come! May God bless and enable you to come!

CHAPTER VIII.

WRITING LETTERS FOR THE PATIENTS.

A DYING SOLDIER'S LETTER TO HIS BROTHER — SOLEMN — HIS WILL — "YOURS IN DEATH" — "LETTERS OF DEATH" — "I AM READY" — LETTERS FROM THE BEREAVED — No. 1. THE BEREAVED WIFE — No. 2. THE BEREAVED BROTHER — No. 3. THE WEEPING WIDOW — No. 4. THE DYING HUSBAND'S LETTER TO HIS WIFE — No. 5. A WEEPING SOUTHERN FAMILY — CANVASSING PATIENTS' HEARTS — DIAGNOSIS OF THE WHOLE HOSPITAL — "OH, CHAPLAIN, STAY, AND TALK TO ME MORE ABOUT JESUS!" — "BEFORE, I WOULD CRY, 'FORT PILLOW, AND LET 'EM HAVE IT!'" — "SAVE ME, LORD! SAVE ME, LORD!"

WHEN long deprived of the pleasures of home, the next thing to *seeing* the friends is to *hear* from them. Letter-writing is said to be "a true transcript of the soul;" and, doubtless, it is this (because we can more fully unbosom our hearts in writing than in speaking face to face) that gives letter-writing such an immense power and influence in society. A neat letter from a long-absent, far-off friend, "how *good* is it." See how the happy recipient clasps it to her bosom, with a heart throbbing with joy! To open and trace the beautiful lines all glowing with sympathy and love, bedewed with the heart-gushing tears of an affectionate friend, wife, or mother, would always cheer up and revive the most cast-down and home-sick patient. Hence, writing letters for them was an important part of the chaplain's and delegate's work. This work was profitable, not only morally, but spiritually. For at the close of every letter sent home, it was always a favorable opportunity to draw out the religious feelings, purposes, and prospects of the patient, to send along to comfort his anxious friends at home. And just as we were about closing the letter, the question would come up, "Shall I say, 'Please pray for me, mother?'" and the inquiry would often be replied to with such a meek, God-confiding "*yes*," as often brought the penitential tear from the eye, redolent with faith and hope. And when we come to inquire, at the last, of the brave soldier, "Shall I add 'May God bless you, mother?'" as the soft "yes" dropped from his quivering lips, with a heart throbbing with the deepest emotions, and thinking that probably it was the son's *last* letter to a dear mother, it seemed to draw us both nearer to God. Scenes like these were solemn, and fraught with peculiar touching interest; but when we come to write the letter of a man mortally wounded, when we *knew* it was his *last*, it increased the interest to deep solemnity. We recollect one particular case of thrilling interest. A young man, of talent and wealth, had received a severe wound in the arm. Amputation had been performed, but not until it was too late. Pyemia had set in, which almost always resulted in dissolution in a few days; and, conscious of the near approach of death, the brave hero begins to set his house in order, and prepares to leave this lower world. How solemn the scene! Although facing "the last enemy," with the stern realities of the eternal world rising in full view before him, yet with undaunted courage he fears not. Death stares him in the face; yet he lies calm and serene. He indites a letter to his brother; it is his *last!* How trying the hour! After casting some reflections upon his surgeon for not cutting off his arm sooner, and giving his brother some directions about his temporal affairs, he closes his dying letter with these striking, solemn words, — "YOURS IN DEATH!"

Prayer was frequently made for his salvation. And entreating him to throw himself in the arms of an all-compassionate Saviour, he seemed to let go of the world, and lay hold of Jesus. There he lies. His last sands are running. The mortal conflict rages. Death works; frail nature gives way; the vital cord snaps, and the heroic patriot yields up the ghost!

LETTERS OF DEATH.

But there was another kind of letters to be written. To inform the friends at home of the condition of the sick and wounded soldier was, sometimes, an unpleasant task; but when one died, especially if he gave but dim evidence of preparation, as was frequently the case, and we were made the despatcher of the mournful intelligence of his death to the bereaved mother, widowed wife, and orphaned children, the duty was peculiarly sad and painful. Hence, we always endeavored to canvass the heart and obtain the spiritual condition of every dangerously diseased patient, not only for his own spiritual benefit, but also for the comfort and consolation of his friends at home. To have a patient brought into the hospital, who had sacrificed his life for his country, and die before we could learn his spiritual condition, as was sometimes the case, was very unpleasant. Yet when the influx of mortally-wounded and fatally-diseased patients was so great, it could not always be avoided. Frequently they were brought in dead, without having any account of their religious experience, and sometimes even without a record of their name, company, or regiment.

How severe the ravages of war! At times, when the mortality was very great, I have frequently been called to the bedside of a dying patient who was too far gone to even express a hope in Christ, leaving no record but his life to comfort his bereaved friends. For an anxious, affectionate mother, or devoted wife, to hear of the death of a dear son or husband, by the ruthless hands of infuriated rebels, was trying; but to hear that he died "without hope," was almost overwhelming. When the mighty conflict was raging that decided the fate of our country, and the newspapers were teeming with the accounts of bloody battles and long lists of casualties, all know with what deep anxiety those rolls of honor were searched by every anxious heart, to know if his or her own particular friend was among the fallen. Much similar was the anxiety felt by those at home who had dear friends in the hospital. Hence, when the messenger of a soldier's death reached the throbbing heart of his bereaved friends, the next question was, "*How did he die?* What were his prospects for eternity? What was his disease, or wounds," etc. All such questions were proper and natural; and, when we could, we always answered them with pleasure, and did what we could to console and comfort the bereaved, mourning friends at home. Many of the brave heroes died triumphant deaths, perfectly resigned; and, rising above all doubts and fears, evincing their assurance and preparation in such words as these: "I am ready." "I have no fear of death." "The Lord is mine." "Tell my wife I died happy," etc. When this was the case, to despatch a death notice was not so painful; but when a man died "without hope," sacrificing his life for the salvation of his country, and dying beside the Prince of Life, and yet, doubtless, dying to die the death that never dies, to communicate the sad intelligence was no desirable task. We always made the best we could of such cases, urging the bereaved friends (at home) to be warned, by the death of him who died defending his country, to "*prepare to meet their God.*" And the replies we received to these letters were usually most interesting and touching. Filled with gratitude, patriotism, tenderness, sorrow, and faith, we often read them with tears.

Our letters describing the last hours of the departed heroes, and the answers we received in reply from their friends at home, if collected, would make a very interesting book.

LETTERS FROM THE BEREAVED AT HOME TO THE CHAPLAIN IN THE HOSPITAL.

Letter No. 1.—THE BEREAVED WIFE.

Written with a heart gushing with grief and glowing with connubial affection, it cannot fail to interest every reader.

PEASLEVILLE, N. Y., Feb. 13, 1865.

REV. FRIEND: — With a trembling hand and a downcast heart, I take the liberty to write a few lines to one that has visited my dear husband in his last moments. Oh! is it possible that he is gone, and I am never to behold his form on earth again? Must I — can it be so? God has called, and I must submit to the stroke, though severe. He has a large circle of friends and relatives that deeply mourn our loss. He was beloved and respected, in his northern home, by all who knew him. He was the father of three children — two girls, and a boy twelve years of age. They have looked forward to the time when they could greet him; but their hopes are all blasted with mine. They have no father to look after them now in a cold and unfeeling world. Alone! no eye to pity, no arm to save, but God. By diligence and proper improvement of time, he has accumulated a quiet home for his family. We enjoyed the comfort of his society until his country called for him; he left us in the hands of God, and went forth to lend a helping hand in this great strife which desolates a home which was once pleasant and lovely. The rose may blossom and flowers bloom around my lonely dwelling — the hand that planted them with so much care lies silent in the tomb, and there must rest until God shall wake the sleeping dead. Oh, how many a great and good man has fallen to save and preserve the Union, so the living can have freedom of speech and liberty. May God hasten the time when it can be said, we are victorious; that oppression has ceased, and the cord which bound the oppressed is broken; may the time soon come when the flag of honor and glory may find a resting-place in every State over our great continent; and then may it wave in peace and security until time is no longer — this is my prayer.

N. B. Concerning my husband's precious remains, if it is possible, how glad would I be to have him buried in the family burying-ground with his dear connections; so that when I am done with the afflictions of this life, I can slumber sweetly by his side. Not having the money by me, I wait an answer from you. If you will take the trouble to let me know how much it would cost me, and if it is possible for me to raise the money, I shall. But it is my prayer that there may be a way opened so that his remains can be sent to me. I cannot bear the thought of having him slumber there, away from home and all that was dear to him on earth. Oh, how gladly would I visit the ward where he has endured so much suffering and toil, and spent his last days on earth!

Oh, how can I give him up, and never greet that form again? If thou art a companion, or a father, thou knowest well our feelings. But when the short journey of life is concluded, and I am done with sorrow and afflictions, that we shall meet where separation is unknown forever. My prayer shall not cease for that ward, although my husband is called away by death.

Receive this from the hand of deep affliction, which pen cannot describe. This short epistle to the much-honored chaplain of Hampton Hospital.

LETTER No. 2. — THE BEREAVED BROTHER.

He had just lost his only brother — died far away, in the service of his country. Here are the feelings of his soul, lamenting his loss, and expressions of gratitude for favors shown him in his last sufferings.

NEW HAVEN, July 30, 1865.

MR. BILLINGSLEY, AND FRIEND: — I received your letter containing the sad intelligence of my brother's death, the youngest, and only brother, — my eldest having died only one year and six months ago. Your sympathy for me, in my sad trial and bereavement, I assure you, I appreciate more than pen and ink can describe; while you kindly assure me he fared well, and I am somewhat consoled. I am grieved that I cannot learn the date of death, where and when he was wounded. I wrote to Washington, as you advised, but without the much-desired information. I received an answer. Please accept my heartfelt thanks for kindness in writing the particulars so far as you were at liberty to do.

Your letter, with its contents, will ever be a sad comfort to me. Should you ever visit New Haven, I should be most grateful for a visit from you. I shall bring his remains home as soon as they can be obtained.

Yours gratefully,   ———.

LETTER No. 3. — THE WEEPING WIDOW.

Though written with a pen dipped in grief, and with a soul bowed down with sorrow, yet it breathes such a spirit of *submission* under the heavy stroke, and the writer seems to derive so much comfort in the sad trial from God's word, that it cannot be read without profit.

DONEGAL, PA., April 18, 1865.

MY DEAR BROTHER:—I received your letter of the 4th on the 12th—the sad news of my dear husband's death. Oh! was ever sorrow equal to mine? I cannot describe my feelings when I came to where you said, your dear departed husband. Oh! I thought, can this be so? Yet it is. I thank you very much for your kind letter, and your kindness to my dear companion in his affliction. Your admonitions, your portions of divine truth, they have been read over and over; and, oh, what consolation I find in these lines, Behold, happy is the man whom God correcteth; therefore, despise not the chastening of the Almighty. For He maketh sore, and bindeth up the wounds; and His hands make whole. He shall deliver them in six troubles; yea, in seven there shall no evil touch them.

No tongue can express my grief. My friends here are trying to persuade me to leave his body there, as you say he is buried decent; and they tell me I could not see him if I would have him brought home. But, oh, I think it cannot be! But his remains must come. They tell me it will cost at least an hundred dollars. I am in rather poor circumstances, and know not what to do; but, if you please, see that the board that marks his grave is well put in, so that, after a while, I perhaps can have him home. If you please, be so kind and write me again, and tell me if he said anything concerning me or my poor little children. I am left with four dear children — the oldest not nine, and the youngest two, years old; but I trust that my Father in heaven will be their father and the widow's husband. My hope of heaven is bright. I am a member of the Baptist Church, and have been for near eleven years; and I love all Christians, let them be of what name or order. And please let me know what branch of the Christian church you are connected with; and I hope that we'll all meet in heaven at last.

I am also very grateful to you for a lock of my companion's hair. Your marks of kindness shall never be forgotten while memory lasts; and my prayer is that you may see the work of the Lord prosper in your hands.

I ask an interest in your prayers: we are here in the wilderness, and oft are tempted; but Christ is sufficient to bring us out conquerors and more.

I think now, if my dear husband had only been permitted to get home to die, that I would not murmur. But this is hard.

And then, when I reflect, I think it is all right, and I should feel thankful that he is now happy, and that he did not fall on the battle-field. And may God hasten the day when war shall cease.

I will close by saying please answer this soon.

Your sorrowful friend,
———.

LETTER No. 4. — THE DYING SOLDIER'S LETTER TO HIS WIFE.

It was his last farewell letter. He indicted it himself as he lay on his bed in the hospital, nigh unto death. To see the dying father, with weeping eyes, bid farewell to his far-off wife and children, was peculiarly touching.

HAMPTON HOSPITAL,
FORTRESS MONROE, Nov. 28, 1864.

MY DEAR WIFE: — I am sick — low with diarrhœa; I don't expect to get well. But I feel that I am going to a better world. I feel prepared to die; and hope and trust and pray you will meet me in heaven. Bid farewell to Catharine and David for me. If you live to raise the children, raise them to the religion of the Bible. Religion seems more precious and valuable to me now than ever before. If you choose, come and take my remains home. I have no doubts of heaven. I never felt so happy before. All is bright and clear. "My title is clear to mansions in the skies." That God may abundantly bless you and the children is my prayer. Farewell.

Your Affectionate Husband.

LETTER No. 5. — A WEEPING SOUTHERN FAMILY.

This letter, although coming from the other side of the struggle, and written shortly after "the surrender," yet, being so full of sorrow and grief of a bereaved family, and breathing such a strong *paternal* and grateful spirit, it will no doubt be read with deep interest by many.

MONTGOMERY, ALA., July, 1865.

SIR: — Yours of the twenty-fifth May, addressed to my father, Mr. C. Stokes, informing him of the death of my only brother,

CHRISTIANITY IN THE WAR. 115

Andrew J. Stokes, has just been received. We had already received the bitter intelligence; but are none the less indebted and thankful to you for your note. Although you are an entire stranger to our once happy, but now gloomy, household, on behalf of the entire family allow me to return to you our most *heartfelt* thanks for the attention and care you bestowed upon the deceased. And although in the busy struggle of life our paths may never meet, rest assured, my dear sir, that under whatever suns, or upon whatever seas, it may please an all-wise God to cast *us*, we shall never, never forget you, who pointed the soul of him we loved so well to the brightly-beaming star of Faith and Hope. The day we received your sad, but comforting letter, because it bid us, "Be of good cheer," "It is thy Father's will," was the anniversary of the third year since last he was with us. *Then*, in the prime of his young, but noble manhood, he left us — *now*, poor boy, he sleeps the quiet sleep of death in a far-off, strangers' land. Pardon me for these ebullitions of private grief, but truly, indeed, has it been written, —

> "Oh, what a shadow o'er the heart is flung,
> When peals the requiem of the loved and young."

Again accept our thanks for your very kind attentions, and believe that when we "bend the knee" to invoke the blessings of Heaven; whenever memory shall revert to the joyous days of yore, we shall ask that same kind and righteous power to shower blessings upon you, so that when your race is run, you may rest in the bosom of the omnipotent God.

With profound respect,
I remain, truly yours,
—— ——.

CANVASSING THE PATIENTS' HEARTS.

One of the most laborious and important duties of the hospital chaplain was to canvass the hearts of the patients. And at one time we knew the *spiritual diagnosis* of almost every patient in the hospital. This was all-important; for it matters but little who has the head, if Satan has the heart. The heart governs. True religion is heart-work. Christianity is the religion of the heart. Hence the divine injunctions, "*Give me thy heart*," "Thou shalt love the Lord thy God with all thy heart," and "Keep thy heart with all diligence, for out of it are the issues of life."

Hence, in talking with the patients, we always endeavored to get at and get down deep into their hearts. And although, with some, it is difficult to reach the heart, yet we scarcely ever found it so with the soldier in the army. Accustomed to acts of heroism, soldiers are generally less ashamed, and more free to talk about religion in the army, than at home. And why should they not be? What a shame to the Christian religion that professors *talk* so little about it. In days of old, it was written, " they that fear the Lord, spake often one to another." Religious conversation is not only instructive, but strengthening and refreshing to the Christian, and very beneficial to the sinner. It warms the heart and fires the soul. Hence we often found it difficult to get away from the sick and wounded soldier. When about to start from the bedside, I have heard them plead thus: "O chaplain, don't go away. Can't you stay, and talk to me more about Jesus?" and giving him a warm shake of the hands, with a hearty "good-by," accompanied with the earnest exhortation, '*Trust in the Lord,*" together with the comprehensive prayer, "*May God bless you,*" it was hard to tear ourselves away from their warm hearts. To sit down, read and explain appropriate passages of Scripture, and enjoy a free, frank, unrestrained, social talk with the brave heroes, and to see the penitential tear trickle down their furrowed cheeks, was always touching and refreshing. They were not afraid or ashamed to unbosom their hearts, and tell us all about their lives and religious experience. If they prayed, they would say so; if not, they would frankly acknowledge it. When we put the question, "Do you swear?" they frankly answered, " Yes," or "No," or "Yes, I swear sometimes, when excited," as the case might be. If they enjoyed religion, they would tell you; if not, they would frankly acknowledge it. If they were seeking it, they were not ashamed to confess it. I asked one lovely boy, severely wounded, under deep conviction, bathed in tears, with anxiety about his salvation, "What *hinders* you from getting religion?" He promptly replied, "Pride, and my hard heart, I suppose," and, wringing his heart with contrition, the big tears flowed down his pale cheeks. With one leg off above the knee, there he lay for many days watering his couch with tears, given up by the ward-master and surgeon to die. He was a noble boy. I wept and prayed much for him; warned and entreated him to come to the Saviour, and, on my entering his ward shortly after, I saw his face lit up with smiles, and on asking, "How are you to-day, Henry?" he replied, "I am better. The burden is removed; I think I have found the Saviour. Oh, what a precious Saviour!" We sent for his father. He came. Henry got better, and went home, leaving one leg and a large portion of his patriotic blood upon the field of battle to water the tree of Liberty.

We often met with soldiers well versed in Scripture, who were rich and fluent in religious conversation. Some of them seemed to have the Bible at their fingers' end. Others, with less knowledge of God in the head, but with more of Christ in the heart; their lips teemed "with words that glow, and thoughts that burn," about the story of the cross, and their own religious experience. To talk and pray with them was a great privilege. I have gone away from their bedsides instructed, encouraged, and much refreshed. To witness the frequent bright conversions, their deep religious experience, triumphant deaths, and bright prospects of a glorious immortality exhibited, by their own language, in such words as these: "I am ready;" "The Lord is mine;" "I have no fear of death;" "Tell my wife I died happy;" "All is well," etc., were truly refreshing to the soul. And often very striking religious expressions fell from the lips of the colored patients. Having fewer religious and theological ideas than white people, what they have seem to take a deep hold and make a very deep impression upon them. More simple and confiding in their views and habits, they seem to *believe more* and *doubt less*, according to the light they have, than the whites. Taking God at his word, they seem to know nothing about doubting or unbelief. And being full of the *warmest* emotions, they often give vent to very vivid and striking impressions, such as the following: "I thank God for my wound: it has knocked the feeling of revenge out of me, and brought me nearer to God." "Before it, I would cry, 'Fort Pillow, and let 'em have it;' but now I would spare a rebel on his knees." Another says, "I am ready to go any time;" "I have got more than all the world can give;" "I don't want." Another earnestly prayed, "Save me, Lord! save me, Lord!" Another says, "When I go into battle, I put Jesus in front, and I don't fear," etc. Speaking right out from the heart, their thoughts are original, quick, and powerful. Many of them are remarkably earnest and powerful in prayer.

CHAPTER IX.

THE WOMEN OF THE HOSPITAL.

Their Valuable Services highly Appreciated by the Patients — Chesapeake Hospital well Supplied — Here Mrs. Mary B. Dully was Directress and Head of Sanitary Department — "She did what she Could" — Miss Amos, of Baltimore, Kind, Faithful, and True — Mrs. Chaplain E. P. Roe — "She went about Doing Good" — Mrs. Meecham and Many Others did Likewise — Mrs. Carver, with her Tent, Cooking-Stove, and Provisions, did much for the Patients — Mrs. Mary Alexander — Plain, Earnest, Heroic, Loved the Soldiers Ardently — "Bury Me with Them, when I Die."

TO the wearied, sick, or wounded soldier, so long from home, and deprived of the affectionate smiles of mother, father, wife, and children, a visit from no one seemed to do them so much good as from a kind, cheerful, sympathizing lady. Made up so much of tenderness, affection, and sympathy, a good woman can cheer and comfort when none else but God can. And so long exposed to the asperities of war, those messengers of mercy always met with a hearty welcome from the patient in the hospital. Hence every well regulated hospital was well furnished with competent matrons. Many a sick and wounded soldier and officer has been greatly comforted in their sick and dying hours by the sympathy and soothing power of woman's kindness. At the Chesapeake, every ward had its own matron, whose duty was to give out medicine, provide suitable food and delicacies for the most needy patients. In this way doubtless, under God,

HOSPITAL SCENE.

they saved the lives of many a patient. Besides this very important work, they did much in cheering up, reading and talking to, and writing letters for, the patients, and in a thousand ways added much to their comfort.

MRS. MARY B. DULLY.

At the Chesapeake, Mrs. Mary B. Dully, directress of this division of the hospital, stood at the head of the sanitary department, and with a liberal, prudent hand gave out the rich supplies of cordials, dainties, clothing, etc., furnished through the liberality of the *Sanitary Commission*, sent chiefly from Pittsburg, Pa. Intrusted with the internal affairs of the hospital, she presided over them with dignity and honor to herself and satisfaction to all concerned. Hailing from Pittsburg, Pa., with a heart full of patriotic ardor, she entered the service, at the beginning of the war, in the old Hygiea Hospital near the fort, and came here when that closed.

Marked for discretion, she succeeded in gathering around her a corps of competent ladies, well qualified for the arduous work of nursing the sick and wounded. With a head "silvered over with age," she always sat at the head of the table, and presided with ease and dignity. Possessing good executive abilities, and wielding a fine moral influence, her administration was a perfect success. But she not only managed the hospital affairs well, but, possessing a heart glowing with kindness, and swelling with compassion for the sick and wounded officers and soldiers, she labored faithfully, and, like Mary of old, "did what she could" to cheer and comfort them. I have seen her sit for hours endeavoring, with all her characteristic tenderness, to ease the pains and soothe the sorrows of the dying hero.

Thus she continued to labor until the hospital closed; and being a warm friend of the freedmen, then fell in and labored for them. She hath wrought a good work. The Lord reward her abundantly for it.

Miss Amos, of Baltimore, was another faithful laborer in this good work, who, in her meek, winning, unobtrusive manner did so much in administering to the wants and comforts of the patients. Mild and prepossessing in her ways, she was always a welcome visitor at the bedside of the patient. For a long while she was a very acceptable matron of one of the principal wards in the officers' division, but was afterward sent to "New Camp" to labor for the well-being and comforts of the private soldier. She was afterward assigned to duty in one of the more prominent wards of the Hampton division of the hospital, where, through her laborious work, she became sick, as did several other matrons, from hard labor and rooming in small rooms in one end of their respective wards. Among many others of equal worth, energy, and self-denial in their painstaking and arduous efforts in caring for and supplying the wants of the patients at the Chesapeake, (as we have not time and space to speak fully of them all,) were *Miss J. E. Bently, Mrs. D. W. Holt, Mrs. Campbell, Mrs. Jane M. Worrell, Miss Preston, Miss E. Wolcott,* and several others whose names we have forgotten.

At Hampton, they acted the same part. But here, the matrons being fewer in proportion to the number of patients, each matron had a much wider field of labor. Sometimes there were but three or four matrons in all the division. Then they went round and visited from ward to ward, paying particular attention to the worst cases.

MRS. CHAPLAIN E. P. ROE,

from New York, for a while in the summer and fall of 1864 took an active part in this noble work. With her kind heart, liberal hand, and cheerful countenance, she went round through the wards, administering both to the temporal and spiritual wants of the patients. Supplied with cordials and articles of clothing, wherever she found a needy patient, she supplied him with these things. And having supplied their temporal wants, she often ministered to them spiritually, in reading and talking to them, pointing them to Christ, and urging them to immediate repentance. With her Christian zeal and characteristic tenderness, she did much to relieve the suffering soldiers. On the opposite page is a picture of her reading to a wounded soldier.

MRS. MEECHAM,

of Cleveland, Ohio, who spent some two or three years in this home of the sick and wounded soldier, by her good sense and adaptedness to the work, was a perfect veteran in administering to the wants and comforts of the patients. She was a sweet singer, and by her enchanting music did much to ease the pains, soothe the sorrows, and cheer the hearts of the suffering. Besides after leading the singing at church, she always went around with the choir to sing in the wards. This exercise, very acceptable and cheering to the patients, was usually conducted by Chaplain Roe, and generally attended to on Sabbath afternoons. The chaplain, accompanied by the choir, would enter a ward, read a suitable passage of Scripture, followed by the enlivening music. After singing two or three pieces, they would go on to the next ward. They usually sung every Sabbath. Part of the time it was omitted.

MRS. CARVER.

Although she was not connected with the hospital, and had no relative therein, she there did a good work. Deeply concerned for the salvation of the country, and deeply interested in the welfare of the soldier, this noble-hearted lady came from Philadelphia, Pa., to Fortress Monroe, Va., to labor for their comfort. Amply provided with cooking-stoves and cooking-utensils, and a rich supply of flour, meats, fruits, fowls, and delicacies, she came here first in the summer of 1864, and located herself in a remote part of the hospital, in the north-east corner of New Camp. Here, through the surgeon in charge, she soon had a comfortable tent erected, put up her cooking-stove, hung out the stars and stripes, and commenced operation on her own hook. Thus prepared, she set about the great work in good earnest, and baking bread and pies, and preparing all sorts of good things in best style, the heart of many a suffering soldier was made glad through her incessant labors and bountiful liberality. And having prepared her rich provisions, she would go round through the wards and look up the most needy patients, and with eagerness administer to their wants. Possessed with a magnanimous spirit and a tender, sympathizing heart and a lofty patriotism, she was a *true friend* of the soldier, and delighted to give and labor for his comfort. The first time I met her was in a tent in New Camp, endeavoring to comfort a distressed, suffering soldier. At her request I went in, read, conversed, and prayed with him, endeavoring to pour into his soul the consolations of the gospel. Here, and in this way, she continued her good work and labor of love until late in the fall, and then went home. But, without growing weary in well doing and with unabated interest in the welfare of the soldier, she returned the following summer, with a fresh supply of provision, and opened out her *Sanitary Tent* again near ward twenty-seven, close by the head-quarters of Hampton Hospital. Here, with renewed vigor and liberality, she prepared and dealt out her good things to the worthy suffering defenders of our country. What she did in the great conflict for the Union in other parts of the army, we do not know; but for what she has done here, she deserves to be enshrined in the memory of every American patriot.

MRS. MARY ALEXANDER.

Of all the matrons of the U. S. General Hospital, Fortress Monroe, Va., for fidelity, self-denial, and devotion to the interests of the sick and wounded, there were none that excelled Mrs. Mary Alexander. Deeply interested in the cause of freedom, she entered the service at the beginning of the war, and sacrificed her life in the noble cause. Born and brought up among the mountains of Switzerland, the principles of liberty were deeply instilled in her mind, and they burned warmly upon the altar of her patriotic heart. *A love of liberty was the ruling passion of her soul.* A true, devoted friend of the soldiers, she nursed them as her own children; and they loved her as a mother. Trusting in God for help and success, when laboring with a patient severely wounded or dangerously diseased, she would say, "*We will try and save him, by the help of God.*" And, doubtless, it was her reliance upon God for help that made her so devoted and successful in her noble work and labor of love. Stout-hearted, heavy-set, with a strong, muscular frame, she was well calculated to endure hardness. Firmness, energy, perseverance, and determination were some of the leading traits of her character. Blessed with good sense and sound judgment, plain and unassuming, she was a woman of few words, distinguished more for her *deeds* than for words. Acting the part of both wound-dresser and ward-matron, when it was necessary for the good of the patient to pour into his gangrened wound the burning, smarting tincture, she possessed the nerve to do it, even though the patient would sometimes scream out with anguish and pain. Having so many bad cases in her ward, and being so much exposed to the impurities of the patients, through her excessive labor and toil by day and night, she contracted a malignant fever, which carried her off in eight or ten days. Devotedly attached to the soldiers while living, she said "*Bury me with them, when dead.*" Her request was granted. In the centre of a small triangular lot, reserved for flowers in the centre of the soldiers' graveyard, her mortal remains were buried with all the pomp and honors of war. Having lived to see the rebellion quelled, the slave freed, and the country saved, patient and resigned she passed away, April 23, 1865, at five o'clock P. M., crowned with the glories of martyrdom. She died in the Chesapeake Hospital. Her funeral was large, solemn, and imposing. The corpse, beautifully decorated with garlands of roses and wreaths of flowers, wrapped in a fine shroud and inclosed in a neat coffin, was placed in the parlor, richly draped in mourning in honor of the death of Abraham Lincoln. And there, standing in the aisle, thronged with officers, ladies, and soldiers, Chaplain E. P. Roe, U.S.A., preached an appropriate sermon from the following words, " Well done, thou good and faithful servant, enter thou into the joy of thy Lord." The exercises were very solemn and deeply impressive. The procession, headed by the hospital band discoursing mournful music, was grand and imposing. Having labored faithfully with the soldiers in the field and hospital, she now rests with them in the grave. There she lies, waiting the voice of the last trumpet, " when all will meet again around the judgment-seat of Christ." There she lies, with her noble soul disembodied, and washed, we trust, in the blood of Jesus, has gone to swell the ranks of the redeemed in heaven, where there will be no more war, where God himself shall wipe away all tears. She deserves a monument more durable than brass. Let it rise.

CHAPTER X.

SKETCHES OF SOLDIERS.

"Past Feeling"—Patchwork won't do for Eternity—"Jesus Saved Me Twice"—"I Never Forget My Saviour"—The Blind Exhorter—"I have very Sweet Communion with God"—His Death—Letter from His Wife—Corporal John Creed, 23d Ill., Co. B.—Honored for His Bravery—Soldiers Die Clinched—Courage of Pompey—Joy an Element of Strength—Ananias Montgomery—"He had a Ball in His Side, and God in His Heart"—"I Feel Happy"—The Backslider—"I Lost My Religion"—"Now I am Miserable"—George H. Vanloan—"I do Love Him"—"It would be Hard to Live in the Army without Religion"—The Fixed Heart—"I Pray Often"—"I do Feel Happy"—"I Am Too Wicked for That"—I Swear a Great Deal"—"I Can't Pray"—"It's Too Late"—"I am a Great Sinner"—"I Have Given Up"—"It is Better to Die"—"I am Willing to go"—"All is Well"—Midnight Calls—"O Chaplain, I Feel most Awful!"

"PAST FEELING."

SITTING beside a pale, languid soldier, one day, in ward number seven, endeavoring to probe his conscience and stir his soul upon the subject of immediate repentance, and finding him hard to reach, the kind, compassionate matron came up, and cried out, "Comfort him! *comfort him!*" whereupon I immediately replied, "The soldier's heart, like his wound, must be *probed* before it can be healed or comforted. To comfort the

PITTSBURGH LANDING.

soul while the heart is embedded in sin is *impossible*. What caused this great national disturbance? Why is our country deluged with blood to-day? What is the cause? It is *sin*. Sin is the great disturber in this world. It is sin that robs man of comfort; and so long as it lies on the heart unrepented of, there can be no lasting peace. Sin has dug hell; and God says, 'The wicked shall be turned into hell;' and I wish to say to you, my dear friend, you must soon repent or perish, turn or die. And, as Whitefield says, 'It is better to hear of hell, than to feel it,' we wish to give you fair warning. Patchwork may do for time, but it will not do for eternity. It won't stand the test of the great heart-searching God, whose eyes are as a flaming fire. If you build on the sand, when the floods of God's wrath rise, you will be swept away. The natural heart is such a sink of iniquity that, unless it is deeply probed by God's Spirit, and washed in Christ's blood, there can be no true peace on earth and no happiness in heaven. A wound may be healed over with corruption within, but it will soon break out again; so you may smooth over, and patch the old stony heart, and obtain a little transient comfort; but unless it be thoroughly cleansed, like the troubled sea, that cannot rest, it will continually be casting up mire and dirt. So long as Satan sits enthroned within, and retains possession of the heart, the ebullitions of envy, strife, and unhallowed ambition will continue to rise, and keep the whole man in a continual commotion. A small leak will sink a great ship; and a small sin, unrepented of, will sink the soul to hell. Hence we learn the importance of a change of heart and complete sanctification. Oh, then, we beseech you, my dear friend, give your heart to God! Surrender the old heart, and God will give you a new one. You have had many warnings. God still waits to be gracious. Jesus still cries, 'Come unto me, and I will give you rest.'" I preached to him, conversed and prayed with him; urged and besought him by the mercies of God, by the love of Christ, and by the joys of heaven, to fly to Jesus; yet all seemed to make but little or no impression. His heart seemed barred against the truth. He seemed to be past feeling, and the story of the cross appeared to make no impression upon him. He was frank and free to talk, but seemed to be perfectly careless and indifferent about his salvation. The tender-hearted matron tried him, but, with all her sympathy and kindness, said she could do nothing with him. Profane and careless, he seemed to quench the Spirit and resist the truth. He was now pale and low with chronic diarrhœa, and, from all appearance, was nigh unto death. I said to him, " Are you not afraid you will die, and be lost ? " "No!" he said, without appearing to realize his danger. I urged him by every possible motive, with all tenderness, to look to Jesus; but, dead in sin and lost to God, nothing appeared to touch him. With his conscience seared, he seemed to have sinned away his day of grace, and to have become " past feeling." I said to him, " Were you to feel the torments of hell and to realize the joys of heaven for one minute, think you would remain any longer careless?" He said, "I don't know; but I suppose not." "And yet the existence of these places is as *sure* as though you had felt the torments of the one and realized the joys of the other. Why not then *act* as though you had seen and felt them both?" He belonged to the 169th N. Y. Vol. We urged him by the melting scenes of Gethsemane and Calvary, but all apparently with no effect. He lingered till February 17, 1865, and, so far as we could see, died without hope. Let the careless be warned and entreated to seek the Lord while he may be found. This was a very rare case.

A SICK SOLDIER BAPTIZED.

At our first interview with JOHN W. PHILIPS, of Ohio, we found him tender, and with some degree of anxiety inquiring what to do to be saved. After pointing him to the Lamb of God whose blood cleanseth from all sin, and beseeching him by the mercies of God to come to Jesus, we bid him good-by. Although now quite feeble, his strength was evidently declining. At our next interview we found his spiritual interest increasing, and he seemed to be indulging a hope. Telling him of the goodness of God, of the amazing *love* of Christ, and of his willingness and ability to save even to the uttermost, and endeavoring to explain the simplicity of the plan of salvation by faith, and urging him to let go self, renounce the world, forsake sin, and *at once* to throw himself right into the arms of Jesus, and beseeching the Lord to wash and save his soul, we left him to meditate on these things. Possessing a mild, amiable, forgiving spirit, and apparently resigned to God's will, not a murmur fell from his lips. At our next call we found him sinking physically, but rising spiritually, and, indulging a hope that he had felt the washing of regeneration, he desired to be received into the church, and be baptized. He laid in a tent hard by and facing the bay, from which blew daily a fine refreshing breeze, symbolical of the Spirit that washed, we trust, his soul in a Saviour's precious blood. Pressing his desire to unite with the Presbyterian Church, we brought the pastor and ruling elders of the Annapolis Presbyterian Church, and after the usual examination he was received, and after a brief explanation of the nature and design of the ordinance of baptism, he was solemnly baptized, sitting on his death-bed, beside the blue waters of Chesapeake Bay, May 10, 1864. Rejoicing in the Lord, and overflowing with gratitude, he thanked us most heartily. But his time was short. Lingering some ten hours after his baptism, his soul left its clay tenement, and went, we hope, to dwell with the spirits of just men made perfect on high.

A SOLDIER WITH HALF OF HIS THROAT SHOT OFF.

The army of the Potomac, commanded by Gen. Grant, set out for Richmond, May 3, 1864, and, having crossed the Rapidan, they soon met the bloodthirsty rebels in the fierce, destructive battles of the Wilderness and Spottsylvania, and the wounded soon began to pour into the hospitals here almost daily. Many of the officers, though but slightly wounded or diseased, seemed to be a good deal fatigued, and after a few days' rest were, by the exacting surgeon in charge, sent back to the front. Others, severely wounded and unable for duty, were retained, and received strict attention.

In making my regular visits, one day, I found an unfortunate soldier, sitting alone in his tent, with half of his under jaw and throat shot off. "A very narrow escape, sir! you have made a very narrow escape with your life." "Yes, a little deeper, and I would have been gone." Though severely wounded, he bore it all very patiently without a murmur. With his swallow so badly injured and so much of it torn off, he had to live entirely on spoon victuals. And his vocal organs were so much impaired he could scarcely speak. On approaching him on the subject of religion, he said he trusted in the Lord, and appeared to have a well-grounded hope. After pointing him to the Saviour, and beseeching him to cling to the cross, I said to him, "Shall I pray for you?" and promptly nodding his head, he quickly kneeled down with such a *zest* that manifested a longing desire for the intercession; and kneeling down by his side, we besought God to sustain and comfort him in his trials, heal his wounds, forgive his sins, and save his soul. We visited him often, and always found him patient and resigned, frequently reading his Testament. He belonged in Philadelphia, had no family, and when we left the hospital he was doing well. How he got along afterward, we never heard.

This and the case immediately preceding it, were in the U.S. General Hospital at Annapolis, Md.

"JESUS SAVED ME TWICE."

The shock of battle, the bloody charge, the groans of the dying, and the awful sight of the ghastly dead, together with the pressing danger of the severe conflict, sometimes so deeply stir the soul and fire the heart of the Christian soldier, that when he falls severely wounded upon the gory field, and is carried to the hospital, the first word he utters is one glowing with gratitude to God for his great mercy in sparing his life. Such were the heart-gushing words of George Frederick, 15th N. J., Co. C, as he lay upon his bed with a rebel ball in his shoulder, when he said, with deep emotion and tears, as I first approached him, "*Jesus saved me twice.*" Having twice barely escaped with his life, and ascribing all the glory of his salvation to God, he hastens to give utterance to the deep thoughts of his heart, and exclaims, in words of immortal memory, "*Jesus saved me twice;*" whereupon I replied, "And I hope he will save you again." And George said, with a smiling countenance, "I hope and believe he will."

He was wounded in one of the last great battles near Petersburg, Va., having been shot in the left shoulder, the ball remaining in him; yet, with his strong faith and buoyant hope, his severe wound soon began to improve.

Upon examining a little farther into his spiritual condition, we found him very penitent and unusually prayerful. He was a member of the Presbyterian Church, and, conscious of the great things God had done for him, his heart seemed to flow out with prayer and praise. He prayed much. His wound was so severe, and the shock so great at first, to use his own language, he said, "I thought I would have died on the field, and I requested a friend to write home, '*Poor George is dead.*'" And although exposed to the temptations of the camp, the trials of the march, and the conflicts of battle, yet, says he, "*I never forget my Saviour.*" "Never forget him! Few, very few, can say as much. You must be very happy?" "Yes, I feel happy in the Lord." "And I suppose you find this happy state of feeling, or joy in the Lord, a source of courage and strength in the day of battle?" "Yes, I believe it is. Besides the salvation of the country, the anticipated honor and glory of victory does much to urge men on to acts of daring and courage in the day of battle." "As you never forget your Saviour, George, I suppose the ordinary temptations of army life make but little impression upon you." "No; I try to watch and pray, and by endeavoring to remember the great truth contained in the words of Hagar, 'Thou, God, seest me,' I endeavor to endure temptation as much as possible." And there is nothing tends more to deliver us from temptation than a clear conception of God's presence. A deep sense of the sublime truth, *God is present*, should quench the fiery darts of the wicked and blunt the weapons of hell. If the thief, when he goes to steal, would stop, and call to mind the important truth God is present, his thieving heart would fail him. If the profane swearer, when his lips begin to teem with oaths, would remember that the God whose name he profanes is present, it would stay his swearing. Had J. Wilkes Booth, when he was about to assassinate Abraham Lincoln, stopped, and grasped the awe-inspiring truth, *God is present*, his fiendish heart would have failed him, and his murderous hand would have fallen palsied to his side, and he would have failed to commit that awful deed. Thus, as a check upon sin, let us always remember God is present, and our responsibility unto him, and strive to live so that we will be enabled to say in the words of George Frederick, "I never forget my Saviour." The last we heard of him was in his own words, "I feel happy in the Lord."

THE BLIND EXHORTER.

The Gangrene Camp was the scene of much severe suffering. It was a kind of a depository for the almost hopeless cases of men with gangrened wounds, and other contagious diseases. Yet patients taken there frequently recovered, and were taken back again to their wards. Patients dreaded to go there. But gangrene being considered so contagious, it was considered dangerous to allow cases of it to remain with other wounded patients clear of it. In our "gospel ranging," we often met with very interesting cases of religious experience in this lonely camp. When we first met with Hutchinson Miller, 29th Conn., Co. C, colored troops, we found him low with the erysipelas in the head. His face and eyes were so badly swollen with this fatal disease that he could not see. Wearing a noble countenance, marked with intelligence, integrity, and honor, we find him pleasant and interesting in conversation. Approaching him on the subject of religion, he seemed to be well versed in the doctrines of the cross. Hailing from "the land of steady habits," and being a Presbyterian, he possessed less of the emotional than colored men generally. He said he had been converted fifteen years ago. And as I began to draw him out on his religious experience, he gave me as his creed, "*All my trust is in Jesus Christ.*" "That is a very good, brief, comprehensive, sound, orthodox creed. If you will stand straight and firm on that, it will sustain, console, and buoy you up under all circumstances. With 'all your trust in

Christ,' who is able, willing, mighty to save, you have nothing to fear. He is the rock of our salvation. Besides him there is no Saviour. He is able to save to the uttermost. I suppose you derive much comfort from Him?" "Yes, I have very sweet communion with God." "Communion and intercourse with dear friends is sweet and precious, but it is nothing compared to communion with God. When John Wesley was lying on his death-bed, surrounded with intimate friends, with tender hearts and weeping eyes expressing their warmest sympathies and earnest efforts to comfort him, the faithful old soldier of the cross, realizing that his comfort came from a higher source, exclaimed, '*The best of all is, God is with us.*' Sweet communion with God, together with a firm reliance upon Christ, will drive away every cloud, and enable us to '*rejoice in the Lord always.*' I hope you have no fear of death?" "No, I am not afraid to die." "With all your trust in Christ, you need not fear to die, because, when standing firmly on such a foundation, 'to die is gain.' Christ, when he died upon the cross, deprived death of its sting to every believer; hence Paul said, 'to depart is far better.'" His disease grew worse, and although he could not see, yet, perceiving that an unconverted soldier was lying close by him in the same tent, Hutchinson Miller, being no longer able to wield "the sword of Gideon," now grasps the sword of the Spirit, and fights with it in warning, instructing, and beseeching his dying comrade to repent, and fly to the Saviour. Although his swollen eyes hid from his vision the light of the natural sun, yet, with his soul lit up by the glorious light of the Sun of Righteousness, he exhorted his tent-mates with tenderness and earnestness to prepare to meet their God. Blest with the joys of salvation himself, he felt deeply anxious that his comrades-in-arms should enjoy it also. And to see him, with his swollen head and closed eyes, lying upon his death-bed, with a gushing heart imploring the wayward to be reconciled to God, was enough to stir the soul of the most unfaithful Christian. He said he belonged to the Free Masons. Calm and submissive, he survived the struggles of life till February 25, 1865, when his soul left its clay tenement, and went, we trust, to the home of the blest. His last words to me were, " Christ is precious, and all my trust." The following interesting letter is from his bereaved wife.

READING, PA., March 1, 1865.

CHAPLAIN A. S. BILLINGSLEY: — I take my pen in hand to inform you that I received your letter of the 3d, which revealed to me the sad news — the death of my husband, Hutchinson Miller. So great was the shock to me that I have been unable to answer your letter till now. At present I am laboring under a very severe headache. Whilst this duty is a very painful one to me, your letter was very kind and sympathizing; and I feel under many obligations to you for the interest that you took in visiting him, conversing with him, and also in writing to me so soon. You will please here accept my warmest thanks for all you have done, hoping that God will reward you more bountifully. My loss is exceedingly a very great one; for the last letter he wrote was dated on the fifteenth of February: he then spoke of feeling very comfortable, and up to that time he entertained a hope that he would get a furlough. I had been in the habit of getting a letter every week, and often twice a week. The last one was a very cheerful one, and he spoke much of coming home, and of our poor little children; and when the time arrived for me to get the next, and there was none, I felt confident that he would answer it by his presence. I set up every night till after the late train came in, thinking he would come; but, alas! my waiting was in vain; instead of his presence, the unwelcome news came that he was gone where no traveller was ever known to return. So you can imagine my loss much better than I can express it. At one time he wrote me that he had asked for a furlough, and the reply was that he would get one, but it would be down front, which was very wounding to his feelings. I think that it is very hard that, when a man leaves his home — a comfortable home, like he did — and when they are no longer fit for service, that they are deprived of the privilege of seeing their families, which is their all in this life. At times I think that it cannot be that I am not to see him any more in this life! But I pray earnestly that God will give me grace sufficient to bear with my bereavement. My health is very poor, so that I am not able to labor to raise my family; but still I believe that God will provide a way for me, if I live faithful. I was led to inquire the way to Christ when a Sabbath-school scholar, and at the age of fourteen years I was admitted a member of the Presbyterian Church; and in all my sorrow through life, He has been my comfort, and I still feel to trust Him. So I close, hoping that you will remember me and my family when bowing before the throne of grace!

From your bereaved friend,
———.

N. B. His remains may be sent for; but at present I have not the means. If he was here, it would all be much to my comfort.

SOLDIERS DYING CLINCHED IN BATTLE.

Corp. JOHN CREED, 23d Ill., Co. B, though small in body, possessed a noble, courageous heart. He was an old soldier, and had served several years in the old country before he left Ireland. His physiognomy, manners, and appearance, and everything about him, denoted honesty, frankness, and simplicity. Although he carried with him a medal of honor that he had received from the Government of the United States for his bravery, and had received special marks of respect from President Lincoln, he was very unpretending in his manners. He was shot in both arms at the capture of Fort Craig, Va., just at the close of the war. Though mild, he was also stern and invincible. To hear him recount deeds of valor and bravery on the field of battle would raise the patriotism of the most heroic. He said he saw a Union and rebel soldier bayonet one another, clinch, and die clinched. Said he had seen men die standing on the field of battle. And just here let us stop a moment, and inquire what it is that leads men to do such daring deeds. The fear of disgrace and the love of honor, together with the love of God and a patriotic devotion, constitute some of the strongest motives that actuate men in the discharge of duty. Aside from these considerations, the power of military discipline has a wonderful influence in making men steadfast and resolute. A striking instance of which is given by Dr. Guthrie, in the case of the old Roman sentinel, in the following graphic words:

THE ROMAN SENTINEL.

There was nothing in Pompeii that invested it with a deeper interest to me than the spot where a soldier of old Rome displayed a most heroic fidelity. That fatal day on which Vesuvius, at whose feet the city stood, burst out into an eruption that shook the earth, poured torrents of lava from its riven sides, and discharged, amidst the noise of a hundred thunders, such clouds of ashes as filled the air, produced a darkness deeper than midnight, and struck such terror into all hearts that men thought not only that the end of the world had come and all must die, but that the gods themselves were expiring — on that night a sentinel kept watch by the gate which looked to the burning mountain. Amidst unimaginable confusion, and shrieks of terror mingled with the roar of the volcano, and cries of mothers who had lost their children in the darkness, the inhabitants fled from the fatal town, while falling ashes, loading the darkened air and penetrating every place, rose in the streets till they covered the house-roofs, nor left a vestige of the city but a vast silent mound, beneath which it lay unknown, dead, and buried, for nearly seventeen hundred years. Amidst this fearful disorder, the sentinel at the gate had been forgotten; and as Rome required her sentinels, happen what might, to hold their posts till relieved by the guard, or set at liberty by their officers, he had to choose between death and dishonor. Pattern of fidelity, he stood by his post. Slowly but surely the ashes rise on his manly form; now they reach his breast; and now, covering his lips, they choke his breathing. He, also, was "faithful unto death." After seventeen centuries, they found his skeleton standing erect in a marble niche, clad in its rusty armor — the helmet on his empty skull, and his bony fingers still closed upon his spear. And next almost to the interest I felt in placing myself on the spot where Paul, true to his colors when all men deserted him, pleaded before the Roman tyrant, was the interest I felt in the niche by the city gate where they found the skeleton of one who, in his fidelity to the cause of Cæsar, sets us an example of faithfulness to the cause of Christ — an example it were for the honor of their Master that all his servants followed.

And besides all this, there is a thrilling, buoyant joy in anticipated victory which nerves the soul and urges on in daring deeds, that leads men undauntedly to face danger, and even to bid defiance to death itself. When the friends of the intrepid Pompey dissuaded him from venturing on a tempestuous sea, in order to be in Rome on an important occasion, the fearless hero replied in words of immortal memory: "It is necessary for me to go; it is not necessary for me to live." To Pompey, the joy in the discharge of duty overcomes the fear of death. When Gen. Howard (under Gen. Sherman) was advancing upon Savannah, as he approached the doomed city, he met in the way a small rebel battery which kept up a most galling fire, to the great annoyance of his troops; whereupon the brave general commanded a halt, and called out for twenty-five brave men to storm the rebel stronghold. Animated with a sublime thirst for the fierce conflict, and fired with a noble joy in anticipating the victory, the brave twenty-five quickly volunteered, and rushed up boldly amidst the thick grape and canister, and, staring death in the face, took the courageous battery amidst the loud shouts of ten thousand hearts anxiously gazing upon the grandeur of the sublime achievement. And although man burns with ambition and longs for fame's immortal honors, it is after all the inspiring joy attending these things that impels the ambitious to grasp for them. Hence this animating joy is one of the principal elements of moral strength in all great and laudable undertakings: it is strength to the orator, it is strength to the soldier, and strength to the Christian. It is this buoyant feeling that gives the rostrum and the pulpit such wonderful power, and makes the forum flash " with thoughts that burn and words that glow." It is this wonderful element of strength that holds the martyr to the stake, and enables him to shout victory in the very agonies of death. "For the joy of the Lord is your strength."— Neh. viii. 10. And if it were possible to strip man of this powerful element, the church and the enterprising world would fall into a sudden collapse. What, we ask, was it that led Jesus to Calvary? What enabled him to endure the cross and despise the shame? It was the "joy" that was set before him. Then, if we would be mighty in battle and strong in the Lord, let us so live that we will be " rejoicing in the Lord always."— Phil. iv. 4. Reader, if you would be happy, useful, and successful in the world, cultivate a cheerful disposition.

ANANIAS MONTGOMERY—HE HAD A BALL IN HIS SIDE, AND GOD IN HIS HEART.

In canvassing one of the new wards, on a balmy April morning, we came in contact with Ananias Montgomery, 10th West Va., Co. B, and found him, at our first interview, patient, prayerful, and resigned. His manly form, expressive countenance, frank appearance, led us to set him down for a noble fellow. He was wounded in the capture of Fort Craig, April 2, 1865, in the last great battle of the war. I remarked to him that it seemed hard to fight three or four years, and then receive a mortal wound just at the close of the struggle. "It does seem so," he said; "yet I hope and trust it is all right. God's will be done." "Thank God for such submission! To be resigned to God's will is a very high attainment. Although you have a minie-ball in your side, yet, having God in your heart, you have, I hope, nothing to fear. Do you think you would be afraid to die?" "No; I feel I can die happy." Realizing his need of divine assistance, he said, "Pray for me, that I may hold out faithful till death." "Have you any word to send to your wife?" "Nothing; only I feel happy, and prepared to die." What a consoling message from a dear dying husband to a bereaved, weeping wife! It is more precious than all the victories and honors ever won upon the field of battle. Victory over the enemy is glorious, but victory over death is rapturous; and to the bereaved, heart-broken wife nothing could afford so much consolation. To lose a kind husband at home, under the most favorable circumstances, is very trying to the bereaved widow; but when he dies upon the ensanguined field, or in the hospital, far away from friends, it is far more severe. Having fought a good fight, even with a ball in his side, and feeling that God was in his heart, with the grave yawning before him, sustained by God's grace, he was enabled to say, "I feel happy, and prepared to die." He lingered a few days, and passed away, we trust, where the clanging of arms and the whistling of balls are heard no more.

THE BACKSLIDER.

I have heard men say, in the Rocky Mountains of Colorado, "We can't live out religion here, where sin so much abounds, and where temptations are so strong." Sometimes the same objection and excuse has been urged in the army. And although restraints are weaker, and temptations stronger, in the army than at home, yet, as God is the same everywhere, and as his grace is sufficient for us at all times, and in all places, if we will only trust in Him, he will deliver in every temptation, and sustain us in every trial, as well in the army as at home. If God preserved and delivered Daniel in the lions' den, surely he can sustain the Christian soldier in the army. At our first interview with Harry Stanton, 118th N. Y., Co. C, we found him of easy access, frank and free to converse, and confess his sins. Said he, "I was soundly converted over twelve years ago. I enjoyed religion very well for six months; but then I lost it." "What a long list of sins! Yet we are glad to see you make such a frank and full confession of them. It is good to confess your faults to another. God says, 'If we confess our sins, he is faithful to forgive, and to cleanse us from all unrighteousness.' What led you to backslide?" "My own unfaithfulness. My neglecting my Bible, my closet, the church, and the prayer-meeting. I became lukewarm; my love waxed cold; I forsook God, and he has forsaken me." "Where did your backsliding begin?" "It began in my heart, I suppose, and, taking root there, it soon spread all through my thoughts, prayers, devotions, words, and deeds, until I soon found that I possessed so little strength that I was just 'ready to die.'" "Now do you think you *were* really soundly converted to God?" "Yes, I have no doubt of it." "Although it is the Christian's privilege to *know* that he is a Christian, there is, after all, a possibility of being deceived in this matter. We may think and belief we are Christians, when we are not. Hence, close self-examination is all-important. How are you getting along now? Do you feel happy since you lost your religion?" "Oh, no; I am miserable. God frowns upon me — a miserable backslider! Yes, that's what I am!" "Oh! how strange and awful, that any should ever wander away from such a compassionate Saviour, who has done such great things for us! Take the oath of allegiance to the King of kings, and then turn traitor to God! Forsake Him who suffered, bled, and died for *you?* Oh, how treacherous! What treacherous disloyalty! With your soul once washed in Christ's blood, and then return like a sow that is washed to her wallowing in the mire! Come down from the lofty heights of holiness, of union and communion with God, and return again to the beggarly elements and to bondage — quit praying, and take to swearing; forsake God to serve Satan! Oh, how awful! And is it so? *Is this your condition?*" "Yes, that's it, in strong terms." "And don't you feel sorry for your aggravated sins?" "Yes, [weeping,] I do feel sorry; and I am going to try to do better." "You are not going to live without religion, I hope?" "No; I expect to seek it again when I get home." "Why not seek it here in the hospital now?" "Oh, this is a poor place for it." "A poor place for it here, among the sick and dying, where death is so frequent, where time is so short, and eternity so near? I should think it a very *good* place for it; and it is the very place that you need. Do you see that shrouded corpse; do you see that dear comrade bleeding to death; do you hear the dying groans of that expiring soldier; and what meaneth all this? It is a warning to you; it is the voice of God warning and admonishing you, '*Prepare to meet thy God!*' Oh, then, say not 'this is a poor place to seek religion!' If the awful, terrible charge and the shock of battle don't alarm you; if the thrilling, solemn scenes of the hospital don't arrest you, and lead you to repentance, how can you expect the dull routine of life at home to do it? You *expect*, you say, to seek religion when you get home? What if you should never reach home; how then? Besides, God says, 'The expectation of the wicked shall perish.' (Prov. x. 28.) Many, doubtless, expect to be saved, who are finally lost. Your only safety, then, is in *immediate* repentance. *Now* is God's time, and *here* is the right *place*. Oh, then, we beseech you, repent, repent *now*, — come back, come home to God, and he will heal your backsliding, and restore unto you the joys of his salvation! May God bless you."

GEORGE H. VANLOAN.

Upon canvassing the heart of George H. Vanloan, 3d N. Y. Cavalry, we found him penitent, prayerful, trusting in the Lord. "Do you love the Saviour!" "Yes," he said, with great emphasis, and deep emotion and tears, "I *do* love him." "Love is the principal thing. Without love we are 'as sounding brass, or a tinkling cymbal.' 'And though I bestow all my goods to feed the poor, and though I give my body to be burned, and have not charity, or love, I am nothing. Love is the fulfilling of the law; it is the strongest of all propensities. It holds and binds the Christian to the throne of grace, and the martyr to the stake. Don't you think love to Christ helps in getting along in afflictions?" "Yes, I believe so; for I'd have died long ago, had I not trusted in the Lord." "The calm, composed state of mind resulting from strong faith in Christ, when passing through the deep waters of affliction, is, no doubt, well calculated to sustain and comfort the sick, so that in many cases life has been spared and health restored where death would have ensued without it. I have heard soldiers, who had been brought nigh to death, express themselves to this effect frequently. Faith saves the soul, and is the means of saving the life. It is written of the blind beggar, 'Thy faith hath made thee whole.'" Afflicted reader, if you would bear affliction patiently, and get well quickly, trust in Christ, the great physician, who, in justice, love, and mercy, afflicts his own children, when they need it, for their profit. A deep consciousness of the fact that sanctified affliction's work for our good, and the consequent cheerful spirit resulting therefrom, is doubtless one of the reasons why they tend to restore health.

"IT WOULD BE HARD TO LIVE IN THE ARMY WITHOUT RELIGION."

While it has often been said by the thoughtless and careless, "We can't live out religion in the army;" and although it is often said by a certain class of professors, "the army is a hard place to be a Christian, and live it out," yet at our first interview with James H. Finney, 1st N. Y. Engineers, we found him entertaining a very different view, and being fully conscious of the enjoyments and consolations of the Christian religion, he says, "It would be hard to live in the army without it." Opposed, as we are, by the combined powers of the world, the flesh, and the devil, life at best is a warfare from the cradle to the grave. And although the temptations are greater and the restraints weaker some places than others, yet, since God's grace is sufficient at all times and under all circumstances to guide, guard, and sustain the believer, he can, if he will, at all times walk worthy of his vocation, and so live and act that his life will be an *embodiment* of the great doctrines of the cross of Christ. And it is impugning the wisdom, mercy, power, and grace of God to say that he cannot. Noah, though thrown amidst all the whirlpools of temptation of an antediluvian world, yet, actuated by a living faith, he sustained his character, and moved with fear, when God's wrath and fury were about to be poured out upon a doomed world, " he prepared an ark to the saving of his house." If God gives the martyr grace and strength to burn at the stake, most assuredly he will give grace sufficient to stand the trials and temptations of the march, the camp, and the field of battle. And surrounded with increased exposure in the army, as you say, it would be hard to live without the comforts and consolations of religion. It is difficult to conceive how a man once regenerated, with his sins pardoned, and with the image of God restamped upon his soul, and blessed with the glorious hope of a blessed immortality beyond the grave, could ever think of living without religion anywhere, much less among the asperities and hardships and trials of the army. To sustain under trials, to comfort in distress, and to bind up the broken in heart, is one of the great objects of the religion of the cross. And to hold that we cannot have it, and enjoy it when we most need it, is preposterous in the extreme. The only difficulty in living in the full enjoyment of the sweet consolations of the gospel is in the faithful use of the means. If we will only be faithful, God will bless and comfort as well in the army as in the family circle at home. "Be thou faithful unto death, and I will give thee a crown of life."

THE FIXED HEART.

It was just as the last lingering rays of the setting sun playing on the lofty dome of "old Chesapeake," as we were making our regular round through the hospital, that we came in contact with Henry Bartsher, 58th Pa. Vol., Co. I. And, finding him of easy access, we had no difficulty in drawing him out on the subject of religion. Conscious of the great things God had done for him, he was not ashamed to speak of them. Penitent and humble, and realizing his constant need of God's strengthening grace, he says, "I pray often, and believe God has forgiven my sins." Warmly attached to the Saviour, and feeling him dear and precious, he said, "Christ is on my mind all the time." "Always thinking about Jesus?" "Yes." "You must be very happy?" "Yes, I do feel happy, thank God!" "Your experience seems to be somewhat similar to David's, who, though surrounded with danger, and hotly pursued by enemies, even with his soul among lions, exclaims, with a mind calm and composed, 'My heart is fixed, O God; my heart is fixed: I will sing and give praise.' Here we have the *way* and the *source* of happiness. What is it? *A fixed heart* — a heart stayed and *fixed* upon God. Let the world allure; let the flesh entice; let Satan shoot his fiery darts dipped in sin's poisonous bowl; let the waves of trouble rise, how high soever; let the fires of persecution burn and blaze as hot as they did at the stake of John Rogers — yet, with the heart *stayed* and *fixed* upon God, the Christian can say 'All is well,' and sing and give praise. The heart is a very hard thing to keep; but when you get it fixed upon God, happiness is sure to follow. With a heart stayed and fixed upon God, and with Christ on the mind all the time, the martyr, with composure, faces the scaffold and the stake; and with undaunted courage dies in triumph amidst devouring flames. With his heart stayed and fixed upon God, John Nicholson, with his legs burned to stumps, with two halberds thrust into his sides, with which his cruel persecutors lifted him up as far as the chain would permit, while his fingers' ends were flaming with fire, exclaimed, 'None but Christ! None but Christ!' and, being let down, fell in the fire, and soon expired in the triumphs of faith. With his heart stayed and fixed upon God, Paul, standing upon the verge of the eternal world, exclaimed, 'I am now ready' to be offered; ready to sacrifice his life for the cause of Christ."

Henry Bartsher lived till October 19, 1864, when the silver cord was loosened, and the golden bowl was broken, and his emancipated soul went to the realms of everlasting peace!

"I AM TOO WICKED FOR THAT!"

It was just after sermon, in one of the wards, when I stepped up to John Palmer, 62d Ohio Vol., Co. F, and on my beseeching him to repent, and look to God for strength and salvation, he said, "I am too wicked for that!" "Too wicked? Too wicked to seek God?" "Yes; I feel so." "Although you confess your wickedness, yet I suppose you are much wickeder than you think you are. Could you but see the height, length, breadth, and depth of the depravity and wickedness of your deceitful heart, I suppose you would be driven to despair. God, in mercy, for a while conceals the truth, and opens our eyes gradually, and gives us light as we can stand it. 'Too wicked to come to Jesus?' Oh, what infatuation! How deceitful, bewitching, and blinding is sin! It makes the sinner feel rich and as though he has need of nothing, when, at the same time, he is wretched, miserable, poor, blind, naked. (Rev. iii. 17.) What kind of a life have you lived?" "I have lived a careless and wicked life." "Did you ever feel much interested in religion?" "No; I always lived careless." "Do you swear?" "Yes; I swear a great deal." "Do you ever pray?" "No; I am too wicked to pray." "Be not deceived; God is not mocked. When the Lord saw that the heart of Simon Magus was not right, he commanded him to repent of his wickedness, and pray for forgiveness. Your case is similar; and as God commanded Simon to repent of his wickedness, and pray for forgiveness, so he commands you to repent and pray also. God *now* commandeth *all* men, everywhere, to *repent*. And when God bids you repent and pray, it won't do for you to say, '*I can't*.' Severely wounded, racked with pain, wicked and careless, profane and prayerless, without strength sufficient to pray, or keep from swearing, as you say, your case presents rather a dark picture. Yet it was just such sinners as you, Jesus came to seek and save. Oh, then, don't be discouraged. God says, 'Let the wicked forsake his way, and the unrighteous man his thoughts: and let him return unto the Lord, and he will have mercy upon him; and to our God, for he will abundantly pardon.' Now *fix* it in your mind, you *must* repent, or perish. Turn or burn! turn or die! is one of God's unalterably fixed laws. And, no doubt, you *expect* to be saved?" "Yes, I hope to." "How?" "Why, I expect to *reform*, and do better." "Yes; but you say you are without strength, and too wicked to ask God for it — that 'you can't pray.' Yes, there you are; hanging upon the mercy of God, standing upon the very verge of the eternal world, exposed to all the penalties of a broken and violated law, and liable to sink to hell any moment. There you hang, with heaven and hell before you. Satan seeks to destroy you; Jesus to save you! Oh, then, choose ye this day whom ye will serve! Say no longer you can't pray; you can, if you will. The publican prayed, and God heard his prayer, and forgave his sins. The thief on the cross, no doubt, a much worse man than you, prayed, and the Lord heard his prayer, and saved his soul. Oh, then, be encouraged; your wickedness, your sins and oaths, are no hindrance in coming to Jesus, if you will only repent. God's mercy is infinite, the atonement of Jesus infinite, and God can save a big sinner as easy as a little one. The blood of Christ cleanseth from all sin. Think of what momentous interests are involved in your case. Your wound may get well; and you may go back and fight a few more battles, and help win a few more victories. You may die to save your country; but, unless you come to Jesus, you will die, and be lost. Only think of the goodness of God in sparing you, and of the love of Christ in dying to save you! Go to the garden of Gethsemane, and view Jesus agonizing in prayer for our salvation; view him dying upon the cross; view him going from the cross to the tomb, and from the tomb to the throne — and all that we poor unworthy sinners might be saved! Oh, then, let his Spirit woo you; let his love constrain you to give your heart unto him! Look away from self; look away from your sins, and look directly, and only, to Jesus. He will wash your guilty soul in his own cleansing blood, and you will find your wickedness giving way to holiness. 'Rise, rise, he calleth thee;' here he is, *right here!* entreating and beseeching you, by the mercies of God, come and be saved! Stretch forth thy hand, and grasp Jesus like a drowning man a straw, and he will save you! Just make the *effort;* strike for the cross; make a plunge for Jesus, like sinking Peter, and cry, 'Lord, save, or I perish!' and the crown is yours."

"IT IS TOO LATE!"

Sad, solemn, impressive words to fall from the lips of a dying soldier, as he lay struggling in the agonies of death. As we entered upon the canvass of the heart of Edwin Vanwert, 3d Mich. Regiment, Co. E, we found him, apparently, much concerned for his salvation. It seemed that the light of divine truth had dawned upon his darkened soul, and that conviction had been sealed upon his mind, and feeling, to some extent at least, the depravity of his heart, he says, "I have been very wicked. I am a great sinner." "It was just such that Jesus came to seek and to save," I replied. "Therefore be encouraged. Look and live; believe and be saved. It is an encouraging fact to find that you have found it out that you are such 'a great sinner.' Yet you must never for a moment, however, entertain the idea that the greatness of your sins will be any hindrance to your coming to the Saviour. Jesus is 'mighty to save.' His blood cleanseth from all sin, and he can as easily save one sinner as another, if he will only repent." He seemed to be penitent. And as we urged him to come to Jesus, as though he felt his need of a Saviour, he began to pray, and cried, " God have mercy on me." "That, my dear friend, is a very good, appropriate prayer. It just suits your case. It is very similar to the prayer of the publican, who, when he cried out, 'God be merciful to me a sinner,' he went down justified. Oh, then, look up, and, from the answer of this sinner's remarkable prayer, press your suit for salvation." And although his case did look more encouraging at times, as we conversed, plead, and prayed with him, yet, with all we could do, dark clouds rose before him, his hopes began to fail, and the withering hand of despair grasping his soul, he says, "It is too late; I have given up." "Oh, no, my friend, it is *not* too late, 'it is not too late.' 'While there is life, there is hope.' Don't 'give up.' Man's extremity is God's opportunity. The promises of God run parallel with a man's life. A defeat is sometimes turned into a victory. No, it is not too late There is still balm in Gilead. The river of life still flows at your feet. Step in, wash, and be clean. The Spirit still strives. Jesus still cries, how often would I have gathered you, even as a hen gathereth her chickens under her wings, and must it, *shall* it, be said of you, *ye would not?*

> 'While the lamp holds out to burn,
> The vilest sinner may return.'

God still waits to be gracious. Oh, then, escape for thy life — fly to the cross. Embrace Christ by faith. Come to Jesus just as you are, and he will save you. And to encourage you still further, let me urge you, by faith, to go to Calvary and gaze upon that wonderful scene. Do you see that dying thief hanging beside that dying Saviour? and hanging there upon the very verge of the eternal world, with a soul all stained with blood, guilt, theft, robbery, and murder, it would not have been surprising to hear him exclaim, 'It is too late,' yet with pierced hands and feet, with his life-blood flowing from his wounded heart, moved with the wonderful love, compassion, and meekness of Jesus exhibited on the cross, instead of crying 'it is too late,' he earnestly cries, 'Jesus, Lord, remember me when thou comest in thy kingdom;' and in answer to his prayer, in quick succession, with his guilty soul washed in the Saviour's blood, plucked as a brand from the burning, the dying Saviour responds, 'To-day shalt thou be with me in paradise,' and the praying thief and vile malefactor went from the cross to the throne of God in heaven. Saved at the eleventh hour, in order to encourage just such cases as yours. Oh, then, say not, 'it is too late,' but let the lateness of the hour and the near approach of death arouse and bestir you to arise and come to Jesus at once. Then let the love of Christ constrain you, let the terrors of the Lord persuade you, let the crowns of glory, the palm of victory, and the joys of heaven entice you. Oh, then, delay no longer. And while Jesus is here offering and beseeching you to receive the crown of life, reach forth thy wounded hand and accept it. Remember, you *must make an effort* — you must seek God with *all your heart.* Resolve, like the prodigal son, 'I will arise.' And yet here you lay, like the man with the withered hand to whom Jesus said, Stretch forth thy hand; and no sooner did the command drop from the lips of the omnipotent Saviour, than the man begins to stir, makes an effort, raises and stretches forth his withered hand, and immediately it was restored whole as the other. Jesus healed him, but not without an effort on his part. So, if you will only *make an effort,* and resolve *I will arise,* and go to my Father, while Jesus is standing with open arms to receive you, he will forgive your sins and save your soul. Oh, then, look and live, believe and be saved, and, as you die for your country, let the glorious, cheering news go home to your bereaved friends, and go home to heaven, that you died in the Lord."

The curtain falls, and on the twenty-first day of April, 1865, the same day Macon, Ga., was captured by Gen. Wilson's cavalry, and five days before the final surrender of the rebel army, right in the midst of the fall of the confederacy, while the nation was hotly pursuing the murderers of Abraham Lincoln, the soul of Edwin Vanwert, who, on his death-bed said, "It is too late," went to its long home. Sinner, beware.

"IT IS BETTER TO DIE."

Among many other interesting cases we found in the lonely Gangrene Camp was that of Robert Armstrong, 109th U.S., Co. I. At our first interview, we found him prayerful, tender, penitent, and resigned. Said he, "I prayed at home; but I have got wild since I came into the army. Yet I hope God has forgiven my sins." "Do you think you love the Saviour, Robert?" "Yes, I love him; and he is precious to me." I visited him very often, and frequently read and prayed with him. Though he suffered long and severe, he always seemed to be perfectly resigned. "Think you would be afraid to die, Robert?" "No; I am not afraid to die. I believe I could die happy." Deeply concerned for his wife, he handed me a few dollars, saying, "If I die, send that to her." At another interview, as he appeared to draw nearer to God with meek submission, he calmly said,

"I am willing to go. All is well! and I think it better to die." "Blessed be God for his sustaining, comforting grace! When 'we are willing,' and when 'all is well,' *it is better to die!* Then, as Paul says, 'to die is gain,' and 'to depart is far better.' Death is only a *change*, only a 'departure,' or separation of the soul from the body. We live *after* death; death is an advanced step in our state of existence; hence, if prepared, *to die is gain!* In death we lose 'a vile body,' which, though very useful in this life, is a clog to the soul. The body is not only the occasion of disease, but it is also the source of a great many very expensive cares, fears, temptations, pains, and sorrows. At death, this mortal body is dismissed, and the disembodied spirit, washed in Christ's blood, divested of these heavy weights, is borne by angels to the mansions of the blessed. And 'it is better to die,' because by death the redeemed gain a great increase of knowledge. How great soever may be our mental attainments here, we remain ignorant of a great many things. God's providence is mysterious, and his 'judgments are a great deep.' 'Now we know in part, but then we shall know even as we are known.' 'Now we see through a glass darkly, but then face to face.' Oh, how great the change! how rich the gain! And, in order to realize it more fully, let us contrast the Christian soldier's condition on earth with his condition in heaven. Here all is war and strife; there all is joy and peace; here we have conflict, there victory; here we are in exile, there at home; here we suffer, there we reign; this is the race, that the goal; here we are strangers and pilgrims, there fellow-citizens with the saints. Contrast Paul on earth with Paul in heaven: here he wore a chain, there he wears a crown; here he dwelt in prisons, there in mansions of light and glory; here he hung upon the martyr's stake, there he sits upon the throne of God. Oh, then, let us strive so to live, that, when we come to depart, we may say, 'All is well;' so that it will 'be better to die.'" Robert Armstrong lived till June 2, 1865, when his soul went, we trust, to realize the gain and bliss of dying. It was refreshing to talk with him. "Be ye also ready!"

MIDNIGHT CALLS.

Danger, when realized, will always lead a man to look for refuge and some way of escape; hence "a drowning man will catch at a straw:" yet the careless and thoughtless sinner, blinded by sin and deceived by Satan, lying strongly intrenched in carnal security, feeling that all is well, cries peace and safety when sudden destruction is near. But when death threatens, and the grave yawns, and conscience begins to probe, and the clay tenement begins to give way, it is natural to look out for some way of escape. And thus alarmed, the trembling sinner, instead of flying directly to Christ, will often send for a spiritual adviser to point him to the Saviour. Even the old soldier of the cross, sometimes, getting under a cloud, lying upon his wearisome, lonely bed, would send for the chaplain at all hours of the night. And sometimes the patient would put it off till it was too late, and die; calling for the chaplain, instead of calling upon God for salvation. Although God repeatedly says "*to-day*," the poor, blinded sinner, like Pharaoh, says "*to-morrow*." And it is through this fatal *delay*, the devil cheats many a man out of the salvation of his soul. I recollect the case of a captain, with whom I prayed in an amputation-tent, who was carried back to his bed without being operated upon, whose wound shortly after proved fatal, who desired a call from me; but his attending brother refused until he was almost gone, and when I arrived reason was dethroned, and it was "*too late!*" His wound had bled, frail nature gave way, and to see the brave soldier struggling in the agonies of death, and that too with an ungratified desire to see the chaplain about his spiritual condition, presented a scene solemn and lamentable. I recollect the case of an assistant surgeon of the U. S. army, who seemed to be an humble Christian; yet, while lying in Chesapeake Hospital, through surrounding discouragements, got into the fog, and began to doubt his interest in Christ, and giving way to a desponding frame, and fearing his sudden dissolution with the awful foreboding of dying unprepared, he sent for me about three o'clock in the morning. I got up, and upon hastening to his room, found him in deep distress, cast down, and feeling as though God had forsaken him, he was in deep agony of soul. "What distresses you, doctor?" I said, as I approached him. "O chaplain, I feel most awful bad. I have been a professor for several years, and thought I enjoyed religion; but now I feel as though I had lost it all." "Don't be discouraged, doctor; perhaps God is only *trying* you. Job says, 'Though he slay me, yet will I trust in him.' God afflicts his own children in *love* and *mercy* 'for their profit,' and it is their duty to be resigned. The very fact of your deep concern about your salvation is clear evidence that you have not 'lost it all,' and that God has not forsaken you. Look up, 'be of good cheer;' 'let not your heart be troubled;' 'cast thy burden upon the Lord, and he will sustain thee.' Bring all your troubles, doubts, and fears, and lay them at the foot of the cross, and throw yourself, just as you are, right into the arms of Jesus, and he will lift the burden from your troubled soul. Your soul-trouble, doubtless, arises from your disease of body; and if you will but remember the troubles and sufferings of Jesus, it will help to release you." With a few words of exhortation and comfort, and a word of prayer, we bade him good-night, and left him much releaved of his doubts and fears. Rising out of his slough of despond, the doctor soon got well, and returned to duty.

Another very touching case was that of a private soldier, lying at the point of death in the lonely Gangrene Camp. It was a cold, chilly night in November, when, summoned by the call of this dying soldier, we approached his tent, near midnight. Lit up with the pale light of the moon, and the candle dimly burning, we approached the lonely bedside of the heroic patriot. Gazing upon his placid eye and serene countenance, we soon saw he bore the image of Christ; and, instead of being perplexed with doubts and fears, found him rejoicing in the God of his salvation. And feeling that the time of his departure was near at hand, he said, "I have sent for you, chaplain, to administer a word of comfort in my last hours; and to request you to write a letter of sympathy and consolation to my dear wife and children after I am dead and gone; and tell them that I died happy in Christ, requesting them to strive to meet me in heaven." After a very refreshing interview with him about his religious experience and sufferings of the past, and his bright prospects for the future, closing with reading an appropriate passage of Scripture and a word of prayer, commending him to the God of all grace, we bade him a long farewell. He died next day.

After visiting two other patients close by, we closed our nocturnal visits for the night. These nightly calls were always attended with more than usual interest. The stillness of the night, as well as the peculiar circumstances of the occasion, always added much to the impressiveness and solemnity of the scene. A dying man, a bleeding soldier, an anxious sinner, the fear of death, together with the stern realities of the external world drawing nigh and rising in full view before them, always tended to deeply impress not only the thoughtful, but the most careless and indifferent. But these were not the only impressive sights we saw in our nightly visits; there were others also deeply solemn. "See there! Do you see that corpse wrapped in a winding-sheet carried along on a stretcher by those four men?" "Yes; who are they?" "They are the nurses from one of the wards. One of the patients has died, and they are carrying his body to the dead house." "Who's dead, boys?" "Emanuel Byers, from ward twelve." "What! Byers dead? Why, he was much better this morning!" "Yes; but the tying of his artery gave way to-night, and he soon bled to death." "Gone at last!" He had prayed and wept much; and as death drew near to him, he seemed to draw nigh to God. Among his last words, he said, "I am resting on Christ, sure." And, doubtless, for him "to depart was far better." Though his body was bathed in his own blood, yet with his soul washed in the blood of Jesus, we trust he has gone to swell the ranks of the blood-washed throng in heaven. And as they bore away his pale corpse, by the light of the moon, to deposit it in a red coffin in the dead house, we were deeply impressed with the solemn thought that we, too, must soon die. Yet death was so common, and we all got so used to it, that, while in the army and in the hospital, it seemed generally to make but little impression. When a patient died, the soldiers called it "*getting discharged,*" or "getting his red overcoat," meaning his red coffin.

CHAPTER XI.

SCENES IN ANDERSONVILLE.

The Prison — Its Condition — Cruel Treatment — "Can this be Hell?" — Prisoners' Awful Condition — Mortality One Hundred and Fifty a Day — Apathy of U. S. Government toward Them — Hundreds Died of Broken Hearts — Many went Deranged, and turned Maniacs — A School and Church there Now — "The Dead-Line" — Execution of Union Prisoners — Band of Robbers and Murderers — Six Tried, and Condemned to be Hung — Awful Tragic Scene — They Expected to the Last to Escape — The Crisis of Andersonville — Murder will Out — Patriotism in Andersonville — "I would rather have Died a Dozen Deaths" — "I am not Sorry that I Enlisted" — Your Patriotism never Dies: "It is Stronger than Death" — Died Praying for Victory — Andersonville Hospital: an Awful Place — No Beds but Bare Ground — Rations — Diet — Enlarged — The Food would Produce Disease among Swine — The Moonlight Prayer-Meeting — Religion Sweetens the Bitterest Cup.

ALTHOUGH Andersonville before the war was a small, insignificant village of four houses, one church, and a post-office, situated in Sumpter county, Ga., it has now a world-wide notoriety. And of all rebel prisons, for cruel torture, revenge, wretchedness, starvation, murder, and death, there were none equal to it. Belle Isle was awful, Libby was intolerable, but for double-distilled cruelty, Andersonville excelled all. With thirty-five thousand starved, half-naked prisoners crowded into an area of some twenty-five acres, literally covered all over with lice and vermin; breathing an atmosphere filled with poisonous, fetid odors, arising from sinks and putrid corpses, it presented a scene awfully terrible and horrible beyond description. The very thought of it is appalling. To think of it carries the mind down to the infernal regions, and makes one think of the torments of hell. And so appalling was the scene, and horrible the sight, that the brave heroes captured at Plymouth, upon entering it, out of the depths of their feelings and burning indignation, instinctively exclaimed, "Can this be hell? can this be hell?" and feeling their need of divine help, there arose from many a pious heart the earnest prayer, "Lord, have mercy. May God protect us." Adding to the loathsomeness and wretchedness of this horrible place, was a large swamp of three or four acres, extending half-way across the camp, through which ran a small brook, three or four feet wide, which, with a few small springs and wells, was the only supply of water for all this vast throng of suffering humanity. The water generally was so thoroughly impregnated with filth and excrement, that it was entirely unfit for use; yet, rather than die with thirst, the poor fellows drank it with avidity. Here, into this "slaughter-pen," our brave patriots were dragged in from Belle Isle, Castle Thunder, Pemberton, Danville, and Libby prisons by hundreds and thousands. And when any of these unfortunate sufferers were fortunate enough, by digging immense tunnels, to escape, the rebel tyrants hunted them down like dogs, with fierce bloodhounds, brought them back, and punished them most inhumanly for their struggling to get out. Here, huddled together, without shelter to protect them from the drenching rains, winter's cold and summer's heat, with no bed but the bare ground, and sometimes dying at the rate of some one hundred and fifty a day, and compelled to endure the malignant contempt, abuse, and reproach of the rebel tyrants, their condition was indescribably wretched and awful. But the most unpleasant thing of all to them, says one of their number, was the apparent apathy of the Federal Government toward them, and its want of efforts to rescue them from the iron heel of their unmerciful oppressors. Cut off from all communication with the North, and the rebels laboring to convince them that their Northern friends had forsaken them, they succeeded in fastening the conviction upon the hearts of some that the Federal Government had abandoned them. And to feel themselves thus forsaken in times of deep distress, is one of the hardest things to endure.

Having voluntarily left their homes at their country's call, and ready to fight and die for its honor and defence, and now to be neglected and forsaken, as they felt themselves to be, was enough to crush and break the heart of the most noble and devoted patriot. To endure sickness, hunger, thirst, and rebel contumely was awful hard; but nothing compared to the grief and anguish of soul arising from the conviction — although it was not true — that the Government, the army, the navy, and their friends at the North had forsaken them; and so severe was this trial to them, and the awful cruel treatment they received, that hundreds sank away, and died of broken hearts; many went deranged, and became maniacs; others, filled with despair, and preferring death to such a wretched life, crossed the dead-line in order to be shot. Having suffered there so long and so extremely severe, without knowing of any effort on the part of the Government to relieve them; and the rebels doing all they could to convince them that the Government had forsaken them; and thus try to induce them to join the confederacy, and having no means of ascertaining the feelings of the Government toward them; and struggling along through such horrible scenes of filth, cruelty, and murder — it is no wonder that many gave way to despair, and turned maniacs. This stronghold of cruelty was at first designed for but ten thousand men, and contained but sixteen acres; but it was afterward enlarged to twenty-five acres. And, although there have been volumes written about the sufferings and atrocious cruelties perpetrated upon our soldiers in Andersonville, the half will never be told. Language fails to express it. The fifty acres of graves, and the sacred spot where lie the mortal remains of thirteen thousand heroic martyrs who perished there, will doubtless be guarded, and preserved, and adorned with appropriate monuments, handing down to future generations, through all coming time, the cruel torture there inflicted, and the heroic patriotism there manifested by our unflinching heroes. It is said that, when a train of cars approaches this consecrated spot, every eye is strained to see it, and every voice is hushed in silence as the train rolls slowly by. The power of association is so great while approaching near the precious dust of these immortal heroes, that the heart so fills with sympathy and indignation that the tongue is mute in contemplating the tragic, horrible scenes of their sufferings and death. It is an encouraging, pleasing fact to know that the "American Missionary Association" has recently established a school and a church in this noted place. This is progress in the right direction; and God said, "Let there be light!"

"THE DEAD-LINE."

As our Union soldiers approached Andersonville prison, they were warned by those outside, *"Beware of the Dead-Line."* And "What is that?" said one. It is a slender wooden railing extending all around inside, and about a rod from the inner stockade of the prison, which, if a prisoner approached, passed or attempted to pass, to get a drink of water, or for any other purpose, he met with certain death from the vigilant sentinel, charged with strict orders to shoot every man who attempts to pass that fatal line. There goes a poor thirsty prisoner, just ready to die with thirst; he crawls up to slake his parched tongue, all unconscious of his danger, without knowing of the barbarous law or order; the eye of the bloodthirsty guard is upon him; but encouraged by the sight of the cooling brook, his languid eye sparkles with joy at the bright prospect of a refreshing drink; along he drags his frail body buoyant with hope; but, alas! as he was about to realize his fond expectation, the ruthless rebel raises his gun, takes a deadly aim, and, without a moment's warning, the loyal patriot falls a lifeless corpse, bathed in his own life's blood. And just here let me say to you, my impenitent friend, God has his "dead-line," beyond which, if you go in life, eternal death is your certain inevitable doom. Where is it? Just where the sinner commits "the sin unto death;" grieves and quenches the Holy Spirit, until he ceases to strive with him. Although God is slow to wrath, full of compassion, and abundant in mercy, and *waits* to be gracious, yet he will not wait *always;* for there is a point—a "dead-line"—beyond which, if the sinner goes, he sins away his day of grace; and then for him "there remaineth no more sacrifice for sins, but a certain fearful looking for of judgment and fiery indignation;" and then, being "past feeling," and "joined to his idols," God pronounces the awful sentence, "*Let him alone!*" and then his condemnation is sealed forever. God spared and warned the antediluvian world one hundred and twenty years; but when they had gone on in sin, "treasuring up wrath against the day of wrath," until their cup was full, and the earth was filled with violence, God says, "My spirit shall not always strive with man;" and he issues his decree, and declares, "I will destroy man whom I have created from the face of the earth." But Noah having found grace in God's sight, God commanded him to build an ark to the saving of his house. The ark being finished, "the Lord said unto Noah, Come thou and all thy house into the ark;" and they, and two of every living species went in; and God having shut them in, the closing of the ark's ponderous door upon its huge hinges announced to a dying world the day of mercy is over, and the day of wrath begun. It was then, with those excluded, *too late.* The door was shut. They had passed the dead-line of God's mercy, and God swears, in his wrath, that "they shall not enter into his rest." (Heb. iii. 11.) And now the rain falls in torrents, the windows of heaven are opened, and the fountains of the great deep are broken up, and the whole earth was deluged, and all out of the ark perished in the mighty flood.

Take, for example, the *almost Christian*, one with whom the good spirit and the evil spirit are both striving. Satan strives to drag him down to hell, and the Holy Spirit strives to raise him up to heaven. How critical his condition; how momentous the conflict! It is the *crisis* of the soul. Standing upon the pivot of eternity, seemingly, a small influence decides his destiny forever. Oh, how critical his condition! Another crooked step, one more sinful thrust against the Spirit's wooing voice, may banish him forever from your breast, carry you across the fatal line, and seal your damnation in hell forever. Oh, then, strive that you "quench not the Spirit," but cherish and yield to his impressions; let him come into your soul, and take possession of your heart! A man who has lost his way in a dark, dreary mine, and can only find his way out, and save his life, by a candle he carries in his hand, would be very careful how he carries it, lest it be blown out and let him perish in darkness. So should the almost Christian take great heed, lest he quench the Spirit, and let him perish forever. Oh, then, reader, lest this be your case; let us beseech you, by the mercies of God, by the love of Christ, and by the joys of heaven, yield to the Spirit, and come to Jesus, and come just *now!*

EXECUTION OF UNION PRISONERS.

Man is a creature of circumstances. We are all influenced very much by our surroundings; and whether or not it rose from the hardening influence of the barbarous, cruel treatment our men received in Andersonville, there was a large gang of robbers, who made it their business to beat, plunder, and murder prisoners as they came into camp, and as opportunity favored. This outrageous work was suffered to go on until it rose to such a height it proved its own destruction. As new prisoners came in, those thieves availed themselves of every opportunity to rob them. Seizing a new comer, one day, as he entered the prison, after lacerating his head and beating him most severely, they robbed him of his watch and one hundred and seventy-five dollars in greenbacks. He made complaint to Capt. Wirz, and the fact spread throughout the prison. And filled with indignation at such enormous cruelty, the whole camp became thoroughly aroused, and armed with clubs, etc., a large crowd collected and proceeded to arrest the robbers as fast as possible, and hand them over to the rebel guards outside, to keep them for trial by our own men. On the next day, aided by the rebel quartermaster, sergeants, and guards, guided by a noted character known as "Limber Jim," and his comrades, they soon arrested about fifty, and twelve of our newly arrived men were appointed to try them. Under their tents were found money, pistols, knives, and a few dead bodies. And upon satisfactory evidence, six of them were convicted, and found guilty of robbery and murder, and sentenced to be hung till dead. Those not found thus guilty were sent back into the prison, and made to run the gauntlet between a long row of deeply-incensed men, who so furiously pelted them with clubs and stones, that one was killed in the furious action. The day of execution, July 12, 1864, having arrived, a gallows was erected in the prison, and at half-past four P.M., mounted on horseback, dressed in spotless white, Capt. Wirz came in with the six condemned murderers and robbers under guard, and delivered them up to the vigilance committee, saying, "These men have been tried and convicted by their own fellows, and I now return them to you in as good condition as I received them. You can now do with them as your reason, justice, and mercy dictates. And may God protect both you and them." After their sentence was announced, the Catholic priest came and plead most earnestly for their lives; but seeing that he prevailed nothing, and convinced that the poor unfortunate men must soon die, he began to try to induce them to "prepare to meet their God." He talked and prayed with them. And yet, believing that the whole affair was disguised merely to frighten them, the whole doomed six exhibited a degree of wonderful unconcern about their awful impending crisis. Vain, delusive hope! Blinded by sin, hardened by crime, and deceived by their false hopes, like the careless sinner, they cried peace and safety when sudden destruction was near. How awful and tragic the scene! Tried, condemned, sentenced to be hung dead, and standing at the foot of the gallows, gazed upon by tens of thousands, and yet expect to escape. And it was not until they ascended the gallows that they began to feel that it was a reality, and that they were about to be executed. "*Be sure your sins will find you out.*" "*Murder* WILL *out.*" As they were about to mount the scaffold, one of them made a desperate lunge, broke away, and ran through the swamp to the opposite side of the prison. But mark ye, it was no escape. The decree had gone forth, "you *must hang;*" and the enraged crowd, eager for his execution, soon arrested and brought him back, with a countenance filled with wretchedness and despair, and securely placed him with his condemned comrades. Oh, how awful and lamentable the tragic scene! *There they stand —* six American soldiers, prisoners of war, sentenced to be hung for robbing and murdering their own fellow-soldiers and captives in Andersonville prison! What a foul blot upon American soldiery; and what a deep disgrace to the United States army! An opportunity was given them to speak, but they had but little to say. After a few words of advice, and requesting their comrades to take warning by their sad fate, meal-sacks were drawn over their heads, and the dreaded ropes being adjusted, all is ready. A short pause ensues; all eyes are fixed. It is the crisis of Andersonville, and to the condemned the crisis of the soul. The awful form of death seems to stand out before them. "The door of the eternal world is swinging open;" the grave yawns to receive them. Crime, judgment, and stern retribution are making their terrible impressions. "Swift, vivid thoughts are in every heart, and the prayer, God have mercy on them, falls from many a lip." The hour is up; their time is out. The drop falls, and they are launched from time into eternity. There they hang, swinging in the air, gone to reap the fruits of their own doings in their eternal reward. How sad! "The way of the transgressor *is hard*." Let him take warning.

PATRIOTISM IN ANDERSONVILLE.

With all the excruciating torments inflicted on our brave patriots in Andersonville, with few exceptions, their heroic devotion to their country never abated; though surrounded with filth, cruelty, starvation, murder, and death, they still clung to the dear old flag with unyielding pertinacity, choosing rather to die martyrs than traitors. While a few took the oath of allegiance and joined the confederacy, expecting thereby to escape and flee to our lines, the great body of the men stood, with unshaken confidence and unflinching hearts, for God and their country! This was the true spirit of martyrdom. To face the belching cannon, to storm batteries, make charges, and capture forts, requires pluck and strong courage; but to face starvation, hunger, and murder, to drag out a life more intolerable than death itself, amidst such fiendish cruelty and barbarity as characterized this slaughter-pen, required something more than pluck and courage. And to endure all this, when the Government, which they had so nobly volunteered to defend, treated them, as they thought, with such a spirit of indifference as led them to believe it had forsaken them, manifested a self-sacrificing heroism unparalleled in the history of the world; and sometimes, when a number reduced to the extremity of want, with death staring them in the face, did go over to the confederacy, the feeling of the great mass of the soldiers was, "*I would rather have died a dozen deaths than be guilty of such disloyalty.*" After they had been years in the army, and several months in Andersonville, we hear them say, "*I am not sorry that I enlisted.*" No; true patriotism, like true love, never dies out: it is stronger than death. And with the unquenchable fire burning in their bones, and blazing upon the altar of their hearts, thirteen thousand brave martyrs, rather than turn traitors, chose to die amidst the devouring cruelties and torments of Andersonville, and left their uncoffined bones to tell the tragic story of their sad fate. Being excluded from the world, and deprived of all news from the army and the progress of the war, except what they heard from prisoners coming in, their condition was not only inexpressibly wretched, but dreary and lonely; yet, like the captive Jews in Babylon, they never forgot their country. Dejected, discouraged, and heart-broken as they were, yet, methinks, I can hear them exclaiming, in the language of the Psalmist, "If I forget thee, O my country, let my right hand forget her cunning!" etc. (Ps. cxxxvii. 5, 6.) Hence, with all their cruelties, when any encouraging news came from the army, crowds would collect, and sing with joy a few patriotic songs, such as " Red, White, and Blue," " My Country," and " Star-Spangled Banner;" at which the rebel guards were surprised and somewhat confused, as though they hardly knew what it meant. Devotedly attached to their country, and having so long shared each others' hardships and misfortunes, they became warmly attached to each other; and, says one of them, " We loved each other as brothers." Even in the hospital, while racked with pain, and writhing in agony from the most malignant forms of diarrhœa, dropsy, and scurvy, they expressed their trongest desires and *most earnest longings* for success and victory to crown our arms. Their patriotism was of the undying kind.

With the same heroic devotion with which they went forth to fight the battles of their country, firmly clinging to the dear old flag, they died the most excruciable deaths possible for rebel tyrants to inflict. The severe shock of battle, and all the unutterable horrors of starvation, death, and murder of Andersonville, failed to lessen their unfaltering devotion to their bleeding country, and dying even by starvation and torture, martyr-like, their last prayers were for victory and Union.

ANDERSONVILLE HOSPITAL.

The word hospital usually means a place where sick and wounded are nursed and cared for; but here it seemed more like mockery. The hospital, at first, was inside the stockade, on both sides of the run passing through the prison. The indescribable filth, the pestilential air, and the utter want of comfort and attention to the patients was perfectly awful. The very sight of the inside was sickening and horribly revolting. With a poor, scanty, sickly diet, and many with nothing fit to eat; with but little medicine, and no beds but the naked ground; with no tents, and but very scanty covering of any kind, the very thought of going into such a horrible place was enough to make a well man sick. The number of patients was never large, seldom much over two hundred; not because there were but few sick, but because they died as fast as they took them in, and because, if a sick man had any friends, he preferred to run his chance outside. It was almost certain death to go there, and they never went until the very last resort. To come out alive was wonderful. And yet, withal, there was little or no complaint among the patients. About the first of June, 1864, a much more comfortable hospital, containing about four acres, was fitted up outside the stockade, near one hundred rods from the prison. Regularly laid out with a few shady trees and inferior tents, and with a stream of water passing through it, the accommodation and comforts were far superior to the former. About a month later, it was again sufficiently enlarged to accommodate twenty-five hundred patients, and seven hundred were admitted in one day. To be admitted into the hospital, the patient had to attend the *sick-call*, to which one thousand or twelve hundred poor lingering sufferers would come out daily, seeking relief. Hundreds were brought in blankets; and the number received into the hospital corresponded with the number of vacancies occasioned by death the past twenty-four hours. And here the poor sick fellows, scorched with burning fevers, were often left standing in the hot sun all day without anything to eat or drink. How awful their sufferings! Stern indignity, heartless cruelty, and ruthless inhumanity seemed to characterize every act of treatment. A shivering sufferer was shot by the guard, and had his leg broken above the knee, for warming himself by the guard's fire; his leg was amputated, and he died shortly after. Such cases of extreme cruelty were frequent. The nurses would often search and rob the dying patients before they were entirely dead. The rations per day were two ounces of meat and a piece of coarse corn-bread, about two inches square, made of corn and cobs all ground up together. In very bad cases, they were allowed two gills of flour, and occasionally a little loathsome rice. What a mess for sick men in a land of plenty; not better than ordinary hog feed! Some of the surgeons often complained, and said, "*Some of the food furnished the patients would produce disease among swine.*"

The principal diseases were chronic diarrhœa, scurvy, dropsy, and typhoid fever; all in their most malignant forms. In cases of dropsy, the sufferings were extreme. Sometimes the limbs of the poor sufferers would burst open and fill up with maggots; and the pain would become so severe, they would cry out with agony for some one to come and kill them. In other cases, it would affect the extremities, and disable the patients from walking; with others, it would settle in the mouth, and so affect the gums that the teeth would all drop out at once, and leave the patient entirely toothless. Says a prisoner: "I have seen hundreds of cases in this disease, where the men have actually starved to death, because they were unable to eat the coarse food furnished them by the confederates."

Living among such awful filth and impurities, the blood of the men generally became so impure that the least break of the skin usually led to gangrene, subsequent amputation, and consequent death. Exposed to the hot rays of a scorching sun, the upper surface of the foot often became blistered, which would break, and leave the foot all raw; and, becoming gangrenous, a loss of the foot was inevitable, and death generally ensued from amputation. The patients subjected to amputation averaged six or seven daily, and they almost invariably died. A great many suffered most cruelly from the use of poisonous vaccine matter and from the exposure to the burning rays of the sun, and, from a combination of cruelties, many went totally blind. Raining for twenty-one days in succession, in June, 1864, tended much to increase the suffering and mortality. With fifteen thousand prisoners, without any shelter, huddled up together in such a slaughter pen as this, where it took the healthiest prisoner three hours each day to divest himself of the abounding pestiferous lice, together with the awful surroundings, must have presented a scene the most appalling and horrible the eye of mortal man ever beheld. Nearly three thousand died during August, 1864. Some of the surgeons complained of their fare in strong terms to the higher authorities; but their cries were disregarded.

The men seemed to cling to life with a wonderful tenacity Fired with heroic zeal for the salvation of the Union, hope buoyed them up until life was almost extinct. With a gradual, constant decline, they usually passed away at last so suddenly and unexpectedly that they often failed to realize the approach of death, and said but little about dying. Almost dead and dying for days, they seemed to pass off without much pain. Some gave bright evidences of preparation, and, leaving their dying messages to be sent home, died triumphant deaths, and, with their souls washed in Christ's blood, went from this awful scene of suffering to "where the wicked cease to trouble, and the weary are forever at rest."

Such, reader, is but a very faint description of the untold and awful cruelties and sufferings of Andersonville Hospital. But the HALF is not told. The facts beggar all description.

THE MOONLIGHT PRAYER-MEETING.

Notwithstanding the intolerable suffering and untold cruelties of Andersonville, though distressed, forlorn, and cast down, many of the suffering heroes often met for prayer and supplication. Although the rebels cut off their communication with the outer world, yet they could not prevent their communion with God. Deeply realizing their need of Divine help, with no covering but the canopy of heaven, and no light but that of the moon, yet enlightened by God's spirit, and constrained by Christ's love, they often met, read God's word, sung and prayed; and pouring out their souls and hearts unto God in prayer for protection and deliverance, they enjoyed precious times of refreshing; and, says one of them, "We could pray as well, or better, there, than at home." And there, like David, with their "souls among lions," yet, like him, with their hearts stayed and fixed upon God, they sang and gave praise. (Ps. lvii.) There, like imprisoned, fettered Paul and Silas, though encompassed with a strong stockade, an insolent guard, and a terrible "dead-line," yet, like Daniel in the lions' den, drawing nigh unto God, they felt that the Lord of hosts was with them. There, surrounded with the dead and dying, and feeling that the salvation of their comrades, under God, depended upon their prayers, and becoming so deeply interested and praying so earnestly for their salvation and protection, they almost forgot their imprisonment. In this we see the power of the Christian religion to sustain, strengthen, and comfort. With warm, ardent love to Christ, and strong faith in Jesus, religion will lighten the heaviest burden and sweeten the bitterest cup.

CHAPTER XII.

THE EXCHANGE.

Long Looked for — Many Exchanging Time for Eternity — They Cheer the Old Flag — "It never Seemed so Dear" — They Wept Profusely — Rejoicing — Sung the "Battle-Cry of Freedom" — What a Happy, Grateful Crowd — Furloughed Home Thirty Days — The Departure — "Be Ready to Depart" — Filled with Rejoicing — They Cried, "Thank God! Thank God!" — "The Year of Jubilee is come" — Loud Shouts of Joy burst from Thousands — Farewell, Andersonville — Sad Disappointment — It was no Exchange: Only a Removal — "Hope Deferred maketh the Heart Sick."

ALTHOUGH they had been sadly deceived, disappointed, and made heartsick by frequent false promises of release, at last a day of deliverance arrives. To the poor half-starved, suffering heroes, it was a glorious day. Deliverance from the atrocious cruelties and tyranny of Andersonville, Florence, Milan, etc., was almost like life from the dead. It is one of the great events of the war. Behold the brave heroes, ten thousand poor half-starved, shoeless, hatless, shirtless men, almost naked, whose blackened skin, blackened by filth and dirt, hung loosely upon their protruding frames. There they are, the maimed, the halt, the blind — the sons, brothers, husbands of the North. Brave, heroic men! some who have dragged out a life more intolerable than death itself, but at last to be exchanged; but with many, alas, it is too late! They are *dying*, exchanging time for eternity. But with the great mass it is a day of ecstatic joy and rejoicing. As they drew near and saw the glorious old flag, they gave it three most hearty cheers. And when they stepped upon the steamers, and fully realized that they were finally cut loose from rebeldom, they gave three more grateful cheers, and began to sing "The Battle-Cry of Freedom," "Rally Round the Flag, Boys," etc. The men divest themselves of their filthy

CHRISTIANITY IN THE WAR. 165

rags and throw them into the river or furnace, wash off, and, after putting on new and comfortable clothing, they rejoiced with joy unspeakable! A large lot of prisoners from Florence sailed down from Savannah to Venus Point, the place of exchange, in the *Beauregard, Gen. Lee,* and *Jeff. Davis.* The *Beauregard* bore the flag of truce, carried the officers; and the other two steamers, the privates. Rounding Fort Jackson, they hove in sight of the splendid Union fleet waiting to receive them, with the dear old flag waving its beautiful folds, welcoming them back to its protection. "Never before," said one, "did it seem so dear." Grateful for their deliverance, and rejoicing over their exchange, gazing upon it, they wept profusely. After the commissioners of the two fleets, Col. Mulford of the Union, and Capt. Hatch of the Confederates, had a short interview, an arrangement was agreed upon, and the rebel boats soon sided up to the Union transports, *Star of the South,* the *Crescent,* and the *New York,* and the long-wished-for exchange began. They first stepped on the *Star of the South,* the "receiving ship," hence to the *New York,* the "clothing ship," where, after bathing, and casting off their lice and old tattered garments, once very valuable to them, they all received new and comfortable clothing. Then going aboard of the *Crescent,* the "feeding ship," their craving appetites were once more satisfied, with gratitude inexpressible, upon a good army meal. "What a feast it was," exclaimed one half-starved fellow; and "that pint of hot coffee," to them, was like nectar. They were one of the happiest crowds on earth. Rescued from an untimely grave, the chilly rains of autumn, and the scorching sun of summer, and delivered from the tyranny of Capt. Wirz, and sailing homeward-bound under the glorious stars and stripes, language fails to express their gratitude and joy. They sung, danced, and rejoiced exceedingly. Those too feeble to participate were highly cheered by looking on. Getting aboard the regular transports, they bade a final farewell to Dixie, and sailed for Annapolis, Md., where they were joyfully and heartily received with the cheering strains of Hail Columbia, by the Marine Band. Thus ended their prison-life; for heart-rending cruelties, atrocious barbarity, and fiendish tyranny, unequalled upon the face of the earth. Receiving two months' pay and a commutation for rations, all that were able received a thirty days' furlough, and away they went in haste to see the loved ones at home. This exchange took place about the eighteenth or twentieth of November, 1864, at *Venus Point*, near Savannah, on the Savannah River, Ga. Many had been in captivity from nine to fifteen months. What a glorious deliverance!

THE DEPARTURE.

After many warm, earnest, pathetic appeals to the Government in behalf of the prisoners perishing for relief; after many false promises of a speedy exchange from Capt. Wirz; and having so often realized "that hope deferred maketh the heart sick," at length the decree *"Let my people go,"* went forth, and the heart-cheering order, *"Be ready to depart,"* spread throughout the camp like wild fire. It put new life in everybody. All are now on tiptoe with rejoicing; and overflowing with gratitude and joy upon the glorious deliverance, with gushing hearts many exclaimed, "Thank God! thank God!" and began to fix up, and make ready to depart. Fooled and disappointed so *often*, soon doubts begin to rise in their minds; and, as the encouraging news spread throughout the camp, the anxious inquiry, *"Is it so? is it so?"* went forth from many a throbbing heart; and, as it met with a speedy respond, "Yes, yes!" by the messenger, loud shouts of joy and rejoicing rose in quick succession from thousands of glad hearts —

> "The year of jubilee is come,
> Return, ye ransomed sinners, home!"

It inspired everybody with fresh life and courage. To be delivered from Andersonville was almost like deliverance from hell. What a stir throughout the camp; what a shaking among the dry bones! Every one is astir, on the alert, gathering up his *few* things, and making his last call with his frail comrades too weak to go! (It is about the first of September, 1864.) And while all this excitement and preparation to leave Andersonville for exchange was going on, many are just exchanging time for eternity. To struggle through all the torments of Andersonville up to the hour of exchange, and *then* die, seemed unusually hard. But it seemed "thus it must be!" (Matt. xxvi. 54.) Others too weak to go, it seemed hard to leave. To bid a final farewell to a dear comrade, with whom they had so long shared the hardships and horrors of war, amid such awful circumstances, was indeed trying; it was hard for those going, and much harder for those left. A hearty, warm sigh and a gushing tear, a good wish and a hearty "May God bless you!" was all they could do; and while they were pronouncing the final "*farewell*," the cry, "*There they go!*" flashed across the camp, and thousands of the heroic braves, together with the maimed, halt, and blind, were seen marching up and passing that gate which had so long held them in captivity, and through which thirteen thousand brave patriots brought in alive had been carried out dead. Farewell, Andersonville; farewell, thou hell of earth and "plague-spot of creation!" let thy name go down to posterity as synonymous with cruelty, starvation, atrocity, death, and murder! Thou wilt be remembered only with the saddest associations. The awful sufferings there endured, and the reproach, gross insult, abuse, and vindictive revenge there poured out upon the brave heroes by those malignant rebels, will never be forgotten. As they marched out, they were divided into small companies of sixty each, and tottered over to the depot, the stronger supporting the weak. With sixty in a car (freight-car), with a little corn-bread and rancid bacon for their rations, and a bucket to get water, away they went through the beautiful scenes of Georgia. Shut up so long as they had been, the green trees, beautiful foliage, thrifty grass, and fine flowers, and the pure air, to them appeared most lovely and delightful. By sunset, next evening, they arrived at Augusta, where they were detained a long while, and were much refreshed through the great kindness of the generous citizens, who did what they could to administer to their wants in supplying them with good water, biscuits, meat, and delicacies for the sick. They were received with the warmest gratitude, without knowing whether they came from loyalists or disloyalists. How very striking the contrast between the tyranny and cruelty of Andersonville and the warm sympathy and kindness of Augusta! Here all was kindness and good-will, there all was hatred and revenge; here the kind people labored to save the lives of the prisoners, there they labored to destroy them; here they were treated like men, there like hogs and wild beasts!

Here our captive heroes met a confederate prisoner from the North (from Johnson's Island), who, when asked by our men how he fared while a prisoner, promptly replied, "*Very well, indeed*, sir! We had plenty of good food, and vegetables 'quite often;'" and to compare his stout, robust, healthy appearance with our half-starved, pale, feeble, disheartened men, the contrast was most striking. The next day, at three P. M., they arrived at Charleston, S.C., and, to their great surprise and most sad disappointment, they ascertained that "it was *no exchange* after all;" it was only a hurried remove upon the sudden anticipated approach of Sherman's army. And again they felt "that hope deferred maketh the heart sick," and sorrow and sadness again filled their hearts. Such is life—full of ups and downs; and the downs are often greater than the ups! Here the fare was hard, but far superior to Andersonville; here they were visited by two sisters of charity, who did much to relieve the sufferings of both Catholics and Protestants. Having put in a few weeks at Charleston, they were taken to Florence early in October. Here the suffering and barbarous cruelties were about equal to Andersonville. The hospital here was literally awful. To see brave soldiers, the heroes of a hundred battles, lying nigh unto death, with no beds and no coverings, and turning idiots from suffering and starvation, and dying at the rate of twenty-five a day out of seven hundred, or about four percentage, was horrible in the extreme. But at last the day of deliverance came, and they were let go free.

CHAPTER XIII.

ANDERSONVILLE CEMETERY.

Contains Fifty Acres — Thirteen Thousand and Seven Hundred and Five Graves — Who are the Dead? — What did They Suffer? — How did They Die? — As They Lived and Fought — The First Prisoners Buried There — The Last One — The Stars and Stripes Wave Over Them — Captain Wirz — His Birth — Entering the Rebel Army — Promoted for His Cruelty to the Prisoners — Proven Guilty of Conspiracy against the United States — "I will Give You Bullets for Bread" — He Shot a Prisoner — "Oh, Do let Me Down!" — His Last Days — Found Guilty — Received Sentence to be Hung very coolly — Attended by the Priest — No Signs of Sorrow — His Execution — Hurries to the Gallows — The Closing Scene.

IN a well-selected spot, half a mile north of the prison stockade, lie the heroic martyrs of Andersonville. Containing some fifty acres of level land in an elevated old field, surrounded with dense forests of pine, and lying close to the South-western Railroad, it is a beautiful situation. Inclosed with a white-washed picket fence, and laid off in four sections, with streets crossing in the centre, it presents quite a neat appearance. Entering at the south gate, and passing up the main street, there are three sections of graves on your right, of about three-quarters of an acre each, divided by two alleys; and on your left are two more of equal size. The dead all lie facing to the east. At the head of every grave is a plain *head-board*, ten inches wide, two and a half feet high, painted white, with the prisoner's name, company, regiment, and date of death, lettered on it in black. The dead lie very close together in trenches and in rows, each body occupying only fourteen inches, with only four inches between the head-boards. The graves are finished in a common level, and are neatly grassed over.

Who are the dead? whence came they? From almost every

State in the Union; but chiefly from the North. There they lie, from the green mountains of Vermont to the golden shores of California and Oregon. There lie the uncoffined bones of the dear husband of many a crushed, heart-broken widow, and the precious dust of many patriotic sons, whose weeping mothers refuse to be comforted, because they are not. There lie thousands of brave veterans, who, at the tap of the drum, voluntarily rushed to the defence of the old flag, at the beginning of the rebellion. The heroes of one hundred battles, they were a part of the very bone and sinew of the army; not bounty-jumpers, but noble, heroic, patriotic men, who fought, suffered, and died; not for *mere pay*, but from *principle*, for the glory, defence, and salvation of the country; not stragglers, but *soldiers* thirsting for victory, rushed into the thickest of the battle, and unfortunately were captured, and dragged into the slaughter-house at Andersonville.

What did they suffer? Tongue cannot tell; heart cannot conceive, and language cannot describe it. The severity of their sufferings beggars all description; they not only suffered cruelty, hunger, thirst, starvation, robbery, torture, death, but atrocious contumely, dire reproach, and fell revenge from rebel tyrants. It was proven in Capt. Wirz's trial, that some ten thousand died from torture, neglect, cruelty, hunger, and want maliciously inflicted; "that numbers died from the dead being left too long in the prison; that numbers died from wearing the ball and chain; that many died from being tied up by the thumbs, and from torture in 'the stocks;' that a number were shot and killed upon the dead-line; that a large number died from the bite of ferocious dogs or bloodhounds, and from poisonous vaccination ordered by Capt. Wirz; "and," says Col. Chipman, Judge Advocate, in his closing remarks on the trial, "Capt. Wirz *murdered eighteen,* and one died from his jumping upon, stamping, and kicking him."

How did they die? Having no regular spiritual adviser generally, but little is known of their prospects, or preparation for the future. A number "made perfect through suffering" gave bright evidence of repentance; for whom to die was gain. And from the patient suffering, calm submission, and humble resignation, and true patriotism they exhibited, doubtless many hundreds of them died happily, and have gone beyond the reach of rebel tyrants, "where the wicked cease to trouble, and the weary are forever at rest." The first prisoner buried there was J. S. Warner, Co. H, 2d N. Y. Cavalry, died Feb. 27, 1864. The last death was R. Hanson, Co. F, 1st Wis., died April 28, 1865. The exact number buried there is 13,065, including one hundred and fifteen rebels from the garrison, and sixty-five who died from small-pox. There they lie, waiting the sound of the last trump summoning them to judgment, when all will be rewarded strictly according to their works.

In the centre of this vast depository of the patriotic dead is to be erected a suitable *monument* to the memory of these heroic martyrs. Let it rise. *They most richly deserve it. Let it rise,* that it may tell to future generations the patriotic heroism, the ardent devotion, patient endurance, and unyielding perseverance of those thirteen thousand heroic martyrs.

Again we say *let it rise,* and engrave upon it the opprobrious name, "ANDERSONVILLE," that it may tell to future ages the extreme suffering, the despotic tyranny, the gross indignity, the fierce cruelty, the severe punishment, hunger, want, and starvation endured by the immortal heroes lying beneath it. *Let it rise* of material lasting as time, so that if our American patriotism should ever grow cold, and we become unmindful of the rich boon of civil and religious liberty established by the blood of our fathers, and redeemed by the blood of half a million of their sons, we may go and stand around the graves of these departed heroes; that we may think of the horrible sufferings they endured, and of the awful deaths they died, that we and our country might live; that the world may know that man is capable of self-government, and that all men are created free and equal. In the centre of this large depository of the lamented dead stands a flagstaff, one hundred and twenty feet high, from which the stars and stripes float every day. Cared for by a superintendent appointed by the Government, who keeps two hands employed in dressing it, the cemetery is kept in good order. A few marble stones have been placed at a few of the graves by friends. The main entrance is at the south; and on the east side of the gate is printed in large capital letters:

NATIONAL CEMETERY, ANDERSONVILLE.

Opposite these words are inscribed the following touching lines:

> "On Fame's eternal camping-ground
> Their silent tents are spread;
> And Glory guards with solemn round
> The bivouac of the dead."

A little farther down stand the following graphic words:

> "The hopes, the fears, the blood, the tears,
> That marked the bitter strife,
> Are now all covered by victory
> That saved the nation's life.
>
> "A thousand battle-fields have drunk
> The blood of warriors brave:
> And countless homes are dark and drear
> Through the land they died to save."

In one corner, by themselves, lie six more buried, marked below their names — "Hung, July 12, 1864."

CAPTAIN WIRZ.

And now, in closing those wonderful scenes from Andersonville, the reader will no doubt feel anxious to hear a little more about the perpetrator of those awful crimes and the inflicter of such severe punishments.

Capt. Henry Wirz was born of respectable parents, in Zurich, Switzerland, Nov. 1823. In early life he manifested a strong desire to study medicine, but, his father objecting, he was placed in a commercial house in his native town. Desiring to try his luck in a new country, he came to the United States in 1849, landing at New York, where he again resumed the study of medicine. During the first stages of secession, Wirz obtained some notoriety by his severe denunciations of the Federal Government, and declaring his warm attachment to the South. But failing to get a commission as surgeon in the rebel army, he enlisted as a private soldier under the flag of treason. But having served a short time in that capacity, and being of a cruel disposition, and possessing the requisite qualifications to execute the atrocious designs of rebel leaders upon our prisoners, he was, early in the war, put in charge of Libby Prison. Here the sergeant-major soon so distinguished himself for cruelty and barbarity to the unfortunate captives, that he was promoted to the rank of second lieutenant. In the spring of 1862, he was sent to the front, while Gen. McClellan was bringing to bear his battering-rams upon the strongholds of Richmond, and receiving a wound in the arm, by the stroke of a fragment of a shell at the battle of Fair Oaks, he obtained a furlough to visit his native home in Europe. After having spent over a year on his furlough, he voluntarily returned to the United States in the spring of 1864. Shortly after his return, he was ordered to assist Gen. G. H. Winder in carrying out his cruel atrocities perpetrated upon our unfortunate men incarcerated in Andersonville. Here he was again promoted, and honored with the rank of captain. Having full sway, and giving loose rein to his cruel, bloodthirsty disposition, he went on in his barbarous work until he was proven guilty of confederating, combining, and conspiring with Jefferson Davis, Howell Cobb, and others, in leagued rebellion against the United States; and that he did maliciously and traitorously, contrary to the laws of war, so cruelly neglect and treat some ten thousand Union prisoners under his care in Andersonville, that they died from hunger, torture, cruelty, and want. What a long black catalogue of crimes! How deeply seared must have been the conscience, and how awfully hard must have been the heart, of the atrocious perpetrator! Before such monstrous iniquity, the sensitive heart recoils and humanity shudders. Such heights and depths of deep, double-distilled wickedness are seldom, if ever, equalled. On a certain occasion, when a poor starved soldier asked Capt. Wirz for a little more bread, the hard-hearted tyrant contemptuously replied, "*I will give you bullets for bread.*" On another occasion a frail, prostrated sufferer mildly asked permission of the unmerciful captain to go out to get fresh air, when Wirz indignantly replied, "What do you mean?" drew out his revolver from his pocket, and shot him down. He died in two or three hours after, watering the tree of liberty with his patriotic blood.

The *prison punishments* were all most cruelly severe. The idea of mercy or kindness seemed never to have entered the hearts of those unrelenting tormentors. For a prisoner to attempt to escape was almost always certain death. The fact is, the institution was got up, and kept up, to weary, abuse, starve, and destroy Union prisoners. Capt. W. S. Winder said, when he was laying out the stockade, "*I am going to build a pen here that will kill more Yankees than can be destroyed at the front.*" And Capt. Wirz said to the Union men who were burying the dead, "This is the way I give the Yankees the land they come to fight for." What deep-seated malevolence and murderous revenge underlies such devilish expressions! Wirz often told the prisoners " that he *intended* to destroy them."

"On passing by the guard-house, one day," says Major Kellog, "I heard a most pitiable, distressing outcry; and upon looking around, I saw a prisoner, who for attempting to escape had been brought back and strung up by the thumbs to the beam of the guard-house, paying the unrighteous penalty of honorably attempting to flee from impending starvation and death. And there, swinging in the air, with his body roasted with pain and a soul writhing in anguish, in the most compassionate, pitiable manner, he begged with his cruel tormentors for mercy. Hanging there with the ruthless cords tightening around his swollen thumbs, he exclaimed, in the most heart-rending manner, 'Oh, for God's sake, have mercy on me; oh, do let me down. Oh, mercy, mercy, mercy!' But, alas! he begged without mercy." There he hung. Oh, how awful! Humanity shudders at the horrible cruelty. A wicked world gaze and look on with astonishment, and in summing up this double-distilled cruelty, atrocious torture, fell revenge, and fiendish murder, it would seem that God had withdrawn all restraining grace, and that Satan had poured forth his bitterest vials of wrath to fire the malicious heart of Wirz to perpetrate those most damnable deeds, that the world might see how low and deep the depraved heart is capable of sinking in iniquity. And yet, doubtless, as this monster of iniquity was only a tool in the hands of higher officers, his crimes must be small when compared with theirs.

THE LAST DAYS OF WIRZ.

After the fall of Richmond and the surrender of Johnston to Sherman, when bloody treason was lying low in the dust, and the shouts of victory gushing from every loyal heart throughout the land, Wirz endeavored to flee the country; but was arrested, and brought back to Washington, and confined in prison to await his trial for his numberless deeds of cruelty and murder.

After the assassins of Abraham Lincoln were executed, charges and specifications were brought against this monster of iniquity, and a military court was convened, and the guilty tyrant was made to look at himself in the eyes of the law and justice. He took a deep interest in the trial, and closely watched every movement and every word of testimony brought against him. The trial, though long and tedious, was at length closed; the pleadings heard, the testimony canvassed, and the sentence, "guilty," brought in; and on the sixth of November, 1865, he was informed by Gen. Winder that he was sentenced to be hung on Friday the tenth. Wirz received his sentence with remarkable coolness and with great unconcern, remarking only, "Well, I suppose it must be done;" and with a stern indifference he went immediately to the door of his cell, and announced the fact to Gen. Briscoe, who was occupying the opposite side of the cell, in the following words: "General, I am to be hung on Friday!" And as Gen. Augur was retiring from the cell, he said, "After I am dead and gone, I will come back and haunt you all."

Being a Roman Catholic, a priest was sent for to administer to his spiritual wants, and warn and entreat him to prepare for death. And, notwithstanding his enormous sins, his historian says he gave no marks of sorrow or contrition for his iniquitous crimes. Scoffing at the Federal Government to the last, on the night before his execution he said "the American Eagle was a turkey buzzard." Undisturbed about his approaching end, he slept soundly the last night of his life, until he was aroused at three o'clock by his spiritual comforters, to pray with and for him, and beseech him to prepare for the solemn scene. He listened to their prayers, but, insisting on his innocence, manifested no signs of forgiveness.

Touching his personal appearance, wearing a dark complexion, Wirz was a man of about five feet ten inches high, "of a thin, spare figure," with black hair, beard and mustache mixed with gray. Dressed in black, with an old silk hat, he presented, during the trial, a rather shabby, genteel appearance.

THE EXECUTION.

At length the day of execution dawns. On the morning of the tenth of November, with the preparations at the gallows all completed, fifteen minutes before ten the doomed man was led out of his cell, supported by Fathers Doyle and Wiget. And although he manifested no regret for his crimes nor sorrow for his sins, yet, realizing the stern laws of retribution beginning to play upon him, he now begins to feel that the way of the transgressor is hard. And wrapped in a black robe, carrying his right arm in a sling, with hands and feet unmanacled, with a light, careless step he made haste to the gallows and ran up the steps, and sat down upon a chair, sitting upon the deadly drop, over which hung the fatal noose dangling in the air, ready to crush the forfeited life lingering in "the demon of Andersonville." Guarded by a battalion of soldiers, formed into a hollow square, there he sits, hanging upon the verge of the eternal world, just running his last sands. With death standing out before him, and the grave yawning to receive him, there he sits, wrapped in the hardness of his own insensibility. Major Russell, taking his station directly opposite the gallows, read aloud the charge, specifications, and the sentence. Wirz listened attentively, but shook his head with an occasional smile, without a ray of sorrow or remorse flashing from his stern brow. At the close of the reading, he was asked if he had anything to say. He replied, "No; I have nothing to say to the public." After a silent whisper and parting exhortation of the priest, the black cap being drawn over his face, he was requested to stand up, and the rope was adjusted around his neck, and his hands and feet bound with cords. And now the fatal hour draws nigh. At twenty minutes past ten, the commanding officer gave the signal, and Capt. Henry Wirz hangs suspended between heaven and earth. The roofs of the surrounding houses were crowded with spectators, anxiously gazing upon the solemn scene; and, at the fall of the fatal drop, a loud yell rose from the crowd without. After a few convulsive jerks, the soul of Wirz winged its flight to the eternal world, and the tragic scene closed. At seven o'clock his body was taken down, examined by the attending physician, and officially pronounced dead. The corpse was placed in a coffin, and delivered into the hands of Father Boyle, and the excited crowd dispersed.

CHAPTER XIV.

SKETCHES OF SOLDIERS.

"My Heart is so Hard, I Can't Pray"—Converted on the Field of Battle—"I Went to Church Cursing, and Came away Praying"—"I Can't get Religion"—"I Can't help but Pray"—A Hero of Andersonville Saved by His Wife—A Boat-Load of Andersonville Prisoners—"Converted on Picket by Two Men Talking to Me"—"I am Resolved to Quit Swearing"—Died Calling for the Chaplain to Pray for Him—"I am Ready to Die"—"Tell Them I am Happy"—"Converted through a Sister's Letters"—"If I go to Hell, I will go Praying"—"Prayer is a Great Privilege"—"Oh, that I had Ventured Before!"—"I am Guilty of Everything but Theft and Murder"—"I Expect to get Religion when I get Home"—Bleeding to Death, yet "Resting on Christ"—"Praying for Sport"—"I Gave My Heart to Jesus"—"Christ is Everything to Me"—"My Sins are Great and Heavy"—"Satan is Often at My Heels"—James Ward, 81st N.Y., Co. I—A Soldier's Creed—"I See so much Bad Christianity, I am Discouraged"—"Jesus is Still Precious"—"I Still Hold on to God"—"I Pray much in Battle"—A Soldier with Seven Wounds—"I can Afford to Suffer"—A Happy, Shouting Soldier—"I would Like to be a Christian, If I could Keep It"—"I Can't Live without Prayer"—"The Lord is Mine"—"I Can't Pray"—"I Found Jesus"—"I Leave it all with the Lord"—A Swearer Brought to Tears.

"MY HEART IS SO HARD, I CAN'T PRAY."

JOSEPH P. NICHOLS, 39th Ill. Vol., Co. K, was severely wounded in one of the last battles near Petersburg, Va., and was soon after brought to Hampton Hospital. His wound soon became gangrened, and he was taken to the Gangrene Camp. At first we found him a profane, prayerless sinner, and yet honest and frank to confess it. Said he "had been a Methodist, but had wofully backslid." He said, "I have been a great swearer. I have sworn to such an extent that I am ashamed of it." "We are very glad to hear you confess your sins, and your shame for swearing. And are you sorry for it now, Joseph?" "Yes, I feel sorry; but not as I ought to." I preached to him; pointed him to Christ; told him of his love and compassion; that he waits to be gracious; that he is "able and willing to save, even to the uttermost;" and urged him to repent, and come to him. He became very anxious; and as I urged him to pray and to turn his oaths into prayers, he said, with deep emotion and tears, "My heart is so hard, I can't pray." I told him to "tell the Lord so;" to go to God with his hard heart, and he would soften and change it. He now seemed to feel deeply the greatness of his sins; and as I urged him to pray, and throw himself right into the arms of Jesus, he cried, with eyes filled with tears, "God be merciful to me a sinner!" "Lord, save, or I perish!" Thus, with his soul stirred, pleading and begging for mercy, we left him, and made special prayers for him that night at the public service, and ere the sun set on the nineteenth of May, 1865, he closed his eyes in death. Gone, we trust, to reap his reward in heaven. Let backsliders be warned, and take care. "Return unto me, and I will return unto you, saith the Lord."

CONVERTED ON THE FIELD OF BATTLE.

"Good-morning, Henry! how do you do to-day?" "I am somewhat better to-day, I thank you, chaplain." "Very glad to see you so well. How are you *spiritually?*" "Well, I have been a very great sinner; but I believe, now, God has converted my soul and forgiven my sins." "Where do you think you were converted?" "In the battle of Hatcher's Run. There, amidst the shock of battle, I saw so many falling around me, and thinking how soon it might be my turn, and what an awful thing it would be to die for my country, and lose my own soul; there, with balls and bullets whistling close by me, and shells bursting around me, together with the groans of the wounded and dying, I cried to God for mercy; and there, I believe, he changed my heart." "Did you feel afraid in battle?" "No, not much; we never expect to get hit. I felt anxious about my soul; my sins rose up before me, and seemed to be very great. The battle raged. 'On we went, giving it to the rebels hot and heavy;' but I kept on praying, 'Lord, have mercy, and save me!' We drove the rebels, and gained a glorious victory." "But I suppose your greatest victory was a victory over Satan." "I 'spose it was." "Satan has a very strong fort in every sinner's heart, and to storm and take that fort requires nothing less than the omnipotent power of God. And you still think you were converted, then, during that battle?" "Yes, I believe I was." "Do you now feel like holding fast, and going on in the Lord's service?" "Yes, I do; by the grace of God I will try, and be faithful till death." "Do you pray often now, Henry?" "Yes, I pray two or three times a day." "When did you begin to pray?" "While we were at Petersburg." "May God bless you, Henry. Cling to the cross; trust in the Lord; and all will be well!" It was Henry McElvain, 118th U. S., Co. A.

"I WENT TO CHURCH CURSING, AND CAME AWAY PRAYING."

Upon canvassing the heart of HENRY FERGUSON, 39th Ill., Co. E, we soon saw that he bore marks of the new creature. The pleasing smile upon his countenance bore evidence that the image of God had been enstamped upon his heart. And upon further inquiry, he said, "I have a hope that I would not exchange for the world." "Do you think you are a converted man?" "Yes, I believe that I am." "When do you think you were converted?" "About fifteen months ago." "Where?" "In church. *I went to church cursing, and came away praying.* While there, I was deeply convicted and smitten down. My sins rose like mountains before me, and I felt very unhappy and awful. I thought I saw the devil, that he was all black and dreadful. The encouraging promise, 'Resist the devil, and he will flee from you,' rushed to my mind; and all of a sudden light dawned upon my mind, and I began to pray to God for mercy; and all at once a feeling of joy came over me, and I felt glory in my soul." "How have you lived since?" "I still trust in the Lord and try to be faithful, and I feel happy ever since. I have no fear of death." "How does the Saviour appear to you?" "Dear and precious; he has done great things for me." "Do you still pray daily?" "Yes; I read my Testament, and pray two or three times every day." "Do you ever feel like swearing now?" "No; swearing never comes into my mind now." "*Be faithful.* War a good warfare. Watch and pray, and may God abundantly bless you." From the example of Henry, let the wicked and profane be encouraged to go to church. Men often receive a blessing when they don't expect it. A man once went to hear John Wesley preach, with a stone in his pocket to break his head, but his sermon broke his heart, and resulted in his conversion.

"I CAN'T GET RELIGION."

As I approached HENRY W. CHASE, 96th N. Y., Co. H, he wept profusely, and exhibited distress and deep anxiety of mind. I said to him, "Do you want anything?" "No. *I can't get religion.*" "Would you like to have it?" "Yes," he said. "Oh, yes," trembling, and weeping with deepest emotions. "I am glad to see you so anxious. Salvation is free — free as the air you breathe. Jesus says, 'If any man thirst, let him come unto me, and drink. Ho every one that thirsteth, come; and whosoever *will*, let him come and take of the waters of life freely.' What hinders you from getting religion?" "Pride, and my hard heart," he said, weeping most bitterly. Oh, how I felt and prayed for him. Jesus, thou son of David, have mercy on him. "Do you feel sorry for your sins?" "Yes; but I fear God has not forgiven them." "Do your sins seem to be great?" "Yes, *very great.*" "The blood of Christ cleanseth from *all sin.* Look and live. Only believe on the Lord Jesus Christ, and thou shalt be saved. Just come to Christ *now.* Throw yourself right into his arms, and he will save you. Come *just as you are.* Don't wait to get better. There is no work to be done; no preparation to be made to go to Jesus. No, *all* things are *now* ready; come and be saved." I preached occasionally to him and his ward, and warned them to flee the wrath to come, fly to Jesus, and cling to the cross. He grew worse, and the ward-master gave him up to die. How interesting the scene. Gather round and gaze upon the brave, lovely boy as he lies upon his bed, with one leg off above the knee; with a fine countenance and a pale face, there he lies, bathed in tears, weeping for his sins, and pleading for salvation. Calling on him a few days after, he said, weeping, "I have not found the Saviour yet." "Oh, Henry, are you willing to die for your country, and die and be lost? Only think of the love of Christ. View him in Bethlehem. View him in Gethsemane, agonizing for our salvation. View him on Calvary, groaning, bleeding, dying, that we, that *you*, might have eternal life. And *will* you, CAN you refuse such a Saviour? Having sealed your heroic devotion to your country with your blood, now only look to Jesus, and he will seal the salvation of your soul with his blood. *Step right out upon the promises of God*, and grasp Christ by the hand of faith, and salvation is yours. Look away from your wound; look only to Christ, and he will break and melt your hard heart, and give you a new one. Jesus cries to you in tones of love and mercy. 'My son, my son, give me thy heart.' Remember, my dear friend, you must surrender or be lost; you must repent or perish; turn or die. Jesus cries, 'How often would I have gathered you, and *will* you not come?' May God help and bless you." He suffered long, and bore it all very patiently. Not a murmur fell from his lips. At my next call his wound was better, and he was indulging a hope, and said, "Prospects are brighter." "Do you still pray, Henry?" "Yes, I pray very often." At our next call we found him still more encouraged, and he said, "I think now I have found the Saviour, and God has forgiven my sins. Christ seems precious now. My sins before seemed heavy, now they seem light." He wept. I wrote to his father: he came. Henry got well, and went home.

"I CAN'T HELP BUT PRAY." "I GO FORWARD."

On canvassing the heart of Joseph Smith, 38th U.S., Co. I, we soon found him evidently a devoted Christian, and seemed to be filled with the Spirit. "I suppose you think and meditate much about the Saviour?" "Yes, I think on God all the time." "Do you pray much?" "Yes, I prays very much: I can't help it." "Can't you *help* it?" "No;" pointing to his breast, he said, "there is something within me that draws me to the throne of grace." "What is it?" "I suppose it is the Spirit of God that prompts me to it, or the love of Christ drawing me." "Do you love Jesus?" "Yes, I loves him; and he is very dear and precious to me." "Do you find it difficult to live out religion in the army?" "No; God is the same in the army as he is at home." "You don't backslide, then?" "No; I go forward, and still keep trying to do my duty to God and my country, and God helps and blesses me." "Be faithful, Joseph; live near to God, and cling to the cross." Reader, if you would reach that high Christian attainment, where you *"can't help* but pray," "think on God all the time!" To the devoted Christian, prayer is no *task*. No; filled with the Holy Ghost, and constrained by the love of Christ, "he can't help but pray!"

A HERO OF ANDERSONVILLE SAVED BY HIS WIFE.

PHILIP HARTEL, 51st Pa. Vol., Co. I, an exchanged prisoner from Andersonville, was brought here from Wilmington, N. C., April 2, 1865. When he came in, he was completely run down with chronic diarrhœa and starvation to a mere skeleton. He looked like death, and for a long time we despaired of his life; but with kind treatment he got along. We preached to him and his ward of prisoners, and tried to comfort them with the consolations of the gospel, and besought them, by the mercies of God, to trust in Christ and cling to the cross. He belonged to the Lutheran Church, and seemed to be an humble, meek, good Christian soldier, looking to God for help and strength. Perfectly resigned, not a complaint or murmur fell from his lips. He said, "I hope and trust, if God willing, to get home and see my wife and child (eight years old)." He gained a little, and in a few days his good wife came and tenderly and most faithfully nursed him; and, after a good while, he got well enough to go home. But it seemed like life from the dead. I believe his faithful wife, under God, saved his life.

A BOAT-LOAD OF ANDERSONVILLE PRISONERS.

One hundred and sixty were brought in April 2, 1865, from Wilmington, N. C. They had been at Florence and Andersonville, and many of them were reduced to mere skeletons from disease and starvation. Although they had spent a few days at Wilmington, and recruited up considerably, yet some of them seemed to look more like dead men than living ones — with hair dishevelled, ghastly eyes, faces pale, and nothing but skin and bones, they looked like living corpses. A great many died at Wilmington. Many of them died here in the wards after lingering a few days.

"CONVERTED ON PICKET BY TWO MEN TALKING TO ME."

Upon conversing with THEODORE BRADLY, 7th Conn., Co. H, we soon found him indulging a good hope. After a short conversation about religion, and the trials and temptations of army life, I asked him if he was an old soldier of the cross. "No," he said. "I was converted by two men talking to me one night on picket at Bermuda Hundred." "What did they talk to you about?" "About Jesus Christ and the way of salvation, and the awful danger of living in the army without religion." "Did they urge you to repentance, and beseech you to come to the Saviour?" "Yes; they talked to me in an earnest, humble, simple manner, and urged me to become a Christian." "How had you lived before that time?" "Careless and indifferent: I went to church at home, but felt no particular interest in religion." "Have you ever read the Bible much?" "Yes, considerable: I went to Sunday-school at home." "Do you feel sorry for your sins, now?" "Yes." "How do your sins appear to you?" "They appear great; but I believe God has forgiven them." "And you still believe you were converted there that night on picket?" "Yes, I believe I was. I still trust in Christ, and I pray daily. Yes, there, standing between two mighty armies, exposed to death from the rebel sharpshooter, I believe God changed my heart and washed my soul. Now, if I know my own heart, I feel prepared to go whenever God calls." "God is everywhere, and can as easily convert a sinner on picket as in the church. Oh, how important to talk about religion, and thus hold up the cross to a dying world! 'Hear, O Israel; the Lord our God is one Lord; and these words shall be in thy heart; and thou shalt *talk* of them when thou sittest in thy house, when thou walkest by the way, when thou liest down, and when thou risest up.' (Deut. vi. 4, 6, 7.) '*Talk* ye of all his wondrous works.' (Psalm cv. 2.) How lamentable that we talk so little about religion! How very common in the social circle, to hear Christians talk all over the world, and talk *all* around the cross, and never utter a word for Jesus. Of old, it was written, 'They that feared the Lord, spake often to one another.'"

"I AM RESOLVED TO QUIT SWEARING."

GEORGE H. TRACK, 6th Conn., Co. K, was severely wounded at the fall of Fort Fisher, where our men did such brave fighting. Upon my grasping him by the hand, and trying to lead him to the cross, he wept most profusely, and seemed to feel his sins very deeply, and appeared to be very penitent, hopeful, and anxious. "Do you pray?" "Yes; and I have resolved to quit swearing." "May God bless you richly. Think you can quit it?" "Yes, I think I can." "I know you *can*, if you *will*. Have you sworn any since you resolved to quit it?" "No, not an oath." To see the big tears rushing to his eyes and rolling down his cheeks encouraged us to talk and pray with him. After singing a beautiful hymn, and commending him to the God of all comfort, we bade him good-by, and left him. Reader, if you swear, resolve to quit it, and you *can*. Remember the words of Him who says, "Swear not at all."

DIED CALLING FOR THE CHAPLAIN TO PRAY FOR HIM.

Upon our first interview with JOHN S. BURKET, 13th Ind. Cavalry, we found him inquiring "what to do to be saved." I replied, "'Believe on the Lord Jesus Christ, and thou shalt be saved.' Salvation is free; and it is ready. Only believe, and you will enjoy it. Faith implies two things: forsaking all else, and receiving and relying upon Christ alone for salvation. It is taking God at his word, and acting as though you believed what he says." He gave signs of penitence; said he "trusted in Christ, and was not afraid to die." "If you only have faith, you need have no fear of death. To die is gain, if you die in faith." Toward the last he became very anxious, and died praying to God for mercy, and calling upon the chaplain to pray for him. He indited a letter to his wife shortly before he expired. Many careless, with the hope of long life, grow anxious about salvation at the approach of death, when it is too late. Delays are dangerous. Oh, then, reader, be warned, and "*prepare* NOW *to meet thy God!*"

"I AM READY TO DIE,"

Said JOHN WEEKLY, 4th U. S., Co. I, after a few minutes conversation with him about his spiritual condition. He seemed to be very tender, penitent, humble, and resigned. "Are you not afraid to die?" "No; I trust in Jesus, and I don't fear death." "Do you love the Saviour?" "Yes; I love him, and he is very good to me." "Perfect love casteth out fear. It is a great blessing," I said. "Oh, yes," he replied, and began to pray, "Jesus, have mercy on me. Save me, Lord, for Jesus' sake." Continuing in prayer, he cried *more earnestly*, "Save, save me, SAVE me, O Jesus." How direct, simple, comprehensive and earnest his prayer. Standing upon the verge of the eternal world, like sinking Peter, he goes directly to Jesus, pleads for salvation, and most earnestly cries, "*Save me, Lord.*" He seemed to live right beneath the throne of God. And with a heart all alive with the love of Christ, it was no wonder he had no fear of death. It is *readiness* to depart that banishes fear. If prepared, "to die is gain," and to depart is far better. "Be ye also ready." Reading and praying with him, and commending him to the God of all grace, we bade him farewell, and left him.

"TELL THEM I AM HAPPY."

When I first visited MAHLON SPANOGLE, 205th Pa., Co. A, he was careless and prayerless, yet a regular attendant at church at home. Beseeching him to be reconciled to God, we left him. His severe wound grew worse, became badly gangrened, and, consequently, he was taken to the gangrene camp. At our next interview, we found him still careless and unconcerned; and we noted him down in our book, "indifferent, and don't pray," and he said, "he swore when excited." After pointing him to the cross, we bade him good-by, and went on to the next poor sufferer. I preached to and prayed with him often, explaining the way of salvation, and besought him to repent and fly to Christ; and after a while he became interested in religion. I often read the Bible to him, lying on his very sore back, and explained to him the penalties of the law and the precious promises of the gospel. By-and-by he became attentive and tender, and gave some signs of repentance. By the examples in the Bible and by the promises of God, I urged him to pray earnestly, to think of the love of Christ, and of the mercy of God in sparing him through so many narrow escapes, and what an awful thing it would be to die for his country, and lose his own soul; and tears trickled down his pale cheeks. The Spirit of God moved upon him, and he said he was sorry for his sins, and seemed deeply penitent. He failed gradually; his mortal frame gave way; and shortly before he expired, when he saw he was going, he threw his arms around the nurse, embraced and hugged him very affectionately, and said, "I am dying; Lord, help me! Tell them I am happy. The gates are open, and I am going home." The wheel at the cistern stood still, and his disembodied spirit went, we trust, where there will be no more sorrow, pain, and death. His bereaved wife arrived half an hour ere his departure, and brought some good things for him to eat; but it was too late. His understanding had failed, and he could not recognize her. What a severe trial! Yet his dying message, "Tell them I am happy," was calculated to afford her strong consolation. May God abundantly bless and comfort the soldiers' widow, mother, orphan. He died Feb. 28, 1865. Reader, when trials, hardships, and suffering surround you, go to the gangrene camp, and think what was there endured for our imperilled country.

"CONVERTED THROUGH A SISTER'S LETTERS."

Canvassing the heart of CHARLES E. SMITH, 148th N. Y., Co. K, we soon saw that he bore marks of regeneration; and, after a little further conversation upon the subject, he said, "I was converted in the army through a sister's letters. They *turned* me," he said. "You mean they were the means of your conversion?" "Yes; for God only can change the heart." "You seem to have clear views of the plan of salvation: what is conversion?" "It is a change of heart." He appeared very penitent, humble, and prayerful. "Do you still feel like going on in the Lord's service?" "Yes; I read my Testament, and pray two or three times a day." "Do you find it difficult, surrounded with the temptations of the army, to live out religion?" "No; if we only strive to be faithful, God will help and sustain us." "Yes; he says, 'My grace is sufficient for thee.' How does the Saviour appear to you now?" "He appears dear and precious." "Peter says, 'To you, therefore, which believe, he is precious.' He is precious in his names, offices, and promises. I suppose your sister wrote you very religious, kind, and affectionate letters, urging and beseeching you to repent, and give your heart to God?" "Yes; she seemed to feel deeply, and to pray very earnestly for me." Let sisters and friends at home be encouraged to write and pray very often for their friends abroad. Persons at home cannot at all conceive what great encouragement and consolation a good letter affords to one long from home.

"IF I GO TO HELL, I WILL GO PRAYING."

At our first interview with WILLIAM S. BULLOCK, 89th N.Y., Co. B, we found him very much concerned about his salvation. He said, "Chaplain, I want to get religion. I thought I had it once, but guess I was mistaken. I have been trying to pray, but it seems rather hard work. Blinded as we are by sin, about our spiritual condition, we are liable to be deceived. Hence Paul says, ' Let a man examine himself, and prove his own works.' I have prayed frequently in the army for some three years, and often with tears; but I do not meet with that change I wish." I preached to him and prayed with him often, urging him to exercise implicit faith in Christ, and recounted to him some of the evidences of the gracious state, and gave him *James's Anxious Inquirer* to read. After reading it, he said he thought he had been deceived, and his anxiety seemed to increase, and his chief concern was to know what to do to be saved. Suffering much from his severe wound in the left arm, he had many ups and downs, and sometimes we almost despaired of his recovery. But he persevered, prayed on. God worked in him; light burst upon his soul; and plucking up courage, and feeling determined to fight on in the good fight, he says, "*I will pray on, pray till I die, and if I go to hell, I will go praying.*" "That's right! May God help and bless you. Make up your mind, by grace, to become a Christian, and God will help you. When the prodigal son made up his mind and resolved, 'I will arise, and go to my Father,' he soon came home. Jacob said, 'I will not let thee go, except thou bless me;' and God blessed him there." His good wife visited him often; with a tender, anxious heart, he would often weep profusely. He continued to pray and read, got better, was promoted, his doubts were removed, and God's smiles restored, and I left him rejoicing in the God of his salvation. If doubts encompass, if clouds of darkness surround you, do not be discouraged! Look to Jesus! pray to God; pray earnestly; pray in faith, and God will hear and bless!

"PRAYER IS A GREAT PRIVILEGE"

That "My dear husband is dead!" is very sad news to the affectionate wife; but it was very common news from the army and hospital. But that he died for his country lessens the sorrow and sadness very much; and that he died happy in the triumph of faith lessens it much more. How great the loss to the family! though gain to the departed. Michael Shawley, 206th Pa., Co. K, at our first interview, wept profusely, and was very tender and penitent. Said he had been praying for years, though a non-professor. He said, "I feel, if I were called away to-day, I would go to heaven. I feel happy. I thought I could go to heaven without joining church." Apparently perfectly resigned, he said, "Not my will, but God's be done. If I die, tell my wife I die happy." "Oh, how exalted the privilege; dying upon the altar of your country; dying at the foot of God's throne, resigned to his will, and dying happy in the Lord! What kind of a heart have you now?" "A bad, wicked heart; yet, if it don't deceive me, I have given it to God." "Do you find it easy to pray?" "Yes; prayer is a great privilege." "Though a non-professor, you seem to be a Christian; yet the Saviour's sweet command, 'Do this in remembrance of me,' I suppose you never obeyed?" "No; I never went to the Lord's table, but I often desired to." "It is a great *privilege*, refreshing to the soul, and strengthening to the heart, which no Christian should deny himself. It is his *right*, it is his *duty*, and to disobey is *sin*. When God, through his great mercy, converts a sinner, he ought to acknowledge it before the world. 'Come out from among them, saith the Lord, and I will receive you.'" He lingered till March 3, 1865, and no doubt went home to heaven.

"OH, THAT I HAD VENTURED BEFORE."

This was the *weeping lament* of a brave, patriotic soldier who had put off repentance till brought to the verge of the grave. His name was Richard Delling, 8th Maine, Co. E. We visited him often, preached to and conversed with him, and urged him to *immediate* repentance. He seemed penitent, tender, and anxious, and wept freely. We could but weep to hear him recount the heroism and losses of his regiment in battle. His chief lament was his putting off religion; and sometimes, with most intense earnestness, he would exclaim, "Oh, that I had ventured before. If I had only thought of it a year ago. If I had only known of this sickness when I was in health, how much better." He resolved to do better Mr. Martin, from New York, of the Christian Commission, did much for him temporally and spiritually. I plead with him, and besought him by the mercies of God to come to Jesus, and come *now*. He desired a good book to read. I gave him one. The Spirit of God seemed to strive with him, and he said, "I have a firmer hold on God than I have on the devil." "Do you feel the devil tempting you?" "Yes, I do." "'As a roaring lion, he walketh about, seeking whom he may devour,' yet if you resist him, he will flee from you. Only meet him with prayer and the sword of the Spirit, and he will flee at once. Martin Luther, when tempted by him, simply prayed, 'Get away, thou infernal spirit,' and he fled immediately. Just hold on to God; cling to the cross; throw yourself right into the outstretched arms of Jesus, and he will rescue you from Satan's grasp, wash your soul in his blood, and save you in spite of the devil. Just cut loose from Satan *at once*, and surrender yourself, heart and all, to Christ, and he will give you a kingdom of righteousness, joy, and peace." "How very striking your warning words. Oh, that I had ventured before." "Ventured before?" "Yes." "It is not too late *now*. The Spirit still strives; the blood of Christ still cleanseth from all sin. Jesus still cries, 'How often would I have gathered you,' and beseeches you look and live, believe and be saved: just come to him *as you are*, and there is no *venture* about it. VENTURE! VENTURE, in going to Jesus! No; thank God, there is no venture about it. *It is a* SURE *thing*. God's promises, made in infinite wisdom and backed by omnipotent power, are all sure. Only believe, and you'll be saved." He seemed to be coming to Christ, growing in grace, and said, "I see a light;" and among his last words to me were, "I am happy in the Lord." Lingering along till February 27, 1865, his mortal frame gave way, and he went, we hope, to dwell with God in heaven.

"I AM GUILTY OF EVERYTHING BUT THEFT AND MURDER,"

Said LAWRENCE MCGAVERN, 2d Pa. Heavy Art.,Co. G, as we were conversing about the value of the soul, the wickedness of the heart, and the love of Christ. He was very low and dangerous with the phthisic. "What kind of a life have you lived?" "I have lived a very wicked life. I am guilty of everything but theft and murder. I am a great sinner." "Truly you are a great sinner. But Christ is a great Saviour — a greater Saviour than you are sinner; more willing to forgive than you are to commit sin; more mighty to save than even you or Satan is to destroy. Guilty of everything but theft and murder?" "Yes." "Your sins are great, yet Christ's love is greater. Christ's love is stronger than death, sweeter than life, and vast as eternity. The love of Christ constraineth us. At the tap of the drum, the patriot soldier leaves home, goes forth, fights, bleeds, and dies to save his country. Christ left heaven, and came to earth, to die upon Calvary to save sinners. He has wrought out salvation, fulfilled the law, made an atonement for sin, bought us with his blood, paid the price of our redemption, and, in a word, made *all things* ready, and now beseeches you look and live, believe and be saved. He saves the greatest sinners. He saved the thief on the cross; he saved some of his own murderers at the foot of it, and he will save you, if you will repent and trust in him." As I talked, read, and prayed with him, the Spirit seemed to strive and the word to sink deep into his heart. He appeared to be deeply penitent, and anxious to be prayed for. Thanking me heartily for my prayers, he said he prayed, felt penitent, and trusted in the Lord. "How long have you been in the army?" "Almost three years; my time is out to-morrow." "Out to-morrow? And what if your time on earth should be out to-morrow? Do you feel willing and prepared to go?" "I hope so," he said, with deep emotion and tears. "My sins are great, yet I believe not unpardonable. I find it easy to pray now, and Jesus seems more precious." "This is the crisis of your soul. Without doubt your last sands are running, time with you will soon be no more. Oh, then, we pray you, we beseech you, by the agonies of the Son of God, escape for thy life, fly to Jesus, and salvation is yours." He lingered along until January 1, 1865: his time was out, and his soul took its flight. A voice seemed to say, "The battle is fought, and the victory is won."

"I EXPECT TO GET RELIGION WHEN I GET HOME."

In our interviews with HENRY LUCAS, 39th Ill., Co. H, we always found him disposed to procrastinate and "put it off." He said, "I expect to get religion when I get home." "Why not get it here *now?*" "This place is unfavorable; there is so much wickedness, profanity, etc., here." "Still, the Lord is here, waiting to be gracious, and give you eternal life. Repentance will be just as easy here as at home; the way of salvation is the same here as at home; God and Jesus Christ are the same here as at home; and your disposition to put it off is a delusion of the devil. Delay is the devil's verb; *Now* is God's time. What if you should never get home? Then, according to your own plans, you will be lost. Oh, how unreasonable and dangerous! If a friend were to offer you a gift of one hundred thousand dollars here, to-day, would you wait till you got home to receive it?" "No; I would accept it now." "Why, then, refuse the gift of eternal life now, which is infinitely more valuable? If you were a deserter, sentenced to be executed, and the President would offer you pardon, would you refuse it?" "No; I would most gladly receive it." "You have deserted God; and you have been arrested, tried, and condemned to eternal death. Jesus now offers you pardon and eternal life, and you refuse it — refuse it at the peril of your soul. Is it wise? is it reasonable? is it safe?" "No." "Are you willing to risk it?" "No." "Then seek ye the Lord while he may be found. May God help, bless, and save you."

BLEEDING TO DEATH, YET "RESTING ON CHRIST."

EMANUEL BYERS, 116th Ohio, Co. D (ward number twelve), was severely wounded in the left arm at the last great battle near Petersburg, Va., which resulted in the fall of Richmond, the flight of Jeff. Davis, Lee's surrender, and the death of the confederacy. At our first interview, we found him very tender and anxious. He said, "I am going to become a Christian when I get home." "What if you should never get home?"

I said; and he began to think and reflect. I visited him very often; prayed with and preached occasionally to him and his ward, warning them "to flee the wrath to come," to repent, and fly to Christ. He read his Bible much, and when I talked to him about his sins, the mercy of God, and the love of Christ, he would weep like a child. He said, "I started once to go to the mourner's bench, burdened with sin and a heart ready to burst; but a friend called me back, and I did not go. The feelings wore off, and I have never felt the same since." Yet he was not "without hope." Time fled: he lived on, got better, prayed, and bled occasionally. On May 1st, he said, "My prayers were answered last night, and I now feel more comfortable." Calling on him two days after, he seemed to be growing in grace and drawing nearer and nearer unto God, and his prospects both temporal and spiritual looked brighter. He prayed on, and I besought him, by the mercies of God and the love of Christ, to make an immediate and entire surrender of himself to the Saviour. Life ebbed away. There lies the brave patriot, with his life-blood gradually flowing from his wound. "It is hard to leave you. Oh, my dear fellow, come to Jesus just as you are, and come now. May God bless, help, and enable you to come. Having shed your own blood for the salvation of your country, come and enjoy the cleansing, saving power of the blood of Jesus!" Reading and praying with him again, we bade him farewell, and left him. Calling again shortly after, we found him indulging a bright hope, and he said, "I think God has forgiven my sins, and that I have experienced a 'change of heart.'" A pleasant smile upon his pale face seemed to denote he was at peace with God. At our next call he bid fair to get well, and said, "I am resting on Christ *sure*." "Thank God! and are you sure of it?" "Yes, I feel so, chaplain." "What a glorious attainment! Dying for your country, and yet dying in the Lord!" He lived along for several days, until the tying of his wound gave way: he bled to death May 27th, 1865, with his body all bathed in his own blood, and his soul, we trust, washed in the blood of Jesus, went home to dwell with God.

"PRAYING FOR SPORT."

While many of the soldiers died triumphantly, some seemed to go "without hope." —— ——, of 67th Ohio, Co. F, a stout, robust man, and a brave soldier, was brought from "the front," mortally wounded with a minie-ball in the left side of his head, into a tent in ward number twenty-four. Though drowsy, he was sensible, but not disposed to talk much. Upon canvassing his heart, he said, "I am not a religious man." "Do you read the Bible?" "Yes; I read it some." "The Saviour says, 'Search the Scriptures.' Do you ever pray?" "I and others have prayed for sport." "Prayed for sport! What! mocking God!" "Yes, I 'spose you may call it that." "Did you not feel afraid God would smite you dead?" "No; we had no fear of God before our eyes." "Pray for sport! oh, how awful! how deep the depravity of the human heart! Do you ever swear?" "Yes, occasionally." "And don't you feel sorry for your sins of profanity and mocking God?" "Yes; I know it is wrong." "Have you ever felt any special interest in religion?" "No, nothing particular; I have lived a careless life." "Though you are a great sinner, yet Christ is a great Saviour. He is more willing to forgive than you are to commit sin. Christ's love is stronger than the sinner's enmity. His blood 'cleanseth from all sin.' Do you feel your sins to be great?" "Yes; they are very great." "Jesus is mighty to save. You have received one wound for the salvation of the country; Jesus received five for the salvation of the soul. That ball in your head is not as bad as sin in your heart; that ball may destroy your life; but your sins, unless you repent, will destroy your soul. Oh, then, we entreat you, repent, look to Christ; throw yourself right into the arms of Jesus, and he will save you. Grasp him by faith, like a drowning man grasps a lifeboat, and all will be well. God calls; Jesus invites, and says, 'Come unto me, and I will give you rest.' Time is short; life uncertain. *Now* is the accepted time. Look, and live!" He lingered a few days, became stupid, and died November 10, 1864, without giving any particular evidence of preparation. Reader, be warned!

"I GAVE MY HEART TO JESUS,"

Said Dwight Williams, 203d Pa., Co. C, as he related his religious experience. "That is a very reasonable, profitable gift: Jesus gave himself, shed his blood, gave his life for us; and it is but a reasonable service that we should give our hearts unto him." "Do you feel that you have given him your heart?" "Yes; I feel so, and he seems very precious to my soul." "Think he has given you a *new* heart?" "I trust he has." "Our hearts are very wicked and deceitful, and the springs of action lie very deep; therefore, lest we be deceived, we should closely examine ourselves, search our hearts, and see if they are right with God, and pray, like David, 'Create in me a clean heart, O God!' Do you ever say bad words?" "No; I detest swearing." "Do you pray regularly?" "Yes; I prayed at home, and I pray in the army too." All about him seemed to bear marks of the new creature, and offering him the consolations of the gospel, and commending him to God in prayer, we bade him a long farewell, November 7th, 1864. He lingered till next day, when his soul was dismissed from its clay tenement, and, washed in Christ's blood, doubtless went home to be forever with the Lord.

"CHRIST IS EVERYTHING TO ME,"

Said Charles Wilson, 16th N. Y. Heavy Art., as he related his religious experience. Though a non-professor at home, he now seemed to have Christ formed within him; and his own dying words seemed clearly to evince that Christ, of God, had been made unto him "wisdom, righteousness, sanctification, and redemption." (1 Cor. i. 30.) "What evidence have you that Christ is yours?" "I think much about him; I love to hear about him, to read his word; and he appears so lovely, and I feel he has forgiven my sins." "How rich the inheritance, and how great the consolation! If Christ is everything unto you, then all things are yours, whether the world, or life, or death, or things present, or things to come — all are yours; and ye are Christ's." "Then you don't want?" "No; the Lord is my shepherd, I shall not want." "You must feel very happy?" "Yes, I feel happy, and am not afraid to die." "With Jesus Christ for your prophet, priest, and king, dying for your country — for the cause of God, liberty, and truth — you have no need to fear death, for then 'to die is gain, and to depart is far better.'" This was October 20th, 1864. John Lambert, who died a martyr at the stake, while his fingers' ends were flaming with fire, exclaimed, "None but Christ; none but Christ!" Charles survived until next day, and with his weeping wife at his side, witnessing his last struggle with the king of terrors, his soul bid farewell to its clay tenement and the world, and went, we trust, where all is joy and peace.

"MY SINS ARE GREAT AND HEAVY,"

Said SMITH A. CONNER, 62d Ohio, Co. I, as I was canvassing his smitten, tender heart. With his soul stirred, he was very anxious, prayerful, penitent, and had a deep sense of his sins. His principal inquiry was, "What must I do to be saved?" He prayed while I stood at his side, and the burden of his prayer was, "God be merciful to me a sinner!" He sent for me, and requested me to pray that his sins be blotted out. "You seem to feel deeply the weight of your sins?" "Yes, my sins are great and heavy." "'The blood of Christ cleanseth from all sin.' Come to him, and 'though your sins be as scarlet, they shall be as white as snow.' Why don't you come to Christ at once? *Now* is the time." "I do try to; but somehow something hinders me." "There is nothing in the way but yourself; Christ is willing, able, waiting. All things are ready. You must let go self, and lay hold of Jesus, and he will blot out your sins, and wash your soul in his own blood. Step right out on the promises of God, and grasp Christ by faith, and he will save you. Jesus is here knocking at the door of your heart, warning, inviting, and beseeching you, by the pains of hell and by the joys of heaven, be ye reconciled to God. Time is short; eternity is near; Death shakes his dart; the grave yawns; hell frowns, and heaven smiles! and *will* you, *can* you delay? How long will you halt? Christ says, in tones of love and mercy, 'My son, my son, give me thy heart!' Just think how lamentable it will be for you to die for your country and lose your own soul; die beside the Prince of Life, and yet die and be lost? Oh, my dear friend, look to Christ, and look *now!*" Preaching and praying with him, and commending him to God, we left him. He lingered a few days, and died full of hope November 7th, 1864.

"SATAN IS OFTEN AT MY HEELS,

"But I keeps him off," said JOSIAH MURDOCK, 4th U. S., Co. H, colored. "How do you keep him off?" "I keeps him off by faith and prayer. I prays, and then he goes away." "Does Satan tempt you often?" "Yes; but I resist him, and he flees. Satan made three bold, imprudent attacks upon the Saviour; but he always met him with the sword of the Spirit, and invariably put him to flight. Paul says, 'Put on the whole armor of God, that ye may be able to stand against the wiles of the devil.'" "How long have you been praying?" "Two years, this fall. I am trying to go to heaven." "The way is straight and narrow. It requires close watching, straight walking, and earnest praying. The Christian's life is a *warfare*. Jesus, our great Captain, commands us to *strive*, fight, contend, watch, pray, and be faithful. Think you have got God in your heart?" "Yes; I think so." "Do you love the Saviour?" "Yes; I try to love him with all my heart." "Pray on, Josiah. Be earnest, cling to the cross. 'Be thou faithful unto death, and God will give you a crown of life.'"

"I WOULD RATHER DIE." — JAMES WARD.

It was a cold, chilly night, late in November, 1864, near midnight, when I was called to see James Ward, 81st N. Y., Co. I, lying in a cold, dreary tent in the Gangrene Camp. At first sight he seemed to be nigh unto death, from a severe wound received while battling for his country. With a strong, abiding faith in Him who giveth life, he manifested no fear at the approach of death. Having been trying to serve God some five years, he said, "Christ is all my hope; and he is growing more and more precious." I asked him what word he had to send to his family. He said, with deep emotion and tears, "Tell them I am happy in Christ. That I would like to live for their sake, if God is willing, and if it would glorify his name; but for myself, I would rather die." To die is gain. How solemn the scene. Gather round and gaze upon the Christian patriot dying for his country; dying in the Lord, resigned to God's will as his rule, and ready to live or die for the promotion of God's glory as his end. What a happy attainment! How consoling his dying message to his bereaved wife and children. "Tell them I am happy in the Lord." And the fervor and affectionate tenderness with which he spoke these words added much to their import. I read the fourteenth of John, endeavoring to comfort him with those consoling words; and kneeling down upon the cold ground, we commended him to God in prayer. On bidding him farewell, he expressed a strong hope and a bright assurance that we would meet again around God's bright throne in heaven.

"Jerome of Prague sung God's praise till choked by the flames at the stake, and with his dying breath said, 'This soul in flames, I offer, Christ, to thee.' You, having sacrificed your life upon the altar of your country, now seem ready to offer your soul to Jesus." His soul seemed to be wrapped in joy and bliss. The serenity of his countenance, his calm, composed spirit, together with his easy departure, seemed to say, "Thanks be to God, who giveth us the victory," and to his weeping wife and children, "weep not," be of good "cheer," and strive to meet me in heaven. He lingered till next day, and God took him home.

A SOLDIER'S CREED.

As I approached JACOB BOSTON, 188th Pa. Vol., Co. C, he grasped my hand *very warmly,* and said, "I trust in God, and shall be saved, and it makes me happy." What a short, plain, comprehensive creed! Would to God every soldier could heartily adopt it. Just look at it. Three blessed things — faith, salvation, happiness. Faith in God as the *source;* assurance, the *privilege;* happiness, the *result.* Strong faith always fills the soul with joy. "Believing, ye rejoice with joy unspeakable and full of glory." "I suppose you have no fear of death?" "No; with faith in God, I fear not." Perpetua was sentenced to martyrdom, and when *most earnestly* besought by her tender father to renounce Christ, great was the struggle in her heart; but grace at last triumphed, and she said, "I am not in my own power, but in that of God;" and when asked, "Art thou a Christian?" she said, "I am;" and when condemned to execution, she returned to her prison filled with joy, saying, "None of these things move me." It was the power of faith. She died in triumph. "Have faith in God."

"I SEE SO MUCH BAD CHRISTIANITY, I AM DISCOURAGED,"

Said GEORGE H. GILBERT, 34th Mass., Co. I, as I was trying to persuade and urge him to come to Jesus. "Blinded by sin since the fall, man's ways have been very crooked, and so prone to evil that, even after regeneration, there is much that is wayward and perverse. We must not expect perfection, even in Christians. What kind of life have you lived?" "I have lived careless and prayerless." "Do you swear?" "Yes, often; but I am quitting it now." "Quitting it? Why don't you quit it *at once?* From the bleeding of your wound, you look pale and weak, and God only knows how short may be your time on earth. You have fought and bled, and are ready to die for your country; and yet you have never *prayed* for it, nor for yourself. God commands us to pray and repent *now!* You should regard that wound as a call to repent, and trust in Him who was wounded for our transgressions. Let every bleeding be a warning to come to Him who bled for you. You seem to stumble over the bad Christianity of professors. This is a sinful excuse. You are excusing one sin with another sin; excusing your own great sin of rejecting Christ with professors' sins. God will never hear such excuses; and if you go to the judgment-seat with them, he will bid you depart — 'depart, ye cursed, into everlasting fire!'

There is much inconsistent practice in professors, we admit; but they are not to be taken as examples. No: take Christ as your example; and remember, if you stumble into perdition over professors' imperfections, it won't lessen the torment any. It is your own fault. 'Every tub must stand on its own bottom;' and, unless we all stand on the 'Rock of Ages,' we will sink to hell. Oh, then, we beseech you, by the love of Christ and by the joys of heaven, repent, and become a devoted Christian, and set the church a good example, and provoke others to good works. Come out from the world. Be 'a living epistle,' and God will save you! May God abundantly bless you! Professor, beware; 'take heed to thyself;' 'keep thyself pure;' walk worthy, lest you be a stumbling-block to others."

"JESUS IS STILL PRECIOUS."

PETER ROBBINS, 203d Pa., Co. F, was mortally wounded in the heroic fight of Fort Fisher, N. C., and brought to the hospital with an arm amputated, and with a bad stump. Though heroic and patient, he never seemed to get along well; he was a calm, harmless, meek Methodist. Though he suffered long and severe, he bore it all very patiently, without a complaining word; prayerful and humble, he said, "Christ is all my trust." "None else is worthy of trust; none but Jesus can do helpless sinners good; he is mighty to save! Throw yourself right into his arms, and he will sustain, bless, and comfort you." I visited him very often, and preached to him occasionally. He said, February 18, "Jesus is still precious." Getting worse, he said, February 21, "I can die happy." "You helped to win a glorious victory at Fort Fisher; but only cling to Jesus, and he will enable you to win a victory far more glorious when you die." His wound became gangrened, and he was taken to the Gangrene Camp, where he suffered, not only from his wound, but from cold. There was no fire in his tent. Lingering till February 26, 1865, death closed the scene, and God took him home to glory. Rev. McClaren said, when he was dying, "I am gathering together all my prayers, sermons, good and evil deeds, and am going to throw them all overboard, and swim to glory on the plank of free grace." Christ was all his trust!

"I STILL HOLD ON TO GOD."

PERRY WELSH, 67th Ohio, Co. A, though rather careless and indifferent at first, soon became deeply interested in his soul's salvation. Becoming prayerful, tender, penitent, and resigned to God's will, he said, " I am not afraid to die." "Do you love the Saviour?" "Yes," he replied. " Love is the fulfilling of the law — the very heart, soul, and core of Christianity. And if you love Jesus, you need not fear death, for then heaven is sure. What a glorious attainment, to rise above the fear of death! It requires courage to face the enemy on the field of battle; but to face death, God, and eternity, requires far greater courage." He became more anxious, tender, and earnest; and at my last call with him, he said, " I still hold on to God's will." "That's right! Hold on, hold on to the cross, and stand by the flag; hold on to Jesus; hold fast; be steadfast! When waves of trouble rise, hold on; when the world allures, and temptations press, hold on; when you go to face the enemy amid the shock of battle, hold on to the flag, and cling to the cross! Above all, hold on, when you come to face death and fight the last great battle of life! Be faithful; go on; never let go the cross, and you will surely win the crown!" Lingering till January 5, 1865, he let go the vital cord, and went home, we trust, to glory.

"I PRAY MUCH IN BATTLE."

At my first interview with JOSHUA SMITH, 11th Western Va., Co. F, I found him a decided Christian. Having passed the sea of doubts, he now seemed to enjoy full assurance. He said, " I have no doubt God will make it all right with me:" said he, " I pray much in battle, on the march, and everywhere." He seemed very tender and penitent, and wept as we talked about these things. "And did you find time to pray in battle?" "Oh, yes; I would load and fire, and pray at the same time." "What!

pray much in battle, when so much depends upon every man doing his utmost with his musket and sword?" "Yes; for the victory is of God, after all." " Pray much in battle, when your captain commands you to fight?" "Yes; for the great Captain commands us, 'watch and pray!'" "How striking the difference; you pray much in battle, and many never find time to pray! You are right; with the grave yawning, eternity approaching, and comrades falling and dying, it is a needy time to pray. We should pray as though God did everything in battle, and fight as though man had everything to do himself." He lived till June 4, 1865, and passed away to where there will be no more war, pain, nor death. Let the prayerless be warned and admonished. "What," said the Saviour, "could ye not watch with me one hour? Watch and pray, lest ye fall into temptation."

A SOLDIER WITH SEVEN WOUNDS.

JOHN WERTZ, 23d Ohio, Co. D, received seven wounds in one of the last battles near Petersburg, Va. Patient, brave, and patriotic, though he lay on his back for several months and suffered severely, he took it all very calmly. His recovery at times was doubtful, but with extra care and with his strong nerve and composed disposition, he gradually improved. Penitent, prayerful, resigned, he said he enjoyed religion, and seemed to enjoy a well-grounded hope. "You have received seven wounds to save your country; Christ received five to save the world. If you look to him, he will save you." I preached to him and his ward often, warning them to flee the wrath to come, and accept of the great salvation. At my last interview with him, he said, "I still pray and trust in the Lord." He was gaining strength and improving, when I left him with his seven scars of honor.

"I CAN AFFORD TO SUFFER,"

Said JUDSON SPALDING, 10th N. Y. Art., Co. H, as we talked about Jesus and his prospects of heaven. He seemed to be rooted and grounded in love, and, blessed with patience, said, "I can afford to suffer, since Christ has suffered so much for me. I trust in him, and he is all my hope." "I am very glad to find you in your sufferings looking unto Jesus, who, for the joy that was set before him, endured the cross with such perfect resignation. Since the immaculate Son of God suffered and died for us, well may we afford to suffer and die for him and for our country. If you grow impatient while suffering, go to Calvary, and learn of Jesus how to bear it. Think of the heroic martyr dying at the stake rather than turn traitor to the cause of Christ. And when called to suffer, it will help us to bear it patiently to remember that Jesus Christ, who hath gone before us as our example, 'hath borne our griefs and carried our sorrows;' so that if we suffer with him, we shall also reign with him in glory. 'No cross, no crown.' Jesus, filled with compassion, even prayed for his own murderers on the cross, and cried, 'Father, forgive them; for they know not what they do.'"

A HAPPY, SHOUTING SOLDIER.

"I have God in my heart, Christ in my soul, and heaven for my home," said PETER JONES, 36th U. S., Co. B, colored, as he related his experience. "You seem to be very happy, Peter?" "Yes, thank God, chaplain; I am happy." "When were you converted?" "Last March." "Where?" "At Point of Rocks, Va. I rose up about three o'clock, got out of bed, and shouted glory to God for nearly an hour. The nurse tried to hold me, but when they saw that I was not out of my head, they let me go." "Think you *have* God in your heart?" "Yes, I have no doubt of it." "Do you feel like holding on?" "Yes; by the grace of God, I mean to stand fast." "It is *all* of grace. Christ says, 'Without me, ye can do nothing;' but if you trust in him, he will give you grace to conquer. With God in your heart, and Christ in your soul, you must be very rich, Peter." "I suppose I must be rich, chaplain, yet I feel very poor and weak." "Christ says, 'Blessed are the poor in spirit.' And with all your assurance, Peter, let me say to you, *beware, watch, and pray.* Our hearts are very deceitful. God says, 'Let him that thinketh he standeth, take heed lest he fall.' The boasting Apostle Peter thought he could stand everything; yet he trembled before a little maid, and thrice denied his Master with cursing and swearing. May God bless you, Peter."

"I WOULD LIKE TO BE A CHRISTIAN, IF I COULD KEEP IT,"

Said ABRAHAM WEED, 58th Pa., Co. E, as we besought him to be reconciled to God. Anxious and hopeful, he said, "I have quit swearing pretty much; and I would like to have religion, if I could keep it." "First attend to getting it, and never fear losing it. If you only get it, the Lord will help and enable you to keep it. We are kept by the *power of God* through faith unto salvation. Jesus Christ is mighty to save, able to save unto the uttermost. Only trust in him, and he will be as a wall of fire round about you, and keep you as the apple of his eye, and make all things work together for your good, and let no evil touch thee. For he says, 'When thou passest through the waters, I will be with thee; and through the rivers, they shall not overflow thee. When thou walkest through the fire, thou shalt not be burned, neither shall the flame kindle upon thee.' Only embrace Christ and cling to him, and there is no danger of losing him." With a tender, smitten heart, he wept as we urged him to go to Jesus. "Come to him *now, just as you are*, and he will forgive your sins, save your soul, and be with you always to guide, guard, sustain, bless, and comfort you." He died May 27, 1865.

"I CAN'T LIVE WITHOUT PRAYER."

GEORGE E. CLEVELAND, 5th N.Y. Cavalry, Co. F, at our first interview, seemed to be a decided Christian. He said, "All my hope is in God;" "I have much faith in prayer;" "Christ was all my hope while in prison," and "I believed that he would bring me home." He was much given to prayer; he said, "I think I could not live through the night without it." "I suppose your religion gave you strong consolation in Andersonville, amid so much suffering, starvation, and death?" "Oh, yes; it was a great comfort." "How very encouraging to find you indulging such a strong hope 'in Him who is our only hope.' We are prisoners of hope. Hope is the anchor of the soul. God is our refuge and strength; a very present help in trouble. Jesus says, 'Lo, I am with you always.'" He lived till April 16, 1865, when death severed the vital cord, and his hope, we trust, was lost in full fruition.

"THE LORD IS MINE,"

Uttered HENRY A. LATHROP, 8th Conn., Co. I, in a low, feeble tone, as he was standing upon the brink of eternity, while I was trying to point him to the blessed Saviour. He was too weak to talk but little; it was too late to get his history. Although apparently seized with death, he was able to say, "I am happy!" "I want nothing." "I feel that 'the Lord is mine, and all is well.'" How very comprehensive, and how clearly those few sentences evince the gracious state! With the love of Christ shed abroad in his heart, and the Spirit bearing witness, the brave Christian soldier rises above all doubts, and to the waiting crowd announces his dying words, "I am happy, and 'all is well.'" There, with the grave yawning to engulf him, and Jesus waiting to receive him, having given his life for his country, and now grappling with death, he is enabled to say with a decided though weak tone of voice, "The Lord is mine." How great the loss! how incomparably rich the gain! Life is lost, but heaven is gained! How sweet and consoling the language of assurance, "My Beloved is mine, and I am his!" Ownership in God; and it is mutual—"The Lord is mine, and I am his!" How rich the inheritance "All things are yours!" hence, "All is well." A death message is sad news to send home to weeping friends; but when accompanied with such a happy, triumphant death, when "all is well!" it soothes the sorrows and calms the troubled breast. He expired September 29, 1864.

"I CAN'T PRAY,"

Said CHARLES A. HINKLE, 130th Ohio, Co. D, as we urged him to pray and repent. "Did you ever try to pray?" "No;

I never felt like praying, and never tried it." "I hope you have a praying mother?" "No; I am of a prayerless family." "Do you swear?" "No; I never swear. I go to church, and try to live a moral life." "Morality is very important, but it is not enough. You need not swear, lie, or get drunk, or murder, in order to be lost; no, only *neglect* salvation, and you will be lost sure. 'How shall ye escape, if ye neglect so great a salvation?' 'Except ye repent, ye shall all likewise perish.' You must turn, or die; believe, or be lost. You say you *'can't* pray;' you *can*, if you *will!* Prayer is very simple. It is asking God for what you want in Christ's name. Do you want to be saved?" "Yes." "Then ask God for salvation, and he will save you. 'Ask, and ye shall receive.'" "But I don't know how!" "Ask God to teach you. Pray, 'Lord, teach me how to pray;' pray, like the publican, 'God be merciful to me a sinner;' pray, like sinking Peter, 'Lord, save me!' Will you try it?" "Yes." "The Lord help and bless you."

"I FOUND JESUS."

REUBEN ALEXANDER, 29th U. S., Co. D, was a man of bright talents, and fluent in conversation. He was wounded in his left arm, and possessed much firmness and decision of character. On canvassing his heart, he said, "I have been converted eleven years; and although I have enjoyed much comfort in religion, I still want more and more: I am never satisfied." "What were the circumstances of your conversion?" "My father, mother, and brothers were sold from me, and I wondered where I'd get more good friends. An old man told me of Jesus. I prayed to him, 'Lord, *Lord*, LORD, have mercy on me!' God heard my prayers, and I found Jesus, and then I had glory in my cabin. And, oh, I was so happy then! God has been very good to me." "Do you ever backslide?" "No; me never backslide. I clings to Jesus, watch and pray." He seemed to be an earnest Christian, with clear views of the plan of salvation. He said, "To be a Christian and live it out, we must plough deep and plough straight." "That is so," I said; "it requires close watching and straight walking. The Lord says, 'Love mercy, deal justly, and walk worthy.' 'Do unto others as you would have them do unto you.' Be faithful; keep your lamp trimmed and burning, and be a burning, a shining light. May God bless you."

"I LEAVE IT ALL WITH THE LORD."

On approaching PHIL CORTEGE, 19th U. S., Co. C, lying on his bed, I asked him how he did. He said, "I suffer, and am sick for want of food." He seemed discouraged, and said, "I don't expect ever to get out of this till I am carried out on a stretcher." I said to him, "'Be of good courage, and God will strengthen your heart.' (Ps. xxvii. 14.) Let not your heart be troubled; be of good cheer. Only believe, and God will make *all things*—all these trials, deprivations, wounds, and afflictions—work together for your good. Do you trust in the Lord?" "Yes; I trust in him. I leave it all with the Lord." He seemed to be very honest, penitent, and humble, and yet how resigned. Prostrated upon a sick-bed, away from home, and with a deep, anxious care for his dear wife and children, with a heroic patience he said, "I leave it all to the Lord." And the *manner* in which he said it added much to the resignation conveyed. It was a *voluntary* expression of his submission to God's will, and a mark of very high Christian attainment in weeping Philip. "Do you pray?" "I prays all de time. I makes praying my *business*." He said he had served God twenty-four years, and appeared to be a decided Christian. I pointed him to the consolations of the cross, and he soon got well. John Fletcher received on his death-bed such a manifestation of the full meaning of the words, *God is love*, he said, "It fills my heart every moment," and he exclaimed, "Shout, shout aloud." His last words were, "I leave it all to God."

A SWEARER BROUGHT TO TEARS.

It was on a warm afternoon, July 24, 1864, while visiting ward No. 26, I heard a man groaning from pain occasioned by his wound being dressed. We were all strangers. As I approached his tent, in the presence of a kind mother, whose son lay by her side, shot in the head, this groaning man swore awfully. I spoke of his swearing in his presence, and went away. Presently, the anxious mother requested me to talk to her wounded son about his salvation. She wept and I wept. After visiting and reading and praying with a few suffering boys in another tent, I returned to see this swearing man; and after a hearty shake of the hand, he gave me his religious experience. Said he had been in a revival, and was put down for baptism, but ran off before his turn came. On telling him of his wickedness, and beseeching him to repent, and flee the wrath to come, he apologized for his profanity. Turning from him, I began to talk of the joys of heaven to the next poor sick fellow, whose brother John was waiting on him, and he requested me to pray for him; and his brother burst into tears and wept like a child. As I rose from prayer, we found the great swearer all bathed in tears. James wept, and as John bade him farewell, he hoped, if they met no more on earth, to meet in heaven. It was really a time of refreshing. Sailing round to New York with a ship-load of patients, I met James again; and he was so glad and thankful, he warmly and affectionately kissed my hand, as he lay upon his back, unable to set up. The soldier wounded in the head, accompanied with his parents, went on the same ship to New York, and got worse, and when his weeping mother asked permission to take him to the City Hospital, the surgeon refused her request. It seemed very hard. I supposed he died soon after.

14

CHAPTER XV.

SKETCHES OF SOLDIERS — CONTINUED.

The Bomb-Proof Prayer-Meeting — "Are You Ready to Go?" — Little Lizzie's Letter — "I Prayed in the Street" — "I Love Everybody" — "I Have no Fear" — Sergeant James Tustison: "I am Dying, but I am very Happy" — "I have got It!" — Satan Repulsed by Prayer — "Hell Seems to be Gaping for Me" — "I am Happy in the Lord" — "Converted in the Army through Sin" — "Do You Trust in the Lord?" — "Urge Him to Come to Jesus" — "Thank God for My Wound" — Sergeant Dwight Kneeland: "My Work is Done" — Died Calling for the Chaplain — "Just as God Wishes" — "Tell My Mother I Died Happy" — "It is Easier to Serve Satan" — "I am Better in the Army than at Home" — William J. Johnson, 142d N. Y., Co. D — "All is Well" — "Old Jacob," the Grave-Digger — "The Bible Better than Greenbacks" — "Somehow it Worked upon Me" — "God Still Sticks to Me" — "O Chaplain; What Will I Do?" — "I am on the Devil's Side" — "Pray for Me, Chaplain, till I Die:" His Bereaved Wife's Letter — "I would as soon go to my Heavenly Home" — "I am Too Wicked to come to Jesus" — "God Grabbed Me into His Heart at Once" — "I Prayed on, and God Changed My Heart" — "The Devil Coaxed Me Off."

THE BOMB-PROOF PRAYER-MEETING.

AS a number of the delegates of the U. S. Christian Commission were passing by Fort Albany, then guarded by the 14th Mass. Volunteers, one of the brave boys said to them, "Look here!" (pointing to a deep hole in the ground;) "what is that?" "It's the bomb-proof, where we hold our daily prayer-meetings, down twelve feet under ground." "Do any come?" "Oh, yes; sixty or more." "Do you find the Saviour there?" "Yes; we find him here as well as at home." "So you go down to get up?" "Yes; and that is one of God's fixed, unalterable laws, 'We must go down to get up;' for God says, 'Before

THE COOPER SHOP VOLUNTEER REFRESHMENT SALOON, PHILADELPHIA.

honor is humility,' and 'He that humbleth himself shall be exalted.' Christ was exalted to heaven because he humbled himself, and became 'obedient unto death.' (Phil. ii. 8, 9.) So it is with all of us; we must humble ourselves, if we would be exalted; if we would ever reach the joys of heaven, we must start at the foot of the cross. And do you get very high, and draw very near to God, down there?" "Yes, sir; and when we meet down there, we come away strengthened and refreshed, and feel that it was good to be there." "I suppose you all flee down there when the rebel balls and shells fall thick around you?" "Yes, that is our refuge in time of extreme peril. But when the devil, the first great rebel, shoots his fiery darts, we can't find refuge in bomb-proofs, forts, or behind earth-works, because he can very easily shoot his poisonous darts through all these. No refuge from him is found but in the cleft-rock, Christ Jesus, the believer's only stronghold of defence and protection." "I suppose when the balls and shells fly thicker, and the danger becomes greater, you plead harder for deliverance?" "Yes; realized danger tends to help us to divest ourselves of self, and to draw us nearer to God. The greater our sense of want, the harder we can plead for help. Hence, nothing but great emergencies will develop and draw out the latent powers of the soul. When were the grandest exploits of military genius displayed? Under some great pressing emergency, when the glories of victory, or the salvation of the country, hung upon the decision of an hour and the action of a moment. When were the greatest and most eloquent speeches delivered? Under some very great crisis, involving the interests of nations and the destiny of the world. When were the most earnest and powerful prayers put forth? Under some pre-eminently great emergency involving the redemption of a kingdom and the salvation of the world. Where, we ask, was Jacob, when he plead with that intense importunity and assured confidence that enabled him to exclaim, 'I will not let thee go, except thou bless me?' He was in a case of imminent danger, with his life exposed to the direful revenge of his incensed brother, whom he was going to meet. When did the devoted Daniel plead with such wonderful assurance and power, that his prayer was heard even while he was yet speaking and praying; what were his circumstances? It was when he was deeply concerned for the deliverance of the captive hosts of Israel. It was there, while pouring out his soul and heart unto God, crying, 'O Lord, hear! O Lord, forgive! O Lord, hearken and do! defer not, for thine own sake, O my God,' that the angel flew from heaven, and announced that the decree had gone forth liberating the Jewish captives. What were the circumstances that gave rise to the Saviour's agonizing prayer in the garden of Gethsemane, which brought the bloody sweat from every pore, and led him to exclaim, 'Father, if thy will, let this cup pass from me!' Whence this most intense importunity and anguish of soul? It is the preparation for the agonies of the cross. Jesus is going to Calvary, and feeling the billows of God's wrath rising about him, and realizing the fierce conflict before him in working out our salvation, he goes to God, and prays for sustaining grace. Where, we ask, was the dying thief, when he offered up that effectual prayer that snatched his soul from a yawning hell, and landed it safe in heaven? He was hanging upon the cross, in the very agony of death, and with the flames of eternal fire kindling at his feet, in the most extreme peril. There he hangs; and, standing upon the pivot of the eternal world, feeling that it is the last opportunity, that it will soon be salvation or damnation, he earnestly prays, 'Jesus, Lord, remember me!' and his soul, plucked from the jaws of Satan and washed in the Saviour's blood, went home to heaven!" I heard a soldier say he could pray better while facing the rebel cannon's mouth. Thus we see that, when we are closely pressed and more fully feel our dependence upon God, the more earnestly we can pray. "So, I suppose, when the balls and shells fall thick around you, you draw nearer to God, and pray more fervently, than when all is peace?" "Yes, chaplain, that's so."

"ARE YOU READY TO GO?"

Although over three hundred thousand loyal patriots tasted death during the rebellion, yet many more have fallen since from wounds inflicted and diseases contracted during the war. To fight and die on the gory field, in putting down treason, even when crowned with victory, is hard. To get sick or wounded, and linger and suffer severely for months, and then die in the hospital, far away from friends and from home, is harder; but to linger and suffer for *years* from wounds received, or diseases contracted in the service, and then die, seems harder still. Such was the fate of Samuel S. Brown, late member of the 3d Reg. Ohio Cavalry, Co. B, who entered the service of his country, January 1, 1864, and after enduring much hardness in Sherman's memorable campaign, contracted a severe cold at the long and bloody siege of Atlanta, through exposure to the weather, from the effects of which he never recovered. Having served his country a little over a year, and being unable to serve longer, he was honorably discharged February 8, 1865, when he returned home to his father's house in Cardington, Ohio, where he spent the remainder of his days, and died February 14, 1868, aged twenty-three years and three months. Born and brought up by religious parents, he received a religious training, which seemed to have resulted in his conversion. Quiet and unassuming in his disposition, he was warmly attached and strongly devoted to his parents. Although he suffered long, he bore it all very patiently. Not a murmur was heard to fall from his lips. And when approached by a brother upon the subject of religon, shortly before he died, he seemed calm and collected, and gave good evidence of being at peace with God. When asked, "Do you trust in Jesus?" He replied, "Yes, and have for some time." "Would you be afraid to die?" "No." "Are you ready to go?" "Yes; and the sooner the better." "*The sooner the better?*" "Yes!" "How glorious the attainment! Dying for your country, and dying in the Lord. Not only *ready*, but, like Paul, even *longing* to depart. *Waiting* to hear the summons, 'Come up higher.' *Waiting* to bid farewell to this sinful world of troubles, conflict, and trials. *Waiting* to lay aside this vile body, to go and dwell with the ransomed of the Lord in heaven. To be ready to go when your country calls to defend her honor, is glorious. To be ready to go when the command, "*charge*," is given in the heat of battle, is glorious. But to be ready to go, when it comes ours to die, is more glorious. Victory achieved over the enemy on the field of battle is glorious, but victory achieved over the last enemy, death, is the most glorious of all victories. To be able to face the king of terrors, gazing into the eternal world, and be able to say, 'O death, where is thy sting?' is the very acme of perfection on earth." Mr. Brown lived but a short time after the above conversation, and during his last hours his voice was heard in prayer. *Be ye also ready.*

LITTLE LIZZIE'S LETTER.

PHILADELPHIA, April 17, 1863.

MY DEAR SOLDIER:—I send you a little Testament. I am a little girl seven years old. I want to do something for the soldiers who do so much for us; so I have saved my pocket money to send you this. Although I have never seen you, I intend to begin to pray that God will make and keep you good. Oh, how sorry I am that you have to leave your dear mother. Did she cry when you bade her good-by? Don't you often think of her at night when you are going to bed? Do you kneel down and say your prayers? If I were you, I would not care if the other soldiers did laugh; God will smile upon you. I am sorry, very sorry, that you are sick. I wish that I could go to nurse you. I could bathe your head, and read to you. Do you know the hymn,—

"There is a happy land?"

I hope you will go to that land when you die. But remember, I will pray that you may get well again.

When you are able to sit up, I wish you to write to me, and tell me all about your troubles.

Enclosed you will find a postage-stamp. I live at No. —— North Ninth Street, Philadelphia. Good-by.

Your Friend, LIZZIE S——.

Lizzie's letter and the Testament she sent proved the means of the soldier's salvation who received them.

NASHVILLE, TENN., April 24, 1863.

DEAR SISTER LIZZIE:—I received your kind letter from Mr. C. I. M. A beautiful present indeed, and I trust it will be one of the means of converting others, as well as the receiver. May God bless the giver. You have done a good work. Continue to pray, dear sister, and God will answer you. He says so in his word.

My dear mother is in the grave. It is nearly eleven years since she died; but she died happy; and I trust I shall meet her in heaven. I will try and pray for myself. Have been in the hospital four months, but am now nearly well; will be able to join my regiment to face the enemy; and if I should fall on the battle-field, I may have the blessed assurance of meeting my Saviour in peace.

Yes, "there is a happy land." May we meet in that happy land. I do not think that my fellow-soldiers will deter me from serving my Master. There are many others here that his Spirit is striving with.

I expect to go home to see my dear friends once more. Am very thankful that the privilege is granted, and I trust we shall have a happy meeting. Dear Lizzie, I must close. May God bless you, is my prayer. Write me again.

Address your friend, S. L. N.,
Fourth Mich. Cavalry, Nashville, Tenn.

"I PRAYED IN THE STREET."

"Man's extremity is God's opportunity." Coming to Christ is the sinner's last resort. Blinded by sin and deceived by Satan, man, lost, will go to a thousand refuges before he will flee to the safe one; and it is only when he finds that all other refuges are, in the language of the prophet, "refuges of lies," that he flees to Christ, "the only stronghold." In canvassing the heart of Charles A. Morton, 7th N. H., Co. K, we found him much interested in religion, at our first interview. He seemed to be indulging a bright hope, and said he had been converted in a revival. He appeared to have been powerfully wrought upon by the Spirit; and said he, "I became so earnestly engaged in seeking Christ, that I prayed in the street, and afterward I felt so different that I went home and told my wife." "When an anxious sinner is brought to feel his awful exposure to endless woe, and to realize his own helplessness and utter dependence upon God for salvation, it is perfectly natural and reasonable to fly to God in prayer immediately, even 'on the street,' or, like sinking Peter, 'on the water.' The interests involved are so vast, and the emergency is so great, he *can't* wait; he *must* pray; he *can't help it;* and it is in just such emergencies as these that the most powerful and effectual prayers have been offered up. I suppose when you prayed in the street, you felt that you could not wait till you got home?" "Yes; I felt such a pressing necessity, that I could not wait." "Under that state of feeling, how easy, and, oh, what a great privilege, it is to pray! How have you felt since?" "I feel much altered, and happy." "Regeneration is a great change — a change from darkness to light, and from the power of Satan unto God. In it, the old man is put off and the new put on; old things pass away, and all things become new; so that when a man undergoes it, he will 'feel much altered,' as you say. And although many Christians can't tell the precise time, place, and circumstances of their conversion, yet they will know something about it. Others profess to know all about the circumstances, the time when and the place where the great change, wrought by God's Spirit, was brought about. And how can we know it? Love to the brethren is one distinguishing mark. Hereby 'we know that we have passed from death unto life, because we love the brethren.' 'He that loveth not his brother, abideth in death.' Another evidence is secret prayer:

> 'Prayer is the Christian's vital breath,
> The Christian's native air;
> His watchword at the gate of death:
> He enters heaven with prayer.'

If a man has experienced a change of heart, he will feel so grateful to God that he will often repair to his closet, and thank the Lord for the great things he has done for him. David prayed three times a day. The Saviour prayed all night; and it is said John Welch prayed eight hours out of twenty-four; and that he would often rise at midnight and pour out his soul to God in prayer for the people of his congregation. How is it with you?" "I have been praying ever since my conversion. I pray that my arm may heal fast, and it does." "You seem to have strong faith in prayer?" "Oh, yes, I believe God answers prayer. He says, 'Seek, and ye shall find.'"

"I LOVE EVERYBODY."

It was on a beautiful evening, in the summer of 1865, in the U. S. General Hospital, near Fortress Monroe, Va., while making my daily calls with the patients, that I fell into an interesting conversation with R. Brown, of the 7th Regiment S. C. Cavalry, Co. F., confederate troops. He gave me a hearty welcome to his bedside, and we found him free to converse about religion and his own personal experience. He seemed to be a decided Christian, not only enjoying a well-grounded hope, but even full assurance of his acceptance with God; and, to use his own language, he said, "I know I have passed from death unto life."

What a glorious attainment! It is worth more than all things else. "How long have you been trying to serve the Lord?" "Some fifteen years," he replied. Touching his love to Christ, he said, "I love everybody." "Would you be afraid to die?" "No." "'Perfect love casteth out fear.' 'Love is the fulfilling of the law.' 'Thou shalt love thy neighbor as thyself.' Do you love God's word?" "Oh, yes," he said; "I have read my Testament through thirty times in the army." "Do you find it difficult to live out religion in the army?" "No; I can live as well in the army as out of it?" "Christ, who is our strength, says, 'My grace is sufficient for thee;' hence he says, 'No evil shall touch thee.' With God's Spirit to guide us, and his everlasting arms beneath us, we have nothing to fear." I visited him frequently, and always found him prayerful, patient, and resigned. I heard not a murmur fall from his lips. He manifested a strong desire to see his wife. Administering to him the consolations of the gospel, he lingered along, and died full of hope June 15, 1865.

"I HAVE NO FEAR."

In visiting the sick and wounded, we were daily cheered by the patience and heroism they manifested. We often found them not only resigned, but buoyant and jovial, with hearts glowing with courage and patriotism. At my first interview with John

Lestur, 38th U.S., Co. D, we found him in patience possessing his soul; and although severely wounded, he was jovial and lively as a cricket, and yet full of fight. In describing the hot fight near Chapin's Farm, close by Richmond, he said, "With my finger shot almost off, while going it at double quick, I pulled out my jack-knife, cut it off, threw it down, went on, loaded and fired eight or nine times while charging the fort near the above place." Eager for victory, he said, "With my bleeding hand, I mounted the fort, raised the stars and stripes, and fought on till I received a ball in my thigh, which brought me down." "Were you not afraid in such a warm fight?" "No; I trust in the Lord, and I am not afraid." "You have the right remedy for fear." "What?" "Trust in the Lord — there is nothing equal to it. David said, when surrounded with hosts of enemies, 'What time I am afraid, I will trust in God.' Faith as a shield is a sure defence against the wiles of the devil and all the fiery darts of the wicked." He said, "If I die, I believe Jesus will save me." "Would you not be afraid to make another such charge?" "Oh, no; I would cut off another finger under similar circumstances. I came out to fight and, if need be, to die for God and my country. I have no fear." "No fear? no fear of death?" "No." "'O death, where is thy sting! Thanks be to God, who giveth us the victory through our Lord Jesus Christ.'" How grand the perfection to rise above all fear! Said the celebrated Robert Hall, in his dying hours, "I fear pain more than death;" and he soon passed into glory, praying, "Come, Lord Jesus, come quickly." Dr. Taylor kissed the stake as he approached it, and in meek submission died, sealing the doctrine he taught with his own blood. At our next interview, John Lestur said, as I approached him, "Here I am, waiting on the Lord. Had not Jesus been nigh my side, I'd have died when I got wounded." "Do you think Jesus saved you?" "Yes; I feel so." "Christ is a covert in the storm. The name of the Lord is a strong tower; the righteous runneth therein, and they are safe. The Lord is as a wall of fire round about them that fear him. How does the Saviour appear to you to-day, John?" "He seems dear: Jesus is close by my side, and I am happy in him."

"What sweet words! Happy in Jesus! To such there is no condemnation. And you think you would be willing to lose another finger, 'in a pinch,' for your country; aye, John?" "Oh, yes; the loss of fingers, legs, and lives is nothing to the loss of our country." Such courage and patriotic devotion deserves great praise. To see men cut off a finger, load and fire as they run, charging a rebel fort, shows great pluck and bravery. He got better, and was transferred North.

SERGEANT JAMES TUSTISON.

Fired with a lofty patriotism, JAMES TUSTISON consecrated himself to the service of his country shortly after the outbreak of the rebellion. Though a native of Crawford County, Ohio, he moved to Iowa in 1854, and at his country's call enlisted as orderly sergeant of Capt. Holson's company, of the Tenth Reg. Iowa Volunteers, at Richmond, August 24, 1861, and was mustered into the service, September 6, at Iowa City. And as the rebellion had not reached Iowa, his regiment was soon ordered to St. Louis, and before they had time to procure their uniforms there, they were ordered to Cape Girardeau, where they arrived October 2. Time rolled on, and as the rebellion spread itself, the noble-hearted sergeant met the enemy in a severe skirmish at Charleston, Mo.; and although he was so fortunate as to come out unhurt himself, two of his company were killed and several others wounded. At the close of the fall campaign, his regiment went into *winter-quarters* at Bird's Point, Mo., and the sergeant, being unaccustomed to camp life and that very unhealthy climate, was taken with a severe attack of diarrhœa early in February, 1862. And although he had comfortable quarters, they were made more comfortable by the graceful presence of his kind, affectionate wife, Mrs. Tustison, who, with her characteristic tenderness, went all the way from home to see him, and carefully nursed him through all his sickness. Blessed with an early religious training, he united with the Presbyterian Church when seventeen years of age, and by his consistent life was an ornament to the church, and adorned the doctrines of the cross. His disease assumed the chronic form, and he suffered severely, yet, sustained by an unseen Hand, he bore it all very patiently. Not a murmur was known to fall from his lips. Failing so rapidly, and despairing of his recovery, on application of his friends, he was examined by a board of physicians and honorably discharged from the service, and, accompanied with his faithful wife, he bid farewell to his regiment and started for home. On arriving at Mattoon, Ill., he became so feeble he was unable to go any further, and they "put up" at a hotel. Being a member of the Masonic fraternity, upon (his) making himself known to the lodge of that place, they kindly assisted in taking care of him. The Rev. Mr. McFarlan and Dr. Bridges were especially attentive in administering to his wants; yet, with all their attention, he grew worse. A few days before his departure he became delirious, but on the evening ere he expired, his reason was restored, and he awoke from his unconscious state, wrapped in the sweet smiles of his heavenly Father. As the struggle of death came on, and fully conscious of the approach of "the last enemy," sustained by Him who "hath abolished death," he said, calm and undismayed,

"I AM DYING, BUT I AM VERY HAPPY!"

And filled with filial affection in his last moments, his thoughts fly home to his mother, and wishing to leave her a word of comfort, the dying soldier said, among his last words, "Tell my mother that, when dying, my trust was in Christ."

Lingering until the afternoon of March 27, 1862, the wheel at the cistern stood still, and in the thirtieth year of his age, in the presence of his weeping wife and brother, his blood-washed soul left its clay tenement, and went, we trust, home to swell the ranks of the redeemed in heaven. How sublime such a death— dying for his country, and dying in the Lord! How consoling to his bereaved wife and friends! Though your loss is heavy and your affliction severe, yet, if you will listen, you will hear the soothing voice of the good Shepherd saying unto you, "*Weep not;*" "be of good cheer." "Let not your heart be troubled, for all is well." "Be ye also ready!"

"I HAVE GOT IT."

Having preached in ward twenty-three, as I was passing up the aisle, Thomas Warren, 199th Pa., Co. D, being under deep anxiety of mind, called me to him, and said, "I want to get religion, and I want you to pray for me." He seemed to be very anxious, and on telling him of the goodness of God and the compassion of Jesus, and of his ability and willingness to save, and urging him to repent and pray, he began to pray, and cried, "Lord, have mercy on me! Cast me not off! O Saviour, take me now — just as I am!" and, weeping profusely, and praying with intense earnestness, he exclaimed, "Oh, if I had only religion *now!*" He said he had been swearing, but now seemed deeply penitent. Urging him to look to Jesus, I left him all stirred up. His severe wound became gangrened, and he was taken to the Gangrene Camp; and, calling upon him there soon after, he exclaimed, "I have got it! *I have got it!*" and clapping his hands, shouted, "Glory to God! glory to God! hallelujah!" Several gathered in to see him. He said, "I feel light; a great burden has rolled off of me." Upon my next call, he seemed very much changed; he prayed and wept much. When I left, he was improving.

SATAN REPULSED BY PRAYER.

We found CHARLES WILLIAMS, 5th U. S., Co. C, at the first, prayerful, humble, penitent, anxious, crying like the trembling jailer, "What must I do to be saved!" "When did you begin to pray?" "Since I got wounded." "How do you feel on the subject of religion?" "I feel that I am a great sinner; and I am afraid I won't get through. The devil came and told me I would be lost, if I do trust in Christ." "Yes; but the devil is a liar, and you must not believe a word he says, nor indulge a thought he suggests. Mother Eve believed the devil and disbelieved God, and fell. Do you believe the devil?" "No; when he tempted me I called on the Lord, and he went away." "So you repulsed the devil with prayer?" "Yes, he left me." "That proves the great power of prayer. You will always find it true, 'resist the devil, and he will flee from you.'" Calling upon him again, we found him indulging a strong hope; and I said to him, "Do you think you are a Christian?" "Yes; I believe God has converted my soul; and I expect my wife won't know me when I go home, I will be so changed." "Was it your wound that led you to pray, which has resulted in your hopeful conversion?" "Yes, I believe it was." "A stroke of lightning led to the conversion of Martin Luther, and no doubt the stroke of balls and shells has led to the conversion of many a soldier. Think you could die happy?" "Yes; I feel that I could." "Be faithful. Stand up for the flag, and cling to the cross!"

"HELL SEEMS TO BE GAPING FOR ME!"

Exclaimed JACOB MULLINCUP, 13th Ind., Co. D, as he related his religious experience. He seemed to be very anxious and tender, but said he, "I have not followed Christ; but I want you to pray for me," weeping profusely. "Jesus Christ came into the world to save sinners, and died for the ungodly, just such as you are. He is mighty to save; able and willing to save, even unto the uttermost. His blood cleanseth from all sin: 'Look, and live!'" It was on December 4, 1864, I visited him again at five P.M., and found him writhing with a deep sense of his sins. "You seemed to have lived a wicked life?" "Yes; I have sworn, and done everything that's bad; and my mother brought me up good." "Have you ever been troubled with skepticism?" "Yes; but there can't but be another world." "Why, what makes you think so?" "Not only because God reveals it, but because I feel such a load of guilt upon my conscience." "Do you really feel your sins to be so great?" "Yes, I do. Oh, my sins! my sins! hell seems to be gaping for me! Oh, chaplain, what will I do?" "Just throw yourself right into the arms of Jesus, and cry for mercy, and he will save you. Pray, like the thief on the cross, 'Jesus, Lord, remember me;' pray, like the blind beggar, 'Jesus, thou Son of David, have mercy on me!' What are you going to do with your sins; how do you expect to get rid of them?" "I don't know. I try to pray, and trust in the Lord, but my heart is so hard: I know God is able to save me, but I am so faithless." "Jesus is the only sin-bearer; he hath borne our griefs and carried our sorrows: only believe, and he will wash your soul and cleanse your hard heart. Do you feel sorry for your sins?" "Oh, yes; very sorry." "If you repent, God will forgive. 'Let the wicked forsake his way, and the unrighteous man his thoughts: and let him return unto the Lord, and he will have mercy upon him; and to our God, for he will abundantly pardon.' Jesus is here, full of pity, love, and power, knocking at the very door of your heart, crying, 'Come unto me, and I will give you rest!' May God bless you."

"I AM HAPPY IN THE LORD!"

I visited JAMES REED, 188th Pa., Co. D, very often, and at first he manifested some interest in religion, but gave no satisfactory evidence of piety. He was badly wounded in the knee, and suffered long and very severe. Lying so long on his back, he had very bad bed-sores. I preached, read, and prayed with him very often, and he appreciated it highly. He would say, "Come and see me often, chaplain." He became concerned about his salvation, and gave himself unto prayer. Several days before his death, he seemed to undergo a great change. On the evening of November 27, he was much engaged in prayer, and said, "The Saviour was dear and precious." He seemed to long for heaven, and said, "I feel prepared to go, and am not afraid to die. I pray and hope to meet my father, mother, brothers, and sisters in heaven." He had two books, and said, "Give one to my sister Nancy, and the other to Mary," and again engaged in earnest prayer. November 30th: He prayed fervently to-night. I read and prayed with him, and sung,

"I am going home, to die no more!"

The doctor had given him up some time. He lingered with much pain till December 1st, and death closed the solemn scene.

Dying for his country and, we trust, dying in Christ, he said, "I am happy in the Lord. To die is gain; to depart is far better."

CONVERTED IN THE ARMY THROUGH SIN.

At my first interview with EDWARD BURNETT, 118th N. Y., Co. G, he seemed to be an humble, prayerful Christian. Said he had been converted in the army from seeing so much sin and wickedness, and seeing so many dying soldiers. "Sin led you to forsake sin, did it?" "Yes; hearing so much profanity, and seeing so much wickedness, led me to consider my ways, and led me to seek God in prayer, which has resulted in my conversion." "How do your sins appear to you now?" "They seem very great; but I believe God has forgiven them all." He had a very deep sense of his sins, and gave bright evidence of being a regenerated man. God often brings good out of evil; but this is an unusual case. Such heights of wickedness and streams of profanity, as were common during the war, were enough to alarm the most thoughtless. God's ways are not our ways. He can make one word of truth, the minie-ball, the lightning's flash, and the sinner's sin, result in the conversion of sinners. The wrath of man shall praise him. Edward grew worse, and died November 25, 1864, full of hope.

"DO YOU TRUST IN THE LORD?" "NO,"

Said BENJAMIN R. TILTON, as we tried to urge him to repentance. "Do you pray?" "No." "Do you swear?" "Yes, occasionally." "No prayers, no faith, no Saviour, and shot through the mouth, and scarcely able to speak: what a dark picture! How glorious to die for your country! how awful to die, and be lost! What mean these daily deaths around you? It is the voice of Jesus, warning you to prepare to meet thy God: you must turn or burn; believe or be lost! Oh, then, go to Bethlehem; go to Gethsemane; go to Calvary, and there behold the Lamb of God praying, bleeding, dying, that you might live! Just think of the matchless love of Christ in exchanging

CHRISTIANITY IN THE WAR. 225

the glories of heaven for the agonies of the cross, that we, unworthy sinners, might have eternal life. Think of the prayers and tears of an anxious mother for your salvation, and will you let it all be in vain?" "*I trust not!*" "Your creed, 'I trust not,' is not enough; it will not save you: no, it is quite too scanty to carry you to heaven. Paul's creed delivered to the trembling jailer was short, plain, and orthodox; but it was very comprehensive — a creed which, if heartily received, will carry you safely through the shock of battle; through all the fire, temptations, trials, and storms of life, and finally give you a triumphant death, and take you safely home to heaven." "What is it?" "'Believe on the Lord Jesus Christ, and thou shalt be saved.' There it is. Do you understand it? It is the very thing you need: it is the Bible and the plan of salvation in a nutshell. With Christ for its object, and salvation for its end, it will just suit you. To benefit you, you must receive it by faith. It is the only thing for those who have 'no Saviour,' and no prayers. Only believe, and you have nothing to fear." "Yes; but what is faith?" "Faith is to the Christian what courage is to the soldier." "What?" "That which always carries him through. Faith is letting go of all things else and laying hold of Jesus, and clinging to the cross with all your heart. Let me illustrate it for you. There is a man away down in a well, with his satchel of valuables and gold; he can't get out himself, and therefore cries for help. Two men passing by with a rope, heard him, and ran to his relief. 'Can't you climb up and get out?' 'No; I have nothing to catch hold of.' 'Can't you get a foothold on the stones in the wall of the well?' 'No; it is all too smooth, and the water is deep, and I have nothing to stand on.' 'Nothing to stand on?' 'No.' Just like the sinner without Christ — building without a foundation, and nothing to stand on. 'Can't you touch the bottom?' 'Oh, no; the water is deep, and I am afraid I will lose my satchel. *Oh, DO lift me out!* I am almost out of breath, and I can't keep up much longer. If not soon saved, I am gone forever. And will you let me drown?' 'No; here is a rope: now you grasp it firmly with both hands.' 'With both hands?' 'Yes.' 'But what will I do with my satchel?'

15

'Why, let it go; let it go quick, and grasp the rope with both hands with all your might, or we will let you sink and be drowned.' He grasped the rope with one hand, clinging to the satchel with the other. The men gave a strong pull; but the poor worldling, having reached about half-way up, let go, and down he went again into the water, deeper than ever. 'There! he's gone!' exclaimed one man to the other. 'Stop! wait: let's see if he won't come up again!' Presently he rises again, just ready to perish, exclaiming '*Lord have mercy on me! God be merciful to me a sinner!* Oh, brethren will you let me drown?' And again they let down the rope, beseeching him to drop his satchel, and grasp the rope with all his might with both hands. He did so. They gave another pull, and up came the drowning man, saved at last.' This, Benjamin, is an illustration of faith. It implies two things: first, letting go of the world, and, second, laying hold of Jesus. Do you see it, Benjamin?" "Yes, I believe I do." "Will you try it?" "I will." "May God help and bless you."

"URGE HIM TO COME TO JESUS."

JOHN GOFF, 142d N. Y., Co. D, though rather careless at first, soon became interested, and enjoyed religious services very much. At our next interview, though somewhat anxious, he said, "I don't think I am a Christian, but would like to be one." Apparently penitent and prayerful, he repeatedly said, "God bless me." With a *very severe* wound in the left arm, and increasing in anxiety about his salvation, he seemed to enjoy my visits very much, and would usually exclaim on my entering his tent, "God bless you, chaplain; God bless you. Oh, how glad I am that you have come." He appeared to grow in grace, and several days ere he died he said he loved the Saviour; that he had been converted in the hospital, and that he felt a deep concern for his unconverted brother. He suffered long and severely, and seemed to be an humble, sincere Christian. When I wrote a letter to his brother, he said to me, "*Urge him to come to Jesus.*" Deep concern for the salvation of others is an evidence of the gracious state. He seemed very happy, and his oft-repeated prayer was "God bless me; God bless me." If every man urged his brother to come to Jesus, there would not be so many without hope. Reading and praying with him very often, he lingered a long while, and fell with the autumn leaf in 1864. To depart is far better.

"THANK GOD FOR MY WOUND,"

Said MILES JAMES, Corporal, Co. B, 36th U. S., colored, as he related his religious experience. He was a backslidden Methodist, yet, with his left arm off near the shoulder, he was *very grateful* for liberty; full of fight, full of courage, and with a heart burning with heroic patriotism, he was lively and rich in conversation. Sprightly, and hot with zeal to quell the rebellion, he seemed to "glory in tribulation," exclaiming, as his heart seemed to glow with gratitude, "Thank God, *thank God*, THANK GOD for my wound! It has brought me nearer to God, and knocked the feeling of revenge out of me. Before it, I would have killed a rebel on his knees before me, but now I would take him prisoner. Before it, I would cry, 'Fort Pillow, and let 'em have it,' but now I would spare 'em. My wound has brought me nearer to God, and I thank him for it. Before it, I was full of revenge against the rebels, but this wound has taken it away. I praise the Lord for it. I feel very happy lying here on my bed. *Oh, I am so happy!* But if I get well, I will go and fight again." This was on October 11, 1864. At another interview, he said, "My wound has brought me to the point." "Brought you to the point, aye?" "Yes." "What point?" "Why, to the point of repentance and contrition; it has brought me, chaplain, to the foot of the cross." "Then stick to it, James. By *all* means stick to it. It is *sticking* to the point and clinging to the cross that makes us happy even under the most adverse and trying circumstances. Daniel, when surrounded with hosts of fierce enemies, said, 'My soul is among lions;' yet, with his heart stayed and fixed upon God, he was happy in prayer and praise. Cranmer, brought to the point, with his heart stayed and fixed upon God, because he had subscribed to popery, when at the stake, held his unworthy hand in the flames till it was burned to a cinder, before his body was scorched, exclaiming, 'This hand, this unworthy right hand.' There he hung, apparently insensible of pain, praying, 'Lord Jesus, receive my spirit,' until the flames choked his utterance. How glorious, James, to see you so happy, with your arm riven from your body, that not one star should be riven from the dear old flag. Fight on, James, for God and the country, and the Lord will reward you. Do you pray much?" "Yes; I prays very often. It is very good to pray." "Do you like to hear the gospel?" "Yes; I liked to jump out of my bed when you preached to us last Sunday night." "Pray on, James. Be earnest; stick to the point and cling to the cross, and Jesus will at last raise you to his throne."

SERGEANT DWIGHT KNEELAND.

Sergeant DWIGHT KNEELAND, of the Signal Corps, U. S. A., was brought to the hospital, in Feb. 1865, from near Petersburg, Va. Worn out by nearly three years' service in his country's cause, he was very much reduced in flesh, and sinking with consumption. Pale, tall, slender, and well dressed, he presented a dignified, genteel appearance when he entered the ward. He lingered along for several days with but little perceptible change, yet failing gradually. On approaching him on the subject of religion, we found him rather careless, yet not entirely indifferent. Says he, "I have been a great sinner." But he soon gave signs of concern for his salvation, and became somewhat penitent and prayerful. God worked in him, and on our next interview we found him more deeply concerned, and praying in the language of the publican, "God be merciful to me a sinner." The Spirit strove with him, and, becoming more resigned and contrite, he prayed, "Not my will, but God's, be done." This was on February 26, 1865. I preached to him and his ward on the Sabbath, from the Saviour's compassionate words, Matt. xxiii. 37. It was his last sermon, and he listened very attentively. Time fled, life ebbed away, and three days after, conscious of approaching death, he said, in the language of the immortal Brainard,—

"MY WORK IS DONE!"

I am going to die; I don't want to live; I feel prepared to go. Tell my father, 'I die happy, and that I bid them all farewell! Send my things home to him.'" Thoughtful and faithful to his country and to his trust, he requested us to burn his *Signal-Book*, lest secrets might be revealed; and we burned it in the stove. On approaching him the next evening, he seemed better; and, after reading to him the Saviour's consoling words (John xiv.), and praying with him, we bade him "good-night," expecting to visit him early next morning. But on entering the ward, we found that he had finished his course, and his place in the ward was made vacant! Gone from time to eternity; gone, we trust, from earth to heaven, to join the redeemed, blood-washed throng, where there will be no more war, no more death, neither sorrow nor crying. We saw him next in the dead-house. Patient in all his sufferings, he uttered not a murmuring word. Resigned, and with his work done, and, we trust, prepared to die, his quiet departure seemed to say, "To die is gain; thanks be to God, which giveth us the victory through our Lord Jesus Christ!" He died March 1, 1865. His mortal remains were taken home to Connecticut.

"DIED CALLING FOR THE CHAPLAIN."

At our first interview with JOHN H. DUNHAM, 117th N.Y., Co. D, we found him careless, and rather indifferent about religion. "Do you pray?" "Not much. I feel a little sorry for my sins at times; but it soon passes away like the wind." This was on November 10, 1864. I preached to him and prayed for him, and commended him to God, and urged him to fly to Jesus. "You may get well, but life is very uncertain. How sad the thought to see a brave soldier lose his limb, and shed his blood, and die for his country, and die and be lost! Oh, then, let me beseech you, repent, repent! Let the loss of your leg be a call from God to repent, and seek the salvation of your soul. Only think of the goodness of God in sparing your life; giving you time to repent, while many others fell dead without a moment's warning! Look to the cross; look to Jesus; behold him in Gethsemane; see how he pleads, agonizes, and sweats as it were great drops of blood falling down to the ground, for our salvation! Behold him hanging upon Calvary, groaning, bleeding, and dying that ignominious death, that you might live and enjoy eternal life! How wonderful the scene: the earth quakes; the rocks rend; the graves open; the dead rise; and the sun refuses to shine before the awful grandeur of the solemn scene! And for whom, and for what did he suffer all this? It was for us, poor sinners, who have rebelled against him; it was for you! It was to make an atonement for sin, that you might enjoy forgiveness and eternal life! You have shed your blood for the salvation of your country, Jesus shed his for the salvation of the soul; you die for his friends, Jesus died for his enemies. Oh, John, just think of his matchless love, and be no longer impenitent! Does his compassion move you? does not the very thought of these things touch your heart?" "Yes, chaplain, they do; but my heart is so hard, I can't feel my sins forgiven." "Do you feel sorry for your sins?" "Yes, I do; but not as I ought." "Would you not like to be a Christian?" "Oh, yes, I would; but my heart is so hard." "Yes, but Jesus can soften and change it." "Can't you trust him?" "I will try." "He is able, willing, mighty to save! Just forsake sin, and let go self, and throw yourself right into the arms of Jesus, and he will save you. Only 'believe on the Lord Jesus Christ, and thou shalt be saved.' Pray, pray, like the publican, 'God be merciful to me a sinner!' Pray, like sinking Peter, 'Lord, save me!' and just come to Jesus now, just as you are, and salvation is sure." Calling on him again in a few days, we found him indulging a hope, and said, "He thought he would not be afraid to die, and that he could die happy." He grew worse, and died November 18, 1864, exclaiming, "Where is the chaplain?" Patients often called for the chaplain at the approach of death.

"JUST AS GOD WISHES."

It was on a cold, cloudy day in November, with the whistling wind whirling around the patient's narrow bed, when we approached Wm. Brown, Co. I, 117th N. Y., lying quite low with a severe wound in the leg. But upon canvassing his heart, we found him, though weak in body, strong in faith, clinging to the cross, with bright prospects of a glorious immortality beyond the grave. Resigned and submissive, he said, "Though life is sweet, I am not afraid to die. I can say, God's will be done. *Just as he wishes.*" "How precious the attainment! Just as God wishes, whether I live or die. I suppose you feel very happy?" "Oh, yes; I am happy. To die is gain." "Have you any doubts about your salvation?" "No; I *know* in whom I have believed, and am persuaded that he will grant me a seat at his right hand at the last day." Lying in the arms of Jesus, he seemed to say, with Paul, "I am now ready. I have fought a good fight, I have finished my course, I have kept the faith: henceforth there is laid up for me a crown of righteousness." Oh, how sublime the consummation! How glorious the victory! willing to die for your country, and just waiting to die in the Lord. Just waiting to drop the garment of mortality and be clothed with a glorious immortality. Lingering till December 10, 1864, God gave the word, and said, "Come up higher," and, robed in white, doubtless he went home to glory. "Be ye also ready, for in such an hour as ye think not, the Son of man cometh."

"TELL MY MOTHER I DIED HAPPY,"

Said Lorenzo D. Steward, 11th Me., Co. K, as we were canvassing his tender heart. It was his dying message to an affectionate mother. He freely confessed his waywardness in the army; but at our first interview seemed quite penitent and anxious about his salvation. "I would like to be saved," he said, "and meet my Father in heaven." "Seeing you are so anxious about salvation, I hope you have correct views of the way to be saved." "I trust I have, sir." "What must we do to be saved?" "Believe on the Lord Jesus Christ." "Yes, that's it. Salvation is *free*. Yes, free as the air we breathe. God says, 'Look and live.' Do you feel sorry for your sins?" "I trust I do." "How does the Saviour appear to you?" "He appears dear and precious." "Think you love Jesus?" "I believe I do." "Love is the *principal* thing. 'Love is the fulfilling of the law.' Love to Christ is the *essence* and the very *core* of Christianity. We may say our prayers, shed our tears, make the loudest professions, unite with the church, go to the Lord's table, bestow all our goods to feed the poor, die for our country, and give our bodies to be burned, yet without *love to Christ*, we are as sounding brass or a tinkling cymbal; yea, '*we are nothing*.' The great, heart-searching question the Saviour put to Peter, was, '*Lovest thou* ME?' The question is not do you love your wife, children, parents, or sister. It is not do you love your country? No; it is higher, purer, holier, and more important far than all these. It is do you love the SAVIOUR? Nothing but supreme love to God will ever raise the soul to heaven. The question is not do you *profess* to love. It is not do you *hope* or *expect* to love. No; but do you love *now?* Think you can answer the question as did weeping Peter? 'Yea, Lord, thou *knowest* that I love thee.'" "I believe I can." "Do you feel the love of Christ constraining you?" "Yes; it seems to draw me nearer and nearer unto him. Oh, the love of Christ! *Oh, the love of Christ!* How VAST! how great and powerful! How *precious* is Jesus to my soul. I feel so happy. I have no fear of death. I believe to die will be gain, and to depart will be far better." Outriding the storms of life till November 28, 1864, the silver cord was broken, and, with his soul washed in Christ's blood, he went, we trust, home to heaven. "Blessed are the dead who die in the Lord."

"IT IS EASIER TO SERVE SATAN."

Upon entering a ward of colored patients, one day, and while canvassing the heart of Charles Pearson, 22d U. S., Co. H, colored, and finding that he was still "out of the way," I asked him why he chose to serve Satan? He promptly replied, "It is easier." "Easier? What! is the devil an easier master than the Saviour? is the service of him who walketh about as a roaring lion, seeking whom he may devour, easier than the service of Him who came from heaven to earth to seek, suffer, bleed, and die to save? is 'the snare of the devil' easier than the cross of Christ? is the road to hell easier than the road to heaven? is it easier, Charles?" "It is easier, chaplain, till you get in the right way." "It is always easier to swim down stream than to swim up against a strong current. Lost by the fall, blinded by sin, led captive and deceived by Satan, to the unrenewed to serve him is more natural and easy, although Christ's yoke is far easier and his burden far lighter. Yet Satan is a hard master. Contrast him with Christ: Satan is a liar, Christ is 'the truth;' Christ was always a Saviour, but the devil was always a murderer; Satan seeks to destroy, Christ to save; Satan will lead you down to hell, Christ will lead you up to heaven! Oh, then, choose ye this day whom ye will serve! Cut loose from the world, divorce thyself from Satan, let go self, escape for thy life, fly, fly to Jesus; look and live; believe and be saved! Sin hath its pleasures, but 'at the last it biteth like a serpent, and stingeth like an adder.' Look to God for strength; go forward in Christ's name; and if Satan assaults you, charge against him with the sword of the Spirit, and you will always put him to flight. But to triumph over the devil is not enough. To be safe, you must embrace Christ. Only enlist under his banner, and you will find his yoke easy and his burden light. In his presence there is fulness of joy, and at his right hand there are pleasures forevermore."

"I AM BETTER IN THE ARMY THAN AT HOME."

Notwithstanding the distressing apprehensions and the awful forebodings entertained by some patriotic mothers at home, when their sons entered the service of their country, dreading the contaminating and corrupting influences of the army, and greatly fearing lest they would come home "spoiled and ruined," they almost refused to let them go; yet we find that the army was not such a great *demoralizer* after all. At the close of the war, one million of soldiers go home, receiving the most hearty welcome, accompanied with sumptuous dinners and the most enthusiastic demonstrations of joy upon their safe return, and the glorious victory they achieved. And each one going to his respective home, again enjoys and mingles with his old surviving friends, exerting his influence upon them, and still the moral stamina of society does not seem to have diminished. It is true some became worse, but many were made better by army life. The fact is, the religious interest in the army, in many places, was far greater than ordinarily at home. Hence we not unfrequently hear soldiers express themselves as did Marquis Davis, 118th N. Y., Co. A, "I am better in the army than at home," as we talked about the trials, deprivations, and temptations of army life. Said he, "I have quit swearing in the army. I pray daily; all my trust is in God; and the Saviour is dear and precious." "Pretty well for the army, Marquis! Better here than at home?" "Yes; I have quit swearing, and tried to reform and do better." "Think you have been converted in the army?" "I hope so; but the evidences are not quite as bright as I would like." "You have some doubts, eh!" "Yes; but I have a strong, abiding hope." "Jesus says, 'Come unto me, and I will give you rest.' Just go to God with your case, and make a full, complete surrender of yourself to him who gave himself for you, and all will be well. Ask God for brighter evidences, and he will give it. 'Open thy mouth wide, and I will fill it.' Thomas had doubts, and said, 'Except I shall see in his hands the print of the nails, and thrust my hand into his side, I will not believe. And Jesus said unto him, reach hither thy hand, and behold my hands; and reach hither thy hand, and thrust it into my side; and be no longer faithless, but believing.' And Thomas answered and said unto him, 'My Lord and my God!' His doubts were removed by looking to Christ. Thomas looked with the natural eye; but if you only will look with the eye of faith, Jesus will remove your doubts, and you will be enabled to say, 'My Lord and my God!' Many good Christians at times have doubts;

UNCLE JACOB.

yet it is the believer's privilege to rise above them, and say, with Job, 'I know that my Redeemer liveth.' Pray on, brother; strive to grow in grace; 'go on unto perfection,' until you shall be made complete in Christ and filled with all the fulness of God. If you will only be earnest and faithful, army life will tend to help you on to God. The shock of battle, the stare of death's grim visage, the dreadful carnage, the groans of the wounded and dying, and dear comrades falling around you, together with the stern realities of eternity rising in full view, and the solemn thought, 'I don't know how soon it may be my turn to fall,' are all well calculated to quicken and arouse the most thoughtless sinner. Hence we feel like saying, that doubtless many have been converted in the army who never would have been reached at home. God has his own way of doing his own work."

WILLIAM J. JOHNSON, 142D N. Y., CO. D.,

Was severely wounded during the last year of the war, and brought to Hampton Hospital, and put in a tent, ward number twenty-three. Shot through the left breast, the ball passing through the lungs, he lay for several months upon his back, and suffered severely. William was a kind, good boy, and highly esteemed by all who knew him. Genteel, patient, and neat in his person and manners, everything about him was calculated to win: he was a particular favorite of the matron and ward-master. On approaching him on the subject of religion, he said, "God has done great things for me." "What has he done for you?" "I hope he has forgiven my sins; and I believe he will save me. I put my trust in him, and hope and pray he will raise me." "If you will only trust in God, and believe on the Lord Jesus Christ, your salvation is sure. Salvation is free and ready, and offered without money and without price, upon the conditions of faith and repentance." "Do you feel sorry for your sins?" "I trust I do." "God says, 'Except ye repent, ye shall all likewise perish.' We must all turn or die, believe or be lost." We visited him very often, reading and praying in his tent, urging him to give his heart to God, and cling to the cross.

Brave and patriotic, William bore all his sufferings like a young hero. Patient and resigned, he was always cheerful and happy. Although other patients died around him, William lived on, notwithstanding his severe, dangerous wound, always lively and hopeful. We left him getting better.

"ALL IS WELL."

"Well, William, how are you to-day?" "I feel tolerably well to-day, chaplain." "Gaining a little, eh?" "Yes, a little." "How are you spiritually? Are you soldiering for Christ as well as for your country?" "I don't know: I have lived rather a careless life; but I feel somewhat interested in religion now." I visited him very often, and preached, talked to and prayed with him, and he enjoyed it very much. Though a non-professor, he seemed now, March 20, 1865, on my second visit, to be indulging a good hope. On my approaching him, he wept, and, raising his frail hand, grasped mine most heartily, and appeared to be very happy, and said, "I feel that I could fly away to Jesus." As he saw and felt death approaching, he said, "This (*i. e.* approaching death,) will fetch 'em." "Fetch who?" "Fetch sinners to repentance." "Yes, the approach of 'the king of terrors' often brings men to their feelings, and makes them think and feel very differently from what they had ever done before. I suppose, as you feel as though you could fly away to Jesus, that you are very happy?" "Yes," he said, with deep emotions, "I feel happy in the Lord." Lingering along till March 25, his mortal machinery gave way, and with the dying, consoling words "All is well!" he left this sublunary world, and went, we trust, to dwell with the sanctified above. His name was William F. Smith, 7th Conn., Co. D. How consoling to surviving friends, to die with the happy, "All is well" on the lips! "To depart is far better."

"OLD JACOB," THE GRAVE-DIGGER.

"It takes all sorts of people to make a world," and although "God hath made of one blood all nations of men to dwell on all the face of the earth," yet he has made every man with his peculiar traits and peculiar fitness for some particular position in life. Some are born to rule, others to obey. Some to wield the sword, others the pen. Some to fight and make war, others to reconcile and make peace. When God was about to publish the moral law, and deliver the captive hosts of Israel from Egyptian bondage, he raised up a Moses well fitted for the great work. When a new world was to be discovered, God raised up a Columbus to search and find it. When the gospel was to be sent to the Gentile world, a learned Paul, armed with the panoply of heaven, and with a heart burning with zeal, was raised up, thoroughly furnished for the great and arduous work. When 4,000,000 of slaves were to be emancipated, an Abraham Lincoln steps upon the political arena, walks into the presidential chair, and with a stroke of the pen cuts their bonds asunder. When Dr. Eli McClellan, assistant surgeon of the U. S. A., and surgeon in charge of the U. S. Gen. Hospital, Fortress Monroe, Va., noted for his executive ability, wanted a man to superintend the digging of graves for the departed soldiers, he made a wise choice in the selection of "Old Jacob," of Hampton, Va. With four or five other colored men, under his care, he was entrusted with this laborious work. Always known by the familiar name, "Old Jacob," I never learned his proper name. But judging from his history and from his appearance, his frank, open countenance, the simplicity of his manners, his meek disposition, and marked piety, we suppose he possessed many of the distinguished traits that characterized Jacob of old. At the burying of the soldiers, he always behaved with marked reverence and propriety. With his hoary head bared, with his spade in one hand and hat in the other, he always listened to the funeral services with profound attention, and, judging from his deep sighs and profuse tears, he was evidently very deeply impressed with the solemn scene. There was something noble and prepossessing in his appearance. In fact, he possessed so many marked features and striking traits of character, that the distinguished Abbott, in getting up illustrations, and in preparing a lengthy article on the hospital, for Harpers' Monthly Magazine, put in his portrait, accompanied with a brief sketch of his life. If you look in the August Number of 1864, you will see "Old Jacob," natural as life, with his big white eye, broad-brimmed hat, with his spade in hand, standing beside a soldier's grave, in the soldiers' graveyard at Hampton, Va. Besides digging graves, and burying the dead, he had the supervision of exhuming the dead to be sent home. And so great was the pressure in this unpleasant, sickly work, in the fall of 1864, that "Old Jacob" worked himself to death. At least he got sick, and died December 4, 1864, at Hampton, Va. Gone, we trust, to realize the blessedness of dying in the Lord.

"THE BIBLE BETTER THAN GREENBACKS."

Although the great mass of our soldiers were Americans, we found in the ranks men from almost every nation of the earth. The Germans and Irish were numerous. With a small sprinkle of English, French, and Scotch, we frequently met with the Swiss, the Italian, the Polander, the Russian, the Dane, and the Canadian, and, in a few instances, with "the poor Indian," wearing the soldier's garb, with Uncle Sam's large glittering "U. S." sticking upon his blue cap. While visiting the brave boys of ward No. 27, we accosted John Nichols, of the Oneida tribe, and belonging to the 29th Reg., Co. B, of Conn. Vol.; and as we were conversing about religion, the war, and the country, we were somewhat surprised to learn his high appreciation of the word of God. He said, "Instead of giving the recruit greenbacks, the Government should give him the Bible. The country is too much for greenbacks," he said. Deeply impressed with the horrors of war and of the value of human life, he said, "It is not right to fight and kill so many." Possessed with a humane spirit and being tired of the war, and failing doubtless to realize the great interests involved in the great struggle, he said, "I wish I had never enlisted." He was the only soldier I ever heard express his regret for having entered the service. And although there may have been, in some cases, an undue thirst for greenbacks among this war spirit, yet we did not expect such a reproof as the above, "The country is too fond of greenbacks," from an Oneida Indian. And how very significant the suggestion, "Better give the recruit the Bible than give him greenbacks." "Although money answereth all things," as Solomon said, yet "the love of it is the root of all evil." Money, as "the sinews of war," is good and important; yet the poor Indian says, "for the recruit the Bible is better." And so it is. Armed with the weapons not carnal, which it provides, man is made mighty through God to the pulling down of strongholds. "As you seem to think so much of the Bible, I suppose you read and study it carefully?" "Yes; I carry one along with me, and read it every day." "Do you try to live up to its precepts?" "Yes, I try; but not as I ought." "God says, 'In keeping them, there is great reward.' The Bible says, 'Watch and pray.' Do you pray?" "Not much now. I prayed at home." "Prayed at home; but not much now! In the army is the very place, above all others, where we all ought to pray. Here, where we are exposed to so many temptations, we should pray always." Warning him of his danger, and urging him to immediate repentance, and beseeching him to fly to the Saviour, we bid him good-by. He got well.

"SOMEHOW IT WORKED UPON ME."

"Good-morning, Stephen! How do you do to-day?" "I am some better to-day, chaplain, I thank you. My wound is better, and my appetite is improving; and I am gaining strength, and coming up every way." "How are you religiously?" "I am all right religiously, I think, sir. I have been a great swearer and an awful wicked man, but I feel that I have undergone a great change lately." "Be not deceived, God is not mocked. Our hearts are so deceitful, we may think we are all right when we are all wrong. It is a very nice point to be 'all right.'" "Yes, I know it is, chaplain; but I feel that I am a converted man." "When were you converted?" "About three months ago." "Where?" "In Chestnut Hill Hospital, near Philadelphia, Pa." "What were the means of your conversion?" "A worldly man read a chapter in the Bible in the ward, one day, and *somehow it worked upon me*, while we were playing bluff. I went to church, and prayed, and thought on God." "You seemed to have been deeply convicted by hearing that chapter of the word of God?" "Yes, my sins seemed very great and heavy; but I believe now God has forgiven me; and I feel prepared, and am not afraid to die. God is all my trust; besides him there is no Saviour; neither is there salvation in any other, for there is no other name under heaven given among men whereby we must be saved." "There is only *one* way of salvation. That is enough. Jesus says, 'I am the way.'" "Yes, chaplain, that is enough. I feel that the Lord has done great things for me!" "And all brought about by that worldly man reading a chapter in the Bible?" "Yes, that has been owned and blessed of God, I believe, to my salvation." "What a glorious work: 'A great swearer' saved through a worldly man's reading a chapter in the Bible! How clearly this demonstrates that 'the word of God is quick and powerful;' that 'the law of the Lord is perfect, converting the soul.' Somehow it worked upon you?" "Yes." "But I suppose you cannot tell how?" "No, I cannot tell particularly; light seemed to flash upon my mind; I saw and felt my sins were great, and, realizing my need of a Saviour, I cried to God for mercy; and I believe he has changed my heart and washed my guilty soul." "Yes, it is all mysterious. The word of God is the instrument, and the Spirit of God is the agent, in conversion. We know, in this great change, that the mind is enlightened, that the will is subdued, and the heart changed; but as to the manner how it is effected is mysterious. The Saviour compares the operations of the Spirit in regeneration to the blowing of the wind, which 'we can't tell whence it cometh or whither it goeth; so is every one that is born of the Spirit.' All we can tell about it is, as you say, 'Somehow it worked upon me.' We know it by the effects produced, as we know that the wind blows, because we can feel it, and see its effects; so we may know that we are converted, although we cannot tell *how* the change was brought about." And, as we see in such a striking manner the power of God's word in this case how all-important is it to "Search the Scriptures." And inasmuch as this "great swearer" was converted through the instrumentality of "a man of the world," how strong are the inducements for sinners to labor for the conversion of sinners; or, in the language of the Spirit and the bride, "let him that heareth say, come."

"GOD STILL STICKS TO ME."

During the last few months of my labors in the hospital, I very frequently conversed with JOHN JONES, Co. E, of the 10th Reg. Western Va. Vol. He lay in the western end of ward number two, noted for containing so many badly wounded patients. He was severely wounded in one of the last battles near Petersburg, Va., and brought to the hospital soon after. He said he had been converted in the army, and that he enjoyed religion, and that he derived much comfort from it. When I asked him, "Do you trust in the Saviour?" he promptly replied, "I will trust in him till I die. Jesus is my guide until death." Conscious of his need of help, and realizing his dependence upon God, he was very anxious to be prayed for. I preached to him, conversed and prayed with him very often; and he seemed to grow in grace until May 27, when he appeared to rise above all doubts, and was enabled to say, "All is well; I am going to die." "Would you be afraid to die?" "Oh, no; I have no fear of death. When 'all is well,' to die is gain, and to depart is far better." Wrapped in a kind of vision, he said, "I heard singing in heaven last night, as I awoke out of sleep." Patient, humble, meek, and resigned, although his sufferings were long and severe, not a murmur was heard to fall from his lips. He was so submissive that he seemed to lie passive in the arms of Jesus. At another interview, among other strong expressions of his faith, he said, "God still sticks to me." "Do you *feel* his presence?" "Oh, yes; he is very near to me." "And do you still try to stick to him?" "Yes; though he slay me, yet will I trust in him." "May God bless you, and enable you to 'stand fast in the Lord.' God commands us to 'war a good warfare,' to contend earnestly, to fight, and strive to enter in at the straight gate. 'Jesus is a friend that sticketh closer than a brother.' Just cling to and hold on to him, and he will bring you off more than conqueror. How grand and glorious your position!" Gazing into the eternal world, with its stern realities rising in full view, with death knocking at his door, he was able to say, "All is well." What an all-comprehensive word! Spiritually, it implies pardon, resignation, peace, joy, readiness, and willingness to die and go home to glory. John Jones stood the battle of life until June 21, 1865, when it seemed the victory was complete, and his blood-washed soul, we trust, went home to heaven. "Blessed are the dead who die in the Lord."

"OH, CHAPLAIN! WHAT WILL I DO?"

Most earnestly and piteously exclaimed JOHN CURRY, when I approached him as he lay upon his long occupied bed in the corner of a tent in the north part of "New Camp." "Do you ask what to do to be saved?" "Yes," weeping profusely. "Trust in the Lord. Believe in the Lord Jesus Christ, and thou shalt be saved. There, John, is the plan of salvation in a nutshell. '*Only believe.*' Renounce and let go of everything else, and throw yourself right into the arms of Jesus, and he will save you." I had visited him often before, and as I approached him this time, he warmly grasped my hand, threw his arm around my neck, and hugged me up to him very affectionately. He seemed very penitent and prayerful; and after pointing him again to the Saviour, holding him up to him as one able, willing, and mighty to save, and beseeching him by the mercies of God to come unto him, at his request I read and prayed with him. He belonged to the army of the James, but having forgotten to note down his company, we cannot tell to what regiment he belonged. He was wounded May 9, 1864, in battle, and had his leg cut off on the field. "Johnnie" was a good boy, generous, kind, and affable; he was highly esteemed by all who knew him. Indeed, he was a favorite of the camp. His long, severe sufferings elicited the sympathies of the matron, and she took good care of him. Chaplain Raymond visited and prayed with him also.

At my next call, finding him still anxious about his salvation, I urged him still stronger to surrender himself to the Saviour, and besought him, by the example of the prodigal son, to make up his mind to become a Christian. " Look at that poor prodigal, John. He had everything plenty at home, but becoming dissatisfied, he demanded his fortune, and, on receiving it, took a journey into a far country, where he wasted his substance in riotous living. By-and-by there arose a mighty famine in that land, and he began to be in want. After a while he began to consider, and when he came to himself, he said, 'How many hired servants in my father's house have bread enough and to spare, and I perish here with hunger.' He makes up his mind, and says, in words grave and sublime, 'I will arise, I will arise, and go to my father, and will say unto him: Father, I have sinned against heaven, and in thy sight. I am no more worthy to be called thy son,' and feeling his unworthiness, he prays to be made as one of his servants. Here are two very encouraging facts, John. *First*, the perishing sinner, or the wandering prodigal, *resolves* to return, and says, 'I *will* arise;' and *second*, as the *result* of his resolution, we *soon* find him at home in his father's house. Oh, then, John, let me entreat you this day to resolve to come to God. Now, *will you* arise? Your country called, and you obeyed. You have already lost your leg, and will probably soon lose your life. But the loss of a limb and the loss of your life are both great, but nothing compared with the loss of your immortal soul. Oh, then, look and live, believe and be saved. Think of the *love* of Christ in suffering and dying to save you. And here he is, here in your tent, crying, ' Come unto me, and I will give you rest.'

'Jesus ready stands to save,
Full of pity, love, and power.'"

He was much engaged in prayer, and, though brought up a Catholic, he now seemed to be a converted boy. Surviving the warm months of summer, he fell with the autumn leaf, about the middle of October, 1864, and went, we trust, to swell the ranks of the redeemed in heaven.

"I AM ON THE DEVIL'S SIDE."

Although there is some similarity in the religious views, feelings, and experiences of the soldiers, there is also something new and peculiar in almost every case. In canvassing the stony heart of Henry Campbell, 13th Tenn., Co. B, though frank and free to talk on religious topics, we found him indifferent about the one thing needful. When I questioned him about his manner of life, he frankly replied, "I have lived a careless and prayerless life; but I have recently quit swearing." "To quit swearing is a very encouraging step; it is a sign of a purpose to reform. And yet we may reform to some extent outwardly without any reformation at heart. The world is divided into two great parties. Satan has his party, and Christ has his. And as Moses, when he came down from the mount, filled with indignation upon beholding the idolatry of the children of Israel, exclaimed, 'Who is on the Lord's side,' here let me ask 'on whose side are you, Henry?'" "I am on the devil's side," he replied. "Why don't you come over?" "Oh, I don't know; I mean to do better hereafter." "You mean to do better hereafter? Why not now? God says, '*Now* is the accepted time;' God '*now* commandeth all men everywhere to repent.'" "Yes; but I don't want to be in a hurry, sir." "You ought to be. Time is short. David made haste, and delayed not to keep God's commandments." "I don't suppose I am ready to become a Christian now." "You say you are on the devil's side; and you know the certain result of dying in his service is endless torment. Are you making any efforts to become a Christian?" "Yes; I try to pray, but cannot make much out." "Perhaps you do not try much, or it may be you pray better than you suppose. Prayer is not eloquence of speech, but brokenness of heart and contrition of soul. It is the heart that prays. You may have fine words and beautiful sentences, and have no prayer. Prayer is very simple. It is asking God for what you want. If you are hungry, you know how to ask for bread. If you want salvation, ask God, believing, and he will grant it. Prayer is really a means of power. In answers to the prayers of the church,

Peter was released from prison. In answer to prayer, fire falls from heaven, the blind see, the lame walk, devils are cast out, the lost are saved, and the dead are made alive. The publican prayed, 'God be merciful to me a sinner,' and his sins were pardoned. Sinking Peter prayed, 'Lord, save me!' and immediately Jesus rescued him from a watery grave. The dying thief prayed, 'Jesus, Lord, remember me!' and his soul was snatched from a gaping hell, and wafted home to heaven. And if you will pray earnestly, God will save you."

"PRAY FOR ME, CHAPLAIN, TILL I DIE,"

Exclaimed the noble young SAMUEL RUFENER, 116th Ohio, Co. E, as his life was rapidly ebbing away, from wounds received in one of the last great battles at Petersburg, Va. I had gone over to the boat, and while searching for mortally wounded men, the brave-hearted Rufener caught my eye, as he lay upon his narrow bed, with his mangled body bathed in his own blood. Seeing that he was nigh unto death, I canvassed his warm heart, and took down his spiritual diagnosis, on the boat, before I left him, lest he might die before reaching the hospital. Upon examining the grounds of his hopes for the future, he said "he trusted in the Lord." "He is the only way of salvation," I replied. "How does the Saviour appear to you?" "He seems dear and precious to me; he is a very present help in trouble." He seemed to enjoy religion, and said that he loved the Saviour. Pointing him to the cross, and commending him to the mercy of God, we left him and passed on, looking for others. He was always of easy access, pleasant, and free to talk. Conscious of his dependence upon God, he was prayerful, and accustomed to hardness, suffering, and death, and entertaining "a good hope," he seemed composed and resigned. He was carried on a stretcher to ward number two and laid on bed No. 35, where I again talked and preached to him and his ward a few hours before he died. He was very anxious to have me remain with him. And although it is now six years since he fell, and although I visited hundreds of patients daily, we remember his case very well. Asking him again about his spiritual condition, he responded, "I feel happy in the Lord;" and believing in the power of prayer, he anxiously said to me, "Pray for me till I die." This was April 7, 1865, his last day on earth, as he departed that night; and, having laid down his life for his country, he went, we trust, to dwell with Him who laid down his life that we might live. Though he lived through the war, and fell in the last great struggle, it was a satisfaction to see the rebellion quelled, notwithstanding it cost him his life. The following touching letter was received from the family to which he belonged, soon after his death. It is full of sorrow and affection.

HANNIBAL, MO. COUNTY OHIO,
May 5th, 1865.

CHAPLAIN A. S. BILLINGSLEY.

MY DEAR FRIEND, AND BROTHER IN CHRIST: Grace be to you!—Again I take the pen to inform you that we received your letters which contained the sad message of our dear son and brother Samuel, that he died at Fortress Monroe, Va. It was surely a hard stroke for us. But we know the Lord makes everything right; we therefore say, "Lord, not our, but thy will be done." We feel very thankful to God that we can hear that he was happy in the Lord, and enjoyed religion; this is of more worth to us than if you could tell us he owned ten worlds, and died without it. We know, if we hold out faithful till our end, we shall all get to see him, and "meet to part no more." Oh, how I long for the time to come! I often felt, to say so, homesick for my eternal home; but now I feel it more and more, my dear brother is there! Oh, that I was there! I know my dear Saviour will come, and will take me home sooner or later. I will still try to make my way to heaven. Jesus is the best friend I have: I know that my Redeemer lives; he saved me from my lost estate. I hope to find you once in heaven, where I can tell you my feelings better than now. We hope and pray to God that he may repay you richly for your love and kindness which you have showed so kindly toward us, but most to our dear Samuel. We hope you will find the fruit in heaven which you have sowed at Fortress Monroe.

Dear friend: we received a letter from Mrs. Capt. A. Ingram, from the eighth of April, 1865, in which she told us that he gave her his pocket-book to send home, which contained ten dollars; but she gave it back to him. If it is there, get it. We wish you could take some of it for your trouble; and if there will be something left, if you please, send it by mail to us. His other effects, we think, are not much of any account. The remains of his body we will let lay where they are. Jesus will find and call them there as well as here. Last Sunday, Rev. J. C. Kopp, German Methodist preacher, preached the funeral for him over the text recorded in the Revelation of St. John, 14th chapter, 13th verse. It was a blessed time for our souls. I must close.

Dear sir: I would like to know where you live when at home; it might happen that I could see you once yet on this world; therefore I would like to have your direction, if you could send it. My father would have wrote to you; but we are German people, and he cannot write English; excuse him therefore. Excuse my bad writing and mistakes.

We all love you dearly, and feel thankful to God and to you. May God bless you richly. Our best love and respects to you.
     Your true
           Friends.

"I WOULD AS SOON GO TO MY HEAVENLY HOME."

"The power of association is great, and the exercise of that power often produces feelings both pleasing and mournful to the soul." Returning, for example, after a long absence, to the grave of a beloved father, mother, brother, sister, little babe, and how do the mournful scenes of the past crowd upon you! Pierced with sorrow, bathed in tears, and hushed in silence, you stand around the sacred spot, and, under the influence of heightened emotions, you are ready to speak to the very dead, and say, "Farewell to the dearest object of your tenderest affections." I have seen the bereaved widow, riding in the cars, suddenly burst into tears upon passing the fatal spot where her dear husband had been accidentally killed by striking his head against a telegraph post. And I have seen soldiers, whom you could scarcely touch with the melting scenes of Gethsemane and Calvary, melt into tears when you would begin to talk to them about mother, and the pleasures of home. Merely to *speak* of that sweet word, would stir his soul and touch his heart, and so far, for a time, transfer him back to old scenes and associations that he would revel in the sweet recollections of past enjoyments. "And yet," said Hiram Dickson, 112th N. Y., Co. D, "I would as soon go to my heavenly home as to my native home," as we were conversing with him about his spiritual interests. "That is a very wise choice, Hiram; heaven is always preferable to earth, notwithstanding all its grandeur and glory. Paul, when lying and suffering severely in a dingy prison at Rome, in view of his expected speedy departure, with a full foretaste of heaven, exclaimed, 'To die is gain, and to depart is far better.'" At our first interview with this heroic patriot, we found him exhibiting every mark of penitence and resignation. He said that he had sought and found the Saviour in the low lands of Florida, and that he had been enjoying a bright hope for several months. At his request, we often read and prayed with him; and being full of faith, he derived such a degree of comfort from God's promises and a Saviour's love that he preferred his home in heaven to his home on earth. And well he might, because, with all the endearments and enjoyments of home, it is nothing compared to heaven. Here, we are infants; there, perfect men in Christ Jesus. Here, we are soldiers in battle; there, kings and priests unto God, crowned with glory and honor. Here, we suffer and fight; there, we reign and rejoice forevermore. The Christian sometimes on earth gets so near to God, and enjoys such a bright manifestation of his presence, that he realizes "a joy unspeakable and full of glory." Enjoying this in a high degree, Payson said, "I seemed to swim in a flood of glory, which rolled around me like a sea of light." Edwards, while alone in a solitary mountain, enjoyed such a sense of God's presence, that he seemed entirely detached from the world, and lost and "swallowed up in God." John Welsh exclaimed, shortly before he died, "Lord, hold thy hand: it is enough; thy servant is a clay vessel, and can hold no more." Oh, what unspeakable bliss there is to be enjoyed here on earth. And yet all this is but an earnest of heaven. Here the wicked trouble, but the moment we pass "the threshold of glory," they cease, and the rest remaineth undisturbed forever. There, enshrined in God, and wearing crowns of glory and palms of victory, the redeemed will sit down upon God's throne, and forever rule and reign with him in glory. And even there, bathed "in seas of heavenly rest," will doubtless advance from strength to strength and from glory to glory, and, like two mathematical lines, be forever drawing nearer and nearer unto God, without ever reaching that which is inaccessible. There are no stations in heaven. No: doubtless it is one *eternal progression* in light, joy, and glory. There, even the angels, with all their knowledge and perfection, desire to learn and look into the mysteries of redemption. How much soever we may know and enjoy of Christ here, our cry still is, "My soul thirsteth for God." And doubtless, when we will have been there ten thousand years, our cry will still be the same, "My soul thirsteth for God." Moses, with all his glorious sights, near approaches, and close communions with God, still longs for more, and earnestly prays, "God, I beseech thee, show me thy glory." Paul, though twenty years in Christ, when caught up to the third heaven, and saw what was not possible for man to utter, yet, like a babe in Christ, still prays, "That I may know him." Glorious, wonderful progression! Seated on God's throne, and yet rising higher and higher. Dwelling in God, and yet forever drawing nearer and nearer unto him. Filled with all the fulness of God, and yet forever filling. And even there, upon these lofty heights of grandeur and glory, will be heard a voice issuing from the throne, "Come up higher! come up higher!" And it was, no doubt, Hiram Dickson's clear conception of the happiness and glory of heaven that led him to prefer "his heavenly to his native home." He had seen something of worldly and military glory. He had seen one mighty army fight and vanquish another, and retire from the gory field crowned with glory and honor. But what, we ask, are these and *all* earthly glory, compared with "the eternal weight of glory at God's right hand." Contrast earth with heaven. How is earth dwarfed, eclipsed, and cast into the shade. Lying tranquil in the arms of Jesus, he lingered until January 18, 1864, when his disembodied spirit, washed in a Saviour's blood, went home to dwell with God. "To die is gain."

"I AM TOO WICKED TO COME TO JESUS."

"What! too wicked to come to Jesus! Oh, no; what makes you think so? Christ's love, mercy, and power are all infinite, and he can save a big sinner just as easy as a little one. His atonement is of infinite value. His blood cleanseth from *all* sin." "I know he says so; but I am such a great sinner." "Yes; but Christ is a great Saviour: he is able, willing, mighty to save, even to the uttermost, all that cometh unto God by him. David urges the greatness of his sins as an argument for pardon, and prays in these remarkable words, 'For thy name's sake, O Lord, pardon mine iniquity; for it is great.' Then, don't be discouraged; your great wickedness is no hindrance in coming to Jesus. No; the greater your sins, the greater your need of a Saviour. If you had no sin, you would have no need of a Saviour. Jesus has saved some of the vilest sinners. Paul, the blasphemer and persecutor, called himself the *chief* of sinners, but Jesus saved him. Manasseh was a great sinner, guilty of witchcraft, gross idolatry, and murder, and even made the streets of Jerusalem run red with blood, yet Jesus forgave his sins, washed and saved his soul. Jesus saved the thief on the cross. Jesus saved some of his own murderers who put him to the shameful, ignominious death of crucifixion. And do you think you are worse than they?" "Well, I suppose not." "Oh, then, be encouraged; despair not; 'while there is life, there is hope.'

'While the lamp holds out to burn,
The vilest sinner may return.'

"What kind of a life have you lived?" "I have lived careless and thoughtless about religion." "Do you ever pray?" "No." "Now do you really *feel* that you are so 'wicked'?" "Yes, I feel so." "Sin is so blinding and deceiving, that sometimes the greatest sinners have but very little conception of their sins. This, I suppose, is probably the case with you. When you deeply feel the weight of your sins, you will begin to pray, and ask God for 'pardon.' If you only *felt* your sins to be as great as you acknowledge them to be, you would begin at once to pray like the publican, 'God be merciful unto me a sinner,' or cry, like sinking Peter, 'Lord, save me.' Your great want, then, is *light* — light to see yourself as you are, and to understand the way of salvation. Oh, then, go to God in prayer. Pray like David, 'O Lord, open thou mine eyes, that I may behold wondrous things out of thy law.' You can't get rid of your sins unless you do come to Christ. He is the only sin-bearer. That dying thief, while hanging on the cross, simply prayed 'Jesus, Lord, remember me,' and the Lord saved him. Then be encouraged, and begin *now* to pray. Your sins are not so great as his were. Jesus is the same now that he was then. His blood is as efficacious now as then; and if you will only throw yourself upon his mercy, he will save you. Remember, my friend, if you ever get to heaven, you must make the start. You must forsake your evil ways; cease to do evil, and learn to do well. When the Saviour commenced preaching, he began by saying, 'Repent, repent ye; for the kingdom of heaven is at hand.' It is noble to be a soldier of your country, but it is far more important to be a soldier of the cross. You may die to save your country, and yet die and be lost. It is a very easy thing to be lost. Just live on as you have been doing, in your wilful neglect of the Saviour, and your damnation is sure. Oh, then, rise out of that thick darkness that makes you think you are 'too wicked to come to Jesus.' Such thoughts come from the devil. He is always laboring to deceive us, and keep us away from the cross. And the only remedy is to fly to Jesus just as you are. Yes, come to Jesus just as you are. You can't become any better by delay. No:

> 'The longer wisdom you despise,
> The harder is she to be won.'

Oh, then, fly to the Saviour; step right out on the promises of God, like sinking Peter, and lay hold of Christ by faith, and he will save you. May the love of Christ constrain you. May his Spirit woo you until you yield to the riches of his grace, and bow to the sceptre of his saving power. Will you try?" "I will." "The Lord help you."

"GOD GRABBED ME INTO HIS HEART AT ONCE."

It was just as the last lingering rays of the setting sun played upon the broad stripes of the dear old flag waving over the hospital, that I fell in conversation with Edmund Johnson, 37th U. S., Co. G, as he lay upon his bed in his ward. We held up before him the law, with its precepts, threats, and penalties, and the gospel with its promises and rewards. But he frankly replied, "I don't know much about it in de books; but I know something about it in my heart. I labored hard to get it into my heart." "It is well to have the law and gospel in the head; but it is far better to have it in the heart. When the Saviour said, 'Thy law is within my heart,' he exclaimed, 'I delight to do thy will, O my God!' It is having the law in our hearts that brings about our salvation; for it is the heart God seeks. It matters but little who has the head, if Satan has the heart. The heart governs. This is what gives the Christian religion such power; it takes possession of and controls the *heart;* and if you take the heart out of it, you leave it a lifeless corpse. How very wise, therefore, to 'labor hard to get it into our hearts.' How did you labor to get it into your heart? what did you do?" "I prayed; I called loud on de Lord, and he grabbed me into his heart at once." "Think you have got God in your heart?" "Yes, I think so." "Then endeavor, by all means, to hold on to him. You *in* God, and God in you; what an exalted privilege! God in us, and we in God! You must feel very happy, Edmund?" "I do feel happy, chaplain, thank God!" "Snatched from the kingdom of darkness and grabbed into God's heart, with Christ formed in you the hope of glory, you need have nothing to fear; for 'there is no condemnation to them who are in Christ Jesus.' The relation, or union, existing between Christ and the believer is very close and intimate. Christ is the vine, and the believers are the branches; hence he says, 'Because I live, ye shall live also.' Again he says, 'I in them;' therefore let us 'abide in him.' And as you have labored hard to get 'the word' and God into your heart, strive to keep it there. The way to be happy is to be faithful. 'If ye know these things, happy are ye if ye *do* them.' The connection between fidelity and happiness is inseparable. "No cross, no crown;" no fight, no victory; hence the Saviour says, 'Be thou faithful until death, and I will give thee a crown of life.'"

"I PRAYED ON, AND GOD CHANGED MY HEART."

"How do you do to-day, Jacob?" "Not very well, chaplain." "What ails you?" "Got misery about my heart, and I have no appetite to eat." "How is your heart with God?" "So far as I can judge, my heart is right with God." "Where did you get it fixed?" "In Camp Nelson, Kentucky." "When?" "One year ago." "By a right heart, I suppose you mean a *new* heart, or that you are a converted man?" "Yes, that is what I mean." "What were the means of your conversion?" "I saw men dying around me. I began to consider; and the thought struck me, I don't know how soon it may be my turn to go; and the more I thought about it, the deeper I felt concerned about my soul's salvation. The chaplain came in, read a chapter, and talked to us poor sick and wounded soldiers about Jesus, and prayed for us; and I was so deeply impressed, that I began to pray, and seek God myself. I prayed on, and sought the Lord, and, two months after, God changed my heart." "And how have you felt since?" "I feel very happy; sometimes I feel like flying away to heaven. Praying is now my daily business." "Do you have much liberty in prayer?" "Oh, yes, thank God! I feel as though I get very near the throne of grace sometimes." "A 'fixed heart' is the source of great rejoicing. David, when pursued by fierce enemies, ready to swallow him up, yet, with his heart stayed and fixed upon God, rises above all fear, and says, 'My heart is fixed, O God! my heart is fixed. I will sing and give praise!' Paul, with his heart fixed upon God, though encompassed with conflicts and trials, says, 'None of these things move me.' With his heart stayed and fixed upon God, the martyr unflinchingly burns at the stake; with his heart stayed and fixed upon God, Jesus undauntedly went forth to Calvary, longing and thirsting for the mighty conflict by which he was to rescue man from the ruins of the fall, and effect the salvation of the world." From this case, let the prayerless be encouraged to pray. The unconverted often excuse themselves from prayer, and, to maintain their position, they say, "The prayers of the wicked are an abomination unto the Lord;" yet it is the bounden duty of all to pray. God commanded Simon Magus to pray, when he was in the gall of bitterness and in the bond of iniquity. The unconverted publican prayed, "God be merciful to me a sinner!" and God heard his prayer and forgave his sins. Jacob Ellison, 114th U. S., Co. B, prayed, and he says, "God changed my heart." Therefore let none excuse themselves from this delightful duty because they are not Christians. God says, "Seek, and ye shall find." If your heart is not right with God, pray to have it fixed.

"THE DEVIL COAXED ME OFF."

Talented and shrewd, the soldiers often "got off" some sharp things. Although many of them were limited in their education, yet we frequently found among them the thoroughly educated graduate. Upon our first interview with Charles R. Akin, 4th Mass. Cavalry, Co. B, we found him of easy access, and "full of the gab." Upon approaching him on the subject of religion, he manifested a good deal of anxiety about his salvation, and expressed himself in strong terms of having already passed from death unto life. He appeared prayerful and penitent, and, said he, "I think God has forgiven my sins. God has got me, and has had me for over a year. I have not done right all that time, I know; but God has forgiven my wrongs. My wife gave me good advice at home, but the devil came along and coaxed me off." "You must beware of the devil; he is always ready to tempt and allure us into sin. If you resist him, he will flee from you. Do you feel sorry for your sins?" "Yes; but not as I ought. Yet I feel happy." "Do you think you could die happy?" "Yes, I have no doubt of it; all is bright and clear." "I am glad to see you so happy; yet it is important sometimes to examine very closely the grounds and evidence of our hopes.

Paul says, 'Let a man examine himself.' When the lukewarm Laodiceans thought themselves all right, and said they 'were rich, and had need of nothing,' the great Searcher of hearts describes them as being deceived, and says to them, 'Thou knowest not that thou art wretched, and miserable, and poor, and blind, and naked.' (Rev. iii. 17.) And you know Paul, the pharisee, thought he was all right, when he was all wrong; so it is of the utmost importance to search our hearts, review our lives, and examine very closely, lest we be deceived. Besides, close self-examination tends to growth in grace. You say God has got you, yet, as Satan sometimes 'coaxes you off,' as you say, allow me to warn you; beware, watch, and pray earnestly, lest Satan get you at last." At another conversation, he seemed to possess a confidence still more unshaken, and said, "I am all right; I am happy, happy, the happiest man on earth!" And going on in a strain of ecstatic joy, he said, "There is a foundation to my religion; I mean it." "Then stick to it. May God help and abundantly bless you." How glorious to enjoy such assurance under such trying circumstances! He sent for me, one evening, while conducting the prayer-meeting in the hall, and, on my reaching him, found him still entertaining his bright prospects. After reading a few verses of Scripture, and urging him to be steadfast, and cling to the Saviour, and commending him to God in prayer, we left him. Among his last words to me were, " Tell my wife I died happy in the Lord." This was February 10, 1865. It was very unusual to hear a patient express himself as Charles R. Akin did. Although he had lived somewhat wayward, as his comrades said, yet at the last he appeared not only very penitent, but happy. He died a few days after, and went, we trust, to the realm of peace. He belonged to the Hampton brass band, and the whole band honored him with their deep, solemn strains of music at his funeral.

CHAPTER XVI.

EXTRACTS FROM THE AUTHOR'S DIARY.

PREACHING IN THE WARDS—A MELTING PRAYER-MEETING—HOSPITAL CHURCH ORGANIZED — CHURCH CREED — A WEEPING SCENE AT THE GRAVE — THE NAKED HEART — MORTALITY INCREASING — "TRY AGAIN" — A SOLDIER'S PRAYER-MEETING — CATHOLICS TURNING PROTESTANTS — CHRISTMAS DINNER — HOLIDAYS IN U. S. HOSPITAL — WEEK OF PRAYER—THE LORD'S SUPPER—REVIVAL IN HOSPITAL.

BELIEVING that a few extracts from my army diary will interest our readers, and tend to increase the value of our little book, I here insert a few.

PREACHING IN THE WARDS.

"August 14, 1864. Preached in wards Nos. 1 and 11 this forenoon. Very good attention. First sermon, by request, from the last two verses of Psalm xix. A very good subject. The sermon in ward No. 1 was from Matt. xxiii. 37, Christ's wonderful compassion for sinners; and after the close of the service, as I was walking up the aisle of the ward, one poor sick soldier stretched out his hand to shake hands, beckoning me to come to him; and as I approached him, he said, 'You don't know how thankful I am to you for that sermon, and how much good it has done me.' He seemed very thankful. How very expressive is a warm, tender shake of the hands. Just as we were singing the last hymn,—

'A charge to keep I have,
A God to glorify,'

a sick soldier was brought into the ward dying. They laid him down, gave him a little brandy, and he swallowed it. The nurses began to rub and wash him, but in less than fifteen minutes he was dead. As we were returning from the usual funeral, Aug. 11, I saw a soldier walking close by me, weeping. I said to him,

'Was one of those we buried your brother?' 'No, sir,' he replied; 'but I never want to become insensible to death.'

"Aug. 16. Buried nineteen departed soldiers to-day. The Lord bless the sick and wounded. Prepare them for what is before them. We had a very good prayer-meeting to-night. One of the worst cases in the hospital rose, and said, 'I have been very wicked, almost the chief of sinners, it seems to me, but now I desire to seek God.' Meeting very solemn. 'O Lord, revive thy work.' Lord, humble, forgive, bless us. Another big fight at Deep Bottom. Began last Sabbath. The rebels attacked our forces, and they fought three days. Our men took two rifle-pits, drove the rebels, and took a good lot of prisoners.

"Aug. 19. Buried ten soldiers. Read from last part 1 Cor. xv. It is most glorious; it is so full of the resurrection and victory. Thank God. Visited wards Nos. 4, 5, 6, 7, 8, and led the regular prayer-meeting. Read and spoke from the story of blind Bartimeus, Mark x. 46, etc. Very good, powerful meeting; lasted over an hour and a half. One speaker sat down shouting, 'Glory be to God.' Men say, when they rise to speak, 'I can't sit still.' These meetings were characterized with much heartfelt speaking. Aug. 12. I wrote in my diary, 'It was melting to see the boys rise and speak so tenderly. It was the eloquence of the heart, and it touched the heart.'

"July 8. Visited in the wards generally. Went over to Hampton Hospital; and on approaching a suffering soldier (Spiece), with one leg cut off above the knee, he exclaimed, 'Oh, chaplain, will you pray for me?' After a few words of inquiry about his spiritual condition, and about the compassion of Jesus, I kneeled down on the ground, in the dusty tent, and prayed for him, with his aged father standing by. He is very fond of singing, and when we sung for him, 'Oh, sing to me of heaven,' etc., he went to sleep. He suffered very severely. We often sung him to sleep. And a wounded chaplain hearing our singing, sent for me to come and see him. I went, and found him badly wounded. Sang and prayed with him, comforting him with the promises and consolations of the gospel. Urging him to cling closely to the cross, and bidding him a hearty farewell, we left him with a heart glowing with love to God and gratitude to the chaplain.

"Aug. 17. Three boat-loads of wounded brought down to-day from Deep Bottom. Some four hundred in all. Two officers brought in dead. Great many very badly wounded, with arms and legs off. Met one, whose first words to me were, 'Jesus is precious to me now.' I remained on the boats, pointing the dangerous and dying to the Saviour, till half-past ten that night.

"Sept. 4. Preached three times, and two died in one of the wards where I preached."

A MELTING PRAYER-MEETING.

"To-night, Aug. 22, 1864. It was one of the most melting, contrite meetings we have witnessed for a long time. There was more contrition of soul, conviction of sin, brokenness of heart, and requesting of prayer, than I ever saw at one meeting. Visited a boat-load of sick and wounded, and pointed the worst cases to Christ: then visited New Camp. Received and read five or six letters, and answered one. Wrote a sore-footed man a letter to his wife. Visited the Gangrene Camp, and talked and prayed with the most dangerous cases. Visited colored ward number twenty-two, of sick and wounded. Talked Jesus to a tent of colored soldiers, and an old prayerless, swearing man in ward number two, until he wept tears of penitence. Buried five soldiers this morning. Read and prayed four or five times. Many confessed their sins to-night, asked to be prayed for, and gave their names as seekers and candidates for the organization of a Hospital union church. One of the greatest sinners, as he professed to be, requested to be prayed for, and gave his name as a seeker. One boy, George Moore, said, 'I would not be ashamed nor afraid to pray, if ten thousand bayonets were pointed at me.' Backsliders are returning. O Saviour, draw them nearer and still nearer unto thee!

"Sept. 4, 1864. Sabbath-day. Buried five more departed heroes. Preached three times in wards numbers seventeen, fourteen, and two. Close attention. Meetings solemn and very interesting. They seem to enjoy it very much, and invite me to come and preach again. Preaching is the only way to reach all. Two died to-day in one ward where I preached. One poor fellow, John McMaster, was shot in the throat, and died at six P.M.; the other had his leg cut off above the knee.

"Sept. 3. Prayer-meeting to-night, full, refreshing; not quite so lively and melting as at other times. Many prayed; sometimes three would commence at once, then two had to wait. We had to close with many more willing and waiting to pray. They seem to be thirsting for God, and longing to approach him in prayer. Thank God!

"Sept. 6. Read a few Psalms, Bridges on the 119th Psalm, and '*Imitation of Christ*,' by T. à Kempis; I usually read a few pages of some devotional book once or twice a day; it tends much to strengthen. Visited in wards numbers nineteen, fourteen, and sixteen; and preached in fifteen on the Philippian jailer. At the regular prayer-meeting, to-night, we resolved to organize a Hospital union church. Meeting to-night very interesting. One man rose, and said, 'A patient in ward number nineteen, as I passed by him, called me to his bedside, and requested me to pray for him, and I kneeled down and prayed for him. He seemed very thankful.' Another ward nurse said, as I was conversing with ——, 'I am going to turn a new leaf, and quit swearing, and try to serve the Lord.' Thus we see how God is carrying on his blessed work. Many are hungering for the gospel."

HOSPITAL CHURCH ORGANIZED.

"Sept. 9, 1864. A Hospital union church was organized this evening, with thirty-one members, in the dining-hall. This organization was gone into after mature deliberation between Chaplain Roe and myself, and a free consultation with the patients; and it was found to work well, notwithstanding the unsettled condition of the people. We found our organization tended to give union, action, strength, and influence to the religious element. Soldiers of the cross, like soldiers of the army, do much better, and accomplish more, with than without an organization. Jesus Christ never designed that his followers should live and spend their sojourn on earth alone; hence the organization of the church; and there are the same necessity and advantages for it in the army and hospital that exist at home. Christians of all denominations, and from all parts of the country, united under the 'banner of the cross,' can help, encourage, and protect one another in the bonds of Christian fellowship, better than when standing isolated and alone. Exposed to the strong temptations and asperities of the army, a Christian needs all the props and restraints a church can throw around him."

CHURCH CREED.

Made up of Christians of all denominations, our articles of religion, or confession of faith, were short, plain, and comprehensive. Here it is:

Art. 1. "God being my helper, I will try to the best of my ability to be a Christian."

Art. 2. "I will take the word of God for my guide, and trust in Christ alone for salvation."

Art. 3. "I solemnly pledge myself to abstain from profane language, from alcoholic drinks as a beverage, and from all other vices in the army and camp, and will be a true soldier of my country and of the cross."

Art. 4. "I will earnestly strive to win souls to Christ, and will faithfully try to watch over my Christian brother."

Without affecting other church connections at home, the reader will at once perceive that our creed was broad, orthodox, strong, and comprehensive. Its adoption led to the further development of the religious element, to self-examination, gave tangibility to our efforts, and seemed to be greatly blessed of God to the furtherance of the cause of Christ. This "little flock" increased rapidly, and soon numbered over a hundred. Christians of all denominations, without regard to sects, united in this common brotherhood; and denominationalism was so far swallowed up in the great cause of saving souls, that we but seldom inquired to what church an individual belonged. Wherever we found a man wearing the image of Christ, we were glad to receive him into our society. Even some of the Catholics, giving evidence of a change, were received into our little band of Christian soldiers. A number of the surgeons and ladies of the hospital also connected with us.

"Sept. 9, 1864. It was the evening of prayer, and the meeting was very large; some earnest prayers, and one speech. George W. Moore, 188th Pa., said, 'I went into ward ten; saw a few boys; went up to them, and talked to them about Jesus, and asked them if I might pray for them. They said they "did n't care." I asked the ward-master if I might? He said, "Yes." I prayed, and we had a good, happy time.' Gave away tracts; received five hundred New Testaments and a large box of papers for the patients from New York.

"Sept. 14. Buried four more departed soldiers. Visited seven or eight wards, and found a few willing to join our little Hospital church. Labored a while at my thanksgiving sermon; but, thinking of the suffering patients in ward number one, was constrained to go and see them. Prayed with John R. Small, 37th N. Y., Co. G., and, as I prayed, he followed me, repeating the same words. Visited two wards in New Camp at nine P.M., and a few cases in wards eight and nine. Conversed with one fellow very anxious to get religion; urged him to the cross. How often patients weep! In conversing with Bennett J. Cobley, 58th Pa., Co. I, we found him careless and prayerless. He said his family was so before him. 'Do you swear?' 'I swear occasionally, but I will swear no more, if I can help it.' After a long talk to him about the Saviour, urging him to immediate repentance and to prayer, he said, 'Won't you make a little prayer for me?' wetting his eyes with the penitential tear. His careless brother, standing by, wept profusely. He urged me to call again. Left him praying, 'God be merciful to me a sinner.'

"Sept. 16. No funeral this morning. Five soldiers were buried this evening. Canvassed wards as usual, and preached in ward number two, on 'Christ wonderful.' (Isa. ix. 6.) We had a most powerful prayer-meeting to-night. I never saw such a disposition to pray among the patients. When the chaplain ceased speaking, and picked up the hymn-book to give out a hymn to sing, before he had time to open his mouth, a soldier was on his knees praying. 'We go it' on the voluntary system, and very often the desire to pray is so general, two or three begin to pray at the same time. Eighteen led in prayer this evening. Their prayers were short, plain, direct, earnest. The chaplain read from the last chapter in the Bible. The interest seems to be increasing. 'Lord, help us! O Lord, revive thy work!' B. J. Cobley, referred to in the foregoing record, died to-day, and said he was happy.

"Sept. 17. Eight departed soldiers were buried this evening. Preached in ward five; very attentive. Some two hundred patients brought in to-day; some very sick; two died on the boat. I saw one neglected colored soldier die, leaning up against the side of the boat; no one noticing him but myself; he died easy. They were crowded into a hot, uncomfortable place close by the smoke-stack. I saw another poor soldier dying, whom they said had been partially deranged and very hard of hearing. As I stood by him he grasped my hand, and gave me a most expressive, wishful look; he could not speak. Death soon took him, and the nurses carried his body to the dead-house."

WEEPING SCENE AT THE GRAVE.

"Friday, Sept. 22. Buried five departed soldiers. And just as we closed the funeral services, the bereaved widow of one of them, Henry A. Thurston, 152d N. Y., Co. M, arrived at the grave, and desired to see her dear husband's remains. Of course we all consented at once to a request so reasonable, and proceeded immediately to take up the coffin; but, through some mistake, we took up the wrong one, and opened it to the gaze of the bereaved widow; and as she came forward with a heart smitten with grief, weeping profusely, at the first glimpse of the corpse she exclaimed, 'It ain't him! it ain't him!' and perceiving the mistake, we soon put it back and took up the right one, enshrouded in a plain red coffin, and gathering around it, she wept bitterly. How hard the sad trial! How severe her loss! Yet dying for his country, and giving such bright evidence of dying in the Lord, doubtless 'for him to die was gain.' Corporal Thurston's dying request was, 'Tell my wife I died happy in Christ.' Near his last, he grasped the hands of his cousin, and said, 'I am going home, and praise God for it.' It was quite common to see wives come to see, nurse, and comfort their sick and wounded husbands in the hospital, and find them dead and buried. It was quite common to see anxious mothers come, hundreds of miles, inquiring for their dear sons, and find them enshrouded in their coffins in the dead-house, or lying in the cold grave. Then the next anxious inquiry would be, 'How did he die? What were his last words and dying thoughts? Did he seem resigned? and give any satisfactory evidence of a change?' etc. All such questions we always answered to the best of our ability with great pleasure. To meet a bereaved widow, or mother, or brother, who had sustained the loss of a bosom friend, and have nothing encouraging to tell them about the departed, was, of all duties, the most unpleasant connected with a chaplain's labors in the hospital."

THE NAKED HEART.

"Sept. 27. Visited nine wards in the forenoon and a few in New Camp in the afternoon, where I saw distinctly the throbbings and beatings of the heart of private John L. Reno, 76th Pa. Vol., Co. B, who had been shot through the breast, and left three holes therein. Part of the breastbone was taken out, leaving the heart exposed, so that we could distinctly see every beat of it. Yet this brave soldier was buoyant in spirits and full of courage, and doing well. How vividly this wonderful sight brings to mind God's omniscient, piercing view of the heart. 'Although your heart is uncovered and laid open, we can see nothing but its exterior and the quick throbbings occasioned by the rapid circulation of the blood; but "the Lord searcheth all hearts," and scans every motive, thought, word, and deed; for all of which he will soon call us to give a strict and impartial account. And just here, my brave fellow, allow me to ask how is "your heart with God?" for it matters but little who has the head, if Satan has the heart. The heart governs. How is it with you, John?' 'Well, chaplain, I don't know, but I have a hope.' 'Your heart beats strong and lively to-day, but God only knows how soon it may stop.' David prayed for a clean heart. The Saviour says, "My son, give me thy heart." If you give your life for your country, how reasonable it is to give your heart to God.' In my rounds, on Sept. 30, I saw many badly wounded cases: one poor little fellow with both eyes shot out. Visited them on the boat. They were complaining for something to eat.

"October 1. Three boat-loads of patients brought in to-day, about five hundred in all, and many very severely wounded. Many came with limbs off, some shot in the head, some in the lungs, and one unfortunate colored man shot through the root of the tongue, which swelled so that he could scarcely speak. He wrote his name and address for me."

MORTALITY INCREASING.

With the battles raging at the front, the sick and wounded kept pouring in by boat-loads daily. To go down to the wharf and gaze upon a large steamer thickly strewn with brave, wounded men, fresh from the gory field, with hearts beating with patriotism and blood flowing from their wounds, with here and there one dead, and others dying, the scene presented was solemn and trying. And when you begin to ask, "What meaneth all this?" you were deeply impressed with the value and importance of the salvation of the country. Our forces were now, Oct. 1, 1864, closely investing Richmond; and the conflict waxed warm and heavy. To-day, some five hundred wounded were brought down, many of whom were very severely, and many mortally, wounded. In fact, a good many died on being brought down. Now we buried from fifteen to twenty a day. The dead-house was sometimes full; some lying in their glory, in their plain red coffins, wrapped in their winding-sheets, while others, without coffins, lay on the floor.

"Oct. 2. Preached twice, and visited twelve wards. Sermon at night on 'The Soldier's Guard;' and a soldier was so deeply interested, that he said, 'I could listen all night on that subject.'

"Oct. 3. Buried twenty departed soldiers to-day, four cart-loads; it took all the afternoon. Chaplain Roe, U. S. A., also buried six, making in all twenty-six to-day. Preached twice, and visited some six hundred patients, canvassing the hearts of the sickest ones."

"TRY AGAIN."

Passing up the aisle of one of the wards, one Sabbath afternoon, as we were going round with the choir singing, reading, and praying with the patients in the wards, I stepped up to a soldier of the 10th Reg. of Conn. Volunteers, who had for several days been "trying to pray,"—trying to "trust in the Lord, and trying to believe;" and as I approached his bed, I said to him, "Are you still seeking Jesus?" and immediately he exclaimed, "I have found him! I have found him!" "Thank God, what a precious Saviour! What a glorious discovery! what a blessed privilege to find such a merciful Saviour! Does he seem precious to you?" "Oh, yes; he is so lovely!" Before, it was all try with him. He had tried and tried again, and at last success crowned his efforts. Let the seeker be encouraged; if difficulties rise, pray on and " go forward;" if all seems dark, look to Jesus, and he will give you light; if you feel discouraged, "fear not," God is with you, "be not afraid; only believe, and all is well." "Seek ye the Lord while he may be found."

"Oct. 18. Visited sick, wounded, dying. We had a very good, precious meeting of prayer, praise, and speaking; prayers earnest, warm, tender, touching; speeches earnest, tender, powerful, melting: many wept under one of them made by one who has just professed Christ. Said he, 'I feel ashamed of my levity in the ward: I have been a great swearer; but now I have no disposition to swear; I find it no trouble to keep from it; to swear now never comes into my mind.' A few evenings before, he said, ' We go out into the woods to pray often, and come back refreshed and blessed; my heart seems all broken to pieces. I am thirty-eight years old, and I think it a great sin that I have spent so much time in Satan's service.' The soldiers and officers voted here on October 11, 1864. The following account will show more fully the religious interest at this time among the patients."

A SOLDIER'S PRAYER-MEETING.

"These meetings are always very interesting; but the meeting to-night, October 18, was one of more than ordinary interest and power. It was opened with singing, and reading the ninth chapter of Luke, accompanied with one or two pointed remarks by the chaplain, and again singing that good old hymn:

> 'Come, we that love the Lord,
> And let our joys be known!'

Then the meeting, as usual, was thrown open, and all invited to take part. After eight or ten warm, tender, earnest prayers for the sick, wounded, and dying in the hospital, for our civil and military officers, soldiers 'at the front,' for our Hospital church, and for the 'loved ones at home,' we had a few warm, earnest, heart-gushing speeches from Christian soldiers.

"One stalwart soldier rose, and spoke of the importance of self-examination and fidelity. Said he, 'What we say here in these prayer-meetings is talked over and sifted by the hearers afterwards, therefore let us take heed what we say;' and urged all to stand fast, be firm, decided, rooted and grounded in love, and 'stand up for Jesus.'

"Another spoke of the blessed privilege of attending the prayer-meeting, of his own happy experience, the bliss of heaven, and most earnestly and tenderly besought sinners to come to Christ. His thoughts seemed to soar to heaven and cluster around the throne of God. He seemed very happy, and one who lives nigh to God. In prayer he was very earnest, and seemed to get very near the throne.

"Another spoke of the chaplain, and said, 'I wish we were all under him, that we might do as he bids us,' and said, 'If we hear him, how much more should we hear our great High-Priest, Jesus Christ, who pleads and intercedes for us.' Going on in a very warm, earnest manner, spicing his speech with an occasional shout of 'Glory be to God!' he closed, earnestly beseeching sinners to come to Jesus.

"Another said, 'It is but a short time since I set out to serve God, and I find it good to serve him, and would most heartily recommend it to all.'

"Another young convert said, 'A few months ago I came to this hospital very sick of the fever: the doctors gave me up; but I got well, and here I found the Saviour several weeks ago, and immediately enlisted in his service. Although my praying comrades have ceased to go with me to the bushes to pray, I still go by myself. I find it very refreshing.' He said, 'I went to a tent of colored soldiers, and asked one if he would like to have a little book? He said "Yes." I gave him one. I asked him if he was a Christian? "No," he replied; I told him to pray, and look to Jesus. I went next day, and found him rejoicing in believing.' George spoke with much warmth and earnestness, and closed by urging sinners to come to Christ.

"But the speech that seemed almost to melt the whole congregation into tears, was from one who had just been converted. A few evenings ago he rose and said, 'I came up here to-night to ask an interest in your prayers; something has touched my heart, and I see and feel I am a great sinner, and wish to become a Christian; I have been reading my Bible and trying to pray. To-night I renew my request. Brethren, I hope you will all pray for me. I have been a great swearer; but now I find no difficulty in keeping from swearing, but feel condemned for my levity in joking with "the boys" in the ward. To swear now never comes into my mind. My heart is all broken into pieces. Oh, brethren, pray for me!' He sat down trembling with deep emotions, all bathed in tears. His speech was short, simple, earnest, powerful; coming from the heart, it reached the hearts of many, and brought tears to their eyes. It was good to be there.

"Nov. 6, 1864. After morning devotions, buried the dead; nine in all. A rebel soldier sent for me to come and pray with him. I went. He seemed very penitent, and anxious about his salvation: has a deep sense of his sins; wept freely; prays, but seems to think he is not a Christian, yet he acts a good deal like one. Preached in a ward of colored patients this evening; and visited New Camp, and found a number of colored soldiers in need of clothing.

"Nov. 8. After burying nine soldiers, canvassed the wards as usual. Met one colored patient, who said, 'When I try to pray, my heart wanders away from me: I never saw the beat of it; I never saw the beat of it!' On my asking a colored soldier why so many chose to serve Satan rather than Christ? he said, 'It is easier to serve Satan.' 'What! is Satan's yoke easier than Christ's?' 'Yes; it is easier for the sinner.' 'Very true, it is always easier to swim down stream than up; yet, when you throw off Satan's yoke and put on Christ's, it is much easier to wear Christ's.'"

CATHOLICS TURNING PROTESTANTS.

"To-day, Nov. 10, 1864, two fine-looking German Catholics came to my room to have a talk about Jesus and the Protestant religion, and to consult about joining our Hospital union church. They came from my wing of the hospital. After an interesting interview with them in their ward, they united with the church, and gave good evidence of a change. They were always found at the prayer-meeting. Several Catholics united with our 'little flock.' The army is a good place to reach this class of people. I have often found them free to talk about the Saviour and the way of salvation.

"Nov. 12. Preached to-day to the patients and officers of the fourth division (colored) of the hospital; they were all attention and deeply interested; some few were very old men, contrabands; two very low with disease. Gave out a few books, tracts, and papers; they were very glad to receive them; some can't read; some quite well educated. This division, being about a mile from the head-quarters of the hospital, and being across Hampton Creek, is not visited much by the chaplain or delegates. Spiritually, it is a good deal neglected.

"Nov. 16. Read a few Psalms and a little book called '*Ready.*' Very good. Visited a wounded woman (brought from near Richmond, with three children, in a tent by themselves), in company with Rev. Mr. Crane, and two ladies from Norfolk. She was wounded, near Richmond, with a shell; she is getting well. Preached in a tent of ward number twenty-four on Regeneration, and broke up two squads of card-playing. Visited wards numbers 12, 13, 14, 15, 16, 17, 18, 19, 20, 21, 24, 25, 7, 6, 5, 4, 3, 2, 1, and canvassed the hearts of the sickest ones.

"Nov. 19. Buried five. Visited wards numbers 7, 6, 5, 4, 3, 2, 1, 13, 12, and Gangrene Camp, where I found one suffering colored soldier, in the last stages of life, covered all over with perspiration. Pointing him to the all-compassionate Saviour, and commending him to the God of all grace, with prayer and exhortation, we bid him a last farewell. I usually visited from five to eight hundred patients daily, always conversing with the most dangerous cases. 'Who is sufficient for these things?' 'O God, help me!'

"Nov. 22. Buried ten soldiers, all in old graves out of which dead bodies had been exhumed and taken home. Warned a dying soldier to flee to Christ; read from (Mark x. 46,) story of the blind beggar; urged him to fly to Christ at once; prayed with much liberty. The Lord was with us and helped us. How solemn! After visiting and canvassing a number of wards, wrote letters till eleven o'clock P.M. It keeps me very busy to bury the dead, and to watch, and learn, and keep a record of the dying. Mr. Cole, though careless heretofore, as I urged him to seek an interest in Christ to-day, he wept freely; his last sands are doubtless running. I saw Sergeant Bullock weeping because he could not realize that change of heart he desired."

CHRISTMAS DINNER.

"Dec. 26. Visited patients as usual. Canvassed a while in New Camp. Read and prayed with an old man who said he had been guilty of all crimes but murder and theft. He seemed very anxious about his salvation now. Yesterday I preached a Christmas sermon to a very large, attentive audience in ward C, on the text, 'Glory to God,' Luke ii. 11. One fellow said, going home,

'We had a good Christmas treat to-night.' The Christmas dinner was a sumptuous affair. Through the patriotic liberality of the people at the North, we had some four hundred fine, fat turkeys, which, together with other things in proportion, made up a splendid dinner for all the patients and officers of the hospital, in all some three thousand and five hundred. The soldiers enjoyed it very much. To get a good meal of turkeys, vegetables, etc., was to them a great treat. It was huge feeding. To brave men, who had undergone the asperities and hardships of army life so long, to enjoy such a rich feast was truly gratifying. Such scenes of festivity tend to break up the dull monotony of hospital life, inspire new life, refresh and encourage the sick and wounded. Many of the wards are richly festooned and most splendidly decorated with evergreens, pictures, banners, and flags. Fitted up with so much taste, to enter one would remind you of going into one of the fine halls in New York City. And early in the spring, the yards of several of the wards were fenced off, and sodded over and fitted up in fine style; some of them as neat as the yard of the dwelling-house of any country gentleman. In the beautiful yard of ward number nine you could see in large, beautiful letters of living green, 'RICHMOND FELL APRIL 4, 1865.' Others were adorned with shrubs and fragrant flowers and sweet roses, all tending to make the hospital more cheering and desirable to the patients."

"THEY COULD ONLY SHOUT 'GLORY,' AND DIED,"

Said a brave, honest soldier while he lay on his bed in the hospital, raging with a scorching fever, as he described our poor half-starved, dying, released prisoners, as they were carried from the rebel boat and again placed under the beautiful stripes of the dear old flag of the Union. "And did they shout glory?" " Yes." And no wonder, after experiencing such a glorious deliverance. If the pardoned convict, snatched from the disgrace of the gallows, cries, "glory." If the sinner, rescued from hell, would shout "glory," well might the prisoner released from the untold horrors of Andersonville. Having escaped the cruel revenge, the inexpressible sufferings and excruciating punishments of that awful place of torment, where starving heroes tried to keep soul and body together by eating dead dogs and food that had already passed from the stomach of other men, as those exchanged prisoners themselves stated they had done, it is no wonder they shouted "glory," even when in the agonies of death, when permitted to die under the glorious "stars and stripes." How sad and sickening the thought, to surviving friends, to know that a dear relative had lived through all the inhuman cruelties of that horrible place, and then die at last without seeing home. Oh, the cruelties, horrors, and tortures of the rebellion! Language fails to describe it. What an accumulation of crime, guilt, suffering, misery, cruelty, revenge, torture, starvation, death, and murder is embodied in that awful word *Andersonville*. The heart shudders and recoils at the very thought of it. Its very utterance will always terrify and shock humanity.

HOLIDAYS IN U. S. HOSPITAL.

For a few weeks previous, the "Hampton Glee Club" had been preparing for a "Christmas concert," which came off on Christmas eve. It was a complete success. The spacious hall, finely decorated with flags and richly festooned with wreaths and circlets of pine and evergreens, and ornamented with luxurious berries, "red, white, and blue," and all surmounted with the cheering inscription, "We come with songs to greet you," crowded to overflowing with some nine or ten hundred patients (soldiers), citizens, and officers, presented a sight grand and imposing. The clock strikes eight, and after a cheering "overture," the grand entertainment opens with the stirring strains of the glorious "Star-Spangled Banner," thrilling the whole audience. The Glee Club and others sung many patriotic, sentimental, and interesting songs most sweetly, which were very cheering and gratifying to the patients for whose benefit the concert was gotten up. That everybody enjoyed it richly was evident from the vociferous laughing, stamping, and clapping of hands. The hall being too small, hundreds could not get in; yet, although it was quite cold, many on crutches stood outside and listened to the enchanting music, interspersed with animating interludes by the orchestra.

The Christmas dinner was decidedly *rich* and *good*. With a few fat pigs, a large lot of chickens, and some four hundred or five hundred good turkeys, every patient, attaché, and officer in the hospital "fared sumptuously." The patients particularly were highly gratified. The rich pies and cakes, together with the abundant supply of porter and ale, seemed almost to make many of them forget they were in a hospital. Besides our prayer-meetings, we had two Christmas sermons. With some three thousand patients in all, in the hospital, some one thousand go out to the dining-hall for their meals; the rest eat in their wards, many of which are finely decorated and festooned, presenting an appearance for beauty almost equal to a city drawing-room.

The rich dinner, and the concert, with some variations, were repeated on New Year's day.

The mortality in this hospital is rapidly decreasing. Out of some three thousand patients, only seventeen died last week, which is the least for one week during the last six months.

WEEK OF PRAYER.

This commenced last night with an encouraging prospect. It opened with reading the seventh chapter of Matthew, accompanied with appropriate remarks by Chaplain E. P. Roe. There was a good feeling. It was good to be there. To-night the meeting was opened with praise and reading part of the second chapter of Acts, with remarks upon the great revival recorded there, its extent, depth, power, and influence, and the agency and means by which it was brought about. *Deep* interest to-night. The prayers and speeches were warm, pointed, earnest. Many in tears, and seemed filled with the Holy Ghost. The patients came with wounded heads tied up, and some on crutches.

THE LORD'S SUPPER

Was administered to-day, January 8, 1865, in the chapel at Chesapeake Hospital. Chaplain Marshall preached the action sermon on the text, "What mean ye by this service?" With eight ministers present, some seventy-five persons, soldiers, matrons, and officers communed. The service was deeply solemn and interesting. While our comrades were pouring out their blood, battling for victory, upon the gory field at the front, here, beside the flowing tide of Hampton Roads, we were permitted to celebrate the victory of Calvary. With brave men dying around us, and God's eye upon us, bathed in tears, we commemorated the dying love of Jesus. Oh, what a great privilege!

"How sweet and awful was the place,
With Christ within the doors."

While thousands around us were sealing their attachment to their country with their blood, here, amidst the groans of the sick, wounded, and dying, by renewed vows, we sealed ours to the Saviour. This was the only privilege of this kind we enjoyed during our time of service in the army. The suffused eye and the deep solemnity pervading all present indicated God's gracious presence. It was refreshing to the soul, and we believe many went away strengthened and better prepared for battling in the great cause of liberty and truth.

REVIVAL.

The religious interest from this time onward, for a few weeks, seemed to increase rapidly, and on the evening of Jan. 9 we had a most precious meeting. "Many wept; it was good to be there. The chaplain limited the meeting at the beginning to an hour, but God prolonged it to an hour and a half. It was a real time of refreshing. Several asked to be prayed for. We had one most powerful prayer. The people are getting waked up.

"Jan. 10. Visited wards and canvassed as usual. Very heavy rains. I went through them to visit the sick. Constrained by a sense of duty, I can't omit it. Good prayer-meeting to-night. One man rose, and said, 'Last Sabbath night I began to pray for the first time in my life.' Interest increasing. The next evening I preached from Matt. xxvii. 46. Christ on the cross. The congregation to-night was unusually large and very attentive. All was as solemn as the grave. After an interesting season of prayer, an invitation was given for persons to unite with the church, and a great many stayed in, deeply anxious, lingering around the gates of Zion. The prayer, 'O Lord, revive thy work,' is going up from many hearts. 'Come, Holy Spirit, come with all thy quickening powers.'

"Jan. 13. Buried twelve dead. Prayed with Gibson at his request. He grasped my hand firmly and warmly, and strongly drew me close up to him, unwilling to let me go, exclaiming, 'Oh, don't go away, chaplain, don't go away! Can't you stay with me? Can't you stay and talk more about the blessed Saviour?' He seems very anxious, prayerful, and tender. I have been out late, often till after ten o'clock, every night for several months, laboring with the needy patients. The work is laborious, yet the cause is so noble and glorious, I like it. Rev. Mr. Bingham preached to-night from Acts xvi. 30: the case of the Philippian jailer — a very good, appropriate sermon. 'What must I do to be saved?' The greatest and most important question ever propounded to man.

"Jan. 18. Buried three cart-loads of dead soldiers. Visited and canvassed several wards, and preached in ward four. And after conversing a while with one who is a Roman Catholic, he said, 'Your sermon last night did my soul good.' A ward-master said to-night, 'I would give a hundred dollars to quit swearing. Yes, I would give my arm.' 'And well you might. The Saviour says, "If thy right hand offend thee, cut it off, and cast it from thee; for it is profitable for thee, that one of thy members should perish, and not that thy whole body should be cast into hell." Yea, you had better give your *life* than utter a single oath. But you can, if you *will*, quit it on a far cheaper plan. If you feel unable of *yourself* to quit it, go to God, ask for *strength*, and he will enable you to quit it. Ask, and you shall receive.'

"Jan. 19. Visited hospital transport from Fort Fisher, with two hundred and seven wounded patients,— most of them wounded but slightly; only about twenty or twenty-five stretcher cases. They all seemed very jubilant over the glorious victory achieved; even those who were mortally wounded, you could see their eyes flashing with patriotic fire, and their brave hearts throbbing with heroic devotion to their country. Although they had just come out of a hard hand-to-hand fight, they were all still full of fight. The bullets flew so thick that it seemed they would strike one another in the air. Thank God for the fall of Fort Fisher. The worst cases were put in ward C; and, as I went in a few days after to preach to them, I found them singing, 'My country,' all full of courage. Several of them died shortly after.

"Jan. 21. It rained very heavily all day; sometimes it literally poured down. Yet I visited and canvassed ten or twelve wards as usual, but I got most awful wet and muddy — wetter than I have been for ten years. Saw and conversed with two men nigh unto death, and pointed them to Him whose blood cleanseth from all sin."

But one of our most precious and powerful meetings was on the evening of January 14th. It was a meeting of the church members and anxious inquirers. In my diary I described it in these words: "We had a *Melting Meeting* to-night in ward C." A more full account of it will be found in the following letter.

REVIVAL IN A HOSPITAL.

FORTRESS MONROE, February 4, 1865.

MESSRS. EDITORS: The "Week of Prayer" here has turned out to be a month of prayer. Beginning with the first of January, our prayer-meetings, excepting a few nights' interruption by the arrival of new patients, have been continued to this date. The attendance, mostly soldiers, has been at times very large, reaching about six hundred one evening. Preaching occasionally, the exercises have been prayer, exhortation, and praise. We labor under great inconveniences for want of a comfortable house to meet in. We meet now in the dining-hall, without any fire; and although all is cold and freezing without, the suffused eye, earnest prayer, and warm, earnest exhortation evinced that there is fire within. Here the soldier, upon his crutches and with his wounded head tied up, drags his maimed body to sing and pray. Our "Hospital Union Church," organized September 9, 1864, with thirty members, now numbers about two hundred and ten. Over one hundred united during the month of January, and "still they come!" Conversions are frequent.

Laboring most of the time in Hampton Hospital, or Division No. 1, chaplained by the Rev. E. P. Roe, we endeavor now to get the "spiritual diagnosis" of every patient coming into the hospital. This is a very good plan. To canvass the heart stirs the soul, and often leads men to repentance. The patients are generally very free to talk about religion. Many seem to be inquiring, "What to do to be saved?"

SOLDIER'S PRAYER-MEETING.

It was on a Saturday night, and a meeting of the church members and anxious inquirers. The meeting was opened by reading from John xv., followed with prayer, and a few warm and tender remarks by the chaplain, and we had a "warming time of refreshing." After singing that good old stirring hymn,

> "Stand up, my soul, shake off thy fears,
> And gird the gospel armor on,"

the meeting was thrown open, and all invited to take part in speaking or praying, as they felt. The first speech was by an old soldier of the cross, lately from the North. Requested by the chaplain, with his white locks overhanging his time-worn cheeks, he laid off his over-coat, and slowly rose and spoke tenderly of the prayers and sympathies of the North in behalf of the soldiers, whom he earnestly besought to be faithful; and, trying to impress them with their great responsibility, he says to them, "You are the bulwarks of the nation. Upon your fidelity hangs the protection and salvation of the country." His closing remark was, "Remember, Thou, God, seest me!"

He was followed by the prayer of a young convert, who said "To-night he had won one poor sinner to Christ." We all joined in praise.

Then another aged Christian rose, and spoke of God's goodness to him, and confessed he had "wandered away a little from the Saviour; but to-night I feel my spiritual strength renewed." Urging with tenderness all to be faithful, he asked to be prayed for, and sat down.

Another rises, and says: "I feel happy to-night, and thank God for what he has done for my soul. Though a professor for seven years, I felt myself lost when I came here last spring." Expressing much anxiety about and gratitude for praying friends at home, he sat down, shouting, "Glory be to God!"

Another says, "I was converted three weeks ago, in ward seven, lying on my sick-bed;" and thanking God for what he had done for him, and requesting to be prayed for, sat down.

Another, who, a little while ago "was a great swearer," spoke with much feeling about his man-fearing spirit, and his determination hereafter, through grace, to overcome it, and be more faithful. "When we consider the greatness of God," said he, "what is the fear of a man? Nothing more than a floating thistle in the air." Requesting all to pray for him, he sat down bathed in tears.

Another expressed his surprise at so few being Christians, when we consider the vastness of Christ's love, and what great things he has done for us. Closing with the importance of every Christian *showing his colors*, and letting his light shine, he illustrated the fact by the little drummer-boy, who checked and silenced profanity, gambling, and carousing on a steamboat, simply by kneeling in silent prayer in their presence before he went to bed. "Fellow-soldiers," said he, "let us raise our colors a little higher."

Then a boy rose, and said, "I have resolved to seek the Lord, and be a Christian. I ask an interest in your prayers."

Another visitor, from the North, said, "I was converted February 2, 1835, at nine o'clock at night. I recollect the circumstance very well. The Spirit of God has been running and burning all through me here to-night." He closed by urging the little boy who preceded him, the chaplain, soldiers, and all, to be faithful, and God will reward us.

Another said, "I would not be ashamed to confess Christ, and stand up for his cause, before the world. I hope always so to live that I may win souls to God." He said the fear of man is nothing.

Many others spoke, all saying, "I feel within me that God has blessed my soul, and that it is good to serve him." Nearly every one sat down with the request, "Pray for me." It was truly a time of refreshing. The gushing sigh, the penitential tear, stirring exhortation, and the earnest prayer, all evinced that "The Lord of hosts was with us."

The deep religious interest pervading many of the patients was manifested by their coming to converse with the chaplains about their salvation. On Feb. 6, 1865, after I had closed my sermon in ward twenty-seven, on "halting," a young soldier stepped up to me, weeping profusely, and said, "I ask an interest in your prayers. I feel I am a great sinner; and I have been praying and feeling so about three days. I have a praying mother. I have the heart disease, and am liable to be called away any time." Urging him to give his heart to God, I walked round with him, pointed him to Christ, and by the mercies of God besought him to come to Jesus *at once*, without any preparation. Invoking the blessing of God to rest upon him, we bid him a hearty good-by.

"Feb. 10. Visited a very sick man in ward thirteen. Found him expressing a bright hope. He said, with deep earnestness, 'I am ready,' in an emphatic tone. He sent for me yesterday. I went, read, sung, and prayed with him. Read and wrote a lot of letters; visited and canvassed ten wards; had a long talk with a swearing soldier in ward twenty-eight, endeavoring to expose the folly and sin of profanity, and urged him to quit it. While leading the regular prayer-meeting to-night, I was called away to visit a dying man, and, upon entering the ward, found it was Akin, referred to above. He was still able to converse, and, in a firm and distinct manner, he said, 'I am happy, happy! My religion is built upon a sure foundation. *I mean it.* God has got me. Tell my wife I died happy.' He died that night.

"Feb. 15, 1865. Yesterday we received four hundred and sixteen patients from Point of Rocks, Va. Held the regular semiweekly prayer-meeting to-night in ward eleven because the dining-hall is so cold, there being no fire in it. Mr. Plumb, private of 4th Mass. Cavalry, made us a very good, religious talk. There is an advantage in meeting in the wards for prayer. Here we get the lame, the maimed, and the halt. To-day we buried the remains of Thomas Smith, of the 32d Co. of Veteran Reserve Corps. The funeral was unusually large, as nearly all of that corps present attended. The Hampton Hospital brass band graced the funeral with deep-toned notes of mourning. To-day I received a visit from Gen. Curtis at my room. The general is just so far recovered from his severe wound, received at the capture of Fort Fisher, as to begin to go out a little around the hospital. He is lively, entertaining, and pleasant, and has proved himself a brave soldier in the fierce, bloody conflict at Fort Fisher. Though he lost an eye, he nobly performed his part in achieving that very important victory which cut the rebels' communication with Richmond, and did so much toward hastening the downfall of the rebellion."

CHAPTER XVII.

MISCELLANEOUS FACTS.

CELEBRATION OF WASHINGTON'S BIRTHDAY — RELIGIOUS INTEREST IN NEW CAMP — SOLDIERS' ENTERTAINMENT — THE FALL OF RICHMOND — UNBOUNDED REJOICING — LEE'S SURRENDER — DEATH OF PRESIDENT LINCOLN — LARGEST INTERMENT — DEDICATION OF NEW HOSPITAL CHAPEL — ARRIVAL OF FORT FISHER WOUNDED.

CELEBRATION OF WASHINGTON'S BIRTHDAY.

THIS memorable day was celebrated with much enthusiasm, by the patients and officers of the hospital, in the "Government schoolhouse," hard by the hospital, erected by the Government, under the direction of Gen. Butler, for the education of the colored children. On the morning of the 22d of February, the people began to get ready, and by half-past one o'clock a large procession was formed, near ward four, and marched to the schoolhouse under the direction of Dr. Wolverton, assistant surgeon of the U. S. A., headed by the band, surgeons, and chaplains of the hospital. All comfortably seated in the spacious hall, the exercises were opened by the stirring strains of "Red, White, and Blue," by the hospital band, followed with an appropriate prayer by Rev. Mr. Dinsmore of the Christian Commission. The meeting was addressed by Chaplains Billingsley, Marshall, and Raymond, and Mr. Plumb, of the 4th Mass. Cavalry, with frequent marks of applause. With an audience of some twelve hundred, composed of soldiers with eyes sparkling with patriotism, and a few ladies, with a small sprinkle of colored folks, with the hospital band conspicuously seated in the rear of the stand,— all surmounted by the glorious "stars" of Washington and "stripes" of the Union!— the scene presented was truly grand and imposing. And when we remember that we were standing upon the soil of old Virginia, which, for two hundred and forty-five long years, had been watered with the sweat and blood of slaves, millions of whom are now alive and free, and thousands of them standing around us to-day, the grandeur and glory of the scene were much increased. And what added still more to the interest and glory of that auspicious day and the exercises of the occasion, was, that we were standing almost within sight of the shade of the tomb of him whose birthday we were celebrating, and hard by a whipping-post, tied to which many a slave had received the bloody lashes from an unmerciful master. Cheered by the enchanting music of the hospital band, although we were surrounded with the dead and dying, the meeting was a perfect success; and the patients returned to their respective quarters cheered and encouraged, and better prepared to do and to suffer in the great cause of humanity and truth.

RELIGIOUS INTEREST IN NEW CAMP.

Being now full, February 18, 1865, New Camp contained some eleven hundred colored patients, all comfortably situated in good tents; and, being without a suitable place to meet in, they had but little preaching; hence they engaged more in social worship. It was on a cold frosty evening in February, while I was visiting the suffering patients in the lonely Gangrene Camp, that my ear was greeted with the voice of prayer and praise in the direction of New Camp. As I approached the unlit tents, the sound grew louder and louder until, reaching the interior of the camp, I was agreeably surprised to find prayer-meetings, nearly all led by colored men, going on in eight or ten different tents at the same time. What a flame of thanksgiving, prayer, and praise ascended from the hearts of those earnest suppliants! To see so many, now disabled to fight with the sword, wielding the sword of the Spirit, and the more powerful weapon, *prayer*, for the deliverance of the country and for the salvation of her defenders, was truly encouraging! Ground down so long with the iron heel of slavery, and now, with their shackles knocked off, and elevated to the rank and honor of United States soldiers, fighting for liberty and union, they were full of gratitude and joy; and their thanksgiving and rejoicing were much increased, because their emancipation and promotion were given, as they believed (and doubtless it was so), in answer to their prayers! Approaching one of their tents, I saw a man standing outside, attentively listening to the gushing prayers and praises within. "Why don't you go in?" I said to him. Looking very solemn and anxious, he replied, "I am lookin' for a good meetin' to go to." He waited patiently and listened very attentively, as one sable soldier of the cross, with no light in the tent, gave out the hymn "line upon line;" and they all joined in singing it very impressively. He threatened to go in, but I left him standing there. In several of the tents they had no light; but with their souls lit up by God's light-giving Spirit, richly endued with the spirit of prayer, and deeply impressed with the importance of the subject, they sung and prayed with great power, even as though they felt, "I will not let thee go, except thou bless me." Simple-minded in their nature and habits, with a limited knowledge of the doctrines of the cross, they possess fewer ideas about religion than white folks; but what they have, seem to take a deep hold upon their hearts and to make a deep impression upon their minds. They seem to know nothing about doubting God and his word. Hence, they pray with a child-like simplicity and a noble familiarity with God, peculiar to themselves. And going to God thus, "without wrath, nothing doubting, they seem to get very near the throne, and couching their petitions in the strongest terms, enforced by arguments powerful, touching, and convincing, they prayed with wonderful effect." A servant was once asked by his master, "Tom, how is it that you are always so happy, and I am so miserable?" "Oh, massa, me fall right flat down on de promises, and prays right up. Me is happy in de Lord. You, massa, don't pray, nor trust in de Lord; dat's what makes you so miserable, massa." But to proceed with the prayer-meetings. Passing by and looking in, we often found them conducted by colored men, who were so familiar with the hymns they sung, that they lined them out without a candle. They all seemed to enjoy it very much. The impressiveness of their singing, and the fervor of their prayers, were enough to melt the hardest heart. These prayer-meetings were kept up every night for a long time, with much interest.

This division of the hospital was chaplained by Rev. Dr. Charles Raymond, U. S. A., who, having charge of the public schools of that region, failed to give that attention to the patients they deserved; hence I visited them when I could, and with them I had many very interesting interviews on experimental religion. We often found the colored soldier giving an evidence of a depth of piety that would shame many white Christians. Original and peculiar in their modes of thought and expression, they would "get off" some most striking and interesting things. Speaking right out from the heart, they frequently became very eloquent and powerful, reaching the heart and stirring the soul of every listener. It was a privilege to hear them. Dr. Raymond preached to them occasionally. He had clerks and religious men from the hospital appointed to visit the sickest patients, learn their spiritual condition, get their last words and dying messages of those that died, and send them home to their friends. The delegates of the Christian and Sanitary Commissions did a good work in this camp, both in religious instruction and supplying the temporal wants of the patients. They furnished the patients with a good supply of papers and religious reading, and spelling-books and readers for those wishing to learn to read. A large ward of this camp was occupied with confederate prisoners, who received the same fare as our own men. When this camp was first opened, it was occupied with white patients from our own army. Here many of them suffered and died; some giving directions concerning their bones. After a while they were all taken to division number one, usually called Hampton Hospital; and then New Camp was occupied exclusively by colored patients until July 5, 1865, when it was abandoned entirely, and the patients moved to division number one. For several months this camp was well supplied with faithful matrons, through whose tender kindness doubtless the life of many a soldier was saved.

THE PRESIDENT'S RECEPTION ROOM DURING THE WAR.

SOLDIERS' ENTERTAINMENT.

What was it? A meeting of rejoicing over the late victory achieved by our armies upon the field of battle. It was the fourth of March, the day Abraham Lincoln was reinaugurated President of the United States. Upon a short notice, the spacious old dining-hall was full before it was dark. At the hour appointed, Chaplain Marshall and myself went over; and the hall was so densely crowded that we found it difficult to make our way through to the stand: such was the desire among the patients to witness and participate in the entertainment. Upon uttering the words, "Please, come to order," all was calm and quiet; and after the audience was entertained with cheering music by the hospital band, the exercises were opened with an appropriate prayer by Chaplain Marshall. After a short introductory speech by the writer, Mr. Marshall entertained the jubilant crowd with an interesting address; recounting acts of heroism, inspiring the brave soldiers with fresh courage to go on doing and suffering in the great conflict before us. At the close of his remarks, we were again cheered by the enchanting music and the facetious remarks of two private soldiers, Corporal Cook, of the Veteran Reserves, and Sergeant Plumb, of the 4th Mass. Cavalry. Got up in a hurry, the entertainment was a perfect success. The patients all seemed highly pleased, and all repaired at the close to their respective quarters, strengthened and encouraged.

THE FALL OF RICHMOND — UNBOUNDED REJOICING.

"The year of jubilee is come! Let the earth rejoice!" Of all scenes of rejoicing since the beginning of the war, that over the fall of Richmond excels all. When all was moving on as usual in the hospital, all of a sudden, about half-past eleven o'clock A.M., we received the glorious news that the rebels had fired and evacuated the rebel capital, and that Gen. Weitzel, commanding the 25th army corps (colored), had entered and taken possession about eight o'clock A.M., on April 3, 1865. The word was sent up from the fort by Dr. McClellan, and soon spread like wild-fire all over the hospital, and such exhibitions of heart-felt rejoicing were seldom if ever witnessed. Convalescents at work in the field threw up their hats and cheered most heartily. Everybody was all alive with enthusiastic rejoicing; vociferous cheer after cheer rolled from the gushing hearts of large crowds of patients and officers assembled at head-quarters, while the hospital band made everything ring with their enchanting music. But the crowning act of the occasion was an old colored man raising his hands and shouting aloud, "Glory to God in the highest!" to which many responded with a hearty "Amen!" With this stirring clap of applause, we dispersed for dinner, and met again, at the call of the surgeon-in-charge, at night in the dining-hall, where we had a most enthusiastic season of rejoicing. The meeting was addressed by Dr. McClellan, Dr. Crane, Medical Director at Fortress Monroe, and by Chaplains Raymond, Roe, Marshall, and Billingsley, and others. Graced with the thrilling music of the hospital band, with an audience of some ten or twelve hundred, all passed off very orderly. Feeling that with the downfall of Richmond the rebellion was virtually quelled, the slave freed, the effusion of blood stayed, and the country saved, we knew not how enough to thank God and the army and the navy for the great and glorious victory achieved.

LEE'S SURRENDER.

But our highest note of rejoicing was reserved for Lee's surrender. We received the news about midnight, April 10, 1865. Immediately the band strikes up music, and hundreds of us, being waked up by the loud cheering, rose to rejoice, and in a few minutes the whole hospital was all on tiptoe with the most enthusiastic jubilation. Loud, prolonged cheering and shouts of "glory to God" burst forth from every heart. "Thank God, the battle is fought and the victory won!" was the pervading sentiment of all. Language failed to give expression to the deep emotions of gratitude and rejoicing. The effect was almost overwhelming. Everybody seemed almost lost in the grandeur, glory, and importance of the victory achieved. Even the aged gray-headed matrons rose after midnight to give thanks to God, and mingle their hearts and voices over the downfall of the rebellion. And being so highly elated with the importance of the occasion, the old band came up from the fort to unite in the jubilations of the auspicious day; and while the jubilant crowd was standing upon the porch of the Chesapeake, listening to the stirring music, Dr. Rush, Surgeon U. S. Vol., was called upon for a speech; but he said, "It is not a time for speaking: the effect is too deep; it is a time to rejoice!" Whereupon the writer was called upon for a speech; but, being so deeply impressed with the importance of the event, that he was only able to say, after alluding to the grandeur, glory, and importance of the victory achieved, that "the war is over, the slave is freed, the effusion of blood is stayed, the rebellion quelled, the Union preserved, the devil whipped, the country saved, and God glorified!" It was received with hearty cheering. Some of the men and officers indulged a little in "old rye," which seemed to increase the jollification. I was very hardly pressed to drink, but I resisted every temptation. The jubilation was kept up until daylight, and all through the next day, and until we received the sad news of Lincoln's assassination, when all most suddenly were thrown into the deepest mourning, lamentation, and woe.

DEATH OF PRESIDENT LINCOLN.

"April 14. Spent the day in visiting the sick and wounded, and pointing them to Jesus, and entreating them to repent, and in writing letters. Buried the dead; four loads. Preached in ward one to a very attentive congregation. Visited a boat-load of three hundred patients, brought down this evening from near Richmond; two boat-loads brought down yesterday with several very severely wounded. The stream of death is rising in the hospital, and it requires close watching to keep run of his ravages. Five brave heroes have died from wounds in ward twenty-two since the capture of Richmond.

"April 16. Sabbath. Chaplain Roe and myself both spoke to-night on the death of President Lincoln; Mr. Roe from Psalm xlvi. 1. I urged the people not to despair; God will protect us. The congregation was the largest I ever saw in the hall,—some eight hundred; meeting very solemn and impressive; many wept."

LARGEST INTERMENT.

"Ten patients died yesterday. We buried twenty-nine to-day (April 20); six cart-loads. There was an accumulation of corpses in the dead-house, for want of coffins to bury them in. Funeral services at the graves unusually solemn and impressive. Read and spoke on the resurrection and general judgment. 'Great God have mercy on the dying soldiers! Save them for Jesus' sake!' The above is the greatest number we buried in any one day during the war at Hampton Hospital.

"May 2. Buried twelve. Preached in ward fifteen; canvassed as usual; went through rebel and gangrene camps, pointing the anxious to the cross, and warning the careless 'to flee the wrath to come.' Visited two confederate soldiers, who wept—one profusely—as I talked to them about Jesus; while I talked to one about other things, he seemed to feel not; but when I touched upon the cross, his heart seemed to swell with emotions. He had been a colporteur for the American Tract Society."

DEDICATION OF NEW HOSPITAL CHAPEL.

The new Hospital chapel, for the want of which we labored for three years under great disadvantages, was dedicated to-day, July 16, 1865. Sixty feet long and thirty wide, with two large wings,—one for a library and reading-room, and the other for the chaplains' quarters,—with stained glass, and a small spire, it presents quite a neat appearance. Rev. Mr. Tisdale, Agent of the U.S. Christian Commission at Fortress Monroe, Va., preached the dedicatory sermon from the prophecy of Jeremiah; Chaplain Roe presided; Chaplain Billingsley made the opening, and Chaplain Marshall the closing prayer upon the interesting and solemn occasion. The congregation was large and attentive. Mr. Roe, who has proved himself to be a very successful beggar in raising some twenty-five hundred dollars in the North, principally in

CHRISTIANITY IN THE WAR. 287

New York and Brooklyn, to erect this much needed house, soon after it was dedicated opened in it a day-school for the colored patients to learn to read, write, and cipher. The first day they had over one hundred scholars, all eager to learn. The hospital library contains some fifteen hundred volumes, many of which are large, fine, valuable, and suitable for the patients.

ARRIVAL OF FORT FISHER WOUNDED.

It was January 19, 1865, when a large steamer, hospital transport, arrived at the wharf, laden with two hundred and seven wounded braves, direct from the bloody field of Fort Fisher, North Carolina. Flushed with victory, though they came with arms and legs off, with limbs shattered, bones broken, and with bodies scarred and lacerated with rebel bayonets, and carrying rebel bullets within them, yet, with hearts throbbing with patriotism and courage, and crowned with glory and honor, they were the most jubilant lot of patients we ever saw enter a hospital. Having just come out of a hard hand-to-hand fight, they were forgetful of their severe, mortal wounds, and conscious of the great victory achieved, they delighted to talk about it. In the language of the immortal Perry, they could say, " We have met the enemy, and they are ours." Enter the boat: there they lie, with their life-blood ebbing away, yet, patient and resigned, not a murmur falls from their lips. Having fought a good fight, and won crowns of glory, though their sufferings were great, they bore it all with heroic courage, without a word of complaint. But, alas! for these brave heroes, though jubilant, and flushed with victory to-day, some are doomed to die to-morrow; having just triumphantly fought one battle, they are soon to fight another; having just vanquished one enemy, some are soon to vanquish another; having just won one glorious victory, they are soon to win another more glorious, even victory over death, the last enemy, and go down to the grave crowned with all the glories of martyrdom; for it was but a few hours ere we saw some grappling with death, and, "having fought a good fight," gave shouts of victory. Thus, dying for their country, sealing the bonds of Union with their blood, they have left the scene of conflict; gone forever, gone from the field of battle, by way of Fortress Monroe, home to glory, to swell the victor's song of redeeming love around the throne of God forever.

CHAPTER XVIII.

BOMBARDMENT OF FORT FISHER.

THE WOUNDED ARRIVE AT THE HOSPITAL — THEY ARE VERY JUBILANT — ADMIRAL PORTER COMMANDS THE FLEET — "THE WORLD NEVER SAW SUCH FIGHTING" — THE SCENE AWFULLY GRAND AND SUBLIME — GREAT SLAUGHTER OF SAILORS — AWFUL HAND-TO-HAND FIGHT FOR HOURS — THE SURRENDER — BUOYANT WOUNDED FROM RICHMOND — DYING THAT THE NATION MIGHT LIVE — HOSPITAL VARIETY MONOTONOUS — DESIRE TO GO HOME.

BUT we cannot drop these brave heroes without giving a brief sketch of the terrible fight in the capture of Fort Fisher, of which, said Admiral Porter, "The world never saw such fighting as our men did." It was on Friday morning, January 13, 1865, about four o'clock, while the pale moon shone brightly upon the placid ocean, that the signal, "get up," flashed from the flag-ship by the firing of a gun, and reverberating throughout the vast fleet, bid the slumbering thousands rise and prepare for the solemn, important work of the day. In a moment the reveille is beating, soldiers and sailors are rising, and in a few minutes the entire squadron is all in action. Breakfast being over at five o'clock, the sagacious admiral cries out, "*Get under way*," and the whole fleet weigh anchor, spread sail, get up steam, and by the first dawn of day the whole armada was in motion. At a quarter before seven, the admiral gives another signal, and cries out, "*Form line of battle!*" Whereupon the *Brooklyn*, bearing twenty-six guns, together with twelve other boats, carrying in all one hundred and sixteen guns, moved up about three and a half miles above Fort Fisher, near the Half-moon Battery, to clear out by shelling a place for the landing of the troops, and ordered to prepare for action, and soon began to shell the adjacent beach. Meanwhile five iron-clads were thrown into position, three-fourths of a mile, and the monitors half a mile from the fort, and opened upon it with a most galling fire, with a terrible effect, with an occasional shot from the fort. About nine o'clock some four thousand men, assisted by the boats, were landed, and planted their flag upon one of the highest sand-hills, amidst the hearty cheering of gazing thousands of the fleet, panting for victory. Not an enemy could be seen.

The bombardment now becomes general, and by four o'clock P. M., the admiral orders the vessels in the line of battle number one to take their position, and join the bombardment; whereupon fourteen vessels, led by the *Brooklyn*, carrying in all one hundred and thirty-six guns, sallied forth fully primed for the mighty conflict. Following in rapid succession was an order to the second line of battle to take their position and join the bombardment; and immediately it moved forward with seven of the largest wooden gunboats (in the service), led by the *Minnesota*, with fifty-two, and in all one hundred and seventy-six guns. There they are, with three hundred and twelve guns, together with the iron-clads and monitors, all fully primed, manned with buoyant hearts, thirsting for the deadly work. At twenty minutes before five, the whole fleet joined in the general bombardment. Now began one of the fiercest, most powerful and destructive cannonades the world ever saw. With one vast sheet of flame, for an hour and a half they poured in their enormous devouring shells at the rate of two hundred and forty per minute, dealing death and destruction among the ruthless entrenched rebels at every blow, and silenced the rebel guns at once. One fifteen-inch shell pierced a bomb-proof, and killed sixteen, and severely wounded twenty-five rebels.

How thrilling the scene! The vivid flash, the belching blaze, the tremendous roar, and the mighty torrent of balls and shells, together with the thick volumes of dust and smoke rising from the doomed fort, presented a scene of terrific grandeur and awful sublimity, beyond the power of language to describe! It seemed as if all the artillery of heaven was let loose upon the doomed crumbling fort! At ten minutes past six P. M. the general bombardment ceases, and the fort, with some three or four thousand shells and balls lodged in and about it, is reduced to a perfect pulp, and well prepared for an attack by land. Hitherto the fight, on our part, has been preparatory to the final assault. As yet, not a life has been lost, nor a drop of blood shed. But Sabbath, January 15, dawns with a clear sky and a placid ocean, and now comes the tug of war in earnest. During the night, the army forces, numbering some four thousand, commanded by Maj.-Gen. A. H. Terry, had gathered round the fort, anxiously waiting the signal to attack. The most perfect harmony exists between Admiral Porter, commanding the fleet, and Gen. Terry; and though they were a mile apart during the assault, they conversed by signs as the emergencies required. With some twenty-two hundred bloodthirsty rebels strongly entrenched in the besieged fort, fully determined to conquer or die, encompassed by five thousand heroic braves thirsting for victory in the cause of God and the Union, how critical the moment! Big with the fate of Fort Fisher, and the destiny of so many valuable lives, and the salvation of the country, how very important the crisis! Gaze upon the tragic scene, swelling with importance, anxiety, and solemnity as the decisive hour approaches. With hundreds, it is the last Sabbath upon earth; hundreds of hearts, now warm and gushing with patriotism and thirsting for glory and honor, are soon to lie cold in death. Oh, how thrilling and critical the hour! "Great God, on what a slender thread hangs the destiny of immortal things!" It is now eleven o'clock A. M., and the vast fleet again open, and continue firing upon the unfortunate fort most furiously for hours. Time flies: the crisis approaches; and now, with all ready, at half-past three P.M. the signal is given, and the awful charge and fearful assault are made, and the mighty struggle begins. At this juncture, with a report louder than seven thunders, all the steam-whistles blow, and the gallant soldiers and sailors rush forward, each one nobly vying to reach the top of the parapet first. Two thousand brave sailors, led on by Capt. K. R. Breese, attack on the sea-front of the fort, and rushing forward, apparently determined to take it by storm; but on reaching the parapet, and there planting their colors, the rebels mistook them for the main body of the charge, and there concentrating their force, repeatedly poured in upon them the most galling, destructive fires of grape and canister. The gallant heroes sallied three times, right in the jaws of death, but were swept away like chaff before the wind; and finding their efforts were unavailing (with all the efforts of Capt. Breese, Lieuts. Cushing and Preston), they were compelled to give way amidst three loud rebel cheers, leaving some two hundred of their number killed and wounded strewn round the fort. Meanwhile three thousand heroic soldiers of the old 10th Corps, led on by the brave Gen. N. M. Curtis, 142d N. Y. Vol., under the immediate supervision of Gen. Terry, made the attack on the rear, and most difficult part of the fort, with complete success. Although the sailors failed in their attack, they did a good work in diverting the enemy from the attack on the rear by the troops, who, upon mounting the parapets and scaling the crumbling fort, and seeing the rebels driving the sailors, rushed in upon them, peppering their backs, and gave them one of the most destructive fires ever discharged; and then ensued one of the most desperate, savage, and destructive hand-to-hand fights the world ever saw. It lasted seven hours. Both sides fought with perfect desperation. Fearless and determined to conquer or die, Gen. Terry entered the fort himself. Gen. Curtis coming in direct contact with the bloodthirsty rebels, slew them with his sword, and had one of his eyes put out in the fight. Col. Moore, 203d Pa. Vol., bearing the flag of his regiment, fearlessly rushed forward, and received several balls which laid him dead at once. On and on waged the terrible conflict. From traverse after traverse the ruthless rebels were driven back by our invincible heroes, fighting like lions. Col. Pennypacker, following Gen. Curtis closely in the assault, was severely wounded. Thus fiercely waged the awful conflict, until the blood-stained fort was strewn with the dead and dying. They fought on till ten o'clock at night, when the rebels were driven out and fled to Federal point, where Gen. Whiting, commanding the rebel forces, surrendered himself and command unconditionally to Gen. Terry, the hero of Fort Fisher, about twelve o'clock. The rebel dead were estimated at five hundred; our killed and wounded about nine hundred. Col. Bell, 4th N. H., died the following morning. Lieuts. Preston and Porter, of the navy, were both killed.

Soon after the fall of Richmond, we received a few boat-loads of patients from that region, many of whom were severely wounded, and coming from the field of carnage, laden with the spoils and glory of victory, they too were highly jubilant and full of rejoicing over the fall of the rebel capital and flight of Jeff Davis. Uplifted with the great victory achieved, and having so nobly done their part in achieving it, although a great many of them had left a limb or two and a great portion of their blood upon the gory field, yet conscious of the greatness and grandeur of the achievement, with hearts throbbing with heroic devotion to their country, although with many their life-blood was fast ebbing away, and with all the stern realities of eternity rising before them, still they were buoyant and cheerful. Having stood so many charges and faced so many rebel cannon, yet trusting in the Lord, and dying for their country, they are not afraid to face death and eternity. To see so many mangled heroes, with sloughing stumps, bleeding wounds, and amputated limbs, strewn over a ward, lying upon their death-beds, and to look around and see this and that brave patriot struggling in the agonies of death, dying that the nation might live, deeply impresses one with the horrors of war, with the great price of liberty, and the solemnity of death. We often received patients mangled all over with six or eight wounds, and so severe that they were unable to turn in bed, and yet with patience and good nursing they would get along and get well. Here lies a man, shot in the mouth, the ball passing out at the back of his neck; yet he is so full of courage, he still lives, jovial and cheerful.

HOSPITAL VARIETY MONOTONOUS.

Notwithstanding the variety of the daily routine of hospital life; the reveille in the morning, and the tattoo in the evening;

the daily carrying live, wounded men in, and the daily carrying dead men out, together with the stirring strains of music by the Hospital band, and the mournful notes of the death march at the soldier's funeral, with muffled drums, etc., yet, withal to the old incumbent, there was much dull monotony. Hence the strong desire among the patients for something new and exciting, and usually having on hand from ten to twelve hundred convalescents, it was no trouble to get up a large meeting almost any time.

SOLDIERS GOING HOME.

Since the fall of the rebellion, we have had a great rush of convalescents to this hospital, to be discharged; and "I want my discharge papers and my pay" has been the ringing cry of the hospital for weeks. This is natural. Tired of hospital life, and anxious to see "the loved ones at home," everybody wants to go first. Hence the familiar "Good-by, Jim," and the warm farewell shake of hands, are of constant occurrence; and it is solemn. It is a farewell, perhaps, to meet no more on earth. And while they are going at the rate of one hundred a day, others here are going to their *long home* at the rate of four or five a day. A good many rebel prisoners have been brought in lately, and many of them being in a bad condition, they drop off rapidly. Many of them come with their Bibles and Testaments, which they have carried through the war; and many of them seem to be religious men, and often ask to be prayed for, and desire to hear religious service. I have seen many a one weep profusely on his death-bed, and give clear evidence of piety. The approach of death seems to knock rebellion out of them. Besides, a great many say they were *driven* into it, and always opposed it.

When I was captured at Plymouth, N. C., they put our wounded in the same room with theirs; and when I went in to see them, a young rebel lying near by, nigh unto death, called me to come and pray for him. I went, and he thanked me heartily, and died shortly after. While many are still rebels at heart, we think it an encouraging fact in reconstruction that so many seem to fear God. Many of them think Davis should be hung.

We still have some three thousand convalescents and patients in the hospital, and more are expected soon.

CHAPTER XIX.

LINCOLN'S FUNERAL.

LINCOLN'S FUNERAL — DEEP FEELING: SOLEMN, IMPRESSIVE — THE AUTHOR'S ADDRESS AT THE FUNERAL — SUDDEN CHANGE FROM REJOICING TO WEEPING — HIS DEATH A LOSS TO THE ENTIRE WORLD — NATIONAL GRIEF UNSPEAKABLE — HIS CHARACTER — THE GREAT EMANCIPATOR AND FRIEND OF THE SLAVE — SELF-MADE — THE SAVIOUR OF HIS COUNTRY — RELIGIOUS CHARACTER: BROUGHT UP TO PRAY, AND READ THE BIBLE — HIS LAST REQUEST: "PRAY FOR ME" — "I LEAVE MYSELF, MY COUNTRY, AND ALL IN THE HANDS OF GOD."

LINCOLN'S FUNERAL.

AT the suggestion of President Johnson, according to an order issued by Dr. McClellan, Assistant Surgeon U. S. A., in charge of the aforesaid hospital, some two thousand five hundred heart-smitten patients, officers, strangers, and citizens assembled, April 19, 1865, to participate in the national obsequies of the lamented President. The meeting, held in the open air, was peculiarly solemn and impressive. Filled with sorrow and anguish, everybody turned out to mingle their tears with a nation crushed with grief under this most severe national bereavement. Every soldier and patient that could get out of bed and crawl was there. There they came, with amputated limbs, broken bones, tender wounds, and frail bodies, limping along on crutches, to unite in the solemn service, with hearts throbbing with grief over the loss of their beloved commander-in-chief. There, too, were hundreds of colored patients and people bathed in tears, wringing their hearts with grief over the invaluable loss of their best friend and great emancipator. There, too, were two companies of the Veteran Reserves, in mourning attire, deeply lamenting the loss of the nation's savior. There, deeply impressed with the solemnity of the occasion, crushed with unutterable grief, waiting beneath a shining sun until the hour appointed, when the exercises were commenced with a solemn dirge by the band, followed with the reading of suitable passages of Scripture, accompanied with a few appropriate introductory remarks by Chaplain Marshall; whereupon Chaplain Billingsley led the weeping assembly in prayer. After singing, Chaplain Raymond followed with an able, appropriate address, analyzing the character of Abraham Lincoln, and highly eulogizing his invaluable services to the country, "when Chaplain Billingsley followed in a strain similar to the previous speaker," in the following speech. The exercises were concluded with brief remarks and an appropriate prayer by Rev. Mr. Craighead, editor of the New York Evangelist, when the vast assemblage dispersed to their respective quarters, deeply impressed with the great loss and the solemnities of the memorable occasion. With the flags all hung at half-mast, business suspended, the hospital buildings draped in the deepest mourning, and every countenance clothed in sorrow and grief inexpressible, all nature seemed to present an aspect of lamentation and woe. The assassination of Abraham Lincoln was the greatest shock America, or the world, ever received.

ADDRESS AT LINCOLN'S FUNERAL.

How solemn and impressive this scene! How deep and pungent the national sorrow! Although it is caused by one man's death, yet the impression is so deep, it seems as though there was one dead in every house. When Washington died, the grief and anguish was very great and national; but that stroke was not so severe as this. The circumstances are very different. Then the country was at peace; to-day it is baptized with fraternal blood, with a martyred President in his coffin. How very sudden the change. Yesterday, the nation was all alive with rejoicing;

to-day, it is wrapped in the deepest mourning. Yesterday all eyes were gleaming with joy; to-day, millions are flashing with vengeance upon the treacherous, fiendish assassin. And is Abraham Lincoln dead? Is he no more? Though dead, he still lives. The bright example he left us, and the great good he done us, will live after him. The great principles he taught and advocated are immortal. No man *liveth*, and no man *dieth*, to himself. Though he met an untimely death, yet, enshrined in the affections and enthroned upon the hearts of the people, he will live embalmed in their memory forever. How very great his loss! Who can calculate it? It is irreparable. None can fill his place. Blessing with his kindness, through his bright example of pure patriotism, stern integrity, and broad, comprehensive principles of humanity, liberty, and justice, the nations of the earth, his death is a severe loss to the entire world. And we are here to-day, in common with millions of weeping hearts all over the land, to mingle our tears with theirs upon this most severe national bereavement. Upon such an occasion as this, it is manly to weep. A great, wise, noble, patriotic, good man is dead. "How are the mighty fallen?" Flushed with victory, yesterday Abraham Lincoln filled the presidential chair, covered with glory and honor; to-day he lies a stiffened corpse, enshrouded in the flag he died a martyr to defend. Gather round, and gaze upon his noble form as he lies in state. Draw down that napkin. Ah, me! see how his visage is marred by the ruthless hand of that vile assassin. Oh, how lamentable and heart-rending the scene! How great the calamity! How severe the rebuke! With the nation's head, with the nation's favorite, with the nation's greatest benefactor, snatched away without a moment's warning, in such a time as this, language fails to express and heart to conceive the unspeakable grief and sadness of a heart-smitten nation.

The murder of Cæsar in the Roman senate was atrocious; hanging Union soldiers by scores for their loyalty in North Carolina was barbarous; the wholesale, cold-blooded massacre at Fort Pillow was fiendish; starving to death thousands of soldiers in Andersonville was horrible beyond description; but these most shocking crimes, culminating in the diabolical murder of President Lincoln and attempted national assassination, are second only to the crucifixion of Jesus Christ upon Mount Calvary! It would seem that hell had disgorged and robbed itself to send forth the blackest devil to scourge and chasten us! And although the earth did not quake, nor the rocks rend, nor the sun refuse to shine, yet, appalled with horror and crushed with grief, everything wears an aspect of lamentation and woe, and wraps the nation in the deepest gloom and mourning.

Yet, fellow-soldiers and fellow-citizens, let us not be discouraged; though our dearest, best personal and national friend is gone, despair not; let not your hearts be troubled; "be of good cheer." Jehovah Jesus still rules and reigns high over all, and head over all things to the Church! God is still our refuge and strength, therefore we will not fear, though our chief executive is removed from us! The wheels of government will still roll on; our armies will march; victories will follow; the soldiers will go home; his widowed wife and bereaved mother will weep; that dear old flag, now dearer than ever, will still wave over the country Abraham Lincoln, under God, redeemed from treason; but from his warm gushing heart we will receive no more proclamations nor kind messages. Touching his character, wisdom, good sense, sound judgment, magnanimity, pure patriotism, shrewd sagacity, moral courage, simplicity, *kindness*, and, above all, *stern integrity*, were among his most prominent traits. Devoted to his country, he was a true friend to the soldier, and made the preservation of the Union the principal object of his administration. The great emancipator and special friend of the slave, he freed millions by proclamation, and gave them the protection of the Government. Born in obscurity and brought up in poverty, through his own persevering efforts he rose from the humblest walks of life to the highest position on earth; and while Washington is "the father," Abraham Lincoln well deserves the title of "the savior," of his country.

The nation to-day is burying the lamented President. Burying him! burying Abraham Lincoln! No: you cannot do it, no more than you can bury the Declaration of Independence, the

Constitution, the Bible, or the history of your country; no more than you can bury the everlasting hills, mountains, lakes, rivers, and oceans! No: he will *live on;* live all over the world, and live through all coming time! Nations, kingdoms, and empires may rise, flourish, fade, and fall; generations will pass away; the bed of the Chesapeake may shift; the Potomac may dry up; the ocean's swelling tide may cease to roll; the blue hills of Virginia may give way to the mouldering hand of time; and every Lincoln monument may crumble to the dust — but HIS NAME and HIS DEEDS will live as long as time rolls on!

Born of a pious mother, and brought up to the Bible, Abraham Lincoln was taught to pray before he could pronounce his Maker's name. Deeply impressed with the responsibilities of his position, and feeling his need of divine aid on leaving home for Washington, his last request of his friends was, *"Pray for me!"* And during his last years, like Havelock, he usually spent from one to two hours every morning in reading God's word, meditation, and prayer. Abraham Lincoln was a man of prayer; and as the difficulties and responsibilities of his position increased, and bore more heavily upon his tender heart, it drove him nearer to God. Hence we hear him, in times of great emergencies, giving vent to his feelings in such words as these: "I have been driven many times to my knees by the overwhelming conviction that I had nowhere else to go. My own wisdom, and that of all about me, seemed insufficient for that day." Filled with sorrow upon the death of his son, he said to a sympathizing friend, "I will try to go to God with my sorrows." Soon after, she asked him if he could trust God; he said, "I think I can, and I will try." Very much distressed about the loss at the second defeat at Bull Run, he said, "I have done the best I could; I have asked God to guide me, and now I must leave the event with him." But the highest expression of his sublime faith and devotion to God is seen, perhaps, in his words to a friend during the dark days of Gettysburg. "I rolled on Him the burden of my country, and rose from my knees lightened of my load, feeling a peace that passes all understanding,— feeling I could leave myself, my country, and my all in the hands of God." These bright manifestations of his fervent prayers, strong, unwavering faith, taken in connection with the purity of his life, his devotion to his country, his meek, forgiving spirit, his unselfish disposition, his "charity for all, and malice toward none," together with the reliance upon God and submission to his will, expressed in his last Inaugural Address, so deeply impresses the unprejudiced mind, that we can no longer doubt that for him "to die was gain, and to depart far better." Having passed away from the thrilling scenes of a most eventful life, and the difficulties of reconstruction and restoring peace, he has gone, we trust, where no vile rebel lurks, and where no foul assassin prowls. Yes, crowned with all the glories of martyrdom, he has gone, we trust, "where the wicked cease to trouble, and the weary are forever at rest;" gone where there will be no more war, no more death, neither sorrow nor crying; where God himself shall wipe away all tears. This being so, how striking the contrast between his condition on earth and his condition in heaven. Here all is war, blood, and death; there all is life, joy, and peace. Here he was surrounded with the dead and dying; there with the redeemed and living. Here he bore a sword, there he wears a crown; here he sat upon the presidential chair, there he sits upon the throne of God. And though dead, he yet speaketh; his tongue, though now mute in death, seems to say to his successor, to every member of his cabinet, to every senator and congressman, to every officer, soldier, and sailor of the army and navy, "Be ye also ready!" "*Prepare to meet thy God!*"

CHAPTER XX.

THE STREAM OF DEATH.

THE FIRST SOLDIERS KILLED IN THE WAR — REBEL CRUELTY TO THE DEAD — DEATH OF COL. BAKER — GEN. LYON'S BRAVERY AND DEATH — DEATH IN THE MISSISSIPPI VALLEY AND ON THE PENINSULA — REMOVAL OF GEN. MCCLELLAN — GEN. ROSECRANS' BRAVERY AT STONE RIVER — "THE BLOODIEST BATTLE OF THE WAR" — THE BATTLE OF GETTYSBURG THE DEATH-BLOW OF THE REBELLION — GEN. GRANT ASSUMES COMMAND IN CHIEF — "ON TO RICHMOND" — DEATH OF GEN. SEDGWICK — BATTLE OF COAL HARBOR — SIMULTANEOUS MOVEMENT OF ARMIES — GEN. SHERMAN AT ATLANTA — GEN. SHERIDAN'S VICTORIES IN THE SHENANDOAH VALLEY — BATTLE AT FRANKLIN, TENN. — GEN. SHERIDAN'S STRATAGEM AT CEDAR CREEK — LINCOLN CALLS FOR MORE VOLUNTEERS — GEN. SHERMAN COMPLETES HIS "MARCH TO THE SEA" — SLAVERY ABOLISHED BY CONGRESS, JAN. 31, 1865 — GRANT'S LAST "GREAT STRIKE" — FALL OF RICHMOND, FLIGHT OF JEFF. DAVIS, AND SURRENDER OF GEN. LEE — MORTALITY DURING THE WAR — THE DESERTER.

AS soon as the war was inaugurated, the stream of death began to flow, and it continued, with slight variations, until the war closed. The first man killed was private Daniel Hough, who fell nobly defending his country at the rebel bombardment of Fort Sumter, April 12, 1861. The next blood shed and lives lost was in an encounter of the 6th Massachusetts with an outrageous mob in Baltimore, while on their way to Washington to defend the President and national capital from prowling assassins. In this severe struggle the immortal 6th, commanded by Col. —— Jones, lost two killed and nine wounded; while the assailants lost nine killed and eight severely wounded. The next patriotic blood that crimsoned the stream of death was that of the brave Col. Ellsworth, which provoked a prompt revenge by Brownell, and the blood of both patriot and assassin ran commingly together in Alexandria, May 24, 1861. The next influx

VIEW OF THE ANTIETAM BATTLE-GROUND.

into this mortal stream was at the battle of Big Bethel, where some three or more brave boys tasted death; among them was Major Winthrop, who was shot by a North Carolina drummer-boy, and fell dead while bravely leading his men into battle. Following down the crimson tide of this widening stream, until you reach the bloody field where Americans first met Americans in pitched battle upon the gory field of Bull Run, and there you see death invading our ranks, and bearing off some five hundred more noble heroes, who sealed their devotion to their country with their blood. At this sad defeat the nation was thrown into the deepest gloom, and thousands were wringing their hearts with grief over the most sad misfortune. Not satisfied with the victory won, to add ignominy to defeat, the rebels buried our men with their faces downward, and took their bones for drumsticks and finger-rings, and their skulls for goblets and punchbowls. From that time on, during the long four years of bloody strife, Death, like a mighty tyrant, reigned through the ranks of our brave heroes, bearing them off by hundreds and thousands at every great battle. .

Tracing down still further the surging waves of this mighty struggle for national life, we see Death, like a stern monarch, going forth conquering and to conquer; and at the terrible slaughter at Ball's Bluff, in a desperate conflict against awful odds, bearing off two hundred and twenty-five more noble heroes, among whom was the brave, noble, and magnanimous Col. Baker, who fell in the heat of battle from the discharge of eight pistol-balls into his body by a red-headed and black-hearted rebel, who also fell the next minute in a similar manner by a prompt avenger, Capt. Beirel, who with one fire of his pistol laid the ruthless traitor brainless beside one of freedom's noblest martyrs.

The next large influx into this rising stream was at the battle of Wilson's Creek, Mo., where the brave Gen. Lyon, and some two hundred and thirty more gallant soldiers, nobly sacrificed their lives upon the altar of their country. In the hot fury of the battle, Lyon calls to his men, "Prepare to charge the enemy," when the brave Iowans, thirsting for victory, cry out, "Who will lead us?" Whereupon Gen. Lyon exclaimed,

"Come on, brave, brave men, I will lead you!" In a moment, the general was at their head, and on they pushed amidst a most galling fire of rebel musketry, slightly checking their advance; but on they rushed, and in a moment the rebels gave way, "the army was saved, *but Lyon was dead!*" Receiving two bullets in his breast, he fell immediately; and an officer, rushing to his relief, anxiously inquired, "Are you hurt?" "Not much," was his faint reply. They were his last words. He expired immediately, covered with all the glories of martyrdom.

But this is only the beginning of sorrows; only, as it were, the first fruits of the ravages of death in "the war for the Union." As the conflict increased, we find the fell destroyer with one vast sweep of his ruthless scythe mowing down thousands in a single battle. Sweeping down the Valley of the Mississippi, the king of terrors made havoc of the nation's defenders; slaying seventeen hundred and thirty-five, and wounding seven thousand eight hundred and thirty-two, with a total loss of near fourteen thousand at the bloody battle of Pittsburg Landing, April 7, 1862, with a rebel loss of sixteen thousand, and twenty-seven hundred killed. At the battle of South Mountain, Md., September 14, 1862, four hundred and forty-three more noble patriots fell out of the Union ranks into the river of death, with eighteen hundred and six more wounded, together with a rebel loss of some four thousand, and five hundred killed.

Going forth on his pale horse, this mighty conqueror, during the Peninsula campaign, swept away thousands and thousands, many of whom left their uncoffined bones bleaching in the dismal swamps of Virginia. At the battle of Williamsburg, Va., three hundred of our brave boys fell beneath his iron grasp; and with one fell stroke of his devouring hand, at the great battle of Antietam, Md., September 17, 1862, he plucked from our noble army two thousand and ten heroic patriots, who left the world to wear a martyr's crown. The wounded numbered 9416; total loss, 12,469: rebel loss, 25,000. Brig.-Gen. Mansfield, U.S.A., was killed in this battle. In the two days' battle of Fair Oaks, Va., eight hundred and ninety more fell at their posts, defending the cause of God, liberty, and truth, with thirty-six hundred and twenty-seven wounded. In the hard-fought battle of Malvern Hill, Va., together with the seven or eight battles fought during Gen. McClellan's retreat from Richmond, including all from Mechanicsville to Malvern Hill, twelve hundred and sixty-five more of our Union braves tasted death, and sealed their devotion to their country with their blood. In these battles our wounded were 7701; total loss, 14,924 : rebel loss estimated at 18,000. The last important battle of the Peninsula campaign was fought at Cedar Mountain, Va., August 19, 1862, in which our loss in killed and wounded was twelve hundred and fifty. Thus Death reigned throughout our armies, spreading destruction on every side.

On August 16, 1862, Gen. McClellan, having failed to take Richmond, moved his entire army from Harrison's Landing, via Fortress Monroe, Va., to Alexandria and Washington.

The next great influx into this raging stream was at the battle of Bull Run, August 29, 1862, where, said Gen. Pope commanding, "our loss was not less than eight thousand killed and wounded, and the loss of the enemy was at least two to our one." Gen. McClellan was then, immediately after the battle of Antietam, removed, and Gen. Burnside took his place. But the stream of death still flowed on. At the battle of Fredericksburg, Va., fought as it was under great disadvantages, our death-defying heroes made three successive charges on the rebels, strongly entrenched behind a stone wall, and were thrice driven back with great slaughter, with a loss of over twelve thousand (12,321), while the rebels' loss was comparatively few, as they fought under cover. Flowing round by the battle of Corinth, three hundred and fifteen more brave patriots fell dead into this sweeping stream, and thirteen hundred more fell badly wounded upon its gory banks. Here the rebels lost fourteen hundred killed and eighteen hundred wounded. The President having about this time called into the field six hundred thousand more men, tended to swell the size of this rising stream.

At the hard-fought battle of Stone River, the rebels, commanded by Gen. Bragg, fighting with great determination, thrice repulsed our men. But Gen. Sheridan rallying his men, and eager for victory, drove them back four times with heavy loss. Still they held on, and, coming up again, they received a most galling fire. At this juncture the rebels fell back, and the firing ceased. The Federal troops, commanded by General Rosecrans, had been worsted in the fight, and lost some three thousand killed and wounded. The enemy had also suffered terribly; yet, not willing to give up, Gen. Rosecrans called a council of his generals, and sternly declared to them, *"We conquer, or die right here!"* and the fire flashing into their hearts, his officers resolved to rally again, and conquer or die on the spot. Confident of success, on came the defiant rebels bold as lions, and our heroic braves, pitching into them mowed them down with great slaughter, and drove them across the shallow river at the point of the bayonet. In this severe struggle, Death plucked from our ranks ninety-three brave officers and fourteen hundred and forty-one privates; officers wounded, 384; privates, 6865. Flowing down the valley of the lower Mississippi, this mortal stream swept away five hundred and forty-five more gallant soldiers at the battle of Vicksburg, four hundred and twenty-six at Champion's Hills, and one hundred and thirty at Port Gibson. And flowing on still further down, at the capture of Port Hudson over two thousand more were killed and wounded. The fall of Vicksburg and capture of Port Hudson again removed the obstructions from the Mississippi River. Burnside being relieved, Gen. Hooker took his place, and soon began the fourth campaign against Richmond. But the river of death still flowed on, and at the disastrous battle of Chancellorsville it was swollen with the blood of some ten thousand more brave heroes bleeding and dying for the country's cause, among whom was Gen. Berry, who fell gallantly leading his men in battle Sabbath night. Gen. Lee pronounced this "the bloodiest battle of the war," and the rebels estimated their loss at from sixteen to eighteen thousand, among whom was the brave Stonewall Jackson, who died soon after from wounds received in this bloody fight.

Not long after the battle of Chancellorsville, Gen. Lee made his great disastrous raid up north into Pennsylvania; and at the decisive battle of Gettysburg, July 3, 1863, the king of terrors, with showers of balls flying thick as hail, streaming forth from some three hundred and fifty guns, blackening the air, swept away, as with the besom of destruction, two thousand eight hundred and thirty-four heroic veterans, leaving thirteen thousand seven hundred and nine bleeding with wounds upon the hotly contested field. Total loss, twenty-three thousand one hundred and eighty-six. The rebels lost over forty-five hundred killed, buried by Union men, with over thirteen thousand prisoners, and an estimated total loss of thirty thousand. Death reigns! Viewed prospectively, and taking it all in all, this was, doubtless, one of the most important battles ever fought in the world. Here the head of the serpent was bruised, and the rebellion, in all its ramifications, was struck with death! Here, beneath the shades of Independence Hall, whence, eighty-seven years before, was issued the "Declaration of Independence," declaring, for the first time, that all men are created free and equal, the decree went forth, amidst streams of blood and death against the rebellion, that, *dying, thou shalt die!*

Thus mortally wounded, the rebellion struggled along several months, and expired April 9, 1865, at the surrender of Gen. Lee, near Appomattox Court-House, Va.

Sweeping round to the West, at the hard-fought battle of Chickamauga, or Chattanooga, sixteen hundred and forty-four more gallant heroes fell beneath his withering grasp, leaving eight thousand six hundred and ninety-eight bleeding on the gory field, with a rebel loss of eighteen thousand seven hundred killed and wounded. Sweeping round his great scythe, Death swept hundreds more from our ranks at the battle of Missionary Ridge. And at the heavy assault upon Fort Wagner, in Charleston harbor, we lost some fifteen hundred in killed, wounded, and missing. Here the 54th Mass. distinguished themselves. Placed in advance of two brave brigades, and giving a fierce yell as they approached the strong fort, on they rushed amidst furious volleys of grape and canister, plunging through a ditch of water four feet deep, and scaling the parapet, and fighting with perfect desperation, left their brave Col. Shaw, with over one-half of their number, dead upon the ensanguined field. The next heavy influx into this swelling stream was at the awful massacre at Fort Pillow; when (April 12, 1864,) the ferocious rebels, under command of Gen. Forrest, indiscriminately butchered, in cold blood, over four hundred men, white and black, after they had surrendered and laid down their arms. "Those who begged for quarter were shot down and bayoneted; even the women and children were killed and wounded."

On March 10, 1864, Gen. Grant, by appointment of President Lincoln, assumed the command of the armies of the United States, with his head-quarters in the field. But still the stream of death flowed on rapidly. On the second of the following May, the Lieutenant-General, with the army of the Potomac, crossed the Rapidan, and commenced the fifth campaign against Richmond, and soon came in contact with Gen. Lee and his determined forces. For two days they fought the bloody battle of the Wilderness, with a Union loss of some fifteen thousand, including Gens. Hays and Wadsworth. The rebel loss was about equal to the Federal. It was remarkable in this deadly battle, fought in the midst of thick woods, with the sabre and the rifle, that each army "claimed to have repelled the fierce attack of the enemy."

But unterrified with these heavy losses, the mighty conflict still went on, and raged with great fury at the battle of Spottsylvania, where both armies fought with great determination. Every inch of soil, drunk with human blood, was fought over with perfect desperation, and with rival bayonets interlocked in the bloody grapple over the entrenchments, lasting for hours, with rebel battle-flags surging up alongside with ours, Death made great havoc in our ranks, and the heroic dead were left upon the gory field in heaps. It was here, May 11, 1864, after six days' very hard fighting, with a heavy loss on both sides, "with much in our favor," the rebels having retreated during the night, after five unsuccessful attempts to drive our troops, that the persistent Grant heroically declared, in words immortal, "I propose to fight it out on this line, if it takes all summer!"

Gens. Rice and Stevenson were killed on the first day of this great battle, and many under-officers on the third. Full casualties not given. But the severest loss was that of Gen. Sedgwick, who was on the advance with his men, where the rebel bullets were flying thick and fast. The soldiers dodged; and one falling to the ground, the general humorously said to them, "Pooh, pooh, men! who ever heard of a soldier dodging a bullet? Why, they could not hit an elephant at this distance." The men laughed; the general smiled; but it was his last smile. The next moment the fatal bullet pierced his face, and passing through his brain, he fell, and expired without uttering a word. "Watch," "be ye also ready!"

Both armies were now largely re-enforced, and Grant, with unconquerable will, swings his brave boys around, and again coming in contact with his formidable adversary at Cold Harbor, they had another desperate struggle. Here the two armies had lain entrenched within one hundred and fifty yards of each other, and one Federal brigade within fifteen yards of the rebels. Thus exposed, panting for victory, our men, with death staring them in the face, boldly assault the rebels behind their breastworks, and were mown down like grass, with a loss of some seventy-five hundred, while the rebels reported a loss of one thousand. Simultaneous with Grant's crossing the Rapidan, and opening his vigorous campaign against Richmond, was Sherman's advance upon Atlanta, Sigel's into the valley of the Shenandoah, and Butler's up the James upon Fort Darling. And while these mighty armies sallied forth with buoyant spirits, thirsting for victory over their inveterate foe, Death went forth upon his pale horse, conquering and to conquer; and while he made such fearful slaughter in Grant's ranks, he also slew his hundreds and thousands in Sherman's and Butler's. At the well-fought battle of Resaca, Ga., managed by the strategetic Sherman, about eight hundred brave patriots fell beneath his iron grasp, and over four thousand more were wounded in the bloody conflict. The next day Gen. Butler's forces, while investing Fort Darling, were attacked in heavy masses by Beauregard's forces, in a dense fog, and were surprised and defeated, with a loss of twenty-five hundred killed and wounded; the rebels sustaining a loss nearly equal to ours. Thus we see "the king of terrors" is no respecter of persons; but, whetting his sword, he enters indiscriminately the Union and rebel ranks, and plucks his victims from the very flower of both armies.

On the 27th of June, 1864, in Sherman's attack upon the rebels entrenched upon Kenesaw Mountain, he was repulsed with great slaughter, with a loss of thirty-five hundred and twenty-one, inflicting but little damage upon the rebels. And although the people prayed for peace and the cessation of bloodshed, yet the stream of death flowed on; and we next see its ravages up in Maryland, slaying hundreds in the battle of Monocacy, where one hundred and twenty-one Union and three hundred rebel soldiers fell into its crimson flood. Then, flowing around over Sherman's great "march to the sea," in the investing and fall of Atlanta, the Federal loss in three battles, on three different days, was ninety-seven hundred, with a rebel loss of twenty-four thousand and five hundred. And in one of these decisive battles, fought July 22, 1864, which raged with great fury, Sherman commanding in person, and when the 15th Corps had been worsted somewhat, the brave general ordered them to regain their lost ground at any cost; and again plunging into the fierce conflict, determined to conquer or die, they drove the ruthless rebels with tremendous shouts of victory and rejoicing, with a rebel loss of twelve thousand, with over three thousand killed, while the Federals lost only thirty-seven hundred. In this important battle, the heroic Gen. James B. McPherson fell, while giving command to his staff. Shot through the lungs by a volley of bullets from sneaking rebel skirmishers, he fell dead from his horse, crowned with the glories of dying for his country. Gen. Sherman, with a force of some ninety thousand men, lost, in his campaign from Chattanooga to Atlanta, thirty-one thousand three hundred and one, while the rebels sustained a loss of forty-three thousand seven hundred in killed, wounded, and missing.

Gen. Sheridan having assumed command of the middle military division August 7, 1864, and after a few weeks of splendid manœuvring to prevent rebel forces being sent south to reenforce Hood at Atlanta, finally, when opportunity favored, he massed his troops, and thirsting for victory, we see the next general rise in the river of death in the Valley of the Shenandoah, where the brave, dashing Sheridan whipped and drove the bloodthirsty rebels, with a loss of some ten thousand in the battles of Opequan and Fisher's Hill, with an estimated Union loss of four thousand.* Still increasing his reign, the next heavy dash "the last enemy" made upon our noble veterans was at the bloody, hard-fought battle of Franklin, Tenn., where the Federals and rebels, coming in close contact, fought each other with bayonets and clubbed muskets, with perfect desperation, for hours, till darkness closed the bloody scene, with a Federal loss of twenty-one hundred, and with a rebel loss of seventeen hundred and fifty killed, and about five thousand wounded, embracing six general officers killed, and six wounded. Still carrying out the decree, "death hath passed upon all men," and swinging around his fatal scythe again in the battles of Nashville, the Federals lost twenty-nine hundred, and the rebels twenty-five hundred, in killed and wounded.

Yet, as though never satisfied, the old tyrant, Death, still rides forth, building up his kingdom; and the next victory he achieves is in the Valley of the Shenandoah, among the unterrified ranks of the indomitable Sheridan, in the battle of Cedar Creek. Having just won two signal victories, Sheridan had gone to Washington, and on his return, upon approaching his headquarters, and hearing the loud roar of artillery in the direction of his army, he soon found them all, to his great surprise and deep mortification, in full retreat, closely pressed by the sagacious Gen. Early; but, galloping up in full speed to the front, he commanded his retreating army to halt, and by the prestige of his power, the majesty of his courage-inspiring presence, together with the lightning flash of his vivid eye, infused fresh courage into his vanquished heroes; and quickly forming them into line of battle, and wheeling them about, charged and drove the conquering rebels in wild confusion, with an estimated loss of ten thousand men and officers, while our loss was only sixty-five hundred, including fifteen hundred prisoners. The Union Gen. Bidwell and Col. Thoburn fell in this battle.

President Lincoln now, December 20, 1864, issued a call for three hundred thousand more troops; and Sherman went on driving the rebels before him like chaff before the wind, simply at his approach, and completed his "great march to the sea," and there achieved a great bloodless victory in the capture of Savannah, and made of it, with all its spoils, a fine Christmas gift to Abraham Lincoln.

Commencing the year 1865 with an army of six hundred and five thousand men, and the rebels with some three hundred and fifty thousand, Gen. Sherman, having made preparations for leaving Savannah, began his long, difficult, and most extraordinary march of near five hundred miles through swamps, and storms, and creeks, and over mountains, deemed by others almost impassable, in the most inclement season of the year. On the 21st of March, with a loss of one thousand in the campaign, his, the army of Gen. Schofield from Newbern, and Terry's from Wilmington, all crowned with victory, and highly jubilant with success, with a happy coincidence all met in conjunction at Goldsborough, N. C., demonstrating the complete success of the triune campaign. But while this happy juncture was transpiring, the stream of death, though having long since been running down, was still making further inroads in our ranks, and we see our unyielding braves coming out of the battle of Averysboro' with a loss of seven hundred and twenty, and out of the battle of Bentonsville with a loss of sixteen hundred and forty-six. And although Congress, January 31, 1865, passed the Constitutional Amendment, abolishing slavery forever in the United States, with tremendous cheering and shouts of rejoicing, and with the rebellion now cut in two, and the great cause of the war removed in the national decree to "let the oppressed go free," with heaven smiling upon the cause of right and liberty, with the rebels fighting in "the last ditch," the speedy collapse of the rebellion began to loom up from all quarters. The rebellion is doomed! "The die is cast!" and the immortal Grant, concentrating his mighty cohorts, fully primed, in his strong embattlements around Petersburg, prepares to make the last great strike; and with the rebellion "on its last legs," and the veteran Gen. Lee trembling for his cause, the fatal hour arrives, and the crisis comes. Grant gives the word, and the final struggle rages with great fury along his whole line of thirty miles; and the disheartened rebels giving way in every quarter, Lee's army was almost annihilated, and the old veteran army of the Potomac again covers itself with glory. Thus, with the battle fought and the victory won, on the morning of April 3, 1865, at four A.M., filled with enthusiastic exultation, our brave, victorious Union saviors entered the long fought for city of Petersburg amid loud shouts of rejoicing.

In this grand, decisive struggle, in the battles of Hatcher's Run, Fort Steadman, and Five Forks, etc., Gen. Grant estimated our loss at about five thousand killed and wounded, and some two thousand prisoners; while the dispirited rebels, fighting with far less desperation than usual, lost some twelve thousand killed and wounded, and about thirteen thousand prisoners. On the same day, Jeff. Davis and his vanquished rebels having evacuated Richmond, with a large part of it wrapped in flames, fired by their own hands, Gen. Weitzel entered it at a quarter past eight A.M., with most enthusiastic expressions of joy from the inhabitants. Thus ended the march "On to Richmond!" and with the "surrender of Lee to Gen. Grant," amidst loud, prolonged cheering, thus ended the gigantic rebellion, conceived in sin and brought forth in iniquity; and crushed most suddenly, it went down with the deepest grief and greatest mortification to them, but with the profoundest gratitude and highest joy to us. And now, with the stream of death drying up, once more "all is quiet on the Potomac."

The average daily mortality during the war was about two

hundred and fifteen, making in all about three hundred and twenty-five thousand (some put it at 316,000) brave heroes who sacrificed their lives battling for God, liberty, and truth. How are the mighty fallen! See how the country is deluged with their blood, and the land ridged with their graves! Over sixty thousand died in rebel prisons from starvation, cruelty, and torture; scores were hung in North Carolina for loyalty to their country; hundreds were burned to death upon the field of battle; some four hundred were atrociously murdered in cold blood, begging for mercy, at Fort Pillow and Plymouth, N. C.; sometimes, in severe battles, the dead lay four or five feet deep, and, in extreme cases, were used for breastworks,—thus making the dead protect the living, fighting for the life of the nation. Three hundred and twenty-five thousand! Oh, what a sad picture! There they lie in scattered heaps; many of whose uncoffined bones lie bleaching beneath the rays of a scorching sun to-day! Though they died, they conquered; though they died, their blood was the price of self-government, liberty, and truth; though dead, they yet speak; dead, yet they live; and with their memory enshrined in the hearts of a free people, they will live through all coming time. There they lie under the dominion of death; conquerors, yet conquered. Over their precious dust Death now reigns supreme! The saviors of the nation, yet crushed beneath the king of terrors. How mighty is Death! How vast his dominions! But, glory be to God! there is a Mightier: Jesus Christ hath abolished death, and brought life and immortality to light; Jesus, the mighty conqueror, hath robbed the cruel spoiler of his sting, and vanquished him from the tomb, and when he shall say the word, the sea, death, hell, and the grave shall deliver up the dead; and then from the green-turfed grave of every veteran will be seen rising a living form coming to judgment, to be rewarded according to the deeds done in the body.

The rebel loss was about two hundred thousand, making in all over half a million lives sacrificed in the bloody conflict.

THE DESERTER.

The command, by regiments, marched to the appointed ground and wheeled into a hollow square, in the centre of which was the place of execution. The music ceased. Silence and soberness pervaded the vast assembly. Thoughts of the soldier's position and responsibilities were in every bosom.

Presently a solemn dirge is heard from the approaching band. The death procession comes in sight. It enters the square with slow funeral tread: the band; the guard; the coffin borne by four comrades; the deserter handcuffed between two officers; the chaplain; and the fatal platoon of twelve, eleven of whose rifles are loaded with ball-cartridges.

Moving to the step of that sad music around the entire interior of the square, they wheel to the centre, and halt in front of the staff and commanding general.

The captain in charge reads the indictment and sentence of the court-martial. The culprit had "deserted to the enemy, and was found in arms against his country." Sentence: "He shall be *shot to death!*"

"Proceed with the execution!" is the general's stern command.

The coffin is lowered to the ground; the deserter is brought to its side; earnest prayer is offered in his behalf; a few last words and the farewell shake of hands by the chaplain, and then the wretched young man is seated upon his coffin. Handcuffs are removed, eyes bandaged, one-half of that deadly platoon is held in reserve, while the other is ordered "ten paces in front" of the victim.

He sits upright, and apparently firm of nerve, but both hands are braced hard upon his knees. It is a dread moment. Few nerves around are firm; veterans, who could stand calmly before a hurricane of fire, now tremble. The awful form of Death stands out alone! The door of the unseen world is swinging open! Crime, judgment, and stern retribution are working their terrible impressions. Swift, vivid thoughts are in every heart, and "God have mercy on him!" breathes from every lip.

We had not long to wait. *"Ready!"* and the click of the rifle-locks. *"Aim!"* the poor fellow's heart is the target. *"Fire!"* and before the report is heard, he falls back *dead* upon his coffin. The surgeon approaches and examines: "He is dead, sir!" addressing the general.

Again the solemn strains of the band break forth, and the whole parade forms and passes in review of the corpse, followed by a gloomy ambulance. The body, dripping with blood, is placed in its coffin, and put in the ambulance, with only the guard attending, finds its way to the lonely and dishonorable grave.

The troops, who had witnessed the execution, took up their line of march back to camp and duty, awed with the majesty of violated law, feeling, as never before, how serious a thing it is to be a soldier, and how sacred is the cause of our country.

Such is the sad fate of the *deserter:* a grief and shame to his parents; a disgrace to his country, and a curse to the army. CAST OFF! *cast off* by his country, and cut off by the army! Oh, how lamentable! to be cast off by the world, and by all earthly friends, is terrible and awfully severe! But it is nothing to being cast off by God, and be cast down into hell! And why? Why thus cast off, led out, made to kneel, and be shot dead in his coffin? Simply because he had deserted the flag of his country and gone over to the enemy. That, it is true, is a great sin and crime; but it is nothing, sinner, to your sin in forsaking God and rejecting the Saviour. This poor man, simply because he deserted the army, and took up arms against his country, was arrested, tried, condemned, and executed, shot dead on his coffin, and buried in a lonely, dishonorable grave. And what, O impenitent sinner, have you done? You have deserted God, and rejected the Lord Jesus Christ, and gone over to the service of Satan. And you have been arrested, tried, and condemned; yes, "condemned already!" In mercy, God now waits, delays the day of your execution. He has waited long — is waiting still! But he will not always wait. He says, " My Spirit shall not always strive with man." Oh, then, my impenitent friend, let me entreat you to repent and come to Jesus, and come just now.

NATIONAL CEMETERY, FORTRESS MONROE, VA.

CHAPTER XXI.

THE NATIONAL CEMETERY AT FORTRESS MONROE, VA.

Number of Graves — The Place of Many Prayers, Sighs, and Tears — The Old Man Weeping at His Son's Grave — Who are the Dead? — How did They Die? — Soldiers' Dying Words — The Monument — The Inscription — Burying the Dead — National Cemeteries — General Summary.

THIS large depository of the patriotic dead lies about two miles west of the fort, off Hampton Roads, and hard by the once aristocratic town of Hampton; washed by the swelling tide of Chesapeake Bay, and lying on an arm of the same, fringed on one side by thorn and evergreen bushes, and overlooked by the lofty dome of the Chesapeake Hospital, "it is beautiful for situation." Made sacred by containing the remains of so many brave heroes and dear friends, it is a place of much resort. There lie the dead, close to the sacred spot upon which thousands of them once lived, moved, suffered, bled, and died in Hampton Hospital; there, close by the solemn scenes of their last struggle, where many prayed and wept for the preservation of the country and for the salvation of the suffering, dying soldier, now sleep in death their mortal remains, wrapped in plain shrouds, and cased in rough, red coffins.

Embracing an area of nearly twelve acres of valuable land, and containing four thousand six hundred and ninety-five graves,* all marked with neat head-boards, painted white, containing the name, company, regiment, and date of death of every deceased soldier, and all laid out with fine gravel walks, the cemetery presents quite a neat appearance.

It has been the scene of many earnest prayers, deep emotions, tender sighs, and gushing tears. How often have we here seen the bereaved widow, mother, and father weeping over their lamented dead, watering their graves with their tears, and refusing to be comforted, because they were not.

Here we have seen the sadly disappointed father come all the

* Sept. 4, 1868.

way from New England, laden with cordials and good things for his sick and wounded son, and, on arriving, found him dead and buried in this lonely graveyard. Stung with grief, the weeping father at once asks the chaplain, "When did he expire?" "Day before yesterday," replied the chaplain. "How did he die?" "In the triumphs of faith, giving bright evidences of preparation, saying, 'I am ready; all is peace!'" "Thank God!" exclaimed the bereaved parent. "Is he buried?" "Yes." "Where?" "Over there, in the soldier's graveyard." As the chaplain had not time to accompany him, being engaged in attending a funeral, the old man starts at once in search of his grave. There he goes: see how anxiously he looks for it; see how he weeps as he goes: mark his steps; listen to his throbbing heart as he approaches it: there, he has found it! How solemn the scene! There he stands, hushed in silence, bathed in tears and wrapped in grief. Silence reigns; he looks, sighs, drops the tears of affection, and thinks unutterable things! Pensive he gazes upon the new-made grave, and, in the sadness of a smitten heart, exclaims, "O my son, my dear, only beloved son!" and again the gushing tears trickle down his furrowed cheeks. Deeply moved with sorrow and the solemnity of the scene, the aged sire falls prostrate upon the ground, and from the bottom of his heart pours out his soul in thanks to God for the faithful life and triumphant death of his departed son. Having watered the grave with his tears, and consecrated it with his prayers, the bereaved father starts to go away; but, held and drawn by the tender ties of affection, he rushes back and pours out another flood of tears. And there, overcome with sorrow and crushed with grief, under the influence of a kind of momentary delirium rising in the depths of his emotions of grief, as though his son rose again to life, he exclaims, "Farewell, James, farewell! May God bless you!" And, repossessing his powers, he tears himself away, and leaves the sacred spot. After giving his cordials to other needy patients, and gathering up his son's clothes and assets, with a broken heart the aged father starts again for his home in New England. Such were the frequent mournful scenes of this graveyard.

WHO ARE THE DEAD?

As soldiers, they were a part of the very bone and sinew of the country, the guardians and defenders of the Republic, and the protectors of our homes, fathers, mothers, and orphans. Whence came they? From almost every State of the Union. Those buried here during the war, being principally from the "Army of the James," are chiefly from New England, New York, and Pennsylvania, besides some six hundred colored soldiers, who, except a small sprinkle from New England and Pennsylvania, are from the former slave States of the South. It formerly contained none but those who died in Hampton Hospital; but since the close of the war, all the soldiers and officers that were buried at the Chesapeake, and in the vicinity, have been transferred here. Here are those who died at the old Hygiea Hospital, besides many from the army of the Potomac that passed away in this vicinity during Gen. McClellan's first campaign against Richmond. Here, too, are scores of brave heroes, who fell victims to the untold horrors and fiendish cruelty of Andersonville, who died in Hampton Hospital. Here, too, lie many of the heroic braves of Fort Fisher, of whom said Admiral Porter, "The world never saw such fighting as they did." Here, too, lie many who shared in the glories of the last great victory achieved at Petersburg, which brought down Richmond, put Jeff. Davis to flight, and resulted in the overthrow of the rebellion. Here, too, lie those whose blood has stained, and whose dissevered limbs have enriched, almost every battle-field from Fortress Monroe to and around Richmond.

HOW DID THEY DIE?

It was my privilege to preach to thousands, and to converse and pray with many hundreds of them on their death-beds, pointing them to Christ, and by the mercies of God and the love of Jesus, and by the joys of heaven, to entreat and beseech them to be reconciled to God. As they were free to express their feelings as I canvassed their hearts and wrote down their experience, I had a good opportunity to learn their condition. Patience and resignation were among the most marked features of their deaths. Inured to hardness and toil, with hearts brave and courageous, they rose above all murmur and complaint. Deeply and thoroughly loyal and patriotic, they counted all things but loss for the salvation of the country; so that each one might in truth have said, as he passed away, in the immortal words of Swiss Winkelried: "*I make way for liberty.*" I remember hearing one brave fellow say, when suffering very severely, "I can afford to suffer, since Christ has suffered so much for me." With bodies bathed in blood and racked with pain, yet, with a sublime faith, gazing into the eternal world, I have seen them, with souls apparently swimming in a flood of glory, rise above all doubts and fears, ready, waiting, to die, and even longing to depart. In a word, they died as they fought,— like heroes, without a murmur or a complaint. While some seemed to go "without hope," a great many gave bright evidence of preparation, expressing their assurance and bright prospects in such words as the following: "I am not afraid to die!" "The Lord is mine!" Another, deeply concerned for his companion at home, said, "Tell my wife to prepare for death: I have found Jesus." Another, with heaven in full view, exclaimed, "I am ready; ready to go any time!" Another, full of patience and submission, said, among his last words, "Not my will, but God's be done." The dying request of another good boy, who anxiously cared for his mother, was, "Tell my mother not to fret for me; I died happy." Another, racked with pain, with his leg off above the knee, exclaimed with deep emotions, in the presence of his weeping wife, "This wound is God's rod to comfort me: it is for my good;" and, drawing nearer unto God, he said, "Christ is dear and precious; he is all my life, and I can do nothing without him," and his disembodied spirit, washed in the Saviour's blood, went home to glory. Another, having made a full surrender of himself to the Saviour, said, "I gave my heart to Jesus, and now I can die in triumph." Another, apparently filled with the fulness of God, among his last words, said, "All is well!" and soon passed home to glory. Another, after struggling long under deep conviction in seeking religion, at last exclaimed, at the top of his voice, "I have got it! I have got it!" and commenced shouting, "Glory to God! hallelujah to the Lamb!" Another aged colored soldier, past sixty-nine years old, when I asked him, "What brought you into the army?" replied, "God got me to come in: God called, and I obeyed;" and as his frail bark began to give way, lying upon his bed, patient as Job and meek as Moses, he said, "The Lord is with me; I have no trouble;" and, as his thoughts flit home, he said, "The Lord may spare me to go home; but if not, 'all is well!' 'God's will be done.' 'I can die happy!'" and he soon passed away. Another clear-headed, praying veteran said, as his clay tenement began to fail, "I love my Saviour, therefore I don't fear." "I can die happy: it is glorious; there is nothing like it!" and he continued praying, and exhorting his comrades to watch and pray and be faithful, until his voice was hushed in death. But another who had felt some anxiety and concern about his salvation, but apparently feeling himself lost, exclaimed, a little before he expired, "It is too late!" and his destiny was sealed forever. Then, we repeat it, "they died as they fought, like perfect heroes." Peace be to their ashes. Let their heroic deeds be embalmed in the memory and enshrined in the heart of every American patriot.

With all due honor to the officers, it is, after all, principally the soldiers who fight the battle and win the victory. They have borne the heat and burden of the war. And for their faithful service they deserve monuments more durable than brass. The hardness they have endured, the sacrifices they have made, and the price they have paid in toil, sweat, and blood for our country's salvation, is of such a value that it can never be repaid. The Government may pension their widows, orphans, and heirs with all the vacant land in the country, and with all the gold of California; the people may erect to their memory the most gorgeous monuments of marble decked with rich plates of gold and silver; the historian may write their names bright upon the historic page, and engrave it high upon the escutcheon of the country; every surviving patriot may erect, for each one, a monument of the warmest gratitude and affection in the bottom of his heart; but we can never do enough for them. There they lie; and though dead, they yet speak! A voice from every green-turfed grave and uncoffined bone cries to the surviving patriot, *Be faithful to your trust!* A voice from their mangled bodies, and amputated limbs, and ball-perforated heads, cries aloud to every loyal heart, *Stand by the flag, and cling to the cross!* Yes, there they lie, waiting the sound of the last trump summoning them to rise and come to judgment, when their maimed, mangled bodies, sown in corruption, weakness, and dishonor, will be raised in power and glory, without the loss of a hair or a limb; and the redeemed, with their souls washed in the blood of Jesus, will be caught up to meet the Lord in the air, and dwell with him in heaven, where there will be no more war, "no more death, neither sorrow nor crying, for the former things are passed away."

"The only national debt we never can pay is the debt we owe to our victorious Union soldiers and sailors!"

THE MONUMENT.

Standing in the centre of this vast charnal-house is a splendid marble monument, seventy-one feet high, resting upon a solid base nineteen and a half feet square, well proportioned, gradually tapering to the top. Built of fine granite, it will last as long as "the everlasting hills." Bearing the appropriate inscription:

"IN MEMORY

OF

UNION SOLDIERS

WHO DIED TO MAINTAIN THE LAWS,"

it will hand down to future generations the heroic patriotism and daring deeds of those whose memory it was reared to commemorate. This inscription, surmounted above with a spread eagle, and with cross cannons on the right and cross muskets with fixed bayonets on the left, adds much to the taste and appearance of the monument. Enclosed with a good, substantial iron fence, made of old musket-barrels with fixed bayonets, with six-pounders for posts, it is well secured from all outward encroachments. American patriots guard, protect, *preserve it;* and if, through the mouldering hand of time, it should ever fall and crumble to the dust, let another, more lofty, substantial, and grand, rise in its place; and there let it stand, and forever mark the sacred spot where sleeps in death the precious dust of nearly five thousand brave heroes who fell defending the cause of God, liberty, and self-government. Guard and protect it, so that if ever our patriotism should grow cold, we may go and gaze upon this grand structure, and call to mind the heroic devotion, the severe suffering, and self-sacrificing spirit of those who shed their blood and severed their limbs from their bodies that not a star should be riven from the flag of the Union; guard and protect it through all coming time, so that if ever bloody treason should again lift its foul head against the Government, the heroic example of those whose courageous deeds it commemorates may infuse into the hearts of their posterity that daring courage which will urge them at once to put it down at all hazards. Officers, soldiers, and sailors of the United States army and navy, guard and protect it, that it may stand as a living emblem of the great principles of the *Declaration of Independence,* for which these, and over three hundred thousand other martyred heroes, fought, bled, and died in crushing treason and putting down rebellion; guard and protect it, and hang upon its lofty summit the dear old flag, and there let it forever wave over the precious dust of those noble hearts which once beat high with patriotic ardor, and around whose encoffined bones it was wrapped as they were borne, by cart-loads, from the dead-house to their graves. Yes, *guard and protect it,* and there let it stand forever, not only as a "memorial of the dead," and the principles they died for, but as a standing declaration of a firm determination of the living to maintain them at all hazards, though "blood flow to the horse's bridle," and "death come up to the window."

Its erection was first conceived before the rebellion was quelled. Even while it was in full blast, many of those who now lie beneath it, were pouring out their blood, offering up their prayers, and laying down their lives for their country; yea, while the "irrepressible conflict" was still fiercely raging, and the land was yet drunk with patriotic blood, with the stream of death rising and flowing on at the rate of over two hundred a day, just when ten thousand Union prisoners were escaping from Andersonville prison, and while victory after victory was following our armies at the front, a few officers of Hampton and Chesapeake Hospitals determined upon its erection. We consulted Dr. E. McClellan, Assistant Surgeon U. S. Army, surgeon in charge of the hospital, with reference to it, March 6, 1865; and in a few days he appointed the four chaplains of the hospital to raise money in their respective divisions for its erection, and by March 14 we had collected three hundred dollars, with over as much more on subscription. Most of this was raised by Chaplain Roe and the writer. The soldiers contributed very liberally. One noble-hearted patriot from New England, although he had lost both a leg and an arm in the war, gave five dollars out of eleven, all he had. Some gave ten dollars. At the call of the surgeon in charge, a "monument board" was formed July 14, 1865, with Dr. E. McClellan, chairman, Chaplain Roe, treasurer, and Chaplain Marshall, secretary. Late in July Dr. McClellan left the hospital, and Ass't Surgeon J. H. Frantz, U.S.A., who succeeded him, was made chairman of the monument board; and at the close of the year the funds raised amounted to over one thousand dollars. Special honor is due to Chaplain Marshall for his persevering and self-denying efforts in raising funds, in securing the co-operation of the War Department in establishing the cemetery, and in obtaining a deed for the cemetery ground. The entire cost of the monument was twelve thousand dollars; eleven thousand dollars of which were raised by Miss Dix, who very often visited the hospital during the war, and witnessed something of the severe suffering of the heroic martyrs whose daring deeds and mortal remains she has done so much to honor and protect. She engaged in this noble enterprise at the request of Chaplain Marshall. Eternal thanks and praise to her and to her memory, and to those who contributed of their time and money for this noble purpose.

BURYING THE DEAD.

When a man dies, his body is washed, enshrouded in a clean shirt and drawers, and with naked hands and feet is carried by the nurses, on a stretcher, to the dead-house, and put into a plain red coffin. The soldier's name, company, and regiment are painted on the underside of the coffin-lid, to prevent mistake in identifying the deceased in case of exhuming. At the hour appointed, the escort, drum-corps, dead-cart, pall-bearers, and the chaplain, all being assembled, the funeral begins by placing the encoffined dead into the cart, each one receiving the regular dead salute of a threefold rapping of the drums, and the escort presenting arms. We usually take five at a load, all covered over with the glorious old flag they died to honor and defend. All ready, with a slow step and solemn notes of the death-march of fife and drum, we march to the graves, and with solemn silence consign them to the tomb. Until recently, we have usually buried two loads at once, and sometimes three. When the last coffin is let down, all baring their heads, the chaplain reads an appropriate passage of Scripture, makes a few remarks, — often speaking of the dying messages and bright prospects of the departed, and closes with prayer for the sick, wounded, dying, and for the comfort of the bereaved friends at home; and the escort having fired three volleys over their graves, we leave them alone in their glory, to await the sound of the last trump summoning them to judgment.

The average mortality, out of from three to four thousand patients, during the summer of 1864, was from eight to ten daily. We buried twenty-six one day.

Retiring from the grave, the band plays a lively, patriotic air, and the solemn scene closes, usually without a tear being shed, except when a relative happens to be present. The graveyard at Hampton Hospital, now containing some five thousand graves, is beautifully situated, and kept very clean and neat. A neat head-board, bearing the name, date of death, company and regiment of each soldier, marks the spot where his mortal remains lie undisturbed.

NATIONAL CEMETERIES.

The following extracts from the Quartermaster-General's Report of 1868 show the number of United States soldiers interred in the following National Cemeteries:

MILITARY DEPARTMENT OF THE EAST.

Names of Cemeteries.	Graves.
1. Cypress Hills, L. I.	3,116
2. Gettysburg, Pa.	3,564
3. In and around Philadelphia, Pa.	1,903
4. Woodlawn Prison, N. Y.	2,984
5. Madison Barracks, N. Y.	580
	12,147

DEPARTMENT OF WASHINGTON.

1. Arlington, up to June 30, 1868	15,547
2. Soldiers' Home, D.C.	5,488
3. Alexandria Military, D.C.	3,635
4. At Grafton, W.V.	1,082
5. Annapolis, Md.	2,486
6. At Antietam, Md.	4,496
7. At Pt. Lookout, Md., Rebels	2,466
	35,200

The total number of U.S. soldiers interred in the Department of Washington is 35,500, of which 28,085 can be probably identified.

DEPARTMENT OF BALTIMORE.

1. London Park Cemetery, Md.	1,785
2. The Laurel Cemetery, Md. Colored	229
Total	2,014

Of which 1,828 can probably be identified.

DEPARTMENT OF THE LAKES.

1. Mound City, Ill.	4,923
2. Crown Hill, Indianapolis, Ill.	708
3. Rock Island, Ill.	135
4. Camp Butler, Ill.	647
5. Chicago, Ill.	342

Names of Cemeteries.	Graves.
6. Cincinnati, Ohio	655
7. Columbus, Ohio	426
8. Evansville, Ind.	599
9. Camp Denison, Ohio	339
10. Quincy, Ill.	242
11. Galliopolis, Ohio	158
	9,174

CONFEDERATE PRISONERS' BODIES.

1. Chicago, Ill.	4,039
2. Rock Island	1,928
3. Camp Chase	2,050
4. Green Lawn, Ind.	1,556
5. Camp Butler, Ill.	644
6. Camp Denison, Ohio	31
7. Mound City, Ill.	40
Rebel prisoners of war	10,288

FIRST MILITARY DISTRICT.

1. Richmond, Va.	6,281
2. Fort Harrison, Va.	814
3. Glendale, Va.	1,196
4. Cold Harbor, Va.	1,033
5. City Point, Va.	5,123
6. Poplar Grove (Petersburg)	5,599
7. Seven Pines, Va.	1,349
8. Yorktown, Va.	2,180
9. Danville, Va.	1,316
10. Hampton, Va.	4,654
11. Fredericksburg, Va.	14,848
12. Culpepper C. H., Va.	1,327
13. Winchester, Va.	4,385
14. Staunton, Va.	749
	50,854

Of which 18,428 can probably be identified.

SECOND MILITARY DISTRICT.

1. Beaufort, S. C.	10,000

Names of Cemeteries.	Graves.
2. Florence, S. C.	2,795
3. Wilmington, N. C.	2,059
4. Raleigh, N. C.	3,287
5. Newberne, N. C.	1,187
6. Salisbury, N. C.	12,112
7. At Charleston, S. C.	80
8. At Columbia, S. C.	14
	31,534

All of which have been re-interred. Of which 8,474 can probably be identified.

THIRD MILITARY DISTRICT.

1. Andersonville, Ga.	13,705
2. Marietta, Ga.	9,972
3. Mobile, Ala.	834
4. Barrancas, Fla.	1,008
Total	25,519

Of which 21,040 can be probably identified; 12,519 of these have been re-interred up to date of report.

FOURTH MILITARY DISTRICT.

1. Vicksburg, Miss.	14,185
2. Natchez, Miss.	1,720
3. Little Rock, Ark.	4,050
4. Fort Smith, Ark.	1,583
5. Fayetteville, Ark.	1,202
	22,740

Six thousand more are expected to be interred here; of which 9,645 can probably be identified.

FIFTH MILITARY DISTRICT.

1. Monument at Chalmetta, La.	12,230
2. Baton Rouge, La.	2,891
3. Port Hudson, La.	3,779

Names of Cemeteries.	Graves.
4. Pinello, La.	1,487
5. Fort St. Philip, La.	326
6. Brownsville, Texas.	1,763
7. Galveston, Texas.	383
8. San Antonio, Texas.	186
	23,045

Of which 12,073 can be identified.

DEPARTMENT OF THE CUMBERLAND.

1. Knoxville, Tenn.	3,153
2. Chattanooga, Tenn.	12,924
3. Stone River, Tenn.	6,810
4. Nashville, Tenn.	16,329
5. Cumberland River, at Fort Donelson, Tenn.	656
6. Shiloh, Tenn.	3,582
7. Mississippi River, Tenn.	13,958
8. Union, at Corinth, Miss.	5,589
9. New Albany, Ind.	1,931
10. Camp Nelson, Ky.	2,856
11. Mill Springs, Ky.	707
12. Lebanon, Ky.	864
13. Cave Hill, Louisville, Ky.	3,906
14. Lexington, Ky.	994
15. Danville, Ky.	355
	74,114

Of which 45,189 can probably be identified.

DIVISION OF THE MISSOURI.

1. At Jefferson Barracks, Mo.	8,601
2. At Jefferson City, Mo.	635
3. At Springfield, Mo.	1,519
4. At Fort Scott, Kansas.	417
5. At Fort Leavenworth, Ks.	702
6. At Keokuk, Iowa.	627
	12,501

GENERAL SUMMARY.

Reports have been received from seventy-two national cemeteries, and from three hundred and twenty local and post cemeteries.

The total number of bodies of United States soldiers reported throughout the United States is 316,233. The number of the same which can probably be identified is 175,764, or about five-ninths of the whole number. The number of the same which cannot probably be identified is 140,469, or about four-ninths of the whole number. The number of bodies which have been re-interred up to date of report is 257,250, or about four-fifths of the whole number. The number of bodies which it is proposed to re-inter hereafter is 14,283: thus the total number of bodies which will have been re-interred, in all, is 271,533, or about five-sevenths of the whole number of bodies.

The estimated aggregate of expenditure made by the Quartermaster's Department, on account of interments and other cemeterial operations, up to June 30, 1868, is $2,801,352.49. The expenditures required for this purpose next fiscal year are estimated at $553,655.84. The aggregate amount of expenditures, past and future, will thus appear to be $3,355,008.33.

CHAPTER XXII.

SKETCHES BY CHAPLAIN MARSHALL — THE U. S. CHRISTIAN COMMISSION.

A Theatre turned into a Religious Meeting — Masses of Soldiers in Camp Distribution — Their Profanity — Burlesque Military Drill — The Chaplain's Resolution — A Shout upon his Entrance — Theatrical Preparations — They Black Themselves up — They Sing — Devotion Rises — God Helps — The Chaplain Reads, Speaks, Prays — They Sing with Great Power — They Visit the Reading-Room — Great Good done in a Short Time — "No more Swearing" — Sunday Night with the Dying — The Dying Sergeant sends for the Chaplain — The Weeping Father prays for His Dying Son — The Dying Lieutenant desires to be Prayed for — The Dying Captain's Warm Grasp — The Friendship of Christ — The U. S. Christian Commission — Its Origin — Officers — First Meeting — Its Spirit

AND ZEAL — HEAD-QUARTERS — ITS OBJECT — FIDELITY OF ITS DELEGATES — ITS EFFICIENCY AND CONTRIBUTIONS — ITS POPULARITY — "GOD BLESS THE CHRISTIAN COMMISSION."

A THEATRE TURNED INTO A RELIGIOUS MEETING.*

THE mass of soldiers that came into Camp Distribution, Saturday night, March 18, 1865, left for the front on the following day. On Monday night, over a thousand came in. They formed into a large ring in front of the barracks, and witnessed burlesque military drills by some of the muster. It was dark, and I elbowed through till I got to the circle; but there was no time during the evening when I thought that I could successfully turn the amusement into a religious meeting. When I heard the obscene swearing, and the responsive laugh by the crowd to the low wit of the performers, I was upon the point several times of rushing into the ring, and having my customary say to the boys going to the front. But I failed to see the time when I might be successful, and failure would be worse than silence. "Taps" sounded, and all dispersed, — the soldiers to their bunks, and I went into the reading-room, feeling condemned that I had not made one effort for Christ and the salvation of some of these men who were on their way to the battles then raging; and so I resolved, if they remained another night, that sink or swim, live or die, succeed or fail, I would sound the note of warning in their ears. Some of them were in the reading-room next day. Night came, and the soldiers were still there. It rained so hard that no performance could be held outside; but to my utter surprise, when entering one end of the barracks, the other end was fitted up in a most theatrical style, and all the appointments and amusements of the stage were in full blast. I crowded through to the centre, and found a tall Irishman, as ringmaster or manager, blacked up like a negro, and several soldiers also blacked up as negro men and women, with banjos, violins, tambourines, sticks, &c., and soldiers' blankets suspended forming the screen from the

---

* This and the following two articles are by Rev. James Marshall, late Chaplain U. S. A.

audience. What a shout went up as my coat, Bible, hymn-book, &c., became visible; but with my hand upon the shoulder of the manager, and a word to him, I said, " I have just a word to say to the boys, to-night. They are going to the front in the morning, and though sorry to disturb their amusement, yet I might have no other opportunity." "Certainly, certainly," bowed the gracious manager, while I was upon a stool for the purpose, and with a word and a raised hand, and the help of the black Irish manager, I had a hearing in a moment. Referring to the fact that we were all actors on a terrible stage at the present time, and that many there might fall victims of the enemy's bullets before forty-eight hours, as the battles were then raging, and pointing them to the dead-house of the hospital, within sound of our voice, in which were lying six soldiers, before whom that morning, not the curtain formed by their blankets, but the curtain of death had fallen, these facts confirmed silence, turned their thoughts into a new channel, and joined them almost unconsciously in singing a verse of "Alas! and did my Saviour bleed?" which, perhaps, our friends at home were then singing at prayer-meetings in our behalf. Christian soldiers had confidence, raised their voices, and soon the full tide of devotion seemed flowing, — all fixed in their seats and hanging to their tiers of bunks, one above the other, and the black actors were all sitting motionless upon the floor, and gradually slinking back out of sight. Then was the time when the Holy Spirit told us what to say and how to say it. Reading the first Psalm, and classifying my hearers thereby, I spoke fully an hour, first, because they were so attentive, and again, because I did not want to leave them the time before "taps" to get back into their vile habits. I spoke plainly of their amusements of the night before, and hoped they would give way to me to-night. I told them that the vile epithets they used against our Lord and Saviour were worse than they would tolerate against the vilest wretch in society. We would not justify such opprobrium upon the worst man in the army. He would be unworthy of such disgrace; and yet, when likely to be borne by the chances of war into His presence in a few hours or days, how could we conceive of our reception into His presence. While He was pleading with the Father to forgive us our vile sins on His account, we were unceasingly fitting ourselves for the society of the vile and devilish. And yet His blood is sufficient to cleanse us from all these sins, and give us an interest in eternal life. After speaking an hour, they were ready and fitted to listen to prayer. After which, and singing again, in which went up a chorus of voices that sounded as though the very hosts of the redeemed were rejoicing, our hearts were tuned to the songs of the new life in God. After cordially inviting all to visit our reading-rooms and library the next day, till they were ordered to the front, and also to freely use pens, ink, paper, and envelopes and desks, to write letters to their friends in the North that God in his providence was throwing means of grace across their pathway to the battles, so that they might be without excuse, if they failed to recognize the goodness and mercy of our heavenly Father.

The next morning, the reading-room was thronged till they were ordered to the front. They left solemnly, and with a different spirit from that with which they entered. One man said to me that he did not believe that one man ever did so much good in so short a time before. "There was no more swearing after you left the barracks." I could but weep when the poor fellows were marching away, hurled along by the providences of God like insects in an aerial current, God only knew whither. And thus, day after day, for a year and a half, in which some one hundred thousand men passed through that camp, was God's truth spoken and distributed, leaving the results to the great husbandman that garners for eternal glory the harvests flowing from such spiritual sowing.

SUNDAY NIGHT WITH THE DYING.

One Sunday night in March, 1865, I was conducting a meeting in the Bethesdian Chapel, which was crowded with soldiers. Several ministers were present, and doing the speaking. Among them was Dr. Spees, now of Iowa, and several others whose faces I see in memory, but whose names I do not now recall. At that time, the Hospital was full of sick and wounded. I had seen them all, and knew the worst cases. When the meeting was half out, while a large audience was standing and singing, a soldier entered, and came in haste up the aisle, and told me Sergeant Greenough was dying in the seventh ward, and his father wanted me to come in at once. I handed my singing-book to Chaplain Billingsley, who was present, and requested him to lead the meeting to its close, and hastened to the seventh ward, where I found all the nurses and convalescents standing around Greenough's bed. The ward was silent, and the father with his face buried in the clothes of the cot of his son, by which he was kneeling, and the son in the agonies of death. Such expressions of despair and fear and agony as appeared on his face, and such contortions, accompanied with moans and wails, were more than the weeping father or the strong soldiers could endure. He was unconscious. I could only pray for all present, in which that whole ward joined by their silence, broken only by their sobs. Almost immediately, on rising from my knees, some one told me that Lieutenant Hammond was dying in the second ward in the main building, and wanted to see me. Saying a few words to the father, and promising to return as soon as possible, I hastened to Lieutenant Hammond, found him conscious, resting on his chest, and several others with his father in the room. He said to me at once, "Chaplain, I can't live long. I want you to pray for me." After a few words of comfort, I prayed with him. He seemed so happy and resigned; and while in the position of bending over from my chair talking with him, my back toward the door, some one, whom I did not see, whispered in my ear: "Captain Cameron wants to see you. He is dying." In a moment I went to another ward, found Captain Cameron bolstered up, his eyes catching mine as I entered, looking so pleadingly and imploringly. He was surrounded by several officers and nurses. But he was too far gone to speak. I talked to him of Christ's love, and bid him lay hold of that mercy, by faith, which saves and gives peace even to the uttermost; and asked him to press my hand if he would like me to pray with him; and such was that grasp, that my own emotions almost unfitted me for the solemn privilege, when I realized that a spirit from the eternal world was grasping for mercy. In a short time, Captain Cameron passed away, also Lieutenant Hammond and Sergeant Greenough,— all by midnight were gone from this world of war and sin, to receive the reward promised by a merciful God, according to their fidelity to the claims of the divine Son.

THE FRIENDSHIP OF CHRIST.

Two soldiers, whose limbs were amputated, and whose wounds were gangrened, knew that death was inevitable. They were lying in a tent, in the angle of a large ward in the form of a cross, only a few yards from the beach at Hampton Roads. Having left the large ward filled with wounded, I spent a few moments in conversation and prayer with the two sufferers. They were calm and resigned, and waiting for death, which was gradually approaching as quietly and surely as the darkness follows the twilight after sunset. Stepping out upon the banks of the water in that starry midnight hour, my soul was thrilled with peculiar emotions, as I listened to the soughing winds as they played over the waters, and the moaning waves as they broke against the beach, mingling their sad wails with the groans of the wounded and dying, and the great relief of my heart was these men are the friends of Christ, and, better, Christ is their friend, and nothing can separate them. His triumph over death is the sure pledge they shall be victors. His resurrection is the assurance that they shall enjoy the full fruition of eternal glory.

> "Sweet to look inward and attend
> The whispers of his love;
> Sweet to look upward to the place
> Where Jesus pleads above."

THE UNITED STATES CHRISTIAN COMMISSION.

Besides the labors of the chaplain, the work of the U.S. Christian Commission was the grandest exhibition of Christianity in the war. This Commission rose as if by magic. No sooner was the war inaugurated, and the men in the field began to get sick, wound, kill, and devour one another, than the people at home began to provide for their wants. Organized, November 15, 1861, in New York City, the Commission held its first meeting immediately after in Washington City, and was there fully organized by choosing G. H. Stuart, Esq., chairman, B. F. Mannierre, secretary and treasurer, and G. H. Stuart, Bishop J. S. Janes, Rev. Dr. Cutler, C. Demond, and B. F. Mannierre, an executive committe.

A plan of operations was agreed upon at once, and, having secured the approbation and commendation of the President, Secretary of War, and the Commander-in-chief of the Army, the great work was commenced. Moved, it would seem, by the spirit of God, and with a warm affection for the soldier, and a strong determination to quell the rebellion, the fathers, mothers, sons, and daughters rose almost *en masse* to aid this noble work. The women knit socks, made clothes, prepared provisions, delicacies, and cordials for the needy soldiers, and the men conveyed them to them. The people gave money by the million. And the glorious work went on with a zeal and success unparalleled in the history of the world. The head-quarters of the Commission were first established at New York; but were soon removed to Philadelphia, where, through the liberality of its honored chairman, it obtained office-room, room for storage, the service of clerks, etc., free of charge. With the main central office at Philadelphia, and superintended by the efficient chairman, the affairs of the Commission were conducted with great energy and strict economy.

It was the glory of this noble institution, that its gifts and labors were gratuitous. It was not got up for mere pay; no, it rose from a strong desire to promote the spiritual and temporal welfare of the soldier and sailor, and to save the country. The streams of benevolence, and the disposition to help the soldier, seemed to rise as the exigency of the case required. The faithful delegates, watching the movements of the armies, were always on hand, ready to take off the wounded as soon as they fell upon the gory field. The writer heard Rev. Dr. Stockton, heading a delegation of delegates direct from the battle of the Wilderness, tell President Lincoln that they had given the first cup of warm coffee to the wounded of that battle. And when over sixteen thousand of our brave heroes fell killed and wounded at the decisive battle of Gettysburg, the delegates and the people rushed in by thousands to help take care of them.

The efficiency and success of the Commission were wonderful. Beginning with eighteen members in 1861, before the close of the war it had engaged nearly five thousand delegates laboring for the temporal and spiritual wants of the men. Talking Christ to them, preaching to and praying for and with them, was the principal business of a great part of the delegates. In all, they preached to them over 58,000 sermons, and held with them over 77,000 prayer-meetings, and gave them 1,466,748 Bibles and parts of Bibles, 18,000,000 religious newspapers, 1,370,000 hymn-books, over 8,000,000 knapsack-books, and 39,000,000 pages of tracts, and wrote for them 92,000 letters. The total value of the whole amount contributed in four years was $6,291,107 68. With zealous hearts these noble brethren "went about doing good," relieving and comforting the officer, soldier, and sailor wherever they found them.

The high appreciation of the Commission, and the hearty reception of its delegates by the men, was evinced by their manifest gratitude and the soldier's oft-repeated prayer, "God bless the Christian Commission!" As a soldier was about leaving a delegate, one day, to go to his regiment, he said to him, "God bless you, my dear brother, for coming to work for the soldiers! You have been the means of saving my poor soul!" The high standing of the Commission among the leading officials of the nation was shown by their deep interest in the work, and their attending its annual meetings.

Abundantly blessed of God, its name, its labors, and its good fruits will go down to future generations, and do good through all coming time. Eternity only will reveal the good it has accomplished.

The U. S. Sanitary Commission did a similar, and, in some respects, a much more extensive work. The want of room forbids us to speak of it fully. It labored more for the physical and less for the spiritual wants of the soldier and sailor than the Christian Commission. While the latter spent over $6,000,000, the former spent about $15,000,000, in this good work.

CHAPTER XXIII.

DISTINGUISHED MEN OF THE WAR.

REV. P. D. GURLEY. D.D.

His Birth — Pious Mother — Childhood — Desire for the Ministry — His Education — Works his own Way through Union College — His Piety when a Boy — Studied Theology at Princeton — His Standing in his Class — Graduates at Princeton, and Receives a Call to Preach in Indianapolis — His Marriage — His Ordination — Successful Labors — Accepts a Call to Dayton, Ohio — Leaves Dayton and goes to Washington, D. C. — Summoned to Lincoln's Death-Bed — Impressive Scene — Prays at his Death — Presides at a Meeting of the Clergy of the District of Columbia — Preaches at Lincoln's Funeral — Dr. Hall reads the Episcopal Burial Service — Bishop Simpson's Opening Prayer — "Cling to Liberty and Right" — Composed a Hymn for the Funeral — Bishop Simpson's Sermon at the Grave — Dr. Gurley's Christian Character — His Ability in Prayer — Successful as a Minister — His Gifts — He Comforts the Afflicted — His Popularity — His Death — His Rapturous Foretastes of Heaven — His Dying Requests to his Family and Friends — Last Words — Dr. Sunderland's Remarks at the Funeral — His People's Affection for him.

OF all the ministers of the Gospel who officiated in the late American conflict, none performed a more difficult and important part than Dr. Gurley. Although not formally connected with the army, yet, preaching in the National capital, his influence was deeply felt among the leading men of the nation, many of whom were regular attendants upon his ministrations. He was the intimate friend and pastor of Abraham Lincoln, and officiated at his death and funeral.

Born of parents of limited means in 1816, in the State of New York, he was once a poor country boy. Brought up by a devotedly pious mother, who trained him for God, he met with a bright conversion when he was about fifteen years of age. Strong in faith, and possessing an ardent desire to glorify his Saviour, he soon became convinced that it was his duty to con-

P. D. GURLEY.

secrate himself to the work of the gospel ministry. With his heart fixed upon this important work, he set out to obtain an education, and worked his own way through Union College, in July, 1837, with the highest honors of his class, and entered the Theological Seminary at Princeton, N. J., the following fall. Here he made such rapid progress that he was soon regarded as the foremost man in his class. Constrained by a Saviour's love, even while at college, his life and example were so humble and consistent, that one of the wildest and roughest of his classmates said, "If all Christians were like Gurley, I would give the world to be one." Blessed with good sense and sound judgment, and possessing a mild, genial, sociable, and jovial disposition, Mr. Gurley was very highly esteemed by all who knew him.

Graduating at Princeton Seminary in the fall of 1840, full of vigor and hope, with a strong desire to do good, his oft-repeated prayer was, "Oh, if I only knew where God would make me most successful in winning souls to Christ, there I would go!" and in a few weeks he received a call from the First Presbyterian Church of Indianapolis, Ind. Having married Miss Emma Brooks, of Parishville, N. Y., October 7, 1840, Mr. Gurley and his lady immediately set out for their new field of labor; after travelling over heavy roads in coaches and big wagons some two weeks, they reached Indianapolis, and met with a very warm reception from their new friends.

Mr. Gurley was ordained and installed the following December; and giving himself wholly to the work, although he had the genius and ability of Rev. Henry Ward Beecher to compete with, his labors were abundantly blessed, and his church being crowded to overflowing, the congregation soon built a new house.

After nine years of very successful labor in Indianapolis, Rev. P. D. Gurley accepted a call, and moved to Dayton, Ohio, where, having labored four years with signal success, he accepted a call, and removed to Washington City in 1854; and subsequently became pastor of the New York Avenue Church, where the Lord so abundantly blessed his labors that the congregation soon built him another fine, new house of worship. Preaching to presidents, heads of departments, senators, judges, generals, admirals, and congressmen, and conversing with them about their spiritual interests as occasion offered, his church grew from one hundred and sixty members, when he took charge of it, to four hundred and fifty at his death.

As an example of his popularity as a preacher with distinguished men, President Lincoln said to a friend one day, "I like Dr. Gurley. He don't preach politics: I get enough of that through the week; and when I go to church, I like to hear the gospel."

Amidst all this religious prosperity, great national events were crowding upon us. Richmond had fallen, General Lee had just surrendered, and the nation was all a-glow with the highest rejoicing over the glorious victory achieved. But, alas! how sudden the change! Quick, almost as a flash of lightning, the highest rejoicing was turned into the deepest mourning.

As the out-cropping of the rebellion, an atrocious assassin, reeking with cruel revenge, stealthily inflicted a mortal blow upon President Lincoln, and plunged the nation into the most bitter sorrow. And now it would seem as though God had raised up and expressly prepared Dr. Gurley, by a rich experience, for the solemn and important work before him. He is immediately summoned to the bedside of the dying President. How solemn and impressive the tragic scene! It is most heart-rending, and beggars all description! For solemnity and awfulness, it is unparelleled in the history of the world. The weeping Cabinet gaze with smitten hearts. The anguished wife and son wring their lacerated hearts with grief. The nation is wrapped in mourning and bathed in tears, and Dr. Gurley sits weeping beside her unconscious, dying head. Mute in the agonies of death, the martyred hero never spoke after the fatal stroke.

The clock strikes seven: his breath grows short; and in twenty-two minutes more his noble spirit left its clay tenement, and returned to God who gave it. Dread silence reigns; and after a short pause, Secretary Stanton, turning to Dr. Gurley, said, "Doctor, will you say something?" Whereupon, with a moment's reflection, the doctor, addressing himself to the bereaved friends, said,

"LET US TALK WITH GOD;"

and, kneeling down, he offered up a most tender and impressive prayer, "which seemed to cheer and lighten the burden of every weeping heart." Mrs. Lincoln having been in an adjoining room with some sympathizing friends, when the President expired, the doctor went in, and prayed again with them, commending the bereaved family to God and the riches of his grace.

Two days after President's Lincoln's death, Dr. Gurley, by a unanimous vote, presided over a very large meeting of the clergy of all denominations in the District of Columbia, suddenly convened to express their views and feelings touching the late national bereavement, and their good wishes and sympathies for the newly-inaugurated President. Arrangements having been made, and the time fixed, the meeting, *en masse,* called to see President Johnson; and on their approaching him, after they were severally introduced, Dr. Gurley made a very appropriate, touching, and impressive speech, tendering him their warmest sympathies, and promising him their daily prayers, to which he appropriately replied, with deep emotions, expressing, in strong terms, his thanks to them, his deep sense of the solemnity of his situation, and of the responsibility resting upon him.

At the funeral of Abraham Lincoln, Rev. Dr. Gurley delivered, in the east room of the executive mansion, an address, which, in the language of Rev. Dr. W. E. Schenck, of Philadelphia, "for appropriateness, pathos, and genuine and rich scriptural sentiments, has few equals in the English language."

After the reading of portions of the Episcopal burial service by the Rev. Dr. C. H. Hall, and the offering up of an appropriate, impressive prayer by Bishop Simpson, of the M. E. Church, Dr. Gurley began his sermon in the following impressive words: —

"We recognize and adore the sovereignty of God. His throne is in the heavens, and his kingdom ruleth over all. It was a cruel hand, the dark hand of the assassin, that smote our honored, wise, and noble President, and filled the land with sorrow. But above this hand there is another, which we must see and acknowledge. It is the chastening hand of a wise and faithful God. He gives us the bitter cup; we yield to the behest, and drink the draught. . . . The people confided in the late lamented President with a firm and loving confidence, which no other man enjoyed since the days of Washington. He deserved it well, and deserved it all. He merited it by his character, and by his acts, and by the whole tenor, and tone, and spirit of his life. He was wise, simple, and sincere; plain and honest; truthful and just; benevolent and kind. His perceptions were quick and clear, his judgment was calm and accurate, his purposes were good and pure beyond a question; always and everywhere he aimed to *be* right and to *do* right. His integrity was all-pervading, all-controlling, and incorruptible. He gave his personal consideration to all matters, whether great or small. How firmly and well he occupied his position, and met all its grave demands in seasons of trial and difficulty, is known to you all, to the country, and to the world. He comprehended all the enormity of treason, and rose to the full dignity of the occasion. He saw his duty as chief magistrate of a great and imperilled people, and leaned on the arm of Him who giveth power to the faint, and who increaseth strength.

"Never shall I forget the emphasis and the deep emotion with which he said, in this room, to a company of clergymen and others who called to pay their respects, in the darkest days of our civil conflict: 'Gentlemen, my hope of success in this great and terrible struggle rests on that immutable foundation,— the justice and goodness of God! And when events are very threatening, and prospects very dark, I still hope that, in some way which man cannot see, all will be well in the end, because our cause is just, and God is on our side.'

"Such was his sublime and holy faith, and it was an anchor to his soul, both sure and steadfast. It made him firm and strong; it emboldened him in the pathway of duty, however rugged and perilous it might be. It made him valiant for the right, for the cause of God and humanity; and it held him in steady, patient, and unswerving adherence to a policy of administration which he thought, and which we all now think, both God and humanity required him to adopt. We admired and loved him, on many accounts, for strong and various reasons.

We admired his childlike simplicity, his freedom from guile and deceit, his staunch and sterling integrity, his kind and forgiving temper. . . . But more sublime than any of all these, more holy and influential, more beautiful, and strong, and sustaining, was his abiding confidence in God and in the final triumph of truth and righteousness through him and for his sake. This was his noblest virtue, his grandest principle,— the secret alike of his strength, his patience, and his success; and this, it seems to me, after being near him steadily and with him often for more than four years, is the principle by which, more than by any other, ' He being dead, yet speaketh.' By this he speaks to his successor in office, and charges him to have faith in God; by this he speaks to the members of his Cabinet, to all who occupy positions of influence and authority, and charges all to have faith in God; by this he speaks to this great people as they sit in sackcloth to-day, and weep for him with a bitter wailing and refuse to be comforted, and he charges them to have faith in God; and by this he will speak through the ages and to all rulers and peoples in every land, and his messages to them will be, ' *Cling to liberty and right;* battle for them, bleed for them, die for them, if need be, and have confidence in God!' Oh, that the voice of this testimony may sink down into our hearts to-day, and every day, and into the heart of the nation, and exert its appropriate influence upon our feelings, our faith, our patience, and our devotion to the cause, now dearer to us than ever before, because consecrated by the blood of its most conspicuous defender, its wisest and most fondly trusted friend."

The following graphic lines, breathing a lofty spirit of ardent patriotism, were composed by Dr. Gurley as they journeyed from Washington to Springfield, and sung at Lincoln's grave:

> "Rest, noble martyr, rest in peace;
> Rest with the true and brave
> Who, like thee, fell in freedom's cause,
> The nation's life to save!
>
> "Thy name shall live while time endures;
> And men shall say of thee,
> He saved his country from its foes,
> And bade the slave be free.

"These deeds shall be thy monument;
　Better than brass or stone:
They leave thy fame in glory's light,
　Unrivalled and alone.

"This consecrated spot shall be
　To freedom ever dear;
And Freedom's sons of every race
　Shall weep and worship here.

"O God! before whom we, in tears,
　Our fallen chief deplore,
Grant that the cause for which he died
　May live forever more."

At the close of Bishop Simpson's sermon at the grave, Dr. Gurley made a few remarks, offered the closing prayer, and, after singing the above hymn, pronounced the benediction; and the solemn funeral services at the tomb of Lincoln closed.

"When we come to speak of Dr. Gurley as a Christian," says Dr. Schenck, "we are at a loss to find terms sufficiently expressive." Crucified to the world, he was devoted, earnest, self-denying. Living nigh to God, and wholly consecrated to his service, he was powerful and prevalent in prayer. Many good judges have said they never heard his equal in prayer. A distinguished U. S. senator said that the prayer offered by Dr. Gurley, while standing by the remains of Abraham Lincoln in the executive mansion, just before they started for Springfield, made a deeper impression upon him than anything he had ever heard. Laborious and faithful as a pastor, he was eminently successful. With a burning desire for the salvation of souls, like Jesus, "he went about doing good," "always abounding in the work of the Lord." Said Dr. Edwards, who preached his funeral sermon, "He was all faithfulness and all tenderness." Blessed with wisdom, patience, and forbearance, and possessing a large, loving heart, glowing with compassion and filled with "unction from the Holy One," he was exceedingly well qualified to administer comfort to the afflicted. With all these gifts and graces, Dr. Gurley "was a burning and shining light," and a living embodiment of the doctrines of the cross. Highly esteemed by all, in the language of ex-President Pearce, "He was a great and good man."

HIS DEATH.

From one so faithful in life, we could scarcely expect anything but triumph and glory in his death. The hallowed scene of his last hours was most touching and impressive. Such constancy, such faith and Christian heroism as he exhibited, and such unutterable joy and sweet communion with God as he enjoyed, is very seldom realized on earth. His whole life after he gave up to die seemed more like heaven than earth. At times he enjoyed such rapturous foretastes of heaven that, like the dying Payson, "he seemed to swim in a flood of glory." In the language of Dr. Schenck (who preached his memorial sermon), "His last words were full of Jesus and redemption. With his expiring breath he gave glory to God; the impenitent were entreated to come to Jesus; his family and friends were all commended to the Saviour's care, and his fellow-ministers, who approached him, were exhorted to go on preaching Christ." To Rev. Dr. Byron Sunderland, who visited him shortly before his death, he said, "That Jesus, which we have preached so long to others, is with me now." To an aged relative, Rev. R. R. Gurley, he said, "My dear cousin, I am going home before you. We have a long line of pious ancestry in heaven; soon you will join me there, and then we will talk it all over. God bless you and yours; and now," (raising his emaciated hands), he exclaimed, "Glory be to the Father, and to the Son, and to the Holy Ghost. Amen and amen!" To his son-in-law, Major E., he said, while pressing his face to his own, "My dear son, I love you as though you were my own son. Come out from the world, and cast in your lot with the people of God." To his eldest daughter, Mrs. Major E., pressing her to his breast, he said, "My dear daughter, spend that sweet voice in singing for Jesus. Throw away all other music, and sing only the songs of Zion." To his three sons, who stood near, he said, "My dear sons, I have tried to train you for God; now I must leave you with him. '*Live nigh unto him.*'" To his youngest, a little daughter of nine, he said, "Little darling, *live for Jesus.*" To his beloved wife he said, "My dear, dear wife, you have my heart next to Jesus, my whole heart; you always have had. I have many prayers lodged in heaven for you against the time of trial. Jesus will be your friend. I am only going a little before you. I shall be there waiting for you." When asked, toward the close, "Have you peace? Is Jesus with you now?" he answered, "Yes, oh, yes all is peace!" His peace flowed like a river; and, said Dr. Edwards, in his funeral sermon, "He was strong in faith, like Abraham; patient, like Job; exulting, like Habakkuk." When asked, at the very last, "Are you resting in Jesus?" he answered, "Yes, oh, yes, a thousand times, yes!" And, with his mind clear and bright to the last, thus he lingered until the morning of September 30, 1868, when "the golden bowl was broken," and his happy, blood-washed soul went home to glory, crowned with a martyr's crown. Said Rev. Dr. Sunderland, in his closing remarks at the funeral, "It is natural for us to sorrow. It has been ever thus, when the great and good depart. When the Reformer Œcolampadius died at Basle, the whole city was plunged into mourning. Zwinglé, of Zurich, had already fallen in battle. 'And now,' says the historian, 'there was a great void and a great sorrow in the Church of Christ. Dissensions vanished before these two graves, and nothing could be seen but tears. . . . Luther himself was moved; and, many years afterward, he said to Bullinger, "Their death filled me with such intense sorrow that I was near dying myself."' So does it seem after its kind here to-day. Oh, stricken family! oh, smitten flock! oh, afflicted city! another severe blow has fallen from God's hand, not to make us doubt his faithfulness, but to bring us, we know it, nigher to him, and so nigher to each other!"

In the church, at his funeral, besides many other strong expressions of love and sorrow, they had placed against the wall of the alcove, in the rear of the pulpit, in large evergreen letters, the inscription, "BEHOLD, HOW WE LOVED HIM!"

OLIVER O. HOWARD.

His Birth — Boyhood — Early Religious Training — A Christian Gentleman — He Graduates at Bowdoin College; also at West Point Academy in 1854 — His Patriotism — Appointed Colonel of Third Regiment Maine Volunteers — Is Promoted for Bravery — Joins Army of the Potomac — Wounded at Battle of Fair Oaks — Had his Arm Amputated — Returns Home the Next Day — Lectures the People, and Urges Them to Come to the Rescue of the Country — He Returned in Time for the Battles of Bull Run, Antietam, Fredericksburg, and Chancellorsville — His Position at the Battle of Gettysburg — His Calmness in Battle — Is Temperate — Gen. Sherman's High Opinion of him — His Warm Attachment for Capt. Griffin — He Prays with him, and Bids him a Final Farewell — "It is the Last Time" — Appointed Commissioner of the Freedmen's Bureau — Howard University a Monument of his Benevolent Efforts.

IN exhibiting the individual power of "Christianity in the War," we know of no brighter example in the army than Gen. Howard. Brought up in New England, and thoroughly instructed in the doctrines of the Bible and Puritanic orthodoxy, he has ever been from his boyhood an ornament to the Church. Rooted and grounded in love, he carries his religion about with him wherever he goes. With the law of the Lord written upon his heart, he lives it out in his life. An embodiment of the Christian gentleman and of the heroic soldier, ever earnest and faithful, "he is a tower of strength," and well deserves the title, "The Havelock of America." Even when he entered the army, with all its alluring temptations, he exhibited the same inflexible spirit of steadfastness and self-denial.

Born, November 8, 1830, in Leeds, Me., Oliver Otis Howard was made an orphan by the death of his father when he was about ten years old. Being taken then under the care of his uncle, John Otis, he went through Bowdoin College, and graduated at West Point Academy in 1854. Without fully tracing his military career, we find him, at the breaking out of the rebellion, Assistant Professor of Mathematics at West Point. Burning with patriotic ardor, and desiring to draw his sword in quelling the rebellion, he sought the command of a regiment of volunteers from his own State at the beginning of the war. This request being refused by the War Department, he resigned his commission in the regular army, and was soon after appointed, by the Governor of Maine, Colonel of the 3d Regiment of Maine Vol., in May, 1861. For bravery and worthy conduct at the battle of Bull Run, he was promoted to the rank of Brigadier-General.

Having joined the army of the Potomac in the following December, he was raised to the command of the 11th Army Corps in the fall of 1863, and shared in the glory of all the principal battles of that glorious old army. Having been twice wounded in the right arm at the battle of Fair Oaks, he had his arm cut off; yet, with heroic devotion to his country, he started home the next day, and though weak from the loss of blood and from the severe shock of the wound, he spent two months of his disability for actual service in the army in lecturing the people of his native State, urging them to go forward and fight for the salvation of the country. He returned, however, in time for the bloody battles of the second Bull Run, Antietam, Fredericksburg, and Chancellorsville, where he rendered important service, and fought with undaunted courage.

At the decisive battle of Gettysburg, it is said, Howard's troops held the key of the situation; yet, brave and courageous, this heroic general stood undismayed amid all the shock and terror of that tremendous fight. A soldier, who was with him during that awful conflict, in speaking of his calmness, said, "Gen. Howard stood there as if nothing at all was the matter. He never takes stimulants either. Most of the officers do, but he never does. He was so calm, because he was a Christian." Col. Bowman says, "Gen. Howard is careless of exposing his person in battle to an extent that would be attributable to rashness or fatalism, if it were not known to spring from religion." In all his campaigns with Sherman he was noted for his promptness and fidelity in the discharge of duty, and for his calmness and fearlessness in battle. With all these noble qualities, Gen. Howard soon won the profound respect of Gen. Sherman; and, in speaking of him at the end of one of his campaigns, in his report to Gen. Grant, he said, "In Gen. Howard, throughout, I found a polished and Christian gentleman, exhibiting the highest and most chivalrous traits of the soldier."

During the trials and associations of army life, a very warm personal attachment was formed between Gen. Howard and Capt. Griffin, a member of the general's staff. Capt. Griffin was mortally wounded at the battle of Gettysburg; and when orders came to pursue the retreating foe, it was a melting scene to see the kind-hearted general hasten to bid his highly-esteemed friend a last farewell. The time is short, and the interview must be brief. They had long fought together in defending their country; they had long shared in the hardships, glories, and honors of war; but now they must part to meet no more on earth. "It is the last time." How solemn and impressive the scene! With a few words of tender sympathy, the general reads a few verses from the fourteenth chapter of John, and, bowing his knees, pours out his soul to God in commending his dying friend to the mercy and compassion of an almighty Saviour; and rising from his bended knees, grasps him in a long, tender, affectionate, weeping embrace. And now, with a warm shake of the hands and a hearty "God bless you!" the general bids the dying captain a final farewell. Thus they parted — one to go to fight the battles of the Lord here on earth, the other to swell the ranks of the redeemed in heaven.

At the close of the war, Gen. Howard, having won the full confidence of the nation, was appointed Commissioner of the Freedmen's Bureau, a position for which he was eminently qualified. And having entered upon the arduous duties of this important and responsible position with characteristic zeal, his unremitting and self-denying efforts to help and elevate the poor freedmen have been eminently successful. Supplied by the liberal hand of the Government, he has fed the hungry and clothed the naked of millions of God's poor. The firm basis he has succeeded in establishing for their education, and the great start he has given them in becoming self-sustaining, will prove a great and lasting blessing to this rising race.

Howard University itself will prove a standing monument of

this good man's efforts to educate and elevate the down-trodden freedmen. Eternity only will reveal the good he has done; and for his successful labors, the general deserves the nation's thanks and the freedmen's warmest gratitude.

BISHOP SIMPSON.

His Nativity — His Education — Enters the Ministry — His Popularity — Elected President of Asbury University — Elected Editor of "Western Christian Advocate" — His Success — Elected Bishop — His Success and Administration — His Patriotism and Zeal in Quelling the Rebellion — Lincoln's Trusted Friend — His Prayer at Lincoln's Funeral — His Preaching Abilities — His Oration at Lincoln's Grave — Powers of Discrimination — Delineates Lincoln's Characteristics, and Points out the Secret of his Power — His Style of Preaching — He Preaches Christ — What he Covets — His Tour in the Rocky Mountains — Intimate with the Presidents of the United States — Appointed by President Grant to Visit San Domingo — His Present Standing, Influence, and Power — His Touching Peroration at Lincoln's Tomb.

WHILE the learned Dr. McClintock, when living, stood as the prince of theologians, Bishop Simpson, to-day, stands as the prince of preachers in the Methodist Episcopal Church. And that is a very high attainment. To be a complete orator is the height of human perfection. To be able, with great success, to persuade men to renounce the world and give their hearts to God, is the highest and most honorable position this world affords. It is honorable to occupy presidential chairs, to sit upon dazzling thrones, to command armies and win victories — these are all honorable; but for real grandeur and glory there is no position so honorable and useful as the faithful and successful ambassador of the Lord Jesus Christ. And the life and character of every one who has been eminently successful in this glorious work is well worthy of close investigation.

Rev. Matthew Simpson, D. D., is a native of the State of Ohio. When and where he was born, after much inquiry, we have failed to ascertain. But it don't matter. It is enough for our present purpose to know that he has been born, acted his part in

MATTHEW SIMPSON.

the affairs of the church and the world, and labored hard in quelling the Rebellion. He received his education at Alleghany College, Meadville, Pa., and it is said he afterward studied medicine.

Having experienced a change of heart when quite young, and being sensible of the great things God had done for him, and the consequent obligations resting upon him, after going through a theological course, he entered the ministry under the Pittsburg Conference in 1834. Possessing fine preaching abilities, and being devoted to the work, he improved so rapidly that he soon became known as one of the most impressive and eloquent preachers of the denomination. As his vigorous mind became more fully developed, his popularity and usefulness increased; and being a man of energy and ripe scholarship, he was elected President of Asbury University, Greencastle, Indiana, in 1839; and he discharged the duties of that important position with so much ability, success, and satisfaction, that his reputation and influence, both as a teacher and as a pulpit orator, increased so fast that he was soon regarded as one of the leading men of the State.

Improving in intellectual power and usefulness, and growing more and more in favor with the people, he was elected, by the General Conference of 1848, to the responsible position of editor of the "Western Christian Advocate," one of the most important and influential official papers of the church. To fill this influential position well required rare qualifications and a peculiar tact. Yet Mr. Simpson, conscious of the fact that, while occupying the editorial chair, he was speaking to many thousands every week, and making every one of them either better or worse by every issue of his paper, with his well-cultivated mind and thorough knowledge of human nature and of the affairs of the church, made a very successful editor. But with all his popularity and success as an editor, there was another step for Mr. Simpson to take. The church still kept calling him, "Go up higher;" and thus advancing step by step, more and more developing the great faculties of his head and heart, increasing his usefulness and power, until in 1852 the General Conference elected him to the important office of bishop in the Methodist Episcopal Church of the United States. Blessed with a vigorous mind, an indomitable will, and a persevering heart, Bishop Simpson possesses fine qualifications for an executive officer. And being zealous in the Master's cause, he discharges the duties of his office with becoming gravity and general satisfaction. Being thoroughly acquainted with the polity, the work, and the wants of the church, he makes one of the best and most efficient superintendents of the connection. With a wide sphere of labor, and having the care of so many churches, like other bishops he travels about from place to place, holding conferences, administering discipline, dedicating churches, preaching, and ordaining men to preach the gospel. Progressive in his views, and understanding all the wants and interests of the church, Bishop Simpson's administration has been marked for the breadth and liberality of his opinions on all questions pertaining to the polity of the church. Being strongly in favor of lay representation, he has been identified with this great movement from the beginning. Through his persevering labors, aided by the cooperation of other leading men, their efforts have at last been crowned with success, and the great Methodist Church of the land is now blessed with a lay representation.

Full of patriotic ardor, Bishop Simpson has always stood firm for the flag of his country. He looks upon man's duty to his country as being second only to his duty to his Maker; or, as he has (we believe) graphically expressed it: "NAIL THE FLAG JUST BELOW THE CROSS;" or, as the Saviour says, "Render unto Cæsar the thing that are Cæsar's, and unto God the things that are God's." In importance, the church is the centre of the universe. Around it everything else revolves. For the church, grass grows and water flows; for the church, the sun shines by day and the moon and stars by night. God the Father "gave his Son to be head over all things to the church." Hence the importance of faithfully doing your duty to your country, because a good, well-administered government tends so much to advance the prosperity of the church. Says "Harper's Weekly," "When the civil war broke out, Bishop Simpson exerted himself to the utmost in promoting the work of suppressing the Rebellion. He was the trusted friend of the lamented Lincoln;" and by request he made the opening prayer at his funeral at the White House in Washington. This prayer is remarkable for its being very comprehensive, fervent, and appropriate. The earnest suppliant, having implored the Divine blessing to rest upon Lincoln's bereaved widow, upon his sons, upon his successor in office, prayed, "Lord, let thy blessing rest upon our country. Grant unto us all a fixed and strong determination never to cease our efforts until our glorious Union shall be fully re-established." "Around the remains of our beloved President may we covenant together, by every possible means, to give ourselves to our country's service until every vestige of this Rebellion shall have been wiped out, and until slavery, its cause, shall be forever eradicated. Preserve us, we pray Thee, from all complications with foreign nations. Give us hearts to act justly towards all nations, and grant unto them hearts to act justly towards us, that universal peace and happiness may fill our earth. We rejoice then in this inflicting dispensation Thou hast given, as an additional evidence of the strength of our nation. We bless Thee that no tumult has arisen, and in peace and harmony our government moves onward, and that Thou hast shown that our Republican Government is the strongest upon the face of the earth. In this solemn presence may we feel that we, too, are immortal. May the sense of our responsibility to God rest upon us; may we repent of every sin; and may we consecrate anew unto Thee all the time and all the talents which Thou hast given us; and may we so fulfil our allotted duties that, finally, we may have a resting-place with the good and wise and great who now surround that glorious throne."

As a preacher, Bishop Simpson has but few equals. Being an intimate friend of President Lincoln, he was selected to deliver the closing oration at his funeral at Springfield, Illinois. And his comprehensive grasp of the subject of his sermon on that occasion, and the masterly manner in which he treated the great topics therein discussed, denote a thorough knowledge of the affairs of the world and of the human heart, and an ability to delineate and analyze human character seldom equalled. It is often very difficult to ascertain exactly wherein a great man's strength lies. Sometimes it is found in one faculty, and sometimes in another. And here the skilful orator, exploring the heart and scanning the mind of the martyred hero, points out with wonderful precision wherein his great strength lay. And where was it? was it chiefly in his *head?* No. With all his mighty intellectual grasp and strong powers of quick perception and close discrimination, his great moral strength laid more in the goodness of his heart than in the brilliancy of his mind. "And," said Bishop Simpson, in his funeral oration, "if you ask me on what mental characteristics his greatness rested, I answer, on a quick and ready perception of facts; on a memory unusually tenacious and retentive; and on a logical turn of mind, which followed sternly and unwaveringly every link in the chain of thought on every subject which he was called to investigate. . . . Who that has read his messages fails to perceive the directness and simplicity of his style? And this very trait, which was scoffed at and descried by opponents, is now recognized as one of the strong points of that mighty mind which so powerfully influenced the destinies of the nation, and which shall for ages to come influence the destiny of humanity.

"It was not, however, chiefly by his mental faculties that he gained such control over mankind. His moral power gave him pre-eminence. The convictions of men that Abraham Lincoln was an honest man led them to yield to his guidance. As has been said of Cobden, whom he greatly resembled, he made all men feel a sense of himself — a recognition of individuality, a self-relying power. They saw in him a man whom they believed would do what is right regardless of consequences. It was this *moral feeling* that gave him the greatest hold on the people, and made his utterances almost oracular. When the nation was angered by the perfidy of foreign nations in allowing privateers to be fitted out, he uttered the significant expression, 'One war at a time,' and it stilled the national heart. There are instants which seem to contain germs which shall develop and bloom forever. Such a moment came in the tide of our own land, when a question must be settled which affected all the earth. The contest was for human freedom. Not for this republic merely, not for the Union simply, but to decide whether the people, as a people, in their entire majesty, were destined to be the government, or whether they were to be subject to tyrants or aristocrats, or to class of any kind. This is the great question for which we have been fighting, and its decision is at hand, and the result of the contest will affect ages to come. If successful, republics will spread, in spite of monarchs, all over this earth." [Exclamations of "Amen," "Thank God."]

With a warm, gushing heart, glowing with tenderness and sympathy, Bishop Simpson's manner partakes somewhat of the Whitefield style. Of the three great French pulpit orators, it is said that Bossuet addressed the imagination, Massillon, the heart, and Bourdaloue, the understanding. And while Dr. Simpson sometimes soars aloft in the field of imagination, yet generally he addresses himself more to the understanding and the heart. Full of vigor and life, his fine, charming voice and his plain, vivid, fluent style of presenting the truth give him a wonderful power over his hearers; and, rising with the importance of his subject, with all his majesty of thought, vehemence, and tenderness of manner, and irresistible strength of argument, he carries away his audience with a force almost irresistible.

Bishop Simpson preaches Christ. His sermons, though graphic in description, touching and impressive, abound with the doctrines of the Cross. And in grasping for the soul, he often says some very comprehensive and striking things. In his recent sermon before the New England Conference, he said, "If there is anything I covet in this world, it is the power of making man feel that he stands before the throne of God. I would covet the power to take my audience to the Cross, to let them see Jesus in all his mercy and in all his love." When the church is pressed for funds, if they want to raise a large collection, when Bishop Simpson is present they always put him up to preach; and, by the power of his touching eloquence and earnest appeals in pressing the wants of the church and the claims of the gospel, he never fails to secure a very large collection. During the late

Rebellion the Bishop made a tour to Denver and the Gold Regions in the Rocky Mountains of Colorado, preaching at every opportunity to lawyers, politicians, miners, and gamblers; and he always had very large, attentive congregations.

Sometimes, in times of deep distress and great peril, when the destiny of the nation seems to hang upon the decision of the hour, and when the path of duty seems dark, and you know not what to do, it is good to have a wise, trusty friend to consult with. Such a friend was Bishop Simpson to President Lincoln.

But this eminent divine not only enjoyed the abiding confidence of President Lincoln, which he might have won during the anxieties, reverses, and successes of the war, but he also enjoys the friendship and full confidence of President Grant, who recently appointed him as one of the commissioners to visit San Domingo, to consult with others upon the propriety of annexing that fertile island to the United States. In point of standing, the Bishop still seems to be increasing in usefulness and rising in influence and power.

We close this brief, imperfect sketch with the Bishop's graphic peroration at the tomb of Lincoln. Having quoted a touching sentence of Lincoln, with deep and tender emotion he exclaimed: "Chieftain, farewell! The nation mourns thee. Mothers shall teach thy name to their lisping children. The youth of our land shall emulate thy virtues. Statesmen shall study thy record, and learn lessons of wisdom. Mute though thy lips be, yet they still speak. Hushed is thy voice, but its echoes of liberty are ringing through the world, and the sons of bondage listen with joy. Prisoned thou art in death, and yet thou art marching abroad, and chains and manacles are bursting at thy touch. Thou didst fall not for thyself. The assassin had no hate for thee. Our hearts were aimed at, our national life was sought. We crown thee as our martyr, and humanity enthrones thee as her triumphant son. Hero, martyr, friend, farewell!"

ADMIRAL FARRAGUT.

A new Era in Naval Affairs — Fight between the Monitor and Merrimac — Progress in Destroying and Saving Man — Satan's Whetting his Sword should Arouse the Church — Farragut's Birth — Enters the U. S. Navy — His First and Second Engagements — Heroic Courage — Wounded — Highly Esteemed by his Commander — His Heroism Sleeps — Sails all over the World — Promoted — His Loyalty — Went North — Commands a Naval Expedition *vs.* New Orleans — His Large Fleet — Captures New Orleans — Daring Feats in Capturing Vicksburg — His Stratagem and Heroism in Capturing Mobile — Lashed Himself to the Rigging of his Ship in Battle — Calls upon God for Help and Direction — Severe Fight with a Rebel Ironclad — He Whipped her — She Surrenders — Promoted Again — His Habits — Decorating his Grave — His Prayer in the Battle of Mobile Bay — "Go Forward" — His Religious Life — Testimony of Lieut. Montgomery.

THE late war established a new era in naval affairs. Hitherto the fighting at sea had been done on wooden vessels. But now, in the navy, "old things pass away, and all things become new." Fresh light having dawned upon the inventive genius of Captain Ericsson, he begins to construct war vessels upon a new and improved plan, and the feeble old wooden hulks give way to the introduction of the destructive ironclads. And although with those inferior crafts distinguished victories had been won, yet for speedy destruction of life, for naval skill and naval glory, those achieved under the new era are far greater. The unprecedented, fierce, and bloody fight between the Monitor and Merrimac, off Hampton Roads, Va., astonished the world. It put an end to the use of wooden vessels of war, and very materially changed the naval and military strength of the nations of the earth. And notwithstanding the late great progress made in Christian civilization and in the arts and sciences, the introduction of ironclads into the navy, and the needle-gun and the mitrailleuse in the army, indicate a progress in the art of war hitherto unknown. And when we view the awful carnage in the recent civil war in France, and look upon the sixty thousand uncoffined dead lying unburied in the bloody streets of Paris, we are led to believe that the recent progress made in the art of destroying man is much greater than any made to save him. And as Satan is whetting his sword and devising new means for man's destruction, most assuredly the Church, under God, should search out and devise new measures for his salvation.

In the galaxy of naval glory, no star shines brighter than the subject of this sketch. His father was a naval officer before him, and fought under Commodore Patterson a long while ago, at the battle of New Orleans.

David Glascoe Farragut was born at Campbell's Station, in East Tennessee, in 1801. He joined the United States Navy when a boy of only nine years of age, and served a severe apprenticeship under Commodore Porter. His first naval engagement was under Porter in the *Essex*, with the English sloop-of-war *Alert*, on the 13th day of April, 1812. Eager for action, as soon as the *Alert* saw the *Essex*, she ran violently upon her, and with much loud cheering, opened her entire broadside upon her with great fury. The brave commodore, undismayed, and thirsting for victory, quickly replied with such terrible effect that the sinking *Alert* was knocked into drowning helplessness, and surrendered in eight minutes after commencing the fight.

Farragut's next engagement was in the destructive fight in Valparaiso harbor with the British Captain Hillyar. In this noted combat the young midshipman displayed great courage. The British vessel, with a force double that of the *Essex*, by a gross violation of the laws of neutrality succeeded in destroying the *Essex;* yet Farragut, then but twelve years old, although he received a wound in the fight, stood firmly to his post to the very last. In this brave act of the young hero, you see in embryo the heroic admiral. With his deck strewn with the killed and wounded, the humane Porter, when all hope was lost, surrendered his bloody wreck to save himself and the helpless wounded from a watery grave. With the other officers of the ship, Farragut was sent home on parole, accompanied with words of high commendation from Commodore Porter, who in his report to the Secretary of the Navy expressed his sincere regret that the noble boy was too young for promotion. It is more than probable that no other boy in the world, so young, ever endured with so much courage and firmness a fight so terrible and bloody. And such worthy and noble conduct in the young midshipman so completely won the esteem of Commodore Porter that he at once provided for his military and general education. But Farragut preferred the navy to the army, and as soon as the war was over he went back to sea again.

With these bright displays of bravery, the heroism of Farragut, for the want of opportunities to develop it, was suffered to lie almost dormant for over forty years. For some forty-five years he sailed about, all over the world, from place to place, commanding at different harbors, slowly advancing in rank by seniority, until, in 1825, he was made lieutenant. In 1841 he became commander, and in 1851 he was raised to the rank of captain.

When the rebellion burst upon the world, he had served forty-eight years in the United States Navy, yet with his great genius as a naval officer almost entirely undeveloped, and altogether unknown to the world. Having always lived in the South, it was expected he would secede and go with the South in their rebellion and treason; but having sailed so long under the flag of his country, he had learned to respect and honor it too much to rebel and fight against it. He was living at Norfolk, Va., at the time, and as soon as he publicly declared his principles, and made known his determination to stand by his country, he was met with heavy frowns and severe threats. The hot-headed rebels told him it might be unsafe for him to utter, and remain in the South with, such sentiments. "Very well," he said, "I will go where I *can* live with such sentiments;" and making ready, he left Norfolk on the night of the 18th of April, 1861, the very night before the rebels fired the navy yard of that place.

He sailed for the Hudson River, New York, and stopped for a short time near Tarrytown, where, being a perfect stranger, he was looked upon for a while with a good deal of suspicion.

As the rebellion spread itself, the demand for naval strength increased. Captain Farragut received his first appointment January 20, 1862, to command the naval part of an expedition against New Orleans. After a tedious preparation, with a fleet of forty-six sail, the largest ever known in America at that time, Farragut sailed in his splendid flagship *Hartford*, from Hampton Roads, February 3, 1862, and reached Ship Island, near New Orleans, by the 20th of the following March.

The mortar vessels were commanded by Commodore D. D. Porter. After a short consultation with General Butler, it was concluded to advance. Farragut gave the command, and the vast fleet sailed up to the forts, and on the 18th of April commenced a furious bombardment, which lasted six days. Finding the reduction of the forts rather a tedious job, Farragut concluded to pass them; and, dividing his squadron into two columns, after getting under way, they passed the forts under a most furious fire, in an hour and ten minutes. This was a very dangerous feat. Of all injuries received, the Brooklyn fared the worst, which lost eight men killed and twenty wounded. The enemy's steam-rams ran a fire-raft aboard the *Hartford*, and drove her ashore; but the skilful commodore soon drew her off, but not without being severely injured. The forts having been thus passed, and the enemy's fleet sunk or captured, the Union fleet entered the harbor of New Orleans with but little opposition, and the city surrendered to Commodore Farragut, April 26, 1862.

After things became a little settled, General Butler went in and took possession, and established his headquarters in the St. Charles Hotel, which had been closed for some time. He soon established martial law, instituted and maintained a government, though somewhat severe, admirably adapted to the city of New Orleans. After issuing his proclamation, he made a speech to the people, and gave them to understand, with characteristic firmness, what he meant to do.

Baton Rouge, Natchez, and other points above, yielded without making any opposition, at the approach of the Union forces; and Commodore Farragut, with his vast fleet reinforced, received orders to open the Mississippi River from one end to the other.

But this fiery trial and brilliant victory was only a prelude and a foretaste of what was to follow.

Vicksburg was the next stronghold to be taken; and on the

26th of June the batteries around it were bombarded all day with but little effect. On the 27th, at the command of Commodore Porter, the town was shelled. Meanwhile the daring Farragut was lying five miles below, and while Porter was going on with his bombarding, he succeeded in passing the well-fortified city in the face of its blazing batteries, with eight vessels of his fleet, with a loss of only four killed and twenty wounded. Having got above the town, he was met by Commodore Davis, descending from Memphis, when Farragut determined to open the river by cutting a canal through a tongue of land, and leave Vicksburg far to one side, entirely out of the way; but the falling of the river thwarted his design, and compelled him to sail down the river for deeper water; and the capture of the place at that time was abandoned.

The attack on Vicksburg was resumed the following autumn. Meanwhile, the Federal arms had been crowned with such brilliant victories and successes in the earlier part of 1862, that, for a while, some entertained strong hopes of a speedy termination of the war. The Confederates had been driven out of Missouri, Western and Middle Tennessee had been occupied by Union forces, and with the capture of New Orleans (excepting Vicksburg and Port Hudson) the passage of the Mississippi was now clear. And Vicksburg, as it was strongly defended by nature, and much stronger by rebel forces, being the principal obstruction, an attack was made upon it first. An expedition, under General Banks and Farragut, was to ascend the river from New Orleans to meet one under General Sherman and Commodore Porter from Memphis, while General Grant was to operate in the rear of the city. With this formidable combination, they hoped to take the place. But it failed. And after this and other schemes had failed, General Grant determined upon the very dangerous plan of running a portion of the fleet past Vicksburg to make an attack below. And to aid in this, the fearless Farragut, inspiring his brave men with fresh courage by facing danger and death, attempted to pass Port Hudson with its impregnable fortifications and four miles of blazing batteries, with seven of his vessels — the *Hartford, Albatross, Richmond, Kineo, Monongahela, Genesee,* and the *Mississippi.* With eyes flashing with courageous fire, the heroic admiral gives the command, and the daring fleet, falling into line, sails on through vast volleys of balls and bursting shells spreading death and destruction among the struggling ships and sailors. The awful firing was so severe and destructive that only two of the entire fleet, the *Hartford* and the *Albatross,* succeeded in passing. The *Richmond* was so severely damaged that she retreated. The *Mississippi* was destroyed. About eighty persons of the fleet were killed in the hazardous undertaking. This was on March 14, 1863. The Federal army now being below Vicksburg, and supported by the formidable fleet, the capture of the long sought-for city looked far less difficult. Although the rebels poured in their forces by tens of thousands to defend it, and although it was girded with seven hills by the God of nature, yet ere the setting of the bloody sun of July 3, 1863, it fell into the Federal hands, and surrendered to General Grant.

But Farragut's greatest fight and grandest naval victory remains to be told. With the capture of Vicksburg, and the complete opening of the Mississippi, his next great undertaking was the capture of Mobile. And, in order to understand the greatness of that victory, it will be necessary to know something about the strength of the fortifications to be overcome. Besides three lines of strong earthworks extending five or six miles in rear of the city, and five thirty-two rifled batteries strewn along the bay with immense obstructions of piles stuck in the channel, there played in the waters about the city the impregnable iron-clad ram *Tennessee,* and four large wooden gunboats besides. Yet Forts Morgan and Gaines at the mouth of Mobile Bay constituted the principal obstruction in taking Mobile by sea. But before the unterrified admiral this mighty force was soon made to give way. Early in July, Farragut, with his fleet, accompanied by a land force under Generals Canby and Granger, arrived in Mobile Bay. After a short consultation between the admiral and the generals, it was determined to invest Fort Gaines first.

For this purpose, the fleet covered the landing of a force of some four thousand men under General Granger. Meanwhile, feeling their danger, the enemy kept pouring in troops and supplies into Fort Gaines to strengthen its defence. Early on August 4th, the Federal fleet, twenty-six sail, including two double and one single turreted monitor, and one ironclad, commenced closing in their lines east of Fort Morgan, as though they were concentrating their forces on Fort Gaines. But this was only a feigned preparatory step, and by forty minutes past five on the morning of August 5th, the mighty fleet, two abreast and lashed together, set sail. Grand and buoyant they steamed fearlessly up the main channel of the bay, and by forty-seven minutes past six the ironclad *Tecumseh* fired the first shot. In a few minutes the fort opened upon the fleet, and immediately the action became general. The fort played heavily on the *Brooklyn* and *Hartford*, and the fight began to wax very hot. Buoyant with hope and courage, thirsting for victory, the heroic admiral lashed himself to the mast of his ship the better to give command, and there, standing above the smoke and dust of battle, watched with eagle eye the progress of the mighty conflict. Fighting with perfect desperation, the famous ironclad *Tecumseh*, shattered by a torpedo, careened and sank — nearly all on board sinking with her. Undismayed at this heavy loss, the persistent admiral, calling upon God for help and direction, at once peremptorily ordered up the wooden boats to fill up the loss. The flagship *Hartford* then led the fleet, and, urged on by their brave hero, they steamed steadily forward, maintaining a constant fire, and passed the destructive forts a little before eight o'clock.

But though past, the fight was not ended. The rebel gunboats *Morgan*, *Gaines*, and *Selma*, which had kept up such an annoying fire, were then attacked, and one of them was captured and another destroyed. Then followed a most terrible fight with the *Tennessee*, which at once made for the flagship *Hartford;* whereupon the monitors were immediately ordered to attack her. The *Monongahela*, Commander Strong, struck her first; but received far more injury than she inflicted. The rebel monster then received heavy blows from the *Lackawanna* and the *Hart-*

ford and the *Manhattan,* but with little effect, except a fifteen-inch shot from the latter which broke through her iron plating. Determined upon her destruction, the *Hartford* fearlessly made at her again with full speed, and, with the combined efforts of their united forces, she was now reduced to a desperate condition. With her steering chains gone and smoke-stack shot away, she was compelled to resort to her relieving tackles. And increasing their firing on and on, they waged the furious fight until, seeing the *Ossipee* was about to strike her a tremendous blow, she raised the white flag and surrendered about ten o'clock. During this severe fight with the *Tennessee* and the rebel gunboats, the fleet lost more men than it did in passing Fort Morgan. Admiral Buchanan, commanding the *Tennessee*, was wounded in the leg, and two or three of his men were killed, and five or six wounded. Commodore Johnston, formerly of the United States Navy, came on board the flagship to surrender his and Admiral Buchanan's sword to the victorious Farragut. Thus ended one of the fiercest and most destructive naval engagements on record. Thus, too, for the first time in the history of the world, was a naval officer known to risk the danger of lashing himself to the rigging of his ship on entering an engagement.

In this grand adventure it had been thought, as the ship channel was so very near to Fort Morgan, that it would be impossible for any ships to pass. But by the discerning Farragut this seeming insurmountable difficulty was very soon overcome, and even turned to an advantage to him and a disadvantage to them. Lashing his vessels together, two and two, he diminished the exposure, and secured the safety and integrity of the fleet. This was a most masterly contrivance. On the 7th of August, Forts Powel and Gaines surrendered, and, with another small skirmish, on the 23d Fort Morgan surrendered also. With the surrender of Forts Gaines and Morgan eighty-six guns and fifteen hundred men fell into the hands of the Union forces.

In honor of his distinguished services in these splendid victories, Commodore Farragut was, in July, 1863, promoted to the rank of rear-admiral, and in August of the following year he was raised to the rank of vice-admiral, which grade was created by Congress especially for him.

Being remarkably neat, clean, and temperate in his habits, Admiral Farragut enjoyed very good, vigorous health. He would not even so much as smoke a cigar. And the distinguished favors and the strong testimonials of high regard he has received, both at home and abroad, show in the most decided terms how highly his valuable services are appreciated by the people. Mourned by the nation, his full history would fill volumes. Enshrined in the heart, embalmed in the memory, for his heroic, noble deeds, he will live in the affections of the people forever.

We clip the following from a New York paper of May 30, 1871, which shows how fresh his memory still exists in the minds of the people: "Admiral Farragut's grave at Wood Lawn was decorated at sunrise this morning; the ceremonies being performed by a battalion of marines under Colonel Brooke, with a full band from the Brooklyn Navy Yard, the Farragut Lodge of Good Templars, and the Wadsworth Post of the Grand Army of the Republic, both of Brooklyn. General S. Catlin, of Williamsburg, delivered an eloquent address commemorative of the life and services of the deceased admiral, after which the grave was profusely covered with cut and growing flowers. Admiral M. Smith, commanding the Brooklyn Navy Yard, was also present at the ceremonies." A large portion of the crowd were ladies.

FARRAGUT AT PRAYER.

"Man's extremity is God's opportunity." Deeply impressed with a sense of want, and conscious of his own weakness, in times of great emergency, when all human aid seems to fail, it is natural for man to go to God for help. Sinking Peter, hanging upon the verge of a watery grave, cried, "*Lord, save me!*" The shipwrecked disciples, tossed upon the ocean's raging billows, feeling their awful danger and helplessness, fled to Jesus, and cried, "*Lord, save, or we perish!*"

Farragut, in the depths of a great emergency, and feeling the salvation of his country hanging as it were upon his own success, lashed to the rigging of his ball-riven and mast-shattered ship, with cannon-balls flying thick about him, and with his fleet halting and sinking around him, when hesitating what to do, fled to God for help and direction, and cried, "*O God, my Maker, lead me to do this day, what is right and best for my country!*" * "In answer to this prayer, the admiral said he heard a voice from heaven, which seemed to say, in tones of thunder, '*Go forward!* Go FORWARD!'" He went forward; and for deeds of daring courage, high naval skill, and unyielding perseverance, achieved a victory, for grandeur and glory far exceeding anything ever accomplished in the world!

When we come to speak more particularly of the great admiral's religious life, our data is more scanty. Absorbed with his grand naval achievements, our historian has failed fully to record his religious history. But the admiral has always sustained a good reputation as a faithful, consistent Christian. He belonged to the Protestant Episcopal Church; and the Rev. Dr. Montgomery, who preached his funeral sermon, says another, "alluded, in very strong and feeling terms, to his wonderful character as a Christian hero." With his faith and religious emotions highly wrought up in contemplating the melting scenes of Calvary, Dr. Montgomery says "he always partook of the holy communion with great religious fervor." The purity of his life, his heroic devotion to his country, his great *love of truth*, and his unbounded kindness, together with his earnest prayer to God, in passing the belching batteries at Fort Morgan, speak much in favor of his Christian character.

And says Lieutenant James E. Montgomery, the admiral's secretary, who was with him under all kinds of circumstances, for many years, and who was more intimately associated with him than any one else outside of his family: "I fail to recall *one act* that reflects upon him as an upright, exemplary Christian; and at the same time I bear full testimony to the truth of the well-won and justly deserved reputation he has left to the world. He was always truly religious, and he never forgot or

---

* Related by Rev. Dr. Montgomery in preaching the admiral's funeral sermon.

neglected his duties as a professing Christian." These, together with "his *unbounded charity*, tender-hearted disposition, and child-like simplicity, made him one of nature's noblemen, who was at once the hero of the sea and a model Christian patriot."

Full of years and victories, crowned with unfading honor and glory, this noble-hearted hero left this world August 14, 1870. He died at the residence of Commodore Pennock, in the Navy Yard at Portsmouth, New Hampshire, and was temporarily buried there August 17. His remains were removed to New York, and deposited with unparalleled honors in a beautiful mound in Woodlawn Cemetery, September 30, 1870. "Blessed are the dead who die in the Lord."

GEORGE H. STUART.

Sketch of, by Dr. Wylie — His Birth — Parents — Education — Arrival in this Country — Religious Profession — Elected Ruling Elder — His Christian Zeal and Liberality — Missionary Spirit — A Sabbath-school Worker — Suggested the National Presbyterian Convention, and Presided over it — His Suspension from the Church — Refused a Position in President Grant's Cabinet — A Successful Merchant — His Natural Talents — Christian Character — An Expert Presiding Officer — His Natural Eloquence — Attractive Speaker and Successful Beggar — He always Succeeds — Goes About Doing Good — His Marriage — Family — Personal Appearance — His Labors in the Christian Commission — Its Leading Spirit and President — His Qualifications and Devotion to the Work — Secret of His Success — Distributes Books — Overcomes an Infidel — The People's Faith in him — Money Flows in at his Asking — His Importunity Prevails — His Zeal to Supply the Needy Soldiers — His Kindness to the Rebels — Rebels Weep at Northern Kindness — His Fondness for Army Relics — "His Generalship in Prayer" — He can always have Prayer — "An Eminent Christian at Work" — His Christian Sagacity — His Popularity — An Eloquent Speaker — His Speech in England.

THE wisdom, goodness, and power of God are strikingly manifested in amply providing for every emergency of His people. And His provisions are always according to the exigency of the case. "As thy days, so shall thy strength be."

When the world was about to be deluged, God raised up a Noah to prepare an ark to the saving of his house and two of every living thing. When a great Reformation was to be brought about, God raised up a Luther to bring it to pass. When three millions of slaves were to be led out of Egyptian bondage, a Moses was raised up to do it. When the Church was made to pass through a fiery trial of fierce persecution, God raised up hosts of heroic martyrs to die at the stake to sustain it. When a new nation was to be born, God raised up a Washington and hosts of other heroes to establish it. When a great rebellion was to be quelled, God raised up a mighty army to quell it; and when a great Christian Commission was necessary to sustain that army, God raised up a Stuart to manage it. "Even for this same purpose have I raised thee up."

The following extract is from the pen of the Rev. T. W. J. Wylie, D. D., of Philadelphia, Mr. Stuart's distinguished pastor and friend:

"GEORGE HAY STUART was born at Rosehall, County Down, Ireland, April 2, 1816. His parents were highly respected members of the Associate Presbyterian Church, under the pastoral care of the late Rev. George Hay, whose name he bears. After receiving the usual elements of education, he immigrated to this country, to which several of his family had previously come; arriving in Philadelphia, September 1, 1831. Shortly afterward he became a regular attendant at the First Reformed Presbyterian Church, of which the late Rev. Dr. S. B. Wylie was then the pastor. In connection with this he made a profession of religion April 24th, 1835. On the 7th of August, 1842, he was ordained a ruling elder, an office which he still holds. Mr. S. enjoyed the highest regard of his pastor, who was able to discern in his character even at an early age the germs of excellence which have been subsequently so fully developed. Mr. S. has always been one of the most active, liberal, and useful members of the congregation; and to his munificent contributions, as well as his untiring personal labors, much of its prosperity has been owing. The handsome and commodious edifice occupied by the congregation, and which has historic fame as the place of meeting of the Presbyterian National Convention in 1867, was erected principally by his exertions and received his generous aid. Mr. S. has been an early and warm supporter of the Foreign Missionary cause, and for many years acted as treasurer of the Board of Foreign Missions of the Reformed Presbyterian Church. The Missionary Refuge at Landour, Northern India, was his gift to the Saharunpur Mission, to all of whose operations he has made large donations. He was also, for many years, treasurer of the Theological Seminary of the Reformed Presbyterian Church, which received from him valuable aid. He was early interested in the Sabbath-school cause. Shortly after his arrival in this country he became connected, as a teacher, with the Sabbath school of the First Reformed Presbyterian Church, Philadelphia, and after a few years was elected its superintendent, an office which he filled for about twenty-five years with the greatest success, the number of teachers and pupils in the parent school, and two white and one colored mission schools connected with the congregation, amounting at one time to nearly a thousand.

"Mr. Stuart's efforts to do good have not, however, been restricted to any one denomination. Wherever good was to be done, he has been ready to give all the aid in his power. The delegation of the Irish Presbyterian Church sent to this country during the years of famine in that land, owed to his counsel, co-operation, and contributions much of its success. The Rev. Dr. Duff visited America by his invitation, and the extensive tour he made, and the large amount of money he received for the College in Calcutta, was, in a great measure, the result of Mr. S.'s arrangements. Other deputations from the Presbyterian Churches of Ireland and Scotland were greatly indebted to him. The Presbyterian National Convention held in Philadelphia, November, 1867, which did so much to effect the reunion of the Old and New School Churches, was suggested by him, and he was called by acclamation to act as its president. He has been connected with Young Men's Christian Associations since their organization, and was President of the National Conventions held at Troy in 1859, and Chicago, 1863. He has been for many years an officer of the American Sunday-School Union, and of the American Bible and American Tract Societies, in each of whose operations he has taken an active part.

"In 1868 he was *suspended* by the General Synod of the Reformed Presbyterian Church from his office as a ruling elder, and his membership in the church, on a charge of having sung hymns and communed with Christians of other evangelical denominations, and declaring that he would continue to do so. This was done without any trial, and in his absence in consequence of severe sickness, during which his physician would not allow him to leave his room. This act of discipline was formally condemned and repudiated by about half of the Presbyteries of the Reformed Presbyterian Church, and led to a suspension of their relations to the Synod. The large majority of the congregation with which he was connected, along with his pastor, refused to recognize it, and it has met with severe and almost universal condemnation wherever it has been known.

"The esteem and confidence felt for Mr. S. have led to his being called upon to discharge important public trusts. He has repeatedly and urgently been invited by President Grant to occupy a place in his Cabinet, which he has declined on account of his precarious health. He has, however, been acting as one of the Indian Commissioners whose labors have done so much to protect our aborigines from wrong. He is also one of the members of the Board of Public Trusts of the city of Philadelphia, to which the charge of the humane and benevolent institutions under the care of the city has been committed.

"As a merchant, Mr. Stuart occupies the foremost rank, not only in regard to enterprise and sagacity, but also for an integrity which has never been tarnished by a dishonest or dishonorable action. During the war, while acting as President of the Christian Commission, and attending to the management of his own business, he found time to superintend the details of the Commission with a devotion which secured at the lowest expense the greatest efficiency.

"Mr. Stuart's natural talents are of a superior order, and would have rendered him a distinguished man in any position, whether military, political, or ecclesiastical. Like the good king of Judah, 'whatever he does, he does it with all his heart, and prospers.' It is, however, as an humble, earnest, generous, and laborious servant of Christ that his great eminence is manifested. He is emphatically a man of prayer. Few persons, there is reason to believe, are as attentive to the private duties of religion, and none can excel him in conducting public services. Those who hear him pray feel that his heart rises to GOD. He is very frequently called on to preside at public meetings, which he does with unequalled ability. He possesses great natural eloquence. His style is earnest, direct, and luminous. At times he moves to tears, and again he displays great power of humor. None can command better the attention of an audience, or obtain more liberal contributions to the cause which he advocates. We know not that he has ever failed in anything he has undertaken.

"While doing much in public, Mr. Stuart is remarkable for doing more in private. He is frequently at the bedside of the sick and dying; and avails himself of every opportunity in the car, the steamer, the hotel, the counting-room, the workshop, the crowded street, or the lonely dwelling, to give words of counsel and comfort, and to lead the sinner to the Saviour. To him 'to live is CHRIST.'

"Mr. Stuart has naturally a robust constitution, which his habits of strict temperance have kept unimpaired, although his labors have been so abundant. He has been, however, for many years a great sufferer from spasmodic asthma, which has frequently prevented him for weeks in succession from resting in bed. Even in the most severe paroxysms of pain, he has been enabled to endure all without a murmur.

"Mr. Stuart was married, May 11th, 1837, to Miss Martha K. Denison, of Philadelphia. They have had nine children, four of whom have been called to the heavenly world, three dying in childhood, and one, William David, in his twenty-third year, a young man of remarkable talents, sanctified by an extraordinary measure of divine grace. Mr. Stuart's house has been the delightful resort of the great and good of all lands: few strangers of distinction visiting this country have not lodged under his roof, or sat at his table; while at the same time, multitudes unknown to fame have received his warm-hearted hospitality.

"In person, Mr. Stuart is a man who would attract attention by the benignant expression of his features, along with the intelligence and animation which his countenance displays. He is nearly six feet in height, somewhat broad-shouldered, and stout, though with a stoop recently from the effect of sickness and excessive labor."

The mercantile firm with which Mr. Stuart has been so long connected was first established at Philadelphia in 1827, and has consisted of the brothers, Messrs. John, Joseph, David, James, and George H. Stuart, — the last named being admitted in 1837. It has had establishments in New York, Manchester, and Liverpool, as well as in Philadelphia. The business has always been managed with great ability; and during all the financial crises which

CHRISTIANITY IN THE WAR.   369

have occurred, every shock has been sustained with a reputation for integrity, liberality, prudence, and success, which have never been surpassed.

But it is of Mr. Stuart's arduous labors in the Christian Commission we wish now to speak more particularly.

Aroused by the bombardment of Fort Sumter, and stung by the defeat of Bull Run, with the war-cloud rapidly thickening over the national horizon; and convinced that the quelling of the rebellion was no small undertaking — moved by the warm impulses of compassion and sympathy for the soldier and patriotic devotion — the United States Christian Commission sprang into existence as by magic. It rose from a spontaneous and heart-gushing liberality, and from a burning desire and a full determination of the loyal people of the land to quell the rebellion and save the country. Its object was to aid in promoting the spiritual and temporal welfare of the officers, soldiers, and sailors of the army and navy of the United States.

In this grand movement, the like of which was before unknown to the world, Mr. Stuart was the great leading spirit from beginning to end. At its first meeting he was chosen chairman of the Commission, and so remained till its close.* Embracing men of all the leading evangelical denominations, and embodying a large amount of the best character and talent of the nation, inspired with the noble cause of liberty and self-government, it was at once capable of a glorious work.

Liberal, enterprising, and with an energetic, buoyant heart, and possessing fine executive abilities and a lofty patriotism, Mr. Stuart was eminently qualified for the position of chairman;

---

* The following extract from the "First Annual Report of the Christian Commission" shows its origin: "At a convention of delegates from Young Men's Christian Associations, held in the city of New York, November 16, 1861, the following persons were appointed as a United States Christian Commission: Rev. Rollin H. Neale, D.D., Boston; George H. Stuart, Esq., Philadelphia; Charles Demond, Esq., Boston; John P. Crozier, Esq., Philadelphia; Rev. Bishop E. S. Janes, D.D., New York; Rev. M. L. R. P. Thompson, D.D., Cincinnati; Hon. Benj. F. Manniere, New York; Col. Clinton B. Fisk, St. Louis; Rev. Benj. C. Cutler, D.D., Brooklyn; John V. Farwell, Esq., Chicago; Mitchell H. Miller, Esq., Washington; John D. Hill, M.D., Buffalo."

and enjoying the full confidence of the American people, with his excellent business qualifications, rich experience, and unbounded popularity, he managed the affairs of the Commission with marked ability, strict economy, and universal satisfaction. Aided by the hearty co-operation of a generous, patriotic people and efficient officers, and encouraged by the exigencies of the case and the glory of the cause, Mr. Stuart, under God, has made this noble institution a great blessing to the army and navy, to the Church, and to the world.*

And he not only *managed* the Commission well, but with a heart longing for souls and glowing with compassion for the soldier, he made an excellent canvasser in the hospital and the camp. With a head well stored and a heart well fired with the doctrines of the Cross, he could sit down and talk Jesus to the sick, wounded, and dying soldier with great success. His great-heartedness, overflowing kindness, warm sympathies, abounding charity, and Christian enthusiasm, together with a soul lit up by the spirit of God, eminently fitted him for this great, soul-saving work.

With these winning traits, painstaking labors, and earnest desires for the soldier's welfare, the noble-hearted philanthropist soon won their warmest attachment and love.

Professor Stoever, of Gettysburg, Pa., in describing the battle of Gettysburg to Mr. Daniel Macrea, of Glasgow, said "that Mr. Stuart was there, and prayed with dying men upon the field. He was very much loved by the soldiers. One of our poor boys at Gettysburg lifted his bleeding head, and said to Mr. Stuart, 'Will you let me kiss you before I die?'" With hearts overflowing with gratitude for acts of kindness received, they would frequently kiss the hand of the delegate or chaplain.

But with all these eminent gifts and graces, the great secret of Mr. Stuart's success, under God, was mainly in his unyielding *perseverance.* It lay in the principle that prompted his immortal words: † "I DON'T BELIEVE IN BEING CONQUERED!"

---

* A further account of the labors, expenses, and contributions of the Commission is contained in Chapter XXII.

† Uttered in his speech in the House of Representatives, Washington, February 2, 1864.

"I NEVER GIVE UP *anything that is practicable!*" He was speaking about distributing books, and said, "I have visited many of the hospitals and some of the camps, and distributed many of these religious books, and I can testify that, from the beginning until now, I have never met a man who refused my books, save only one, and he was from my own city (Philadelphia). He told me that he was an infidel, that he did not believe in my books, that he did not need them. Said he, 'I am from Philadelphia; I live at such a number, Callowhill Street; if you will go there, you will find out my character, and that I am as good as you are.' 'I trust, a great deal better,' said I. But the case did seem a difficult one. 'Stuart,' said a friend, to whom I related the incident, 'you are beaten for once.' 'No,' I replied, 'I am not done with that man yet.' I approached him a short time afterward, and he said to me, 'What is the book you wanted to give to me?' 'It was a selection from the Scriptures, called Cromwell's Bible.' 'Oh,' said he, 'I don't want your Bible; I've no need of it; I'm a good enough man without it;' and, with a motion of supreme indifference, he turned his head. Said I, 'My friend, I'm from Philadelphia, too. I know where you live — can find the exact house. On next Sunday evening, if God spares my life, I expect to speak for the Christian Commission in the Church of the Epiphany.' He looked at me with an inquisitive air. 'And what are you going to say?' 'I am going to tell the people that I had been distributing books and tracts all day through the hospitals and camps I had visited, and that I had found but one man who refused to take them, and he was from Philadelphia.' 'Well, what more are you going to say?' the man asked, with a steady gaze, apparently defying my attempts to move him. 'Well, I'll tell them that I commenced my tract-distribution this morning at the White House in Washington; and the first gentleman I offered one of these little books was one Abraham Lincoln; that he rose from his chair, read the title, expressed great pleasure in receiving it, and promised to read it. But that I came to one of his cooks, here in these quarters, and he was so exceedingly good that he did n't need a copy of the word of God, and would n't have one!'

'Well,' said the man, completely conquered, 'if the *President* can take one, I suppose I can,' as he reached out his hand and received it!"

Here we see the glorious results of perseverance. Yes, it is "the unconquerable *will*" and unswerving determination that leads to noble deeds and grand achievements. What, we ask, led to the great success of this great Commission, which began with sixteen members, had in its employ over five thousand delegates, and gave over six millions of dollars, and an infinite number of books, pamphlets, tracts, and papers to the army and navy in four years? It was the energy and perseverance of its liberal supporters, and the zeal of its noble-hearted chairman. His great liberality and burning zeal in this great work were manifested in his furnishing the Commission with office and store room; in giving his own time and labors, and the services of clerks and porters, all free of charge. With his whole soul and great heart absorbed and wrapped up in this glorious work, Mr. Stuart prayed and labored for it as though he felt that the salvation of the country depended upon his own individual efforts.

And to save expense, through his and the combined influence of the other officers of the Commission, railroad and telegraph companies gave their services in transporting stores and delegates and in transmitting telegrams without cost.

Commanding the respect and full confidence of the religious publishing societies of the country, the American Bible and the American Tract Societies, and other publishing societies, gave very liberally of their publications in books, periodicals, tracts, and papers, to supply the spiritual and intellectual wants of the men in the field. Led on by the wisdom, energy, and heroic devotion of its efficient chairman, and having secured the confidence of the people and a strong hold upon their sympathies, prayers, and purses, and inspired by the grandeur and glory of the country's salvation, the Commission met with a success unparalleled in the history of the world.

The people gave money by the million, and they gave Bibles, books, papers, and tracts by tens of millions.

The rapidity with which the people raised money for the Com-

CHRISTIANITY IN THE WAR. 373

mission is seen from the words of Mr. Stuart to his Scotch friend, Mr. Macrea: " We relied," said he, " on the voluntary contributions of the people — and how nobly they responded! After the battle of Gettysburg, when tens of thousands of wounded and dying men were thrown upon our hands, I telegraphed in all directions. To Boston I telegraphed, 'Can I draw on you for ten thousand dollars at sight?' It was stuck up in the Exchange. The merchants at once formed in line to put down their subscriptions. In half an hour the answer came: 'Draw for sixty thousand dollars.' And," said Mr. Stuart, " the little children helped us too. They made tens of thousands of little housewives' comfort-bags, as the soldiers called them, with buttons, needles and thread, comb, cake of soap, and, above all, a little tract or Testament, and sent them on through the Commission to the needy soldiers, and they did them a world of good."

Thus armed and equipped, the Commission had nothing to do but to go forward, labor, and pray; gather up delegates, and collect stores and distribute them as needed in the field. And it is wonderful to see with what great despatch stores and delegates were procured and sent on. They gathered them as by magic, and sent them free by lightning-trains. We give one example. It was a pressing case. A number of delegates and boxes of stores had just been sent to Murfreesborough on Saturday night; and on Monday morning, early, an urgent request reached the central office for another supply. Grasping the situation, without a moment's hesitation, Mr. Stuart decided to send them by the next train, if possible. They had only an hour and a half to get them ready. The delegates were ready waiting, but passes had to be procured for them, and an order for the free passage of the stores also. The time was short, and the depot was three-quarters of a mile away. At Mr. Stuart's request, a letter was despatched to the vice-president of the Pennsylvania Railroad for the passes, and half a dozen clerks were sent to buy the stores, and porters and draymen to gather them into the depot. At ten minutes before eleven the messenger sent to the vice-president for the passes returned, saying, "There are twenty men or more before the door, and the door is locked; it's no use trying to see him." The train will start in thirty-five minutes, and the stores are pouring into the depot. Deeply anxious to have them go, Mr. Stuart at once hurried to the office of the vice-president, and instead of pressing his way in front, he went round through a private way into a communicating office, and said to the gentleman occupying it, "I must see Mr. Scott; I have not a moment to spare; just open the door." The door was opened, Mr. Scott was seen, and, although overwhelmed with business, the passes were signed, and the order for the free transmission of the stores was given — and Mr. Stuart was back before the clock struck eleven! And before the remaining twenty-five minutes had expired, the stores — twenty-five boxes, etc. — were piled into the cars, all numbered, marked, invoiced, and went free, with lightning speed, with the delegates to Nashville!

And so *intense* was the desire and *earnest* the efforts to supply the needy soldiers, that the Commission, through the earnest importunity of Mr. Stuart, sometimes prevailed upon long trains of cars to *wait* to take provisions to the suffering braves. . , . It was for a Thanksgiving dinner for the soldiers at Bolivar's Heights, near Harper's Ferry, Va. Mrs. Dr. Harris wrote Mr. Stuart about the rough, scanty fare of the soldiers there — asking for something more than "dry bread, half-boiled beef, and a poor mixture called tea," for their Thanksgiving dinner. Owing to the great press of business at the office, Mrs. Harris's letter was not read until it was too late to get ready and forward what was necessary for the dinner. But, presuming that railroads would do extraordinary things under such extraordinary circumstances, the articles for the dinner were prepared with great despatch and hurried to the depot to go on the express train. The conductor agreed to take them, and they put them aboard as quick as possible; yet, with all their haste, they failed to get them in due time. But the compassionate conductor waited, and, with Mrs. Harris going along to push them through, they reached their destination in due time, and the poor soldiers had a splendid Thanksgiving dinner. Forewarned of an approaching battle, they always sent stores in advance. And, in order still more to expedite this business, they always kept on hand a quantity of stores packed ready for a battle at any time, marked "Stores for the next battle." And to render immediate living aid, they had a class of delegates they called "*minute-men*," ready to go at any time on five minutes' notice; and, said Mr. Stuart, "If one of them was on the pulpit preaching when the telegram reached him, he must stop, and hurry off to the battle-field."

It was very encouraging to the Commission to see how willingly the soldiers would assist them in anything they could do. Was an army church to be erected, they would turn out *en masse* and help put it up! A regiment would cut the logs, gather them in, and put up a church in a few hours. In this way, the Commission erected fifty churches in one week. Sometimes they would begin and lay the foundation of a church in the morning, and have preaching in it at night.

Founded upon the "Rock of Ages," and deeply imbued with the loving spirit of its cheerful chairman, the Christian Commission was a GREAT COMFORTER. It administered comfort both to the soldier's soul and body. When it found a man suffering for suitable food, it fed the body first, and the soul afterward. To the hungry it offered bread first, and then a Baxter's Call. To the thirsty it offered a cup of cold water before the cup of salvation. Relieving the outer man tends to give access to the inner. It brought the fresh sympathies of dear friends and the sweet pleasures of home close to the camp and the hospital. And, being so long destitute of these cheering attractions, nothing else seemed to do the soldiers so much good. Anything direct from home, (even but a flower,) that would cause the mystic cords of memory to vibrate from the dreary hospital, from the lonely camp, or from the bloody battle-field, to the hallowed scenes of home, and there to linger around the lovely forms of a dear sister, an affectionate mother, or a beloved wife, would cheer and revive the drooping spirits of the most forlorn soldier.

We give an illustration in the language of a soldier: "I was seated in my tent on the banks of the Potomac, weary and worn, heartsick and homesick, when a letter was brought in by the postboy, and handed to me. It bore the impress of a sister's direction. I opened it eagerly. A rosebud from a favorite bush at home fell upon my lap. It was a precious memento of home, and of a sister's love. I forgot the letter. I seized the rosebud, pressed it to my lips with a kiss, and sent up a prayer that God would bless my sister, my home, and all its dear ones who were brought so vividly before me. Ah! had I been called at that moment to draw the sword or shoulder the musket and repair to the field of battle, I would have fought with tenfold valor for my country; for my country is the home of my mother that I love, and the sister who had not forgotten me." * Such is the wonderful power of sympathy. Oh, how important to cultivate and bestow it!

But, endowed with this lofty spirit, and engaged in the holy cause of God, liberty, and truth, the Christian Commission was not only a great comforter, but it was also a great *life-preserver* and *soul-saver*. Under God, it preserved men's lives, and saved their souls. In speaking of the labors of the delegates among the soldiers, Bishop McIlvaine, of Ohio, said, in a mass meeting of the Commission in Philadelphia, " We rejoice that they are able to take stimulants to the faint, and food to the hungry. We think it exceedingly precious that they are able to minister to such necessities; but oh, dear brethren, there is a joy unspeakable above such joys as that, that they are permitted to share. It is precious to hear one say, 'I should have died upon the battle-field but for the supplies that the Christian Commission brought me!' But oh, how unspeakably more precious is it to you and to me, brethren, to hear one saying, in addition to this, 'I should have perished in my sins, had it not been for the precious words which Christ spoke to me through the men whom the Christian Commission sent to me.'"

Abounding in these noble deeds and lofty aims, the Christian Commission was food, clothing, and shelter to the destitute; medicine, nurse, and physician to the sick and wounded; joy and hope to the dying; and strength and encouragement to the Government. Armed with the panoply of heaven, laboring incessantly by day and by night in dispensing the benign influences

---

* Extract from Ex-Governor Pollock's address at the first annual meeting of the Christian Commission in Washington, D. C.

of the gospel, and receiving no pay but the soldier's hearty "*God bless you!*" and most successfully managed by the matchless George H. Stuart, it was the glory of the land and the brightest honor of the Church!

KINDNESS TO REBELS.

The care, compassion, and labors of the Christian Commission were not confined to the men of our own army and navy. Christianity is not selfish and sectional. It is not bounded by continents, oceans, empires, and states; it is not confined to army lines, camps, guards, and pickets. No; Christ says, "Do good unto *all* men;" "if thine enemy hunger, feed him; if he thirst, give him drink." Constrained by a Saviour's love, the earnest Christian's heart embraces and yearns for the salvation of a lost world. The cross of Christ, when heartily received, consumes and annihilates self. Self cannot live at the foot of the cross. There it dies; and there it lies buried. Moved by this Christ-like principle, the noble delegates of the Christian Commission administered to the wants of the soldiers and officers of the rebel army as well as our own. The writer has often done this, and received hearty thanks for it. In telling them of Jesus, we have often seen them weep profusely. They often sent for me to come and pray with them in the hospital. I have often preached to them in their wards; and when they died, we always read and prayed at their graves. They fared just the same in the hospital as the Union soldiers.

When the writer, with a number of other officers who had just been released from Libby Prison, was being exchanged at City Point, Va., we met a number of rebel prisoners just from Johnson's Island; and, seeing them looking so well, one of our men asked them, "How did you fare way up North?" "*First-rate, first-rate!*" was one's immediate reply; and he went on to tell what good things they had to eat.

In speaking of his ministrations to Confederate wounded, who were brought to Martinsburg in the same wagons with our own men, Rev. T. B. Thayer says, in *Incidents of the U. S. Christian Commission:* "As we have ministered to their wants and addressed words of kindness to them, tears have started from eyes unaccustomed to weeping. They fairly overwhelmed us with their thankful expressions. 'This is what I call living Christianity,' one would say. 'This is the religion for me,' added another. 'I can't stand this,' said a rough, hard-looking fellow, badly wounded in the foot, but able to hobble along on crutches; 'I can't stand this, boys; it overcomes me; I give in,' with his whole frame shaking with emotion, and the big tears falling from his sun-burnt face — tears which he tried to conceal from his comrades and us. 'You know,' he continued, 'I am no coward; I can face the enemy, and not wink; but this kindness kills me; it breaks me all to pieces. I tell you, boys, this is no humbug; it's a big thing; it's the gospel for body and soul — just what we all need.' And so he went on in the truest eloquence for some minutes, closing with the ever-recurring soldier's benediction, 'God bless you!'"

In speaking of the rebels found on the battle-field, Mr. Stuart said, "If we found them dying, we took their last messages and wrote to their friends, just as if they had been our own soldiers. It was the same in the hospitals. The poor fellows would sometimes burst into tears. One of them said, '*You fight us like devils, but you nurse us like angels.*'"

Mr. Stuart's fondness for army relics and Christian Commission memorials is seen in his statement to his friend from Glasgow. "When you go to Gettysburg, you must see Round Top, where the battle was fiercest, and where the dead lay five or six deep. Lee said to Barksdale, of Mississippi, 'That height must be taken if it cost you all your men.' Barksdale went, and buried himself and his whole force on that slope. This Testament (holding it in his hand) was found there among the dead."

"He showed me," said Mr. Macrea, "another little Testament that had saved a soldier's life. 'It belonged to one of our boys,' said Mr. Stuart. 'He always carried it in his breast-pocket. In one battle a bullet struck him, and nearly knocked him down. It had struck on the Testament, and pierced it to the back board; there, as you see, it stopped, and his life was saved. There are scores like this scattered up and down the country. Some wives have them with the blood-stains on the leaves. I saw one where the ball had stopped at a verse that struck the man, and which proved the means of his conversion. He was killed afterward, but his wife preserved the Testament. I said to her, 'I would like to own that Testament — what will you take for it?' 'Oh, Mr. Stuart,' she said, 'there is n't gold enough in the country to buy it from me.'"

HIS GENERALSHIP IN PRAYER.

In speaking of the Christian Commission practice of connecting religion with all their operations, Mr. Stuart said to Mr. Macrea, "*I never was in a place where I could n't have prayer.* When dissolving the Commission, we went round (more than one hundred of us) and called on Johnson, Stanton, Grant, and all the heads of Departments, and had prayer with them all. When we went to the White House, some of them said, 'Remember, Johnson is a different man from Lincoln.' I said, 'I know it.' However, before we left, I said to the President, 'Mr. Johnson, you have been called to the head of the nation at a very critical time.' 'Yes, yes,' he said. 'After a man who was the idol of the people.' 'Yes.' 'No man has been raised to a position where he stands more in need of divine help.' 'It is true.' 'Dr. ——— will perhaps ask the divine blessing and guidance for you before we go.' The President made no objection, and we all knelt in prayer.

"But when we went to Culpepper to see Botts, Dr. Kirk and the rest of them said there was no hope there. Botts was a prominent statesman. He had opposed the Democrats of the South, but he had no sympathy with the movements on behalf of the negro. We knew that; and he had the reputation of being an infidel. I thought it all the more necessary that we should, if possible, have prayer. He received us very kindly. When we were preparing to leave, I said,' You have seen a good deal of fighting here, Mr. Botts?' 'Fighting!' said he; 'I have seen fifteen battles from that window.' 'You have run many risks?' 'You may well say that,' he replied. 'Now, gentlemen,' I said, turning to the others, 'Mr. Botts has sacrificed a great deal for the country; he has suffered a great deal; he may have much to suffer still — we cannot tell. Now, I think, before going, Dr. Kirk might lead us in thanking God for having preserved Mr. Botts through so much, and praying that Mr. Botts may be long spared to serve his country, and see it restored to prosperity and peace.' Botts, who had been throwing in prompt words of assent to everything that went before, looked queer at this. We all began to go down upon our knees. Botts looked about with a ludicrous expression of perplexity on his face; but, seeing us all kneeling, he seemed to feel there was no escape, and slipped reluctantly down upon his knees. When we came out, Dr. Kirk said, 'I never prayed in such strange circumstances before.' 'Well,' said I, 'you never prayed more powerfully.' Neither he had. Some of them said that Botts was in tears when he rose." * What an invaluable lecture on pastoral theology! For practical utility it is worth more than whole volumes of ordinary lectures. Like Paul, Mr. Stuart seems to know perfectly "how to be all things to all men." To make such a man as Mr. Botts "feel that there was no escape," but to kneel in prayer, denotes wonderful ingenuity!

If we should attempt to describe Mr. Stuart as a *Christian*, it would be hard to find words sufficiently expressive. The Rev. T. W. J. Wylie, D.D., speaks of him as "that most eminent servant of God!" We do not wish to exaggerate, but when we look at his great liberality, self-denying labors, and his eminent success in managing the Christian Commission, and his heroic devotion to his country, and to his Master's cause, as exhibited therein, as a Christian philanthropist, and as "a *Christian at work*," he is one of the most eminent in the world. His Christian sagacity exhibited in his generalship in prayer was most masterly. We do not believe there is another man in the world that could have succeeded as well. By the winning force of his powerful prestige, genius, and tact, together with his melting kindness, he brought every man to his knees — a place where some of them perhaps had never been before. Such sagacious generalship is exceedingly rare. You may search the records of

---

* Mr. Macrea's *Interview with Mr. Stuart.*

all Christendom, and explore the history of the world, and nowhere, we believe, since the fall of man, will you find such shrewd strategy. Corresponding with his unbounded zeal and popularity, the Rev. Dr. E. R. Beadle, of Philadelphia, delegate from the General Assembly of the Presbyterian Church of the United States to the late General Assembly of Ireland, in speaking to the latter of the distinguished Irishmen in America, after having mentioned the names of the distinguished Dr. McCosh, of Princeton, and Dr. Hall, of New York, said, "There is another humble man, namely, George H. Stuart, a man who has made the whole continent love him."

Bishop Simpson, in his farewell remarks to the Christian Commission, said, "Early in the history of this Commission, when our work had not yet been fully developed, I remember to have spoken of our great leader — our worthy president, Mr. Stuart — as our major-general. But, sir, his works merit promotion, and I nominate him now as Lieutenant-General of the Christian Commission! He shall never wear the stars upon his shoulders; but above and behind yon clouds, which hide the Invisible from view, there are crowns, and there are stars which shall shine in his crown of rejoicing forever!"

As a *speaker*, Mr. Stuart is ready, tender, touching, eloquent, and impressive. With a quick discernment, he always grasps the situation, and makes his speeches very appropriate, eloquent, and powerful. Standing before the annual meeting of the British and Foreign Bible Society, says the "American Messenger," " he thrilled the immense audience by evidences of the divine blessing on the Bible in our late civil war, and closed by saying:

" 'England and America speak the same language, they worship the same God, Father, Son, and Holy Ghost, they are the two great Protestant nations of the earth, and woe to the hand that ever causes blood to flow between them. England and America — there may have occasionally risen up differences of opinion between them; but I say here, what I wrote a short time since to a member of the Washington Cabinet. I said to him, " Sir, I believe, all through this terrible conflict, there are no two agencies which God has so much blessed in the preserving of peace between the two countries as the British and Foreign Bible Society and the American Bible Society." I say, God bless the British and Foreign Bible Society! God bless its honored president! may he be long spared to carry on his work of usefulness. God bless the American Bible Society! God bless its honored president! God bless the Queen of England! long may she reign over a prosperous and a free country. God bless the President of the United States! I long for the coming of that day when all wars shall cease, and when Jesus Christ shall reign over all lands.'

"The President of the British and Foreign Bible Society here rose, and, amid the general applause of the meeting, said that with his whole heart he reiterated the prayer of the last speaker, God bless the President of America! God bless the Queen of England! And may peace ever reign between the two countries." This was in 1866.

HENRY WARD BEECHER.

His Distinguishing Traits — A Great Worker — His Style — Oratory — His Birth — Lost his Mother — Early Religious Impressions — Inured to Hardship — A Bashful, Stammering, Unpromising Boy — His Education — Went to School Barefooted, and Hemmed Towels at Recess — Fond of Flowers, and Full of Jokes — Drilled in Elocution — Tired of School — Wishes to "Go to Sea" — Subject of a Revival — Unites with the Church — Naval Project Given up — Attention Turned to the Ministry — Enters College — Choice of Studies — Preferring Rhetoric, Studies to Know "What to Say," and "How to Say it" — Strictly Temperate — Conducts Prayer Meetings — His Creed — Religious Impressions — Troubled — Relieved — Buoyant — Teaches School — Lectures and Preaches — The Slave's Friend — Graduates — Studies Theology — Perplexed about Entering the Ministry — Marries — First Pastoral Charge — Did Everything Himself — Moves to Indianapolis — Style of Preaching — His Popularity — Revival in his Church — Moves to Brooklyn — Visits England and Europe — Lectures in England, and, Braving all Opposition, Pleads America's Cause Successfully — His London Letter glowing with Joy and Gratitude to God, and Love to his Enemies — Impression Favorable — Affectionate Enthusiasm for him — His War Sermons — Oration at Fort Sumter.

THE prescribed limits of our book will not admit of a lengthy sketch of this renowned genius. Distinguished for tact, foresight, independence, intrepidity, patriotism, and great versatility of talent, he does not need it. Constitutionally buoyant, and naturally disposed to look at the bright side of things, he is always lively and cheerful; self-reliant, pertinacious, and courageous, he cannot be swamped nor easily cried down; peculiar and progressive in his views, he is often far ahead of the rest of mankind, and consequently liable sometimes to get a little off the track. Laborious and energetic, he travels and lectures, preaches regularly, writes books, and edits one of the ablest papers in the country. With a style combining grandeur, energy, simplicity, beauty, and strength, he is one of the most popular writers of the day. Being well posted with a thorough knowledge of human nature, always grasping the situation, and possessing fine powers of illustration, he is one of the most complete orators of the age.

And exhibiting so much genius and talent, it will be interesting and profitable to trace him to his early history and origin. A New-Englander by birth, Henry Ward Beecher was born in Litchfield, Conn., June 24, 1813. He is the son of Roxana and Rev. Dr. Lyman Beecher, so distinguished for his piety, theological attainments, and pulpit power. Inheriting from his parents a perfectly sound and healthy organization of both body and mind, and having lost his mother when he was only three years old, he was brought up with little caressing, and in a way that was calculated to develop both his physical and intellectual powers. Having fallen into the hands of a pious, refined, and highly intellectual step-mother, he was highly favored with a kind, religious, motherly training. It was her custom every Sunday night to take Henry Ward (the eighth child of the family) and two other little ones into her bedroom, and read, talk to, and pray with them. Inured to the long winters, severe storms, and bleak mountains of Connecticut, he was brought up to industry, and knew what it was to endure hardness when a boy. During a New-England winter drought, when but nine years old, he harnessed and hitched up the horse to the sled, went alone three miles over an icy, hilly road to a distant spring, dipped up and brought a barrel of water for the family — and "thought nothing of it." The only thing that grieved him about it was, his step-mother compelled him to wear his overcoat. He put it on, however; but not without "tears of mortification freezing on his cheeks as he went for the water, because he had firmly determined in his own mind to go a whole winter without wearing an overcoat." Although bashful and quite dull when a boy at school, yet the stammering lad, being ambitious, was very sensitive as to praise and blame. Nobody ever expected anything brilliant of him; and with a very poor, indistinct utterance, no one ever thought of his making an orator. Said his kind aunt, "When Henry is sent to me with a message, I always have to make him say it over three times; the first time I have no manner of an idea, more than if he spoke Choctaw; the second, I catch now and then a word; by the third time I begin to understand." And while his elder brother was sharing in the first honors of his class at college, and his elder sisters amusing themselves in writing poetry and enjoying the pleasure of Litchfield society, this unpromising boy went to school barefooted in a little old school-house, and (says his sister Harriet) " with a brown towel, or a blue checked apron, to hem during the intervals between his spelling and reading lessons." And yet, with all his apparent stupidity, Henry was not destitute of serious thought. When once driving his step-mother on an errand, in an old chaise, the town-bell tolled for the death of one of the inhabitants; whereupon she said to the thoughtful boy, "Henry, what do you think of, when you hear a bell tolling like that?" Surprised at so grave a question, he replied, " I think, Was that soul prepared? It has gone into *eternity!*" With a poor memory, he disliked to study and commit the catechism, although he was sure of being seriously talked to by Mrs. Beecher if he failed to recite his questions well. Thus at ten years of age he was a stout, well-grown, obedient boy; and although backward in learning, he was very fond of natural scenery, buds, and flowers, and full of jokes and fun.

At twelve, his father moved to Boston, and, shortly after, Henry Ward was sent to the Boston Latin school, where, urged by a sense of self-respect and regard to his father's entreaties, he set out to study in earnest, and completely mastered the Latin Grammar the first year. But hard study seemed to injure his health, and having become somewhat gloomy and dissatisfied at school, his father thought it best to divert his attention a little from his studies, and suggested a course of biographical reading. Delighted with this, after having read a few naval histories, and the accounts of noted voyages, great commanders and sailors, he made up his mind to leave Boston, and "go to sea." Having heard of this project, his father made use of it as an argument to induce Henry to go to school, and study mathematics as a preparation for his newly devised scheme. Although he had no taste for mathematics, yet being enthusiastic for the sea, he went to Amherst, and studied algebra, geometry, etc., with a good degree of success. Here, too, he was thoroughly drilled in the principles of elocution by Professor J. E. Lovell, to which Mr. Beecher attributes very much of his success as a speaker.

While at Amherst, a powerful revival of religion broke out in the school, and Henry, having enjoyed a good religious training, was very deeply impressed. Upon hearing of this, his father wrote for him to come home, to unite with the church at an approaching communion, at which the anxious boy, with a trembling heart, stood up and took upon him the solemn vows of the Church, and, for the first time, obeyed the solemn injunction, "Do this in remembrance of me."

From this time on, his plans and purposes of life were changed — his naval project was abandoned, and his attention was turned to the pulpit.

Having spent three years at Amherst, he was well prepared to enter the sophomore class at college; yet being deeply convinced of the importance of thoroughness, his kind father, in order to give him ample time for general reading, wisely advised him to enter as a freshman. Finding but little attraction in Greek and Latin, or mathematics, though quite thorough in all of them, he turned his attention more particularly to oratory and rhetoric, and made it his chief business to learn "*what to say,*" and "*how to say it.*" To form and improve his style, he took a regular course in the English classics, and read with great avidity such authors as Milton, Bacon, Shakspeare, Robert Hall, etc.

Strictly temperate and regular in his habits, the new convert was regularly at the class prayer-meetings, and took part in the exercises. Fortunately for his early religious development while at college, he became intimately acquainted with a pious, laborious student, who took him around with him to attend the prayer meetings in the outskirts of the village. And after hearing Henry read and pray a few times, the exhorter left one of the prayer-meetings in his care, while he went away and looked up another. With this little foretaste as a Christian worker, Henry went on in the good work, and, aided by others, kept up the prayer meetings all through his college course. This was his beginning as a speaker.

During his sophomore year, Mr. Beecher's attention was incidently directed to the subject of phrenology; and being unsettled in his views as to the truth of this science, after hearing a few lectures on it, he commenced and read with great avidity everything he could get having a bearing on the subject. He and his associates immediately formed a society for physiological investigation. They bought books, charts, dissecting instruments, and set out in good earnest to know the truth. He was so enthusiastic in this matter, that he bought several books for his own individual use. He not only read the works of Drs. Gall, Combe, and Spurzheim, but also a number of old English authors, besides the renowned works of Locke, Reid, Stuart, etc. The taste formed by Mr. Beecher in this physiological and phrenological research, taken in connection with his studies in theology and metaphysics, has had much to do in laying the foundation of his theory and views through life. From that time forward he has pursued this branch of study with deep interest. And, says Mrs. Stowe, to whom we are indebted for many facts in this sketch, "The depth of Mr. Beecher's religious nature prevented this enthusiasm for material science from degenerating into dry materialism. He was a Calvinist in the earnestness of his intense need of the highest and deepest in religion. In his sophomore year there was a revival of religion in college, in which his mind was powerfully excited. He reviewed the almost childish experiences under which he had joined the church, as possibly deceptive, and tried and disciplined himself by those profound tests with which the Edwardarian theology had filled the minds of New England. A blank despair was the result. He applied to Dr. Humphrey, who simply told him that his present feelings were a work of the Spirit, and with which he dared not interfere. After days of almost hopeless prayer, there came suddenly into his mind an ineffable and overpowering perception of the divine love, which seemed to him like a revelation. It dispelled all doubts and fears; he became buoyant and triumphant, and that buoyancy has been marked in his religious teachings ever since."

To raise money to purchase a library of much-desired books, Mr. Beecher, during his last two years at college, taught country schools during the long winter vacations; and then, as now, he was a great worker. While laboring to develop the intellectual powers of his scholars, he was not indifferent to that which is more important, the cultivation of the heart. Besides delivering an occasional lecture on temperance, he made his appointments, and went regularly, and exhorted and preached to the people. With a broad, sympathetic nature, Mr. Beecher was kind to the poor, and a warm friend to the slave; and, possessing an heroic spirit, he was not afraid, in the early anti-slavery move, to be called an Abolitionist.

Graduating in 1834, he went to Cincinnati, Ohio, and soon after commenced the study of theology in Lane Seminary; and having nearly completed the course, as the time of his licensure approached, he was thrown into a deep feeling of melancholy, and was at times so much distressed and perplexed about entering upon the duties of the sacred office that he seriously thought of abandoning the profession. But during his last seminary year he took a Bible class in Cincinnati, and while studying the evangelists, in preparing his lessons for the class, he found so much to think and preach about, his difficulties were all removed.

Having finished his theological course, Mr. Beecher got married, and immediately took charge of a small congregation in Lawrenceburg, on the west bank of the Ohio River, near Cincinnati. In one of his speeches, in England, he gave the following account of his commencing there: "I began my ministry in a church in the wilderness; there were nineteen women and one man, and I wished him out more times than one; they were the saints, and he the sinner. I was at that time sexton and general undertaker for the church; I swept it; I bought the lamps, and lit them; I would have rung the bell, but there was none. I did the preaching, was superintendent of the Sabbath school, and did everything else there was to do; and though many years have passed, and I have seen other scenes, I have never had happier days since." After laboring a short time at Lawrenceburg, he accepted a call and moved to Indianapolis, Ind., where he labored with great success, devoting three months of each year to missionary work, in travelling about from place to place, on horseback, preaching once every day. In studying theology, he paid special attention to the Bible and to human nature — a knowledge of both he held to be necessary to understand either; and, in sermonizing, he studied closely the style and principles of the sermons of the apostles, and endeavored to imitate them. Full of wit and humor, and possessing fine social qualities and a great tact for close observation, he possessed an ability to analyze man's wants and a genius to know how to meet them, rarely attained by one so young. Unique and attractive in his style of preaching, and drawing largely, both for matter and illustrations, from unexplored fields, his popularity spread abroad, and the people flocked to hear him wherever he went.

During a powerful revival that took place in his congregation in Indianapolis, in 1842, a member of that church says, "The whole town was pervaded by the influences of religion, and nearly one hundred persons were added to the church." And Mr. Beecher was seen " plunging through the wet streets, with his trowsers stuffed in his muddy boots, earnest, untiring, swift, with a merry heart, a glowing face, and a helpful word for every one; the whole day preaching Christ to the people, wherever he could find them."

During a pastorate of eight years in Indianapolis, the church was very much strengthened financially, and increased from thirty-two to two hundred and seventy-five members; and although there existed a very strong mutual attachment between pastor and people, yet, having received a call to a much wider sphere of usefulness from the Plymouth Congregational Church, Brooklyn, New York, he accepted it, and moved thither in the summer of 1847, where he has labored with very great success ever since. His church now numbers over two thousand members, and pays him a salary of twenty thousand dollars. In this move, Mr. Beecher changed his ecclesiastical connection from the Presbyterian to the Congregational Church.

Mr. Beecher's fine colloquial powers, his broad, impartial sympathy and kindness, and his thorough knowledge of human nature gave him access to the hearts of all classes; he had warm friends in every grade of society. When living in Indianapolis, he commanded the respect even of the drunkard and the gambler; and when he left there, some of this class gave him the strongest demonstrations of respect and attachment. Some of those whom he had tried to reclaim, seemed to have gone beyond redemption; and one of them, when Mr. Beecher was about to leave the city, said, "Before anything or anybody on earth, I do love Beecher; I know he would have saved me, if he could."

During the heated anti-slavery discussions, Mr. Beecher always took decided grounds in favor of emancipation; and when the rebellion arose, he heartily went in for putting it down at all hazards. Encouraged by their pastor, his congregation raised and equipped one regiment of volunteers (the First Long Island), and many of the young men of the congregation joined it. Deeply interested in their welfare, Mr. Beecher often went out and preached to them while in camp before they started for the field. Mr. Beecher labored very hard during the war; and, having much to say to the public in connection therewith, he assumed the editorial chair of the *Independent* early in the conflict. Burdened with the war and the cares of his country, together with his incessant labors in writing, speaking, and editing, his health and voice began to fail, and he sought relaxation in a trip to Europe. Here he was met by friends, before he stepped off the steamer, urging him to consent to lecture; but he positively declined. Having spent a few days in England, and some two weeks in Wales, he visited Switzerland, Germany, and Northern Italy. At Paris he was much encouraged in receiving the news of the battle of Gettysburg, and the fall of Vicksburg, and found in those great victories the only kind of logic and argument that would successfully carry the cause of America through Great Britain and Europe.

On returning to England, he was again invited to speak, and again declined; but upon the repeated solicitation of such men as Newman Hall, Baptist Noel, and Francis Newman, constrained by a sense of duty to his country, and our friends over there, he at last consented, and arrangements were made for him to lecture in the principal cities of the Kingdom. And now, realizing his great responsibility, and conscious of the difficult task he had undertaken, to plead the cause of his country in a foreign land, he set about preparing for the arduous work. Thus armed and equipped in the great cause of American nationality and American liberty, he delivered his first speech in the Free Trade Hall, in Manchester, October 9, 1863, to a tumultuous crowd of some six or seven thousand. Taking for his subject the merits of the American cause and the rights of the laboring man, he went on to show that the Southern Confederacy was founded upon the false principle that a strong and superior race has a right to oppress a weak and inferior one. And although Southern sympathizers did rail, and rant, and make great efforts to cry him down, and prevent his speaking; yet, with a buoyant heart and a resolute will, he went on in spite of all opposition, and completed his speech; and the London *Times* did him the honor of publishing it the next day. Thus ended his first effort.

On the 13th of October he spoke again in the City Hall of Glasgow, and discussed the comparative advantages of free over slave labor. The next day he spoke to a very large meeting in the Free Church Assembly Hall in Edinburgh, and gave them an historic outline of the American conflict. But the severest struggle and the most disorderly audience was at Liverpool. This place being more pro-slavery, the opposition was found to be more formidable; yet, with undaunted spirit and unyielding pertinacity, Mr. Beecher braved the storm and delivered his message. In describing the difficulty in speaking to these turbulent assemblies, Mr. Beecher says, "I had to outscream a mob, and drown the roar of a multitude. It was like driving a team of runaway horses, and making love to a lady at the same time."

The following letter breathes so much of the spirit of Christianity in the war, it will doubtless be read with deep interest:

"LONDON, Sunday, October 18, 1863.

"MY DEAR FRIEND — You know why I have not written you from England. I have been so full of work that I could not. God has been with me, and prospered me. I have had health, and strength, and courage, and, what is of unspeakably more importance, I have had the sweetest experience of love to God and to man, of all my life. I have been enabled *to love our enemies.* . . . God awakened in my breast a desire to be a full and true Christian toward England the moment I put my foot on her shores, and he has answered the prayers which he inspired. I have been buoyant and happy. The streets of Manchester and Liverpool have been filled with placards in black and white letters, full of all lies and bitterness; but they have seemed to me only the tracery of dreams. For hours I have striven to speak amid interruptions of every kind — yellings, hootings, catcalls, derisive yells, impertinent and insulting questions, and every conceivable annoyance — some personal violence. But God has kept me in perfect peace. I stood in Liverpool and looked on the demoniac scene, almost without a thought that it was *me* that was present. . . . You know, dear friend, how, when were are lifted up by the inspiration of a great subject, and by the almost visible presence and vivid sympathy with Christ, the mind forgets the sediment and dregs of trouble, and sails serenely in an upper realm of peace, as untouched by the noise below, as a bird that flies across a battle-field. Just so I had, at Liverpool and Glasgow, as sweet an inward peace as ever I had in the loving meetings of dear old Plymouth Church. And again and again, when the uproar raged, and I could not speak, my heart seemed to be taking of the infinite fulness of the Saviour's pity, and breathing it out upon those poor, troubled men. I felt that I was his dear child, and that his arms were about me continually, and at times that peace that passeth all understanding has descended upon me, that I could not keep tears of gratitude from falling for so much tender goodness of my God. For, what are outward prosperities compared with those interior intimacies of God? It is not the path *to* the temple, but the *interior* of the temple, that shows the goodness and glory of God. And I have been able to commit all to Him, myself, my family, my friends, and in a special manner the cause of my country. Oh, my friend, I have felt an inexpressible wonder that God should give it to me to do something for the dear land; when sometimes the idea of being clothed with power to stand up in this great kingdom against an inconvinceable violence of prejudice and mistake, and clear the name of my dishonored country, and let her brow shine forth, crowned with liberty, glowing with love to man — oh, I have seemed unable to live, almost! It almost took my breath away.

"I have not in a single instance gone to the speaking halls without all the way breathing to God unutterable desires for inspiration, guidance, success; and I have had no disturbance of *personality*. I have been willing, yea, with eagerness, to be myself contemptible in men's sight, if only my disgrace might be to the honor of that cause which is intrusted to our own thrice dear country. I have asked nothing of God but this, and this with uninterrupted heart-flow of yearning request: 'Make me worthy to speak for God and man.' I never felt my ignorance so painfully, nor the great want of moral purity and nobility of soul, as when approaching my tasks of *defending liberty* in this her hour of trial. I have an ideal of what a man should be that labors for such a cause, that constantly rebukes my real condition and makes me feel how little I am. Yet *that* is hardly painful. There passes before me a view of God's glory, so pure, so serene, uplifted, filling the ages, and more and more to be revealed, that I almost wish to lose my identity, to be like a drop of dew that falls into the sea, and becomes a part of the sublime whole that glows under every line of latitude, and sounds on every shore! '*That God may be all in all!*' that is not a prayer only, but a personal experience. And in all this time I have not had one unkind feeling toward a single human being; even those, who are opposers, I have pitied with undying compassion; and enemies around me have seemed harmless and objects of charity rather than potent foes to be destroyed. God be thanked, who giveth us the victory through our Lord Jesus Christ. . . . .

"I am, as ever, yours, H. W. BEECHER."

Mr. Beecher spoke again, October 20, in Exeter Hall, London, and, in describing the meeting, he said : " It was a very fit close to a series of meetings that have produced a great sensation in England. The enthusiasm was almost wild and fanatical. I was like to have been killed with people pressing to shake my hand." The press was so great, and " the affectionate enthusiasm" so strong, that the police came to his rescue, and conveyed him into the retiring-room, where many gentlemen brought their wives, sons, and daughters for a "God bless you!" from the distinguished orator and patriot.

These meetings made a very favorable impression upon England and Scotland in favor of the American cause, and, no doubt, did much to prevent their interfering in behalf of the Southern Confederacy. Mr. Scott, (the Chamberlain of London,) the president of the meeting in Exeter Hall, said that a few more such meetings "in some other parts of England, and the question would be settled." In the successful delivery of these powerful, impressive speeches amid such strong, combined opposition, we see in a most striking manner the lofty patriotism, the great energy, and indomitable perseverance of Mr. Beecher. In speaking of it, he says, "I thought I had been through furnaces before, but this ordeal surpassed all others. I was quite alone in England; I had no one to consult with; I felt the burden of having to stand for my country in a half-hostile land; and yet I never flinched for a moment or lost heart."

Although Mr. Beecher did not go to the front, and labor and preach much to the army in the field, yet his incessant labors at home in prosecuting the war, had much to do in quelling the rebellion. He made balls, and others threw them; he preached war-sermons at home that encouraged the soldiers to fight hard on the fields. And upon the fall of Richmond, and Lee's surrender — as the flag of the nation had been traitorously stricken down from the battlements of Fort Sumter, April 14, 1861 — as a fitting emblem of the nation's restored sovereignty, the *same* flag was again, by the direction of the Government, with appropriate religious and military ceremonies and rejoicings, unfurled over the same fort, on the same day of the same month, (1865); and Mr. Beecher was invited by the President and Secretary of War to deliver an oration on the important occasion; and, as he drew to a close in his speech, he uttered the following significant words: "From this pulpit of broken stones we speak forth our earnest greetings to all our land: we offer to the President of the United States our solemn congratulations that God has sustained his life and health under the unparalleled burdens and sufferings of four bloody years, and permitted him to behold this auspicious consummation of that national unity for which he has waited with so much patience and fortitude, and for which he has labored with such disinterested wisdom and self-denial." And scarcely had these memorable words of congratulation passed the lips of the patriotic orator, before the cruel assassin's ball had pierced the head of the noble President, and thus most suddenly turned the nation's highest joy into the deepest mourning.

DWIGHT L. MOODY.

Power of Individual Effort — Earnestness the Secret of Success — A Great Want — The Church and the World Asleep — His Birth — Lay-preaching Encouraged — Paul's Great Success — Labor, Labor! — Moody's Early Religious Views — His Conversion — Joins the Congregationalists — Education Limited — His Labors Successful — A Great Worker in Sabbath Schools — Organized Mission Sunday School in Chicago — Its Growth — Started Prayer Meetings — Labors Blessed — Young Men's Christian Associations Begun — Daily Prayer Meeting — His Trust in God for a Living — No Salary — His Active Labors in the Army — His Zeal at the Battle of Fort Donelson — Goes to God for Direction — Efficient in Building — Calls to go Abroad — Crosses the Atlantic — Organized Daily Prayer Meeting in London — Labors in Sunday-School Conventions — Successful — Deeds, not Words, a True Sign of Principle — His Success as an Organizer; as a Speaker; as a Revivalist — How he "Got up a Revival" — His Large Audiences in Chicago — His Popularity at Home — His Personal Influence over Others.

IT is wonderful what good one man can do, when he sets himself about it earnestly. Earnestness is the great secret of success. One *devoted, earnest* Christian will do more good than twenty of the common run. Why were such men as George Whitefield, John Calvin, and John Wesley so eminently successful? It was because of their whole-hearted earnestness. Why was Paul more successful than other apostles? Because "he labored more abundantly than they all." Whence Mr. Moody's great success? According to his own words, it would seem to lay in his earnest, entire consecration to the Master's cause. Paul says, "Give thyself *wholly* to these things." Moody said, early in his Christian labors, "I have decided to give God *all my time.*"

Full, entire, unreserved consecration is the great lack of the church, and the great want of the world. One-half of the world and one-half of the church is more than half asleep all the time. The Lord says, "Awake, awake, put on thy strength." The power of earnestness is great. It is felt, not only in the additional good accomplished directly by it through the earnest individual, but also in the influence it exerts upon others. The very *sight* of an earnest man is stirring and rousing.

Dwight L. Moody was born in Northfield, Mass., February 5, 1837. He is, therefore, comparatively but a young man, and, with a beginning so fair, encouraging, and successful, he has every reason earnestly to go forward, continuing to give all his time to God in winning souls to Christ.

The church, it would seem, has just entered upon an age of lay-preaching; and with the renowned lay-preacher Richard Weaver in the Old World, and with our distinguished lay-preachers in the New, crowned with so much success, the present prospects for more lay-labor are very encouraging. The Apostle Paul was a lay-preacher. He had no theological training nor ecclesiastical ordination, save the receiving of a new heart and a subdued will. Soon as he was put through "the washing of regeneration," he earnestly cried, "Lord, what wilt thou have me to do?" and filled and fired with the Holy Ghost, he straightway went forth preaching Christ crucified; and, with his deep, logical arguments and powerful, moving eloquence, he made kings and emperors tremble upon their thrones, and, for the salvation of the world and the glory of God, accomplished a work second to no man on earth. Then let the lay-preacher be encouraged. Let Zion arise, and shake herself from the dust, until every remnant of latent power shall be fully developed and called forth to the most lively action. God says, "GO, LABOR IN MY VINEYARD."

Born in the State of Massachusetts, the stronghold of Unitarianism in the United States, Mr. Moody was brought up to that doctrine, until his conversion, when he became a Congregationalist. Of his parents we know nothing, and, with but a limited education, constrained by a Saviour's love, he has gone forth sowing precious seed, which, we believe, has produced an abundant harvest, as history, and the following extract by J. F. B., from *The National Sunday-School Teacher*, edited by Rev. Dr. Eggleston of Chicago, will clearly show :

"Fourteen years ago, I met a young man, and was told he was a clerk in a wholesale boot and shoe house; had recently come from Boston. He came into our school, Sabbath morning, seemed much interested, and talked of *work*. Soon after, I met him, and learned that he had been visiting on the North Side, and had found great destitution. He said, 'I have promised to commence a Sabbath school there.' This was in the days when the 'Sands' were the 'Five Points' of Chicago. A few weeks later, the 'North Market Hall Sabbath-School' was an established fact. Similarity of work brought us often together; and in 'an exchange,' when he came one evening to speak at our mission, I learned his early history. He came to Chicago, September, 1856, a young man, and a young Christian. He desired to work for God. He said, 'I applied to the superintendent of a mission Sunday-school for a class, (there were only three mission schools in the city;) but I was told they had a full supply of teachers. I went to another school, and found *twelve* teachers and *sixteen* scholars. I was told if I would gather a class I might teach it.' The next Sabbath he came with *eighteen* boys.

"Then he commenced the 'North Market Hall Mission School.' The old Market Hall was generally used for a dancing hall on *Saturday nights;* and on Sabbath it took most of the forenoon to clean out the sawdust, and wash up the *beer* and *tobacco* filth. Here the school was held for over six years. The growth continued until over one thousand were enrolled. Of the countless incidents, the encouragements and discouragements, we cannot speak; but there was an auxiliary work, and another room. Finding it almost impossible to conduct a prayer meeting or Sabbath evening service in the hall, Mr. Moody rented a room used for a saloon; boarded up the side windows, and seated it with unpainted pine seats. It was small, (seating about two hundred;) it was dark, it was unventilated; it was necessary to have policemen to watch and guard the place during service. And here Mr. Moody met those young men and women, night after night, year after year. But much more than this: here the blessed Lord met hardened sinners, and here his rich grace was abundantly given. This will doubtless fall under the notice of many a child of God, whose eyes will moisten, and heart grow warm, as they remember that these rude benches were a 'mercy-seat' to them, and this rough room 'the gate of heaven.'

"In 1863, the building on Illinois Street was erected. Its cost with the land was nearly twenty thousand dollars. It was all paid for. Here the work has gone forward, the school has not diminished, and here a church of three hundred souls has been gathered; a few have joined by letter, but a very large proportion have been converted there. Of this church Mr. Moody is the leader.

"The great work of God, during the winter of 1857–58, led to the formation, in January of the latter year, of the Young Men's Christian Association. It also led to the organization of a daily union prayer meeting. The latter was held in Metropolitan Hall, beginning in January, and was attended by many hundreds. In April the number had become small, and in May it was moved to the First Baptist Church, corner of La Salle and Washington Streets. It continued to decline in members, and was by the committee turned over to the Association, and removed to the rooms on Randolph Street. Here it was maintained by a few brethren, sometimes not more than three. Mr. Moody commenced attending this meeting, and by his personal efforts it began to increase, and soon the attendance averaged fifty, often being over one hundred. About this time, Mr. Moody met the writer, and said, 'I have decided to give God *all my time.*' He had at first given his evenings, an occasional day, and the Sabbath. I asked how he expected to live? 'God will provide, if he wishes me to keep on; and I will keep on until I am obliged to stop,' was his reply. From that day to this he has never had a salary from any individual or society. The breaking out of the war brought Mr. Moody into public notice. The devotional committee of the Association of which he was a member was made 'the Army Committee,' Mr. J. V. Farwell being added as chairman. The men, to fill the first call for seventy-five thousand, were so quickly off, that only a fragmentary effort could be made. But the first regiment of the three hundred thousand that encamped at Camp Douglas had not finished the shelter for their first night's rest, when a part of that committee were on the ground, and an hour later a camp prayer-meeting was in progress. Over fifteen hundred of these meetings were held. Mr. Moody seemed almost ubiquitous.

"The news of the battle of Fort Donelson came, and among

the first volunteers to go and succor the sufferers were Dr. Robert Patterson and Mr. Moody. He was at Shiloh, at Murfreesboro', with the army at Cleveland, and Chattanooga; he was one of the first to enter Richmond, ministering to friend and foe, following Christ. Though so often absent on duty, he seemed always at home; his presence in the daily meeting was a felt necessity.

"The Association rooms were then in the Methodist Episcopal Church block, small and overcrowded. The only place for private prayer was a *dark closet*. Coming from one of the meetings, two young men, with Mr. Moody, sat on the Clark Street stairs and consulted about the Association. An hour later, they were in that closet at prayer. In a safe on Water Street is a paper signed by each, pledging continuous effort for a building. Plan after plan was formed and abandoned. One day a young man said, 'The only way to get a building is to elect Mr. Moody president of the Association.'

"In March following, he was elected. At the annual meeting a plan was submitted, the following spring the building was commenced, and in September it was finished. For four years he was president, and then was chosen first vice-president only because he would no longer serve. During these years, his record has not only been national, but it has spread abroad. District, State, and national conventions have called him only too often from home. Twice he has crossed the Atlantic, and among his many efforts in Great Britain, he was permitted to organize the daily union prayer-meeting in London.

"It is necessary to go back a step to bring up the Sunday-school work of Mr. Moody. Our State Sunday-school conventions had been much as others, but had never been sources of religious power. The seventh convention was to be held in Springfield. Mr. Moody presented the matter to several brethren in different parts of the State, and in company with two from Chicago took the train Friday night, and arrived in Springfield Saturday morning. The convention was to meet on Tuesday. Saturday was spent in visiting brethren there. On Sabbath afternoon, a great meeting was held, at which about *seventy* rose for prayers. Sabbath evening, another; and on Monday, at 8 A. M., 4 P. M., and in the evening. God greatly blessed those meetings, and they were held three times a day, during the convention, with blessed results. Many were converted; the delegates caught the fire, and the influence spread over the State. The conventions assumed new shape and power, until the last one, at Quincy, was attended by over five thousand people.

"Mr. Moody was president of the State Association during its eleventh year. His help at the conventions in many other States has often been sought.

"The open-air meetings with the soldiers led to similar meetings on the streets during our State and county conventions. The results from one of these will illustrate one view of Mr. Moody's character. He had twice been invited to visit one of the counties in this State, but had been obliged to postpone his visit. Having a leisure week in summer, he sent word to some one of the pastors that he was coming, and took the next train.

"Arriving, he called on the pastor. Said he, 'I'm sorry you have come; when we wrote you, all seemed fair for a revival; now all promise is gone.' He called on another; he said, 'You might better have stayed at home; winter is the time; in summer people are too busy.' Mr. Moody persuaded a few of them to go with him to the corner of the public square. He tumbled a dry-goods box over from a store across the street, and began to speak. A crowd gathered, they listened — they wept. He invited all who wished to go, to a second meeting in the church near by. The church would not hold all who followed. Meetings were continued. A gracious revival followed. The first pastor said, 'I was mistaken; the Lord knew when to send.' The second said, 'I see, summer is just the time for a revival.'

"Under Mr. Moody's leadership, such meetings have been held in different parts of the city. Some of our best workers have been converted there. The violent opposition of the enemy at the central meetings, held in the City Hall Square, led to a change of place, and the Association lecture-room was chosen. This soon became too small; and on the completion of our second building, meetings were held on Sabbath nights in Farwell Hall.

"Mr. Moody has continued to speak at the Illinois Street

Church, Sabbath morning; to superintend the Sabbath-school in the afternoon, and to speak in the hall in the evening. His audience there, now, averages eight hundred — oftentimes more; mostly young men. Here, as everywhere, and always, his services are given, and God provides in his own way.

"The friends who love him here, now insist that they have the privilege of replying for him, to invitations to labor out of the city, and securing a just acknowledgment of his services.

"Even this hurried sketch would be incomplete did it not give some account of the estimation in which he is held at home. It is perhaps the best evidence, that he is gladly welcomed to most of the evangelical pulpits of the city. He is beloved by Sunday-school workers, and respected by all. That he has enemies and opposers is a necessity. Such a positive life for Christ must develop the positive hostility of some. That this is often the result of wrong judgment, one illustration will show.

"One day the writer was conversing with a prominent physician about Mr. Moody, when the doctor avowed his dislike, in the most decided terms. Some months afterward, the same man called and said, 'I once told you how I disliked Mr. Moody. I now wish to say I have greatly changed my opinion.' Being asked the cause, he said, 'I was called in to see a dying woman who had led a life of shame. She gave me her watch, jewels, and other property, and asked me to send them to her daughter, in a distant place. She died. I wrote the daughter. She came to the city, called, gave me her name and her husband's references, and received the things. Finding her respectable and lady-like, I asked her how she escaped. She said, "I was a little girl; we lived on the North Side. I went to Mr. Moody's Sunday school, and he often went to my mother, and begged her to send me away to a place of safety; and his earnest entreaties prevailed. I was sent. I owe it to him." The doctor added, 'This man must be a Christian, and I was wrong.'

"In his home, with his wife, whose gentleness and love are among God's richest gifts to him, with the two dear children, Emma and Willie, he is as loving and tender as are his own warm entreaties to sinners.

"Of his personal influence over others, I now only say 't has been my privilege to know him fourteen years, to be associated with him in many efforts for the blessed Master. I have travelled, worked, eaten, slept, talked, studied, prayed, and wept with him, and the man who has most influenced my life, and, under God, led me to try and live for Him, is DWIGHT L. MOODY."

A man's principles and zeal in a cause are known by his acts. It matters very little how loud a profession he may make, unless he lives it out. *Action*, not profession—*deeds*, not words, constitute the only true sign of principle. "Even a child is known by his *doings*." "By their *fruits* ye shall know them." Woman's attachment to the Saviour is seen in her being "last at the cross and first at the tomb." Mr. Moody's ardent patriotism and strong sympathy for the soldier is seen in his being one of the *first* to volunteer to go down and take care of the wounded at the battle of Fort Donelson. His being among the first to enter fallen Richmond to dispense the blessings of the gospel, evinces the same worthy principle.

As an *organizer*, Mr. Moody seems to excel. On May 10, 1864, he organized a very successful daily prayer meeting in the Second Presbyterian Church, of Nashville, Tenn., which was kept up until after the close of the war, and resulted in much good. This, together with the daily prayer meeting in London, the Sabbath schools, meetings, and prayer meetings in Chicago, in the army, and in other places, he has organized, attended with so much success, clearly prove his zeal, wisdom, tact, and success in this kind of work.

As a *speaker* and a *revivalist*, we suppose, he has but few equals among the laity of this country. To be able, in the midst of summer, when there were no prospects of an awakening, by one short speech made at the corner of the street to collect a large, attentive, weeping audience, and thus "get up a revival," as they call it, proves an ability and genius for this kind of labor rarely excelled. And to be able to attract an audience of some eight or nine hundred every Sabbath in such a city of churches and distinguished preachers as Chicago, denotes a power of attraction and eloquence very rarely attained by one of nothing but a common-school education. In looking over the reports of the Christian Commission, we find frequent references made to the labors of Mr. Moody among the soldiers, which we might here relate; but, having given enough to answer our end, we close this sketch in the stirring words of Solomon: "Whatsoever thy hand findeth to do, do it with thy might."

GARRETSON I. YOUNG.

Solemn Warning — "Be Ye also Ready!" — His Birth — Parents — Boyhood — Education — A Diligent Scholar — His Academical Course at Calcutta, Ohio — Enters Jefferson College — Graduates — His Habits — Taught High School — Studies and Practises Law — Elected Probate Judge — A Neat Bookkeeper — Marries — Early Religious Training — Read the Bible Daily — Joins the Episcopal Church — His Military Position — Labors in War Department — Resigns, and Returns Home — Purchased "The Buckeye State" — Edits it — His Success — Elected to the Ohio Legislature — His Character — Patriotic — Winning Ways — Noble Traits — "He Made Friends Fast" — His Sudden Death — Impressive Scene at the Capitol; and at his Home — His Funeral — Marked Honors Paid him by the Governor and State Legislature — Eulogies by the Members.

SNATCHED away almost without a moment's warning, how solemn and impressive is the admonition to his relatives, to his friends, and to the Ohio State Legislature, "Be ye also ready!" "*Prepare to meet thy God!*" The entrance of death within the portals of the halls of legislation, most assuredly should deeply impress every reader with the certainty of the divine edict, "Dust thou art, and unto dust thou shalt return!"

Garretson I. Young was born of highly respected parents, at Young's Mills, in the Valley of Achor, Columbiana County, Ohio, June 28, 1827. His mother was brought up a Quaker; but for many years she has been a devotedly pious member of the Baptist Church. His father is noted for uprightness and uniformity of character; and as an evidence of his good business qualifications and popularity at home, he was elected township clerk twenty-one years in succession. Being the only child, Garretson was the object of much kind and tender parental affection. He spent the days of his boyhood in the Achor district school. Born and brought up in the same neighborhood with myself, I have known him well from his childhood. The writer taught him to read, write, and cipher. Garretson was always a good boy, and the boy was father to the man. He went through the arithmetic (*The Western Calculator*) in three months, when he was only about ten years old; he was always a diligent student. The school was taught in a little old log school-house near the village of Achor. Although his father was a miller, Garretson never seemed to have much taste for that kind of business; and having obtained a good district-school education, at the age of fourteen he commenced a course of academical study in the High School at Calcutta, Ohio; boarding with his aunt, Mrs. Hoffstot. Here he remained at school some four years, excepting a few months which he spent in teaching; here he and I recited Greek and Latin to S. W. Gilson, Esq., and enjoyed many seasons of pleasant memory; here, too, Mr. Young formed the acquaintance of a large circle of interesting, worthy young ladies, whose society he often enjoyed with much pleasure and profit, and with some of whom he whiled away the shades of many an evening.

Having completed his academical course, he entered Jefferson College, Canonsburg, Pa., in the fall of 1846, where he soon made many warm friends, rose in standing and influence, and graduated with honor and distinction in 1848. In the college there were two large rival literary societies, with one of which almost every student in college was connected. Mr. Young belonged to the Franklin Society, and, having been elected secretary of the same the last term of the year, he had the honor of officially signing the diplomas of the graduating class. Mr. Young was a very fine penman; he excelled in pictorial penmanship, and I have always thought more of my college diploma because he wrote my name on it. As a student, he was diligent and methodical; he had a time for study, and a time for every department of business. Preferring the languages to mathematics, he excelled in the classics; and, proficient as a scholar, he was selected by the faculty of the college to deliver an oration on commencement day.

With his diplomas in his pocket, and bidding a long farewell to his friends at college, he hastened to see his beloved parents at their beautiful home in Achor. After a short rest, and having visited his friends at Calcutta, he engaged in teaching in the Cottage Hill Academy, Ellsworth, Ohio; where he remained until the spring of 1849, when he commenced the study of law under Hon. S. W. Gilson, of Canfield, Ohio, and was admitted to the bar in 1851, and at once entered into partnership and practised with his preceptor.

Appreciated for his uprightness, and valued for his good judgment, in the fall of 1854, he was elected probate judge of Mahoning County; and having given such general satisfaction, at the expiration of three years he was re-elected, and faithfully discharged the duties of that important office for six years. Like his father before him, Judge Young had a fine tact for drawing up instruments of writing. Pleasing in his manners, order, exactness, and neatness were prominent traits in his character. The records of his office while probate judge, said Judge Johnson, of Ohio, are "models of neatness." Mr. Young was a fine epistolary writer. His letters were always rich and spicy.

Conscious that "it is not good that man should be alone," and having arrived to the mature age of nearly thirty years, Judge Young was married to Miss Susan Bingham, of Ellsworth, Ohio, on the 27th day of March, 1856.

Blessed with the good example of a pious mother and an honest father, Mr. Young enjoyed a good, religious training. While at home, he usually attended the Baptist church, and sat under the faithful ministrations of the pious Rev. Reece Davis. While attending the academy at Calcutta, he attended the Presbyterian church, and sat under the able ministrations of the devoted Rev. William Reed; here he attended the weekly prayer meeting and Sabbath school, in which he taught a class. While at college, he was surrounded by similar religious influences, and, although more exposed to temptation there, we never heard an evil thing of him. Being very deeply impressed with the doctrines of the

Christian religion, and having a very high regard for the Bible, Mr. Young read three chapters in it daily during his student-life. At Canfield, where he studied and practised law, the same wholesome checks and restraints were thrown around him, all of which, blest of Heaven, finally resulted in an open profession of his faith in the blessed Saviour. He united with the Protestant Episcopal Church in 1855, in which he continued an active, consistent member until his death. And says Dr. Brooke, of Canfield, "in the discharge of his religious duties, Mr. Young was as earnest and devoted as when engaged in his own private business, or that of a public character."

At the breaking out of the rebellion, being in somewhat feeble health, instead of going to help to fight the battles of his country upon the field, he accepted the appointment of judge advocate in one of the military departments, and made up his mind to serve his country in that way; but before he had time to enter upon the duties thereof, he accepted the office of military secretary and aide-de-camp to Governor Tod, of Ohio, with the rank of colonel, and served in that capacity during the Governor's administration. Having enjoyed a short respite after the close of his arduous labors as secretary, he received and accepted an appointment in the War Department at Washington, and was placed upon duty by Secretary Stanton. Here, besides performing various other duties, he gave decisions in cases of claims against the Government, in cases of rebel prisoners seeking to renew their allegiance to the United States, and in cases where charges were preferred against military officers. He occupied this responsible and important position until the spring of 1868, when, upon the urgent request of his aged parents, he resigned, and returned to his beautiful "Hillside" home in New Lisbon, Ohio, which overlooks the lonely cemetery in which now sleeps the precious dust of his mortal remains. Thus rolled on, one after another, the important events of his life.

In the following August he purchased *The Buckeye State*, one of the old county papers of his native county; and, going at once into the editorial chair, he earnestly applied the genius, ability, and tact of his well-disciplined mind to make it a paper worthy of its new editor. And with his good sense, extensive knowledge of human nature, and general information, together with his easy, fluent, graphic, and forcible style of writing, he succeeded admirably. In a few months the reputation of the paper had improved so much, and the popularity of the new editor increased so rapidly that, in the fall of 1869, the people of his native county did him the honor of electing him a member of the State Legislature. This was a new era in Colonel Young's life. Though a lawyer by profession, and a judge by practice, he had never acted in the capacity of a legislator; yet, buoyant with hope, and eager to discharge every duty, at the meeting of the Legislature he answered to his name at the first calling of the roll; and although, with few exceptions, he entered the walls of the Capitol at Columbus an entire stranger, yet with his genial, winning ways he soon formed many agreeable acquaintances, and made many warm friends. True, sincere, and honest, with engaging manners and fine colloquial powers, he was one who knew well how to make friends, and how to keep them; in fact, warm friendship, stern integrity, pure morality, ardent patriotism, and a peculiar nobility of soul, were some of the leading traits of his noble character. Colonel Young, being of feeble health, labored under great disadvantages; and yet true greatness does not consist in high intellectual attainments: it lies more in the heart, in self-denial, and moral heroism. And if you analyze closely the character of Colonel Young, you will find that his great power and influence laid more in the goodness of his heart than in the brilliancy of his mind. In speaking upon this point, says his special friend, Hon. Mr. Williams, member of the Legislature from Fayette County, "Admirable as were his qualities of mind, it was, after all, more his qualities of *heart* that attracted and attached his fellow-men to him. No man had a higher sense of honor, or finer sensibilities, or exhibited more uniformly in daily life those accomplishments which mark the perfect gentleman. He seemed to have been gifted by nature, rather than to have acquired by culture, in a prominent degree, those noble traits of heart that win and charm; and inspired with confidence and respect all who came in contact with him. *He made friends fast, and held them long.*"

HIS DEATH.

Sudden and unexpected — it came "as a thief in the night." Like a faithful soldier, he died at his post; that is a great honor. Having dined with Mr. Adair, at the American Hotel, they walked in company to the Capitol. Upon ascending the steps, Colonel Young threw up blood, and complained of pain and oppression at the lungs. Growing worse, he intimated that he ought to return to the hotel, and suddenly beginning to feel very weak, he desired to lie down; whereupon he was assisted into the Comptroller's office, and was at once waited upon by his intimate friends, who spared no pains for his comfort, and immediately sent for his old family physician, Dr. George W. Brooke, member of the House of Representatives from Mahoning County. Other physicians were brought at once, and everything possible was done, but all to no avail. Almost as soon as he was seated, "over a gallon of blood gushed from his mouth." This gave him a little relief, but he never spoke after entering the room. When Dr. Brooke, his old friend, approached him, he opened his eyes, but gave no other signs of recognition. His work was done — his time was out; and, with a few more throbbings of his kind, generous heart, "the wheel at the cistern stood still," and his noble soul, washed in a Saviour's blood, went from the exciting scenes of legislation to the peaceful abodes of the redeemed in heaven. The scene in the Capitol was deeply impressive. At first it partook of great excitement; officials ran from their offices, members from the House and Senate Chamber, and, filled with consternation, large crowds rushed from the streets deeply anxious to know what had happened. The first response was, "Colonel Young is dying." And no sooner had this spread through the vast crowd, than came the more startling announcement, "*Colonel Young is dead!*" Deeply impressed with reverence and awe, the people gathered round, and gazed upon the pale face of the departed patriot — the excitement dies away, and a deep feeling of sorrow and sadness settled down upon the Capitol, and all about it.

But still more sorrowful and impressive was the reception of the sad news of his death at his late home in New Lisbon.

Word had been received a day or two previous of Mr. Young's intention to spend the following Sabbath at home with his family: he was therefore anxiously looked for when the news of his dying reached New Lisbon. Almost immediately following the last flash, the next despatch announced that "Colonel Young is dead." How deep the impression, and sad the disappointment! sorrow and sadness filled every heart! How great the loss and severe the trial to the bereaved wife, the aged parents, and the dear little daughter! And although the transition from sweet expectation to the keenest grief and deepest mourning was very sudden and unexpected — yet to the bereaved, in all such cases, Jesus says, "Let not your heart be troubled;" "Weep not;" "*Be of good cheer*," because, for such "*to die is gain*," and "to depart is far better." The departed, instead of spending the anticipated Sabbath with his beloved family on earth, went, no doubt, to spend it with the blessed "family in heaven." Here, his friends weep and mourn his loss; there, realizing his gain, he joins the ranks and sings the songs of the redeemed in glory. Here he sat in a legislator's chair, there he sits upon the throne of God.

The remains of Colonel Young laid in state in the Governor's office, on Friday, from 8 to 10 o'clock, A. M., and arrived on the train, in charge of the escort, at New Lisbon, Saturday evening about 9 o'clock, and were immediately conveyed to his late residence. There, on the following Sabbath, they were visited by hundreds of friends and a large concourse of people; and at 2 o'clock, P. M., the Rev. Dr. Vallandigham read in a very impressive manner the solemn funeral services of the Protestant Episcopal Church. The remains were then escorted to the cemetery by a large delegation of Free Masons and Odd Fellows, to both of which societies the deceased belonged. The funeral procession was unusually large and imposing. At the close of the burial services, the body was given in charge of the Masons, and buried with their usual forms and ceremonies.

The House of Representatives unanimously passed resolutions expressing, in the strongest terms, their high appreciation of Mr. Young's "varied talents, his public and private worth, and of his exalted character as a Christian gentleman." We here insert a few extracts from the speeches of the members of the General Assembly of the State of Ohio, upon the solemn occasion of Mr. Young's death.

Hon. JOSIAH THOMPSON, of East Liverpool, his successor, said, in speaking of the responsible positions he had occupied: "He leaves a record of which his friends may well be proud! But our friend has gone! Cut down in the meridian of the years ordinarily allotted to man — upon the threshold of usefulness, with a brilliant future before him. His kindly greeting will meet us not again; and that place where he was more highly prized and will be more sadly missed — the domestic circle — will see him and hear his voice no more forever. And, while we mourn for the dead, and sympathize with the surviving widow and relations, let us not forget our duty to mankind and to the State: let us so conduct ourselves, not only through the remaining time of the present session of this General Assembly, but through life, that, when the Governor of the Universe shall sound the gavel which shall be the token for our departure, we shall leave behind us characters beautified with all the Christian virtues of our departed friend."

Mr. CURTISS, of Cuyahoga County, said: "Mr. Young's gentle spirit cast a halo of warmth and brightness around him continually. I can truthfully attest that I have never met with one whom I believed combined purer and more excellent elements of character than he. It is rare, indeed, sir, we meet men of finished culture, enlarged intelligence and firmness, who add to these qualities the finer and ennobling characteristics of virtue, truthfulness, and kindness of decided and marked types. But this was true of him. It can truly be said that he lived not within the sphere of self, but in the great interests of humanity. His moral vision was never dimmed by sordid or mercenary conceptions. Truth was ever his polar star, while mercy and justice lighted his pathway."

Mr. ENOCHS, of Lawrence County, in speaking of Colonel Young, said: " He was true, kind, faithful, patient, honest, and brave . . . With a disease at all times preying on the very vitals of his life; standing, as he knew, on the verge of the grave; yet cheerful and happy. Ordinary men would have sunk in its presence; but when not prostrate, he entered upon life each day seemingly as buoyant as though he had every prospect of a long life before him; and at each step in life seemed to feel —

'O death, where is thy sting!
O grave, where is thy victory!'"

The Hon. S. W. Gilson says, in a letter, that "Judge Young was a close student and an excellent classical scholar, careful and attentive to business; and, while with me as student and partner, he was an agreeable friend, a man of good moral character, of excellent habits, and worthy of the esteem of his companions and friends." He adds:

"With these few words
I say, *friend of former years, farewell!*
May'st thou rest with heroes and sages on
The green banks of the river of Life! FAREWELL!"

CHAPTER XXIV.

FAREWELL TO THE HOSPITAL.

A BRIEF AND SOLEMN REVIEW — NUMBER OF PATIENTS IN HOSPITAL — AVERAGE DAILY AND TOTAL MORTALITY OF THE WAR — INTERVIEWS WITH SOLDIERS — CHAPLAINS MUCH EXPOSED TO DISEASE — SOLEMN TO PART — FAREWELL TO THE CHESAPEAKE; TO THE CHAPEL; TO THE MATRONS; TO HAMPTON; TO THE CHAPLAINS — FAREWELL TO THE CHRISTIAN SOLDIERS — APPEAL AND FAREWELL TO THE IMPENITENT — FAREWELL TO THE DEAD — THE GREAT CHRISTIAN VICTORY — THE REBELLION DISSECTED — SOURCE OF THE VICTORY — MUNIFICENT GIFTS — AMERICANS AND EUROPEANS WHETTING ONE ANOTHER — GO FORWARD.

OFFICERS AND FELLOW-SOLDIERS: — The war is over! the effusion of blood is stayed! "the battle's fought; the victory won!" and the country is saved! The two mighty armies, so long engaged in fierce conflict, have disbanded, and gone home! And the nation, just drenched in fraternal blood, again enjoys peace; and the hospitals, for the last four years thronged with the sick, wounded, dying, and dead, are now closing out. And although a few of us are still here lingering around these old blood-stained wards, made sacred by the long, severe suffering and death of so many brave patriots, to nurse and take care of those patients as yet unable to go home, we will all soon be discharged. As for me, being the last chaplain mustered in, I am the first mustered out. Having labored some fifteen months in this extensive home of the sick and wounded, the honorable Secretary of War drops me a little note, stating that "you are honorably mustered out of the service of the United States; your services being no longer needed." Hence we come, to-day, to bid you all an affectionate farewell. And now, in taking my leave, let us take a brief retrospect of the past. It makes a very solemn review. To recall the severe suffering and the immense mortality endured in these hospitals the past two years is very solemn and impressive. And when we begin to count numbers, the impression is much deeper. The greatest number of patients in the hospital at any one time, was four thousand nine hundred and forty-eight on May 26, 1865. And during my labors here, which have been the hardest of my life, we have received and treated in this hospital some twenty-five thousand patients, some two thousand of whom are now in their graves. The greatest number of deaths on any one day was nineteen. Three hundred died during the month of August, 1864, in the Hampton division. The greatest number buried any one day, was twenty-nine. Others are passing away. The stream of death is still flowing. The king of terrors still reigns. Half a million have died in the war, with an average mortality of more than two hundred a day. Two hundred a day! How impressive the fact! how solemn the warning! Take the world over, about seventy die every minute, over four thousand every hour, and a generation every thirty-three years. We will all soon be in our graves. Time is short; eternity is just at hand. Oh, then, fellow-soldiers, let us now prepare for it. My intercourse with you has been very pleasant. To hear the soldier speak of the thrilling incidents of the war, the weary march, the heavy charge, the bloody fight, and the dreadful carnage, was deeply interesting; but to hear them relate, with deep emotions and gushing tears, their religious experience, was far more interesting and refreshing.

The simplicity, freeness, and frankness with which soldiers and officers have talked to us about these things, their wants, trials, temptations, etc., have always added much to the interest and profit of our interviews. They often became eloquent and powerful, because they spoke right out from the heart, telling us all about their sins, difficulties, sufferings, feelings, wants, and cares. Many a time have I gone away from the patient's bedside instructed, encouraged, and refreshed. Although this work was very laborious, yet we deemed it a privilege. Constrained by a sense of duty to the soldier, to our country, and to God, we enjoyed it, notwithstanding our great exposure to contract disease. Though it is very pleasant to go and see "the loved ones at home," yet we leave the suffering soldier, and these old halls, where we have so often knelt and prayed together and enjoyed such precious times of refreshing, with much sorrow and deep regret. It is very hard to get away. To pack up, and say farewell, seems very difficult. To leave kind friends with whom we have been so long associated in our dreadful work, is peculiarly trying. Yet it is a pleasing reflection to go home crowned with victory and a redeemed country, although it has cost the Union army the loss of over three hundred thousand lives, of whom over ninety thousand were killed in action or died of wounds. "Peace be to their ashes." May God abundantly bless and comfort their bereaved, mourning friends! Farewell, "Old Chesapeake!" thou whose ocean breeze has so often gladdened the heart and cheered the soul of many a suffering hero! Farewell to thy historic walls, which, if they could but speak and record the agonies and sufferings, the patience, the dying groans, the fervent prayers, the bright conversions, and triumphant deaths of our departed heroes, 't would fill many volumes with most interesting matter. Farewell, ye widowed weeping wives and bereaved mothers, whose dear husbands and beloved sons have laid down their lives within these blood-stained walls in honor of the dear old flag and for the salvation of the country. You have done your country a good service. May God richly reward you for your great sacrifices, and abundantly bless and comfort you in your sad bereavements. Farewell, ye self-denying matrons, who have so long stood pensive and watchful around the narrow couch of the sick, wounded, and dying soldier, who, by your tender, affectionate, painstaking nursing, fervent prayers, and soothing sympathies, have ministered so much to the comfort of the dying, and have saved the lives of so many of our surviving soldiers and officers. You have done a noble work in the great struggle for national existence. Although you have not wielded the sword, fired the cannon, besieged cities, nor commanded armies; yet, doubtless, you have done more, perhaps, than some who did all these things, in quelling the rebellion and saving the country. Fare ye well! The Lord reward you abundantly for your work and labor of love. Peace be with you!

Farewell, "Bethesdian Chapel," within whose walls we have enjoyed many a precious hour; farewell, thou sacred place endeared to thousands of soldiers and officers by the sweet songs of praise, the impressive sermon, the refreshing prayer and conference meeting, the soldiers' religious talk, earnest exhortation, and fervent prayers! Long wilt thou be remembered with pleasing recollections, as the sacred spot where many a convalescent soldier, officer, and chaplain enjoyed precious seasons of refreshing, and, doubtless, by many as the place where they first drew the breath of spiritual life.

Farewell, "Old Hampton," with all thy thrilling scenes of suffering, blood, and death; farewell, ye blood-stained wards, into whose oblong barracks and snow-white tents the sick and wounded have come and gone like the ocean's tide: though ye have been the scene of so much suffering, sorrow, and death, yet being the place where we have so often mingled our prayers, sympathies, and tears, with so many brave patriots, and being the battle-field where so many have, through grace, won the victory over the world, the flesh, and the devil, those old walks and wards, headquarters, and halls will ever be held in sorrowful, yet affectionate remembrance! Farewell, ye dingy dining-halls; whose rough tables and sombre walls, if they could but speak and record the solemn, impressive sermons, the interesting and refreshing prayer and conference meeting, the soldier's stirring, heart-gushing exhortation and importunate prayer, the happy religious experience, the sweet communions, and solemn vows, and frequent conversions, it too would form many volumes of most interesting and useful matter.

Farewell, ye chaplains! Though we have been long associated in our arduous work, to-day we separate; and although the four divisions of the hospital are now merged into one; and although the patients are now rapidly hurrying away by transfer, by discharge, and by death, yet your work is still great. The field is still great, white, ready to harvest! God is still saying, "Thrust in the sickle, and reap." There are here yet many soldiers of the army, who are not soldiers of the cross. Some are nigh unto death, yet without hope; others, almost Christians, like the trembling jailer, are anxiously inquiring what to do to be saved. They will require special attention, tender sympathy, faithful instruction, and earnest prayers. Many others, still careless and impenitent, should be faithfully instructed, tenderly warned, and earnestly besought to repent and come to Jesus. Let us endeavor to remember that, although the war is over, and the rebellion quelled, it is still our duty to fight on even until death. Then suffer me, in bidding you an affectionate farewell, to say to you, in the language of Jesus, "*Be thou faithful.*" Let us strive to meet around God's throne, where there will be no more war.

We come now, fellow-soldiers, to bid you a long, affectionate farewell! Our associations have been pleasant and agreeable, and, having so long endured the trials, hardships, and deprivations of hospital life, to separate seems very hard; and although I leave you to-day, yet my prayers, my sympathies, and my heart will still be with you. Farewell, ye soldiers of the cross! We have enjoyed many precious times of refreshing around the throne of grace in these old wards and halls; but we will enjoy them here no longer: to-day we part, to meet no more in this world; and, as we will no more mingle our prayers and praises on earth, oh, let us strive " to strike hands in heaven! " Remember, brethren, that, although the war is over, and the country saved, and you will soon be discharged from the service, yet you still have rebellions to quell, battles to fight, and victories to win. Your great Captain's command is, still to fight, fight on, fight on till death, and you'll receive the crown! Doubtless, many of you have been converted in the army or in the hospital; the thrilling incidents of battle, and the melting scenes of hospital life, through grace, have led you to the cross. God has done great things for you. You owe him a debt of gratitude you can never pay. You have done much for the deliverance of your country, and for the salvation of souls; but your work is not complete; there is yet much work to be done, and, as you have enlisted in this service for life, let me entreat you, brethren, toil on, children of the living God, *toil on!* As you go home, carry your religion with you; keep the doctrines of the cross uppermost in your hearts, and let them shine bright in your lives. As you lay off the armor of your country, gird on afresh " the whole armor of God," and let the Church at home see and feel the power of the religion of the army. May God abundantly bless, comfort, and save you. And now we come to bid farewell to you, my impenitent friends! And what shall I say to you? what more can we say? what more can we do, than we have done? My very heart bleeds for you; my very soul longs for your salvation! And, oh, my dear soldiers, what shall we say more? We have given you many warnings; we have sounded in your ears the terrors of God's law; in our exhortations we have led you down to the depths of hell, and then led you up to the seraphic joys of heaven, and besought you by the thrilling scenes of Gethsemane and Calvary, and by the mercies of God, and by the love of Christ, to believe and be saved — and you still remain impenitent. Though you have proved yourselves loyal to your country, yet, with sorrow be it said, you are still disloyal to God! You have fought well to put down rebellion against the Government, yet you still keep up rebellion against God in your hearts. And now, before I bid you a final farewell, allow me to warn and entreat you once more. It is the last time. It is hard to give you up. How solemn and impressive the scene! To see men, who have done so much to save their country, go home, and doing nothing to save their souls, seems hard. Here we have often met beneath the beautiful folds of that dear old flag, and heard many earnest prayers and impressive sermons; but here we all will meet no more forever. We will all soon go home; the hospital will soon disband; the last bugle will soon sound; the last roll will soon be called, and these old wards, made sacred by the death of so many heroes, will soon be torn away; and though we meet no more on earth, we will all meet at the judgment-seat of Christ, when the trump of God shall sound, when a final separation will take place between the loyal and disloyal to God. Then, once more we beseech you, repent, and look to Jesus; let the thrilling scenes of Bethlehem, Gethsemane, and Calvary stir your souls and win your hearts; yes, go to Calvary, and see the Lord of glory expiring upon the cross — Jesus dying that you might have eternal life. Follow him from the cross to the tomb, and from the tomb to the throne, and all to bring us to God. Oh, then, while standing by the graves of three thousand brave comrades who have sacrificed their lives for their country, we beseech you, give your hearts to God. Dear soldiers, farewell, farewell! It is hard to leave you; it is harder to leave you out of Christ. May the God of all grace have mercy upon and abundantly bless you all! And now, in taking leave of the living, my thoughts go and linger with the dead; and while walking amidst the soldiers' graves, we almost feel like saying farewell to their precious dust. Farewell, thou sacred spot, within whose slender walls sleep the mortal remains of thousands around whose lonely graves many a tear has been shed, many a prayer offered, and many a smitten heart has deeply throbbed with crushing grief. Farewell, ye patriotic dead, whose blood has stained many a battle-field, whose valor and courage have won many a victory, and whose daring deeds deserve to be written on leaves more durable than leaves of brass: let their names be enshrined in the memory and deeply engraved upon the heart of every American patriot; let monuments of marble rise to their honor, so that their heroic deeds may be handed down to the latest posterity. Farewell to their precious dust! May God keep, guard, and protect it until the morning of the resurrection, when the voice of the archangel and the trump of God shall sound, and bid the scattered fragments of broken bones and amputated limbs come together; when those mortal bodies, sown in corruption, weakness, and dishonor, shall be raised in power, honor, and glory; when the redeemed shall be caught up to meet the Lord in the air, and dwell forever with him in glory.

THE GREAT CHRISTIAN VICTORY.

With all the Christian efforts, preaching, praying, and painstaking labor performed by the chaplain and the Christian and Sanitary Commissions, to supply the wants and to save the soldier's soul, the grandest exhibition of Christianity in the war is the victory achieved in quelling the rebellion. Conceived in sin, and brought forth in iniquity, the rebellion was all wrong from beginning to end. If you dissect it, you will find it made up of sin, pride, selfishness, treachery, and treason. And the victory achieved in quelling it, is a victory of right over wrong, of truth over error, of liberty over slavery, and of loyalty over treason. The history of the world affords many great and glorious victories; but, for important results, few equal this. And although the earth did not quake, nor the rocks rend, nor the sun refuse to shine at its achievement; yet, when viewed in all its great, far-reaching, and powerful effects upon the church, self-government, human progress, and Christian civilization throughout the world, it is for grandeur and glory the greatest victory since that achieved by the Son of God upon Mount Calvary or at the tomb of Joseph. And when we consider the length and severity of the conflict, the great sacrifice made in life, blood, and treasure in achieving it, carrying away over half a million of brave men, and filling the land with widows and orphans, and ridging it with soldiers' graves, the victory appears much greater. The restoration of peace after a four years' civil war that caused an average daily mortality of three hundred and sixty brave men, is no small blessing. How much soever is due to the bravery, military genius, and hard fighting of the army and navy, yet the great moral energy, strength, and power by which the rebellion was put down, is, doubtless, mainly due to the Christian principles of the loyal part of the nation. It was *moral strength* that saved the nation and freed the slave. And had we had less of it, the rebellion

INDEPENDENCE HALL, PHILADELPHIA

might have destroyed the nation, and thus thwarted this great effort to maintain self-government in the world. Even while the fierce conflict was raging, when victory perched upon the rebel standard, monarchical Europe rejoiced, and European aristocracy were heard to say in derision, "There goes your model republic, knocked into splinters in the course of one man's life!" And then, with our country struggling for life, and just ready to be wrapped in her winding-sheet, as those European aristocrats supposed, they stood ready to help our American traitors lay her in the grave. But thanks be to a kind Providence, our God-protected republic, then unconscious of her strength, withstood the severe storm, and came out of the awful conflict with her columns of constitutional liberty stronger than ever. And so great has been our progress since, that, were it not for the old battle-fields, the maimed soldiers, their graves, and the mourning widows and orphans, you would scarcely know that there had been any war.

The power and influence of Christianity in the war is seen not only in the great efforts made for the soldiers' salvation and spiritual instruction, but also in the munificent contributions made for their general relief and comfort. The *Missionary Herald*, quoting from Hartley's *Philanthropic Results of the War in America*, says that the total amount contributed for the aid and relief of the soldiers and their families during the war by the States, associations, and individuals, is $211,245,474 58, exclusive of the Government expenditures, and what was given for the freedmen and white refugees.

It has been estimated that one-third of this large amount has been given by professing Christians, which, says the same author, is a great deal more than has been given by the entire church for the conversion of the world since the organization of the Government. These vast contributions show that how much soever the American people may be absorbed in bank-bills, that, in times of great emergencies, such as the salvation of the country, they are capable of great acts of sympathy, and of a noble generosity.

Hitherto our republic has been on probation, and the great question of man's self-government was still undecided; but now, having survived the tremendous shock of the rebellion, it may be regarded as being forever settled. And now, with railroads and telegraphs spanning our continent, bringing the life and energy of the Far West in contact with the commerce, wealth, and talent of the Great East; and linked to the Old World with the ties of commerce, religion, literature, and telegraphic communications, making Americans whet Europeans, and Europeans whet Americans — the United States is to-day a terror to kings and queens, an example and a light to the world, and the emulation of the whole earth.

Although sin abounds in our land; yet, with slavery abolished, reconstruction completed, and with a railroad, commercial, educational, Sabbath-school, and Missionary enterprise unsurpassed in the history of the world, our future prospects are very bright and encouraging. How all-important, then, to wisely improve this victory! Achieved at a cost so great, and involving interests so vast both to Church and State, the *trust* reposed in us as a nation is exceedingly great, and fraught with a responsibility literally immense.

Having thus renewed our strength, and been made more perfect through suffering, and having passed the Red Sea of our progress and trials, in view of the great responsibility resting upon us, God, our past success, and the great work before us, bid us "*Go forward!*" "FOLLOW UP THE VICTORY!"

INDEX.

AUCTIONEERING, Sabbath, broken up, 16.
A dying thief's prayer powerful, 34.
Assurance, secret of, 48.
"A glorious attainment," 47.
Arrival of patients, 89.
An affectionate kiss, soldier's, 91.
Army and Navy Hymn-book used, 96, 102.
"Always refreshing," 103.
An Indian's reproof, 239.
Appeal to the wounded in hospital, 105–7.
Asking a mother's prayers, 108.
Amos, Miss, matron, 119, 120.
Americans and Europeans whetting one other, 420.
Alexander, Mrs. Mary, the soldiers' friend, 122; her death, 123.
Armstrong, Robert, 109th U. S., prayerful; "all is well;" happy death, 146–7.
Andersonville Prison, cruelties, 151; trials in, 152; awful suffering, 153, 165; many died of grief, some went deranged, 153, 270; church and school there now, 154.
American Missionary Association, 154.
Almost Christian, the, 155.
Andersonville Hospital, 160; diet of, 160; "sick call," 161; sufferings in, 161, 162.
Andersonville prayer-meeting, 163.
Andersonville Cemetery, 169; the dead, 169; their sufferings, 170; number, 171; inscription on gate, 172.
Alexander, Reuben, 29th U. S., craving prayers, 207.
A swearer brought to tears, 209.
Aikin, Charles A., 4th Mass. Cav., anxious, happy, 254, 255.
Author's praying with a dying rebel, 70.
———— capture, 20, 69; loss by, 69.
———— preaching daily to men on their death-beds, 98, 104, 105, 128, 132, 185, 186, 188, 246.
———— canvassing through the rain, 275.
———— speech at the fall of Richmond, 285.
———— address at Lincoln's funeral, 295–298.
———— Rocky Mountain letter; value of the Union, 62.

Author's saving a lieutenant's life, 36.
———— receiving letters of thanks, 114, 115, 246, 247.

BAPTISM of blood, country's, 15.
Babcock, Elias, 10th N. Y., co. "B," wounded; his heroic faith, ecstatic joy, dying words, 22, 23.
Basil's prayer: "Give me any cross," &c., 37.
Bowman, Moses, 15th W. Va. Vol., converted in the army; began to pray on the field of battle; "all is bright," 51, 56.
Barnett, John H., 101st Pa. Vol., converted in the army; his zeal, will, assurance, weeping farewell, 48, 49.
"Biggest gun ever fired in America," 16.
Brown's, Captain J. B., bravery at Fort Gray, 63.
Beech, Colonel, requests preaching on the boat, 76.
Bible-class, large, interesting, 19, 43, 81.
Brown, Chaplain W. Y., U. S. A., 17.
Baptized an officer at midnight, 41.
"Brought to the point by wounds," 41.
Battle of Plymouth, N. C., 63–68; casualties of, 68.
Bible picked up and carried through the war, 70.
Bread begged for prisoners, 76.
Belle Isle Prison, cruelties of; fare, 78, 151, 152.
Butler, Major-General, 80, 307, 308.
Barnes, General, Surgeon-General, U.S.A., 84.
Blake, Captain, 3d Pa. Heavy Art., 85.
Brands plucked out of the fire, 89.
Bush prayer-meetings, 102.
Bently, Miss J. E., matron, 120.
"Bury me with them, when dead," 123.
Blind exhorter, 130.
Backslider, the, 136, 137, 138, 178.
Bartsher, Henry, 58th Pa. Vols., heart fixed; joyful death, 140–1.
"Bullets for bread," 173.
Boat-load of Andersonville prisoners, 184.
Bradley, Theodore, 7th Conn. Vol., converted in army, 185.

421

422 INDEX.

Burket, John S., 13th Ind. Cav., anxious, prayerful death, 185-6.
Bullock, Wm. S., 89th N. Y. Vol., anxious, prayerful, doubts; perseveres; comfortable, 188-9, 269.
Bleeding to death, yet "resting on Christ sure," 194.
"Ball in your head not as bad as sin in your heart," 195.
Boston, Jacob, 188th Pa. Vols., his creed, faith, assurance; happy; no fear, 199, 200.
Bomb-proof prayer-meetings, 210.
Brown, Samuel S., 3d Ohio Cav., ready to go; his death, 213.
Brown, R., 7th S. C., prayerful assurance; no fear, 217.
Burnett, Edward, 118th N. Y. Vol., converted in army, through sin, 224.
Brown, Wm., 117th N. Y., submissive, strong faith, 231.
Bingham, Rev. Mr., preached, 274.
Bombardment of Fort Fisher, 288.
Battle of Big Bethel, killed at, 301.
—— Bull Run, killed at, 301.
—— Ball's Bluff, killed at, 301.
—— Wilson's Creek, killed at, 301.
—— Pittsburg Landing, killed at, 302.
—— South Mountain, killed at, 302.
—— Williamsburg, killed at, 302.
—— Antietam, killed at, 302.
—— Fair Oaks, killed at, 302.
—— Malvern Hill, killed at, 303.
—— Cedar Mountain, killed at, 303.
—— Second Bull Run, killed at, 303.
—— Fredericksburg, killed at, 303.
—— Corinth, killed at, 303.
—— Stone River, killed at, 304.
—— Chancellorsville, killed at, 304.
—— Vicksburg, killed at, 304.
—— Gettysburg, killed at, 305.
—— Chattanooga, killed at, 305.
—— Missionary Ridge, killed at, 305.
—— Fort Wagner, killed at, 306.
—— and Massacre at Fort Pillow, killed at, 306.
—— of the Wilderness, killed at, 306.
—— Spottsylvania, killed at, 306.
—— Cold Harbor, killed at, 307.
—— Resaca, Ga., 307.
—— Keneshaw Mountain, killed at, 308.
—— Monocacy, killed at, 308.
—— Atlanta, killed at, 308.
—— Opequan and Fisher's Hill, killed at, 309.
—— of Franklin, Tenn., killed at, 309.
—— Nashville, Tenn., killed at, 309.
—— Cedar Creek, killed at, 309-10.
—— Averysboro, killed at, 310.
—— Bentonsville, killed at, 310.
—— Five Forks, killed at, 311.
—— Hatcher's Run, Fort Steadman, 311.

Battles of Sherman's march to the sea, 308-9.
Baker, Colonel, killed, 301; Captain Beirel slew the perpetrator, 301.
Burnside, General, succeeded McClellan, 303-4.
Byers, Emanuel, 116th Ohio Vol., anxious; prayed; delayed; converted; bled to death, 150, 193-4.
Beecher, Henry Ward, 383, 394.

CONNER, Smith A., 62d Ohio Vol., convicted; tries; dies, 197-8.
Cleveland, Geo. E., 5th N. Y. Cav., prayerful; his death, 205-6.
Cortege, Phil., 18th U. S., discouraged; prayerful, 208.
Converted in the army, through sin and profanity, 224.
—— by a worldly man reading the Bible, 240.
Curry, John, a converted Catholic; good boy; sufferings; death, 243.
Church organized, 259.
Church creed, 260, 276.
Cobley, Bennett J., 58th Pa. Vol., careless; wept, 261-2.
Converted Catholics join the Union Church, 261.
Catholics turning Protestants, 268.
Curtis, General, visit from, 278.
Curtis, General N. M., 142d N. Y., 291.
Craighead, Rev. Mr., Editor *N. Y. Evangelist*, 295.
Christmas gift by General Sherman to President Lincoln, 310.
Christmas dinner, 269, 270; four hundred turkeys; "huge feeding," 272.
—— sermons, 269, 270, 272.
—— concert, 271.
Colored soldiers' prayer-meetings in new camp, 280-1.
Captain Cameron's warm grasp; death, 117, 127, 330-1.
Card-playing broken up, 269.
Conversions in the army, 48, 49, 51, 52, 184, 188, 241, 253, 265, 265, 276.
Conversions in hospital, 41, 42, 28, 44, 45, 187, 194, 197.
Converted in hospital, 221, 223, 224, 239, 267, 277.
—— on picket, 97.
—— by hearing the Bible read in hospital, 97.
—— in battle, 179.
—— on picket, by being talked to, 184-5.
Curtis, Robert, 1st U. S., heroic courage; killed five rebels; bit another's throat; left for dead, 55, 56.
Carlton quoted, 27.
Chaplain McCabe, 55.
Chidlaw, Rev. B. W., 61.

INDEX. 423

Cunningham, Jas. A., 96th Ohio Vol.; "all is well;" his death, 61-2.
Chapin, Captain, 85th N. Y. Vol., his heroic bravery; fighting; mortally wounded, 65.
Converted through a sister's letters, 188.
Compher, Captain, 101st Pa. Vol., 67.
Cuyler, John M., 79, 81.
Camp Distribution, preaching in, 80, 85, 86.
Chapel, Bethesdian, precious meetings in, 80.
Contraband Hospital, preached in, 83.
Church, hospital, organized, 101, 259.
Choice of hymns, 104.
Christ's "I would;" your "Ye would not," 106.
"Come just as you are," 107.
Crane, Rev. Mr., 269.
Canvassing the patients' hearts, 115.
Campbell, Mrs., matron, 120.
Carver, Mrs., 121-2.
Creed, John, 23d Ill., co. "B," brave, honored, 133.
Castle Thunder Prison, 152.
Crisis of the soul, 155-8.
—— of Andersonville, 158.
Catholic priest prays with prisoners, 157.
Crying peace in danger, 157.
Chase, Henry W., 96th N. Y., anxious; weeps; sins great; his conversion; went home, 181-2.
Christian Commission supplied reading matter, 20.
—— delegates, 80, 96, 97, 190, 210, 279, 282-6.
—— a grand exhibition of Christianity in the war, 331.
—— gave first cup of coffee to the wounded at battle of Wilderness, 332.
—— its efficiency and contributions, 333.
—— delegates highly esteemed, 333.
—— saved lives and souls, 333.
"God bless the Christian Commission," 333.
Christian effort among patients, 96.
Corporal Cook, Vet. Reserves, 283.
Craven, Doctor, medical director, 284.

DEVIL outflanked, 16; and whipped, 285.
Dixon, Chaplain, of 16th Conn. Vol., 20, 63.
Duncan, John B., wounded; patient; dying words; will; triumphant death, 21, 22.
Draper, Edward, 45th U. S., conversion; strong faith; no fear; "It is glorious," 51, 52.
Dashiel, Chaplain, weeps over a dying soldier, 26, 27.
Doubts and fears removed; joy restored, 38.
Dying soldier's letter to his wife; farewell, 39, 40.
Dully, Mrs. Mary B., principal matron, 41, 81, 119.

Drummer-boy's affection for his mother, 57, 58.
Davis, Jeff., flees Richmond, 78, 173, 292.
Disappointed friends, wives, 89.
Diagnosis, spiritual, of the hospital, 115.
Doubting, distressed doctor relieved, 148-9.
Dead-line, the, in Andersonville, 154.
—— God's, 154.
"Door was shut," 155.
Departure of Andersonville prisoners, 166, 167.
"Died calling for the chaplain," 185-6, 229.
Disappointed, bereaved wife, 187.
Delling, Richard, 8th Maine Vol., brave, patriotic, anxious; prays; dies, 190, 191.
"Delay is the devil's verb — *now* is God's time," 193.
Deserter, condemned, refusing pardon, 193.
Danger of delay, 193.
Doing essential to *enjoying*, 253.
Dunham, John H., 117th N. Y., rather careless; trying; death, 229, 230.
Dickson, Hiram, 112th N. Y. Vol., longs for heaven, 248-9.
Dinsmore, Rev. Mr., 279.
Dedication of new hospital chapel, 286.
Dodging bullets, 307.
Death mighty; there is a Mightier, 312.
Deaths in rebel prisons, 312.
Deserter, the, his crime and fate, 313-14.
Dix, Miss, visits hospitals, erects soldiers' monuments, 322, 323.
Distinguished Christian men in the war, 334.

EMANCIPATION Proclamation, effects of, 16.
Eastman, Chaplain, rolled to the wounded and dying, 35, 36.
—— carried to a dying officer, 36.
Eloquence of the heart powerful, 101, 257.
Execution of prisoners in Andersonville, 156, 157.
Exchange of Andersonville prisoners, 164.
Extreme cruelty, 173.
Eloquence of freedmen, 282.
Edwards, Jonathan, "lost and swallowed up in God," 248.
Eternal progress in heaven, 249.
Ellison, Jacob, 114th U. S., converted in camp, 253.
Extracts from author's diary, 256, 279.
Ellsworth, Colonel, his death, 300.

FEE, Captain, co. "I," 48th N. Y., his character; wound; requests to be prayed for; his death, 32-35.
Filial affection, strong, 57; unquenchable, 58.
Flusser, Lieutenant-Commander, brave, patriotic; his death, 66.
Fisher, David, 101st Pa. Vol., killed, 67.

INDEX.

Frantz, Dr. J. H. A., Surgeon U. S. A., in charge, 82.
Frederick, Geo., 15th N. J. Vol., prayerful; faithful, 128, 130.
Finny, James H., 1st N. Y. Engineers, "can't live without religion," 139, 140.
Fixed heart, the, 140.
Farewell to Dixie, 165
Ferguson, Henry, 39th Ill. Vol., his conviction, conversion, 180–1.
Father's dying message to his family, 199.
Fort Fisher wounded, buoyant, patriotic, brave, 276, 287.
—— bombarded, 288–290.
Friendship of Jesus, 331.
Farewell to the hospital, 411–418.
—— and appeal to the impenitent soldiers, 416, 417.
Farragut, Admiral, 353–363.

GRIFFITH'S, G. S., kindness; liberal gift, 17.
Gangrene camp, suffering in, 87, 88; and triumphs of, 89.
"Got used to death," 98.
Guthrie, Rev. Dr., quoted, 133, 134.
God's dead-line, 154.
Grant, General, assumed command-in-chief, 306.
—— his unyielding determination, 307–311.
—— starts for Richmond, 127.
—— crossed the Rapidan, 125.
Greenough, Sergeant, dying; dead, 330–1.
Good music; melodeon, 20.
"Good-bye, old arm," a patriotic, weeping farewell, 57.
"Get away, thou infernal spirit," 191.
"God's time — *now*," 193.
Great sinners saved, 250.
Gilbert, Geo. H., 34th Mass., careless, profane, bad excuses, 200.
"Going down to get up," 210.
Great emergencies develop moral powers, 211, 212.
Goff, John, 142d N. Y. Vol., interested; prayed; repented; died, 226–7.
Good effects of a sermon, 256.
Gurley, Rev. Dr. P. D., 334–342.

HOLT, Mrs. D. W., hospital matron, 120.
Howard, General, bravery of his soldiers, 134, 135.
Heroic, unparalleled patriotism, 159, 160.
Hartel, Philip, 51st Pa. Vol., saved by his wife, 183.
Hugged the nurse when dying, 187.
Hinkle, Charles A., 130th Ohio Vol., prayerless; "I will try," 206–7.
Homesick for heaven, 246.
Heaven, description of the joys of, 248–9.
Hospital church organized, 259.

Hospital wards, neatness of, 270.
Hays, General, killed, 306.
Hammond, Lieutenant, requests prayer; death, 330–1.
Hero, a, saved by his wife, 183.
Howard, O. O., General, 343–346.
Hospital, General, U. S., Annapolis, 77; preaching in, 77, 80.
—— General, U. S., Fortress Monroe, Va., organization, 79.
—— Chesapeake, 79, 81.
—— library; papers, 80, 287.
—— General, U. S., Hampton, 81, 102.
Henries, H. C., Chaplain, U. S. A., 77.
Hospital garden, abundant crops, 84.
Hospital hennery, useful, 85.
Hampton Hospital, 81, 102, 178.

JOHNSON, Edmund, 37th U. S., colored; prayerful, 252.
James, Milas, 36th U. S., colored; backslider; penitent; patriotic; happy, 227-8.
Jones, Peter, 36th U. S., happy; persevering; shouting, 204.
Joy, a source of moral strength, 135.
Johnson, Wm. J., 142d N. Y. Vol., genteel, patient, brave, patriotic, 235.
Jacob, old, the grave-digger, prepossessing, devout, faithful, 237–8.
Jones, John, 10th W. Va., patient, meek, humble, pious, happy, 241-2.

KELLOGG, Major, the awful sight he saw, 174.
Kissing the stake as he approached it, 218.
Kneeland, Dwight, Signal Corps U. S. A., rather careless; prays; repents; happy, 229.

LOVETT, Lewis, 2d U. S. colored troops, his heroic faith, assurance, patriotism; how to be happy, 46-48.
Longnecker, Lieutenant, 66, 67, 69.
Leghman, Colonel, 103d Pa. Vol., 19, 68, 69.
Left for dead, yet lived, 55.
Libby prison, going to, 71, 72; reception, life in, 72; fare, 73, 151, 152.
—— hospital, patients, 74; farewell to, 75.
Lambert's, John, victorious death, 88.
Letter-writing for patients, 107.
Letters of death, 109.
Last messages, 110.
Letters from the bereaved at home to the chaplain, 110.—1, The bereaved wife, 110; 2, The bereaved brother, 112; 3, The weeping widow, 112; 4, The dying soldier, 114; 5, A weeping Southern family, 114, 115.
Letter from a bereaved wife, 132.
Letters of a sister convert a brother, 188.

INDEX.

Lucas, Henry, 39th Ill. Vol., "putting it off;" delaying, 193.
Lathrop, Henry A., 8th Conn., "All is well;" victorious, 206.
Little Lizzie's letter, 214; reply, 215.
Largest interment any day, 286.
Lestur, John, 138th U. S. colored; brave, faithful, 218.
Loaded and fired eight times during a charge, 218.
Lord's Supper administered, 272.
Lee's surrender, 284-5, 304-5, 311.
Lyon, General, killed, 301-2.
Lincoln, Abraham, his emancipation proclamation, 16; his character, 296-7; religious life, faith, 298; reinauguration, 283; his death, 157; funeral, 285, 295, 299, 310.

MURDOCK, Josiah, 4th U. S. colored, 217; prayerful, 198.
Morton, Charles A., 7th N. H., 215; anxious; prayed; converted, 216.
Mullincup, Jacob, 13th Ind. Vol., anxious, skeptical, tries to pray, 222-3.
McMaster, John, died, 259.
Mortality increasing: twenty-six buried in one day, 264-5, 286.
Moore, Colonel, 203d Pa. Vol., killed; brave, 291.
Mansfield, Brigadier-General, U. S. A., his death, 302.
Moody, D. L., 395-403.
Massacre at Fort Pillow, 306.
McPherson, General James B., killed, 308.
Mortality of the war, average daily and total, 412.
Maximum mortality of hospital at Fortress Monroe, 412.
Moral strength saved the nation, 418.
Munificent contributions for the army and navy, 419.
Marshall, Rev. Jas., U. S. A., 17, 30, 42, 80, 86, 87, 272, 279, 283, 284, 286, 295.
—— sketches by, 326-331.
—— turned a theatre into a religious meeting, 327-9.
—— did great good in a short time, 329.
—— stopped the soldiers swearing, 329.
—— prays with dying officers, 329-30.
Morris, Rev. Mr., 19.
Merrill, Lieutenant F. L., 3d N. H., converted in hospital; baptism; his will; dying words, 40-42.
Mays, Captain, 101st Pa. Vol., 64.
Massacre at Plymouth, 69, 70.
Mortimer, P. B., 103d Pa. Vol., mortally wounded; resigned, 74.
Moore, John B., 1st Texas, hopes; sufferings; death, 54, 55.
Mother, affection for, 57, 58.
Massachusetts 2d Heavy Artillery, 67, 68.

McClellan, Dr. Eli, U. S. A., Surgeon in charge, 81, 82, 84, 283-4, 294, 303.
Military prison, 86.
Moore, George, 188th Pa., a good boy, 97; refreshed, 102, 103, 261.
Meeting God in the bushes, 103.
Most powerful sermon, 103.
Matrons in hospitals, 117.
Meecham, Mrs., veteran matron, 121.
Miller, Hutchinson, 29th Conn., his strong faith; creed; exhorts sinners, though blind, 130, 131.
McElvain, Henry, 118th U. S. Vol., prayers; conversion, 180.
Montgomery, Ananias, 10th W. Va., ball in his head, God in his heart; resigned; death, 135-6.
Midnight calls, 148.
"Murder will out," 157.
Martyrdom, spirit of, 158.
Moonlight prayer-meeting in Andersonville, 163.
Mulford, Colonel, commissioner, 165.
McClellan, General, 173, 317.
Martin, Mr., delegate, Christian Commission, 190.
McGavern, Lawrence, 2d Pa. Heavy Art., wicked; repents; prays; dies, 191-2.

"NO fear; why? "Because I put Jesus in front," 47, 117, 186.
"None but Christ," 88, 141.
Night-calls, 88.
Nichols, Joseph P., 39th Ill. Vol., prayerless; confesses; prays; dies, 178, 179.
No venture in coming to Jesus, 191.
Nichols, John, 29th Conn. Vol., (an Indian), humane, backsliding, 238-9.
Number of patients visited daily, 6, 269.
National Cemetery, Fortress Monroe, Va., prayers and tears in, 315, 316.
—— who are the dead? 317.
—— how did they die? 317; as they fought, 318.
—— their dying words, 318, 319.
—— the monument inscription, 320.
—— a plea to guard and protect it, 321.
—— its erection, 322.
—— burying the dead, 323-4.
National Cemeteries of U. S., different departments, 324-5.
—— general summary of, 325-6.

OWNERSHIP in God. It is mutual — "The Lord is mine, and I am his," 206.

PATRIOTISM, 25, 26, 28, 30, 40, 123, 133, 218, 275, 309; "I came out to conquer or die," 55, 57.
—— in Andersonville, 158, 159; undying, 160.

INDEX.

Patriotism, "we conquer, or die right here," 304–7.
"Put the bright side out to mother," 57.
Philadelphia Inquirer quoted, 69.
"Past feeling," 124.
Procrastination, evil of, 193.
Prisoners in Andersonville, sufferings of, 152-5, 161, 170-4; execution of, 156.
Preaching to colored troops, 17.
—— to patients, 16.
Preached a Christmas sermon, 19.
—— in rebel hospital, 70.
—— on steamer, 76.
Preaching by Col. A. W. Taylor, 19.
—— by colored people, 19.
—— in the military prisons, 43, 73, 87.
Plymouth, strength of garrison, 19; attacked by rebels under General Hoke, 63.
—— consternation of citizens, 63; siege of, 64-70; surrender of, 68.
Papers and tracts distributed, 87.
Pride hinders in coming to Jesus, 116.
Pivot of eternity, the, 155.
Prisoners, Belle Isle, condition of, 75, 76.
—— exchange of, 75.
—— frozen to death, half-starved, 78.
—— severe suffering of, 170-4.
Plan of salvation in a nutshell, 225.
Payson's flood of glory rolling around him, 248.
Preaching in the wards, 256.
Plumb, Sergeant, 4th Mass. Cav., 283.
Porter, Admiral, bravery, 288, 317.
Pennypacker, Col., 291.
Preston, Lieutenant, and Porter, both killed in battle, 292.
President Johnson, 294.
Prayer-meetings, semi-weekly, large, interesting, 16, 80, 92, 273-6.
—— on voluntary principle, 94, 262, 265.
—— powerful, 95-98.
—— ward, 96.
—— in the bushes, 102.
—— melting, 258, 261.
—— soldiers', 100, 101.
—— refreshing, 102, 257-9, 266.
—— by moonlight, 163.
—— in the dark, 281.
—— bomb-proof, 210.
Power of religion on the mind, heart, 56.
—— prayer illustrated, 99, 100, 102, 130.
—— preaching, 105.
—— God's presence, 130.
—— Christ's love, 232.
Privilege of prayer, 189.
PRAYERS, SOLDIERS':
"O Jesus, save me just now," 45.
"Oh, that I had ventured before," 190.
"O Jesus, come just now," 44.
"Come and pray for us," 63.
"Lord, save, or I perish," 179.

PRAYERS, SOLDIERS':
"Oh, chaplain, don't go away," 116.
"Lord have mercy." "May God protect us," 152.
"Oh, for God's sake, have mercy on me," 174.
"Save me, save me, O Jesus," 186.
"I will pray till I die," 187.
"Lord, have mercy on me; cast me not off," 221.
Prayer-hall, 94.
Patchwork won't do for eternity, 125.
Philips, John W., of Ohio, converted in hospital; baptized sitting on his death-bed; death, 126-7.
Pompey's heroic courage, 134.
Palmer, John, 62d Ohio Vol., "too wicked to pray;" "plunge for Jesus," 142-4.
Praying for sport; no fear of God, 195; with a ball in his head, 195.
Praying Tom falls flat down, and prays right up, 281.

RAWLINGS, Chaplain, 103d Pa. Vol., 20; captured, 68.
Rush, Dr., Surgeon U. S. V., skilful, 81, 285.
Ransom, C. M., Lieutenant, 98th N. Y. Vol., wounded; prays; shouts; dies, 31, 32.
Russell, Lieutenant, wounded, 63.
Rebels prayed with, 70; preached to, 49.
Reading-room for soldiers, 81.
Roe, E. P., Chaplain U. S. A., 82, 84, 94, 96, 101, 121, 259, 265, 275, 282-5, 295, 272, 285.
Raymond, Chaplain Charles, U. S. A., 82, 279, 282-4, 295.
Rutherford's dying words, 88.
Religious work at Hampton Hospital, 93.
Revival, 98, 101, 102, 257-8, 273-6.
Religious experience, soldiers' 101.
—— conversation, important, 116, 184-5.
Revenge knocked out by a wound, 117.
Roe, Mrs. Chaplain E. P., 120.
Roman sentinel, the, 133; pattern of fidelity, 134.
"Resting on Christ sure," 150.
"Resist the devil, and he'll flee," 180.
Rich soldier; no want, 197.
Robins, Peter, 203d Pa., patient, heroic, pious, happy, 201.
Reed, James, 188th Pa., interested, repented, prayed, converted, died, 223-4.
Ruffner, Samuel, 116th Ohio Vol., warm-hearted, happy, 245-6.
Reno, John L., 76th Pa. Vol., buoyant, brave, 263-4.
Raising the colors higher, 277.
Richmond fallen; unbounded rejoicing, 283.
Rebel barbarity; used Union soldiers' skulls for goblets, 301.

INDEX. 427

Rosecrans, General, patriotic determination, 304.

S ATAN whetting his sword, 15.
Snowballs and flowers gathered at once, 16.
Schneider, Edward M., 57th Mass., his heroic patriotism; immortal dying words; patience; will; death; grave, 25, 271.
"Stand by the flag," 25.
"Stand up for Jesus," 27.
Sabbath-school, colored, flourishing, 20.
Soldiers hungry for the gospel, 19.
Slough of despond passed, 47.
Sinner's unwillingness keeps him from Christ, 59, 60.
Sinner's own fault, if lost, 60; urged to come, 60.
Sailors drowned at Plymouth, fired on, 66.
Soldiers' dying messages, 88; affectionate kiss of, 91.
Smith, Dr., Surgeon U. S. V., 91.
Stuck fast on the Potomac, 93, 101.
Soldiers' exhortations, eloquent, powerful, 95.
Sanitary Commission delegates, 97, 119.
Soldier's throat shot off, 127.
Stanton, Harry, 118th N. Y. Vol., a backslider; miserable; confesses sorrow; weeps, 137, 138.
Shot dead for getting a drink of water, 154.
Sin, unpardonable, 154.
Spirit quenched, 155.
Soldier's praying for mother, 108; "Stephen," 239.
——— dying words, messages, 117.
——— frankness; free to give their experience, 116.
——— fluent in religious conversation, 117.
——— colored, their implicit faith, 117.
——— dying clinched in battle, 133.
Smith, Joseph, 38th U. S., prayerful, 181-2.
Sherman, General, 175, 307-8, 310.
Spanogle, Mahlon, 205th Pa. Vol., prayerless; repents; dies happy, 187.
Smith, Charles E., 148th N. Y., converted in army by a sister's letters, 188.
Shawley, Michael, 206th Pa. Vol., tender, prayerful, weeping, resigned; happy death, 189, 190.
Self the greatest hindrance, 197.
"Satan is often at my heels," 198.
"Swimming to glory on the plank of free grace," 202.
Smith, Joshua, 11th W. Va., prayerful; victorious, 202-3.
Spaulding, Judson, 15th N. Y. Art., his faith, 203-4.
Satan repulsed by prayer, 221.
"Sticking to the point," 227.
Steward, Lorenzo D., 11th Maine Vol., anxious, hopeful, 231-2.

Smith, Wm. F., 7th Conn., tender; prayed; died happy, 233.
Simplicity of prayer; it is the heart that prays, 244.
Soldiers talking Jesus to soldiers, 261.
Small, John R., 37th N. Y., prayed with chaplain, 261.
Soldiers' prayer and conference meeting, 266-7.
Sent for to pray with a rebel soldier, 267.
Smith, Thomas, 32d Co. Veteran Reserve Corps, 278; his funeral, 278.
Sanitary Commission, 282.
Soldiers' entertainment, 283.
Shells thrown at the rate of two hundred and forty per minute, 289.
Stream of death; first death in the war, 300.
Struggle of the Mass. 6th Regiment in Baltimore, 300.
Sheridan, P., General, bravery, 304, 309-10.
Shaw, Colonel, 54th Mass., killed, 306.
Sedgwick, General, killed, 307.
Slavery abolished in United States, January 31, 1865, 310.
Schofield, General, 310.
Stockton, Rev. Dr., 332.
Soldiers burnt to death in battle, 312.
——— hung for loyalty, 312.
Solemn review of the war, and hospital, 411-12.
Simpson, Bishop, 346-352.
Stuart, Geo. H., 364-382.
SOLDIERS' SAYINGS AND DYING MESSAGES: The insatiable heart cries, "Give, give!" 23.
"I am in perfect peace; I want nothing," 24.
"I saw Jesus waiting to receive me," 52.
"Jesus is precious to me now," 49, 50, 117, 258.
"Christ is very dear and precious," 53.
"Jesus saved me twice," 128.
"Jesus is all my trust," 130.
"Jesus is close to my side, and I am happy," 218.
"Jesus is all I want," 23, 24, 61.
"Hurrah for Jesus," 46.
"All is bright," 52, 146-7.
"All is well; glory to God," 29, 50.
"I have got the victory," 88.
"He *must* pray," 216.
"It's too late," 106.
"I could not wait," 216.
Incorrigible sinner, the, 125, 126.
"I will give you bullets for bread," 173.
"I went to church cursing, and came away praying," 180.
"I can't get religion," 181.
"I can't pray," 206.
"I have not found the Saviour yet," weeping, 182.

428 INDEX.

SOLDIERS' SAYINGS AND DYING MESSAGES:
"I can't help but pray; I go forward," 182.
"If I go to hell, I will go praying," 189.
"I am ready to die," 186.
"I want nothing," 266.
"I have a firmer hold on God than on the devil," 191.
"I'm guilty of everything but theft and murder," 191.
"I am resting on Christ sure," and bleeding to death, 194.
"I gave my heart to Jesus," 196.
"I prays, and Satan goes away," 198.
"I found Jesus," 207.
"I am happy in the Lord; I would rather die," 199.
"I pray much in battle, on the march, and everywhere," 202.
"I would load and fire, and pray at the same time," 202.
"I can afford to suffer," 203.
"I rose at three, and shouted glory to God," &c., 204.
"I can't live without prayer," 205.
"I have no fear," 217.
"I feel the Lord is mine," 206.
"I leave it all with the Lord," 208.
"I prayed in the street," 216.
"I love everybody," 217.
"I trust in the Lord, and I am not afraid," 218.
"I fear pain more than death," 218.
"Tell them I am happy;" dying words, 187.
"I have got it! I have got it! glory to God," 221.
"All is well," 236.
"Hell seems to be gaping for me; O my sins, my sins," 222.
"I have nothing to catch hold of — nothing to stand on," 225.
"Oh, *do* lift me out," 225.
"My work is done," 229.
"Thank God, thank God for my wound," 227.
"My wound has brought me nearer to God," 227.
"I liked to jump out of bed when you preached," 227.
"Oh, the love of Christ," 232.
"It is easier to serve Satan," 232.
"I am better in the army than at home," 233.
"The Bible better than greenbacks,"238.
"Somehow it worked upon me," 240.
"All is well," 242.
"I will trust him till I die," 241.
"I have no fear of death," 241.
"God still sticks to me," 241.
"O chaplain, what will I do?" 242.
"I am on the devil's side," 244.

SOLDIERS' SAYINGS AND DYING MESSAGES:
"I try to pray, but can't make much out," 244.
"Pray for me till I die; I feel happy in the Lord," 246.
"I'm too wicked to come to Jesus," 250.
"I will try," 251.
"God grabbed me into his heart at once," 252.
"I prayed on, and God changed my heart," 253.
"I am the happiest man on earth. I mean it," 255.
"The devil coaxed me off," 254.
"How thankful I am for that sermon," 256.
"God has got me," 228.
"O chaplain, will you pray for me," 257.
"Tell my wife I died happy in Christ," 263.
"I have found Jesus; oh, he is so lovely," 265.
"My heart is all broken into pieces; O brethren, pray for me," 267.
"They could only shout 'glory,' and died," 270.
"I would give my arm and a hundred dollars, to quit swearing," 274.
"I propose to fight it out on this line," 307.
"God got me to come into the army,"319.

TRESOUTHICK, Captain, fond of Bible and prayers; patriotic; his death, 30-1.
Taylor, Colonel A. W., of 101st Pa. Vol., 18, 19, 67, 70.
Thanking God for wounds, 41.
"The Dying Captain," by Chaplain Marshall, 42-46.
Transferring patients north, 83, 89, 90, 92.
"The last warning," 105, 106.
Too wicked to pray, 142.
Too late, 155.
Tisdale, Rev. Mr., 155.
Track, Geo. H., 6th Conn., resolved to quit swearing, 185.
The martyr's soul in flames offered to Christ, 199.
Tustison, James, 10th Iowa Vol., patriotic, patient, happy; his death, 219-20.
Testament, bloody, given up for mother, 49.
Testaments distributed, 86.
Testament read through thirty times during the war, 217.
Testaments, five hundred, received one day, 261, 293.
The great Christian victory, 418, 420.
The rebellion dissected, 418.
Tilton, Benjamin R., prayerless, profane; pleads for mercy, 224-5.
The rope of salvation, 225; grasped; sinners saved, 226.

INDEX. 429

The snares of the devil and the cross of Christ contrasted, 233.
The world's great want, 251.
Talked a swearing man to tears of penitence, 258, 261.
Thurston, Henry A., 152d N. Y.; "I am going home," 263.
The naked heart, 263.
Tremendous cheering, rejoicing, 284-5.
Terry, General A. H., 290-2, 310.
Triune campaign, success of, 310.
Total loss during the war, 312.
Theatre turned into a religious meeting, 327-9.

VISITING the sick in the rain, 273.
Vanderkeiff, Dr., Assistant-Surgeon, U. S., 77.
Voyage to New York, author's, 91.
Victories on the field and in the hospital, 98.
Value of a good letter, 107; the last letter, 108.
Vanloan, Geo. H., 3d N. Y. Cavalry, pious, 138.
Vanwert, Edwin, 3d Mich. Vol., anxious; wicked; prays; dies, 144, 145.
Victory claimed by both armies, 306.

WESSELS, General H. W., 19, 49, 64, 68, 72.
Winslow, Elnor, 203d Pa. Vols., wounded; earnest prayers; longs to depart; happy death, 28-30.
What Christ is to the Christian, 37.
Welsh, Rev. John, his wonderful prayer, 52.
Williams, Samuel, 104th Pa. Vol., longing for Jesus; feels his inability; "Oh, if I only could!" 59, 60.
Words immortal, 25.
"Whole-hearted faith;" its effects, 48.
"World hollow," empty, 54.
Wounded, Plymouth, visited, 70; preached to, 49; farewell to, 70.
Weeping mother's trials, 92.

Work hard, but pleasant, 97.
"We always came back refreshed," 102.
Writing letters for the patients, 107.
Women of the hospital, 118.
Women's kindness and power to comfort, 118.
Worrell, Mrs. Jane M., matron, 120.
Wolcott, Miss E., matron, 120.
Wirz, Captain, 156, 157, 166, 170, 172, 174-7.
"What a feast!" 165.
Warner, J. S., 2d. N. Y. Cav., a weeping mother, 209.
Winder, General G. H., his threats 174.
Weekly, John, 4th U. S., prayerful; ready; no fear; assurance, 186.
Williams, Dwight, 203d Pa., prayerful; resigned, 196.
Wilson, Charles, 16th N. Y. Heavy Artillery, Christ his; no want, 196-7.
Ward, James, 81st N. Y., "Tell my family I am happy," 199.
Welsh, Perry, 67th Ohio Vol., anxious; comfortable; steadfast, 202.
Wertz, John, 23d Ohio, patient, with seven wounds, 203.
Weed, Abraham, 58th Pa. Vol., anxious; fearful, 205.
Warren, Thomas, 199th Pa. Vols., anxious; prayed; converted; happy, 221.
Williams, Charles, 5th U. S., anxious; prayerful; converted, 222.
Wounds lead to prayer and conversions, 221-2.
Weeping scene at the grave, 262.
Week of prayer, 272.
Washington's birthday celebrated, 279-80.
Wolverton, Dr. A., Surgeon U. S. A., 279.
Wadsworth, General, killed, 306.
Weeping, bereaved father, 316; converse with the dead, 316.
Weitzel, General, enters Richmond, 283.

YOURS in death, 108.
Young, Colonel G. I., 403-411.

THE END.

Other Related Solid Ground Titles

In addition to *From the Flag to the Cross*, Solid Ground is honored to offer many other uncovered treasure, many for the first time in more than a century:

JESUS AND I ARE FRIENDS: *The Life of J.R. Miller* by John Faris
Dr. Miller not only served for over 30 years as a pastor of Christ's flock, but he also served during the Civil War in the United States Christian Commission. Although he was already recognized for his love for Christ and for people, his ministry to the sick and dying on the battlefield lifted him to unusual heights in ministering to those who were facing severe trials in their lives. This is a life worth reading and imitating.

THE FORGOTTEN HEROES OF LIBERTY by Joel T. Headley
This volume, written by the highly acclaimed 19th century historian J.T. Headley, explores the vital, but often neglected, role of ministers of the Gospel to the cause of liberty in the founding of this great nation.

LET THE CANNON BLAZE AWAY by Joseph P. Thompson
The author was living in Germany in 1876 when the United States was about to celebrate its 100th anniversary. He was asked to prepare 6 lectures to be delivered in the leading cities of Germany, Italy, France and England. This he did to the overwhelming applause of the leading ministers and statesman of those countries. In fact, the response was so encouraging that it was insisted that these lectures be placed in a book that could be used as a textbook for years to come.

OUR LIVES, OUR FORTUNES AND OUR SACRED HONOR
by Charles Goodrich "The Declaration of Independence is one of the most important political documents in the history of western civilization. The signers are too often dismissed as dead white men, and their greatness is often disparaged. This book will acquaint you with the great men to whom we owe so much for their willingness to pledge to each other their lives, their fortunes and their sacred honour."
- Pastor David Dykstra

A SOLDIER'S CATECHISM by Michael Cannon
"I highly recommend this tool to encourage our great American Soldiers, Airmen, Sailors, Marines and Coast Guardians. In these days of danger and intense service to our country, a means of reminding our troops of their Hope and Joy is very much needed. This time-honored means of instruction is bound to encourage men and women to "glory God and enjoy Him forever!" - CH (COL-P) Douglas E. Lee, U.S.Army Assistant Chief of Chaplains for Mobilizations and Readiness

THE PASTOR IN THE SICK ROOM by John D. Wells
Written from a wealth of more than 40 years pastoral experience and from a heart deeply concerned for the salvation of those who are dying, this book is instructive, challenging and heartwarming. Even though written more than 100 years ago, the spiritual lessons contained in it are as up to date as if written yesterday. *This book should be in the Practical Theology section of every pastor's library."* - Jerry Bridges

A PASTOR'S SKETCHES (in 2 Volumes) by Ichabod Spencer
These books consist of 77 "sketches" or "case studies" drawn from the ministry of one of America's greatest pastors. It is changing lives in over 25 countries and all 50 States and has drawn high praise from dozens of evangelical and reformed leaders throughout the world, like: Jerry Bridges, Maurice Roberts, Ernie Reisinger, James White, Gordon Keddie, Tom Nettles, Joel Beeke, Conrad Mbewe, Geoff Thomas and Peter Jeffery.

Other Solid Ground Titles

In addition to the book in your hand, Solid Ground is honored to offer other uncovered treasure, many for the first time in more than a century:

NOTES ON GALATIANS by J. Gresham Machen
EXPOSITION OF THE BAPTIST CATECHISM by Benjamin Beddome
PAUL THE PREACHER: *Sermons from Acts* by John Eadie
THE COMMUNICANT'S COMPANION by Matthew Henry
THE CHILD AT HOME by John S.C. Abbott
THE LIFE OF JESUS CHRIST FOR THE YOUNG by Richard Newton
THE KING'S HIGHWAY: *10 Commandments for the Young* by Richard Newton
HEROES OF THE REFORMATION by Richard Newton
FEED MY LAMBS: *Lectures to Children on Vital Subjects* by John Todd
LET THE CANNON BLAZE AWAY by Joseph P. Thompson
THE STILL HOUR: *Communion with God in Prayer* by Austin Phelps
COLLECTED WORKS of James Henley Thornwell (4 vols.)
CALVINISM IN HISTORY *by Nathaniel S. McFetridge*
OPENING SCRIPTURE: *Hermeneutical Manual* by Patrick Fairbairn
THE ASSURANCE OF FAITH *by Louis Berkhof*
THE PASTOR IN THE SICK ROOM *by John D. Wells*
THE BUNYAN OF BROOKLYN: *Life & Sermons of I.S. Spencer*
THE NATIONAL PREACHER: *Sermons from 2nd Great Awakening*
FIRST THINGS: *First Lessons God Taught Mankind* Gardiner Spring
BIBLICAL & THEOLOGICAL STUDIES *by 1912 Faculty of Princeton*
THE POWER OF GOD UNTO SALVATION *by B.B. Warfield*
THE LORD OF GLORY *by B.B. Warfield*
A GENTLEMAN & A SCHOLAR: *Memoir of J.P. Boyce* by J. Broadus
SERMONS TO THE NATURAL MAN *by W.G.T. Shedd*
SERMONS TO THE SPIRITUAL MAN *by W.G.T. Shedd*
HOMILETICS AND PASTORAL THEOLOGY *by W.G.T. Shedd*
A PASTOR'S SKETCHES 1 & 2 *by Ichabod S. Spencer*
THE PREACHER AND HIS MODELS *by James Stalker*
IMAGO CHRISTI: *The Example of Jesus Christ by James Stalker*
LECTURES ON THE HISTORY OF PREACHING *by J. A. Broadus*
THE SHORTER CATECHISM ILLUSTRATED *by John Whitecross*
THE CHURCH MEMBER'S GUIDE *by John Angell James*
THE SUNDAY SCHOOL TEACHER'S GUIDE *by John A. James*
CHRIST IN SONG: *Hymns of Immanuel from All Ages* by Philip Schaff
DEVOTIONAL LIFE OF THE S.S. TEACHER *by J.R. Miller*

Call us Toll Free at 1-877-666-9469
Send us an e-mail at sgcb@charter.net
Visit us on line at solid-ground-books.com
Uncovering Buried Treasure to the Glory of God

www.ingramcontent.com/pod-product-compliance
Lightning Source LLC
Chambersburg PA
CBHW021752230426
43669CB00006B/61